ANNIE BESANT

ANNIE BESANT

Series Editor

M.A. Seewan

Editors

Saud Akhtar **R.K. Singh**

Himalaya Books Pvt. Ltd.

'Ramdoot', Dr. Bhalerao Marg, Girgaon, Mumbai - 400 004

Tel : (022) 23863863. Fax : (022) 23877178

Email : himpub@vsnl.com

First Edition : 2011
Edition : 2015

Published by : H.B.P.L.
"Pooja Apartments", 4-B, Murari Lal Street, Ansari Road,
Darya Ganj, New Delhi - 110 002.
Phone: 011-23270392, 23278631; Reliance: 30180392 to 396
Fax: 011-23256286, Email: hphdel@vsnl.com

Sole Distributers : **HIMALAYA PUBLISHING HOUSE PVT. LTD.**

Branch Offices :

Mumbai : "Ramdoot", Dr. Bhalerao Marg, Girgaon, **Mumbai - 400 004.**
Phone: 022-23860170/23863863, Fax: 022-23877178
E-mail: himpub@vsnl.com; Website: www.himpub.com

Nagpur : Kundanlal Chandak Industrial Estate, Ghat Road,
Nagpur - 440 018. Phone: 0712-2738731, 3296733;
Telefax: 0712-2721215

Bengaluru : No. 16/1 (Old 12/1), 1st Floor, Next to Hotel Highlands,
Madhava Nagar, Race Course Road, **Bengaluru - 560 001.**
Phone: 080-22286611, 22385461, 4113 8821, 22281541

Hyderabad : No. 3-4-184, Lingampally, Besides Raghavendra Swamy
Matham, Kachiguda, **Hyderabad - 500 027.**
Phone: 040-27560041, 27550139

Chennai : New-20, Old-59, Thirumalai Pillai Road, T. Nagar,
Chennai - 600 017. Mobile: 9380460419

Pune : First Floor, "Laksha" Apartment, No. 527, Mehunpura,
Shaniwarpeth (Near Prabhat Theatre), **Pune - 411 030.**
Phone: 020-24496323/24496333; Mobile: 09370579333

Lucknow : House No 731, Shekhupura Colony, Near B.D. Convent School,
Aliganj, **Lucknow - 226 022.**
Phone: 0522-4012353; Mobile: 09307501549

Ahmedabad : 114, "SHAIL", 1st Floor, Opp. Madhu Sudan House, C.G. Road,
Navrang Pura, **Ahmedabad - 380 009.**
Phone: 079-26560126; Mobile: 09377088847

Ernakulam : 39/176 (New No: 60/251) 1st Floor, Karikkamuri Road, Ernakulam,
Kochi – 682011.
Phone: 0484-2378012, 2378016; Mobile: 09387122121

Bhubaneswar : 5 Station Square, **Bhubaneswar - 751 001 (Odisha).**
Phone: 0674-2532129, Mobile: 09338746007

Indore : Kesardeep Avenue Extension, 73, Narayan Bagh, Flat No. 302,
IIIrd Floor, Near Humpty Dumpty School, **Indore - 452 007 (M.P.).**
Mobile: 09303399304

Kolkata : 108/4, Beliaghata Main Road, Near ID Hospital, Opp. SBI Bank,
Kolkata - 700 010, Phone: 033-32449649, Mobile: 7439040301

Guwahati : House No. 15, Behind Pragjyotish College, Near Sharma Printing
Press, P.O. Bharalumukh, **Guwahati - 781009, (Assam).**
Mobile: 09883055590, 08486355289, 7439040301

Printed at : M/s. Aditya Offset Process (I) Pvt. Ltd., Hyderabad.
On behalf of HPH.

Preface

Biography, is now a form of literature, very much in vogue. In fact, biography is a description or account of someone's life and the times, which is usually published in the form of a book. A biography is more than a mention of personal facts (life, education, work, relationships and death), it also portrays the subject's experience of events. Technically speaking, a work is biographical, if it covers, all of a person's life. Biography writing has a long history. A biography is real. Ancient Greeks developed the biographical tradition, which we have inherited, although until the 5th century AD, when the word 'biographia' first appeared, in Damascius' "Life of Isodorus," biographical pieces were called simply "lives". It is quite likely that the Greeks were drawing on a pre-existing eastern tradition. Certainly Herodotus' "Histories" contains more detailed biographical information on Persian kings and subjects. The earliest surviving pieces, which we would identify as biographical are Isocrates' "Life of Evagoras" and Xenophon's "Life of Agesilaos," both from the fifth century BC. "Parallel Lives" by Plutarch, a Greek writing under the Roman empire, is a series of short biographies of eminent men.

The Golden Age of English biography emerged in late eighteenth century, the century in which the terms "biography" and "autobiography" entered English lexicon. The classic works of the period were Samuel Johnson's "Critical Lives of the Poets" and James Boswell's "Massive Life of Johnson". Generally American biography followed English model. By World War I, cheap hardcover reprints had become popular. The decade of the 1920s witnessed a biographical 'boom'. Later, biographical writings developed a lot and today biographies are written and compiled in the finest form of the genre. In India too, biography, as a form of literature has been evolved, cultivated and polished over the years. Here is an effort to promote this tradition further.

This series of biographies of great men, great women and celebrities in all walks of life is an adventurous academic endeavour, in its own right. A team of researchers and compilers has worked for a good period of time to accomplish the project. For this purpose, hundreds of books by eminent authors and editors have been consulted and referred to. We have benefited from various works, liberally, in order to illustrate and enrich this effort of ours. Present book is devoted to the great personality of Annie Besant.

President of Theosophical Society of India; founder of Home Rule League, a pleader of self-rule in India and the first woman president of Indian National Congress, Annie Besant was a social reformer, political leader, women's rights activist, writer and orator. She was of Irish origin and made India her second home. She fought for the rights of Indian people. She had travelled widely in Europe, which had widened her outlook. Annie questioned, not only her long-held religious beliefs but the whole of conventional thinking. Annie Besant fought for the causes, she thought were right. She became interested in Theosophy as a way of knowing God. To serve humanity at large was its supreme goal. She toured the entire country. It gave her first hand information about India and middle-class Indians in particular. She also became involved in Indian freedom movement. She founded Home Rule League which advocated self-rule by Indians. She started a newspaper, "New India", criticised British rule and was jailed for sedition. She presided over an annual Congress session.

This is a compact and comprehensive account of the above mentioned great life, which is bound to attract the attention of scholars, researchers, students and the general readers, alike. Let's hope this humble effort would receive a warm welcome and due applause.

— ***Editors***

Contents

1

An Illustrious Life

Introduction

Annie Besant guided thousands of men and women all over the world in their spiritual quest. She was the second President of The Theosophical Society from 1907 to 1933, was described as a 'Diamond Soul', for she had many brilliant facets to her character. She was an outstanding orator of her time, a champion of human freedom, educationist, philanthropist, and author with more than three hundred books and pamphlets to her credit.

As Annie Wood, she was born in 1847 in London into a middle-class family of Irish origin. She was always proud of being Irish and supported the cause of Irish self-rule, throughout her adult life. Her father died when she was five years old, leaving the family almost penniless. Her mother supported the family by running a boarding house for boys at Harrow. However, she was unable to support Annie and persuaded her friend Ellen Marryat to care for her.

Marryat made sure that Annie had a good education. She was given a strong sense of duty to society and an equally strong sense of what independent women could achieve. As a young woman, she was also able to travel widely in Europe. There she acquired a taste for Catholic colour and ceremony that never left her.

At nineteen she married 26 year old clergyman Frank Besant, younger brother of Walter Besant in 1887. He was an evangelical Anglican clergyman who seemed to share many of her concerns. However, almost on the eve of marriage, she had become more politicised through a visit to friends in Manchester, who brought her into contact with both English radicals and the Manchester Martyrs of the Irish Republican Fenian Brotherhood, as well as with the conditions of the urban poor. Soon Frank became vicar of Sibsey in Lincolnshire. Annie moved to Sibsey with her husband, and within a few years they had two children: Arthur and Mabel. The marriage was, however, a disaster. The first conflict came over money and Annie's independence. Annie wrote short stories, books for children and articles. As married women did not have the legal right to own property, Frank was able to take all the money she earned. Politics further divided the couple. Annie began to support farm workers, who were fighting to unionise and to win better conditions. Frank was a Tory and sided with the landlords and farmers. The tension came to a head when Annie refused to attend Communion. In 1873 she left him and returned to London. They were legally separated and Annie took her daughter with her.

Annie began to question her own faith. She turned to leading churchmen for advice. She even went to see Edward Bouverie Pusey, leader of the Catholic wing of the Church of England. When she asked him to recommend books that would answer her questions, he told her she had read too many already. Annie returned to Frank to make a last unsuccessful effort to repair the marriage. She finally left for London.

Birth and Childhood

Annie Besant was born as Annie Wood on 1 October 1847, and was educated privately in England, Germany and France. She was a devout Christian, and was married at the age of twenty to an English clergyman, Rev. Frank Besant, Vicar of Sibsey, Lincolnshire, by whom she had a son, Arthur Digby, and a daughter, Mabel. However, the awakening of her character made her challenge several of the Christian dogmas. 'It was not the challenge of unfaith', as Jinarâjadâsa was to say later, 'but rather of a highly spiritual nature that desired intensely not only to believe but also to understand.' Unable to make logic out of Christian traditions, she left the Church in 1872 and became a freethinker, thus ruining her social position through her passion for Truth; consequently she had to leave her husband and young son.

In 1879 she matriculated at London University and went on with her studies in science but met obstacles there owing to the sexist prejudices of her time. She joined the National Secular Society in 1874 and worked in the free thought and radical movements led by Charles Bradlaugh, MP. She coedited the *National Reformer* with him and wrote many political and free-thought books and pamphlets from 1874–88. At this point her husband moved court to take their little daughter away from her, alleging that she was 'unfit' because of her ideas. This deprivation caused her profound grief. (But, when the children were older they became devoted admirers of their mother.) She was prominent in the Labour and Socialist movements, a member of the Fabian Society and Social Democratic Federation, and took an active part in Trade Union work among unskilled labourers; with Herbert Burrows she led the path-breaking match girls' strike to a successful conclusion.

Growth and Education

Young Miss Wood received her early education under the guidance of Miss Marryat, the favourite sister of Captain Marryat, the famous novelist, a maiden lady of large means. She had a perfect genius for teaching and took the greatest interest in her work. In her own words, she taught her everything except music, and for this she had a master, practising in composition, in recitation, in reading aloud English and French, and later, German, devoting herself to training her in the soundest most thorough fashion. "No words of mine," Mrs. Besant says in her Autobiography, "can tell how much I owe her, not only of knowledge, but of that love of knowledge which has remained with me ever since as a constant spur to study." With her she travelled very early in her age in France and Germany, and learned to read and write the languages of those countries and laid the foundation for that independence of thought and action for which she afterwards became famous.

Marital Bond and Separation

She was married to Evangelical Anglican Clergyman, Frank Besant in 1867. She had two children Digloy and Mabel. But the marriage broke out after the birth of two children. She fought for the sake of women, for equal wages, right of women and birth control (for women's health) In 1866, she read theosophical books written by Mr. A. P. Sinnet. In 1889, H. P. Blavatsky's "The Secret Doctrine" was given for review. After that she joined Theosophical society in May, 1889, and became Blavatsky's devoted pupil and helper. The Theosophical society was against discrimination of race, colour, gender and taught universal brotherhood.

Service in India

In 1893 she landed in India, made a tour of the country in the company of H. S. Olcott, and, by her splendid presentation of Indian philosophy and her undisguised personal preference for the Indian spiritual heritage, won the support of orthodox Brahmins to Theosophy. The transformation of the religious life in India, particularly among Hindus, is one of the wonders she performed. She was an untiring worker for the upliftment of women, and pleaded again and again for a radical change in social conditions, but never desired any modification of the Indian woman's temperament which she held to be one of the most spiritual in the world.

She soon gathered round her a band of Indians to work for the regeneration of the country and in 1898, after much planning, founded the Central Hindu School and College in Banaras (now Varanasi). A few years later she started the Central Hindu School for Girls. Theosophists from overseas came to help her in the work of the college, which was established with the object of impressing India's past glory on the minds and hearts of the students. A brilliant band of workers gathered round her, including Dr. Bhagvan Das, his brother Govinda Das, Gyanendra Nath Chakravarti, Upendranath Basu, I. N. Gurtu, and P. K. Telang, all of whom worked in an honorary capacity. Later the college became the nucleus of the Hindu University, and in recognition of Mrs. Besant's services to Indian education the degree of Doctor of Letters was conferred upon her in 1921.

As Lord Baden-Powell deemed that Indians were unfit to be scouts, the Indian Scout Movement was founded by her in 1918, the boys wearing Indian turbans! When Baden-Powell came to India and saw how successful was the movement created by Annie Besant, it was amalgamated with the world movement, and she was made the Honorary Scout Commissioner for India. In 1932 Baden-Powell sent her from London the highest Scout distinction, the 'Silver Wolf' medal.

Annie Besant travelled all over India and understood the middle-class Indians affected by British rule and its system of education Many educated class were unaware of the glorious past and religion. She studied about Indian scriptures, religious texts, Bhagavad Gita and Upanishads. She learned Hindu manners and customs. She wore Indian sari and invited British who ever liked India to work in Institutions. She concentrated on character building. The word "Commonwealth" was coined by her. She instilled Patriotism through network of colleges and schools. She developed "Central Hindu college" at Banaras by working endlessly. She attended 'Sabhas' of traditional Sanskrit scholars. Mahamahopadhayaya Pandit Gangadhar Sastri was a famous Sanskrit scholar and called her as "Sarvashukla Saraswathi" as he was impressed by Mrs. Besant's deep knowledge, oration and her sincerity.

Meeting with H.P. Blavatsky

Feeling dissatisfied with the negative approach of free thought, Mrs. Besant now made researches into spiritualism, hypnotism, and so forth. At this juncture Mr. W. T. Stead, the editor of *The Review of Reviews,* sent her Madame Blavatsky's *The Secret Doctrine* to review. As she read the book, it was as if a long lost vision of truth flashed through her mind. She asked for an interview with the author, and from that first sight of HPB, her whole life changed. She abandoned her secularist ideas and also to some extent the socialist philosophy, but the new light which she received inspired her more firmly than ever to the service of the world. Her approach towards the various evils in the world changed and she began to deal with the root causes in the light of the laws which govern all existence.

Meeting with J. Krishnamurti

A new phase of Dr. Besant's activity began when she came into contact with two remarkable Indian boys, and declared that the elder of them, J. Krishnamurti, was destined to be the vehicle of the 'World Teacher', the Bodhisattva Maitreya. In 1910 she assumed the guardianship of J. Krishnamurti and his brother, and despite great difficulties launched him on his remarkable career. Mrs. Besant saw her role in Krishnamurti's life as that of a catalyst: 'Amma never told me what to do', Krishnamurti gratefully recalled in later life. She merely tried to prepare him for a worldwide regenerative mission. He was encouraged to meet people, to give talks and lead discussions. The Order of the Star in the East was organised to pave the way for the very special work he was to do.

Adopted Son

In 1909, soon after Besant's inheritance of the presidency, Leadbeater "discovered" fourteen-year-old Jiddu Krishnamurti on the private beach attached to the Theosophical Society's headquarters at Adyar. Krishnamurti had been living next to the headquarters with his father and brothers for a few months prior to this. The "discovery" started years of upheaval in the Theosophical Society, as the boy was proclaimed to be the likely "vehicle" for the expected *World Teacher*. Jiddu Krishnamurti and his younger brother Nityananda ("Nitya") were brought up by Theosophists from that moment on, and Krishnamurti was extensively groomed for his future "mission" as the new *Christ-incarnate*. The boys were soon placed under the legal guardianship of Besant, following a protracted legal battle with their father. Early in their relationship, Krishnamurti and Besant had developed a very close bond and he considered her a surrogate mother - a role she happily accepted. (His biological mother had died when he was ten years old).

In 1929, twenty years after his "discovery", Krishnamurti, who had grown disenchanted with the whole "*World Teacher Project*", repudiated the role that the leadership of the Society and many Theosophists expected him to fulfil. He denounced the concept of saviours, leaders, and spiritual teachers, and severed his ties with Theosophy. He spent the rest of his life holding dialogues and giving public talks around the world as an unaffiliated individual speaker, becoming in the process widely known as an original, independent thinker on philosophical, psychological, and spiritual subjects. However, his love for Besant never waned, as also was the case with Besant's feelings towards him; concerned for his wellbeing after he declared his independence, she had purchased 6 acres (24,000 m^2) of land near the Theosophical Society estate which later became the headquarters of the *Krishnamurti Foundation India*.

Theosophical Society

Annie Besant joined The Theosophical Society on 21 May 1889, and became a devoted pupil and helper of HPB, pledging her loyalty to the President-Founder, Col. H. S. Olcott, and the cause of Theosophy. She became the most brilliant exponent of Theosophy, both as orator and author. In 1893 she represented The Theosophical Society at the World Parliament of Religions in Chicago.

President of the Society

She first met clairvoyant theosophist Charles Webster Leadbeater in London in April 1894. They became close co-workers in the theosophical movement and would remain so for the rest of their lives. Besant became clairvoyant in the following year. In a letter dated 25 August 1895 to Francisca Arundale, Leadbeater narrates how Besant became clairvoyant.

Together they would investigate the universe, matter, thought-forms and the history of mankind through clairvoyance, and would co-author several books. In 1906 Leadbeater suddenly became the centre of controversy when it emerged that he was engaging in mutual masturbation with boys under his care and spiritual instruction — Leadbeater stated he had encouraged the practice in order to keep the boys celibate, which was considered a prerequisite for advancement on the spiritual path. He resigned from the Theosophical Society over the controversy in 1906. The next year Annie Besant became President of the Society and in 1908, with her express support, Leadbeater was readmitted to the Society. Leadbeater went on to face more accusations of improper relations with boys; none of the accusations were proven, and Besant never deserted him. Up until Besant's presidency, the society had as one of its foci Theravada Buddhism and the island of Ceylon, where Henry Olcott did the majority of his useful work.

A Decisive Turn

Under Besant's leadership there was a decisive turn away from this and a refocusing of their activities on "The Aryavarta", as she called central India. Besant actively courted Hindu opinion more than former Theosophical leaders. This was a clear reversal of policy from Blavatsky and Olcott's very public conversion to Buddhism in Ceylon, and their promotion of Buddhist revival activities on the subcontinent.

Establishment of College

Annie set up a new school for boys at Varanasi: the Central Hindu College. Its aim was to build a new leadership for India. The boys lived like monks. They spent 90 minutes a day in prayer and studied the Hindu scriptures, but they also studied modern science. It took 3 years to raise the money for the CHC. Most of the money came from Indian Princes. In April 1911, Annie and Pandit Madan Mohan Malaviya met and decided to unite their forces and work for a common Hindu University at Varanasi. Annie and fellow trustees of the Central Hindu College also agreed to Government of India's precondition that the college should become a part of the new University. The Banaras Hindu University started functioning from 1 October 1917 with the Central Hindu College as its first constituent college.

As early as 1889, Blavatsky had told a group of Theosophical students that the real purpose of establishing the Society was to prepare humanity for the reception of the *World Teacher* when he appeared again on earth. This was repeated again more publicly by Besant in 1896, five years after Blavatsky's death.

Second Term as President

In 1907, after the passing of Col. H. S. Olcott, Annie Besant became the second International President of the Theosophical Society, an office which she held until her death in 1933. Mrs. Besant had always been a great traveller, having visited in the course of her

Theosophical work nearly all the countries of Europe more than once, and making several visits to the United States and Canada, Australia and New Zealand. Her great organising capacity was used to 'make theosophy practical', and action became her 'slogan'. During her presidentship, the Society grew considerably, with the addition of more than thirty-six Sections or National Societies to the initial eleven.

Dr. Besant continued to tour and lecture all over India, dealing extensively with education. Lodges of the Theosophical Society undertook to open schools wherever they could. She also tried to draw women into the movement wherever possible, for at that time women were not encouraged to take part in public life. Clear explanations of the many enigmas of life and the universe were presented in her outstanding books such as *A Study in Consciousness*, which is used in some universities as a textbook. Another of her major works, *Esoteric Christianity*, has been considered a historical document; and has helped to revive true knowledge of Christianity. Her lectures at Theosophical conventions on the great religions of the world were put into a valuable book entitled *Seven Great Religions*, presenting the core teachings of each one of them. The first edition of her English translation of the *Bhagavadgitâ* was published in 1905.

Dr. Besant was a practical mystic, exemplifying in her life and in all her actions a lofty idealism, and a truly religious awareness — a combination found in very few people. In 1908 she announced the formation of a Theosophical Order of Service, which aimed at banding members together in groups with the motto 'Union of all who Love in the Service of all that Suffer.' From 1908 onwards Dr. Besant proceeded to enlarge the Headquarters estate at Adyar. In order to link Adyar more intimately with the rest of the Theosophical world, she started *The Adyar Bulletin*, which continued until 1929. Presently the Adyar Newsletter fulfils a similar function.

New Phase

Active in Indian Politics

A new period in Annie Besant's life began in 1913 when she became active in Indian politics, and gave a lead by claiming

Home Rule for India. She entered politics because she saw that India's independence was essential for her age-old wisdom to become a beacon for the whole world. The Home Rule movement she organised spread all over India. She used all her resources to bring together on the common platform of the 'All India Home Rule League' the two sections of the Indian National Congress which had been divided since 1907. Later she was elected President of the Indian National Congress inspiring Indians with a dynamic vision of India's future. Since the British government merely suppressed agitation but did little to remove the grievances, she started the Young Men's Indian Association in 1914 to train them for public work and donated Gokhale Hall in Madras as a centre for national awakening and free speech. She also started two journals: *The Commonwealth,* a weekly dealing with issues of national reform; and *New India,* a daily newspaper which for fifteen years was a powerful instrument promoting Home Rule and revolutionising Indian journalism.

First World War: Ten months after she began her political work, the World War broke out. India was called upon to make great sacrifices, which she did gladly but not a single word was said by any British statesman as to India's contribution. It was this blunder of British statesmen that convinced Dr. Besant that the political work in India had to continue, and could not be modified or slackened because the Empire was at war. She was interned in 1917 for three months because of her success in arousing the love of freedom in the Indian people. She took as her motto not only 'strike while the iron is hot', but also 'make it hot by striking'. She taught Indian journalists to write strong leading articles denouncing the action of the government, yet keeping within the letter of the law. As President of the Indian National Congress; she made the office one of active work throughout the year, instead of only presiding over it during the four-day annual meetings, as was the practice earlier.

Madras Parliament: Annie Besant's life was one of incredible activity. By 1918 she had started the Madras Parliament, opened Madanapalle College (now in Andhra Pradesh), inaugurated the Adyar Arts League, started the Home Rule League in Bombay, started the Girls' College in Banaras, founded the Order of the

Brothers of Service, presided over the Women's Indian Association at Adyar — from which grew the All-India Women's Conference at Poona (now Pune) in 1927 and the All-Asian Women's Conference at Lahore in 1931 — and started the Society for the Promotion of National Education (SPNE). Unfortunately, she fell into disfavour with the Indian National Congress because of her opposition to Mr. Gandhi's plan of non-cooperation and civil disobedience as she foresaw the danger of instilling disrespect for the law. Although she had a deep regard for Gandhi as someone whose life was guided by truth and compassion, she herself stood by constitutional methods for achieving political reform. Mr. Gandhi's policies were adopted and the disasters she had anticipated occurred in various parts of India. Though she became unpopular and lost her position as a political leader, she still continued with her work for India.

Home Rule Movement

Along with her theosophical activities, Annie continued to participate in concrete political struggles. She had joined the Indian National Congress. As the name suggested, this was originally a debating body, which met each year to consider resolutions on political issues. Mostly it demanded more of a say for middle-class Indians in British Indian government. It had not yet developed into a permanent mass movement with local organisation. About this time she lost her clairvoyance, and co-worker C. W. Leadbeater felt called to move to Sydney, Australia.

In 1914 war broke out in Europe. Britain needed the support of its empire in the fight against Germany. Annie said: "England's need is India's opportunity," a clear echo of an Irish nationalist slogan. As editor of a newspaper called New India, she attacked the (British) government of India and called for clear and decisive moves towards self-rule. As with Ireland, the government refused to discuss any changes while the war lasted.

Home Rule League: In 1916 Annie launched the Home Rule League, once again modelling demands for India on Irish models. For the first time India had a political party to fight for change. Unlike the Congress itself, the League worked all year round. It built a strong structure of local branches, enabling it to mobilise demonstrations, public meetings and agitations. In June 1917 Annie was arrested and interned at a hill station. She flew a red and green flag in the garden to show her defiance. Congress and the Muslim League together threatened to launch protests if she were not set free. Annie's arrest had created a focus for protest, giving those who wanted long-term independence for India a chance to work together for a simple, achievable goal. The government was forced to give way and to make vague but significant concessions. It was announced that the ultimate aim of British rule was Indian self-government, and moves in that direction were promised. Annie was freed in September to a tremendous welcome from crowds all over India. In December she took over as President of Congress for a year. It was perhaps the greatest honour she received in her lifetime.

Congress President

Annie Besant fittingly became the president of Indian National Congress in 1917. Tilak declared that if we were nearer our goals, it was due to Dr. Annie Besant's sincere efforts. Gokhale considered her a true daughter of Mother India. Subash considered her a doughty fighter for Indian freedom. Jawaharlal Nehru said that in India, her memory would endure, especially for the part she played in our freedom struggle in the dark days of the Great War and afterwards. Sarojini Naidu, had this to say.

"Had it not been for her and her enthusiasm, one could not have seen Mr. Gandhi leading the cause of Indian freedom today. It was Mrs. Besant who laid the foundation of modern India – Dr. Besant was a combination of Parvati, Lakshmi and Saraswati."

Mahatma Gandhi on the Scene

After the war, there could be no going back. A new leadership emerged around Mohandas K. Gandhi- one of those who had written to demand Annie's release. He had returned from leading Asians in a peaceful struggle against racism in South Africa. Jawaharlal Nehru, Gandhi's closest associate, had been educated by a Theosophist tutor. The new leadership too was committed to action that was both militant and non-violent, but there were differences between them and Annie. Despite her past, she was not happy with their socialist leanings. Until the end of her life, however, she continued to campaign for India's independence, not only in India but also on speaking tours of Britain. In her own version of Indian dress, Mrs. Besant remained a striking presence on speakers' platforms. She produced a torrent of letters and articles demanding independence.

Spiritual Power

Those who came into intimate contact with Annie Besant were aware of her spiritual powers and first-hand knowledge of many occult matters. She used certain of her yogic powers to investigate the nature of the super-physical realms, and several books on this recondite subject were written in collaboration with her colleague, C. W. Leadbeater. A remarkable piece of writing done by them was *Occult Chemistry,* in which they described the chemical elements examined by them. The first edition was printed in 1908, when it did not appear possible to reconcile their observations with the scientific knowledge of atomic structure of those times, but recent developments in the field support them.

C. Jinarâjadâsa, a former President of the Theosophical Society, published in 1951 a third, enlarged edition of *Occult Chemistry,* containing descriptions of 111 atoms, including 14 isotopes, and the molecules of 29 inorganic compounds and 22 organic compounds. Dr. Stephen M. Phillips, a theoretical physicist, made a detailed analysis of the Besant–Leadbeater studies in the late 1970s and provided a lucid explanation and reinterpretation of their observations, reconciling them with present-day physics. She tried to accommodate Krishnamurti's views into her life, but never really succeeded. The two remained friends, however, until the end of her life. Annie Besant died in 1933 and was survived by her daughter, Mabel. After her death, her colleagues, J. Krishnamurti, Aldous Huxley, Dr. Guido Ferrando, and Rosalind Rajagopal, built Happy Valley School, now renamed Besant Hill School in her honour.

Last Journey

On 20 September 1933, Dr. Besant laid aside her physical body at Adyar. Her Presidentship spanned twenty-six years full of glorious devoted service to the Theosophical Society and to mankind at large, and she passed away as she had lived — a warrior Soul. Mr. N. Sri Ram, who was then her Secretary, wrote the following tribute:

> Dr. Besant was nothing if she was not wholehearted and whole-souled in all that she undertook, in every aim and every inner impulse. . . . Almost always, as I know from personal knowledge of how she affected various people, they were struck with the extraordinary magnetism that seemed to surround her, the brightest energy, which seemed to leave her at the end of the day almost as fresh as at the beginning.

The Descendants

The family history onward from the era in which Annie Besant lived became quite fragmented by the late 1940s. A number of Annie Besant's descendants have been traced in detail from her son Arthur Digby's side. One of Arthur Digby's daughters was Sylvia Besant, who married Commander Clem Lewis in the 1920s. They had a daughter, Kathleen Mary, born in 1934, who was given away for adoption within three weeks of the birth and had the new name of Lavinia Pollock. Lavinia married Frank Castle in 1953 and raised a family of five (Besant's great-great grandchildren) - James, Richard, David, Fiona and Andrew Castle - the last and youngest sibling being a former British professional tennis player and now television presenter and personality.

2

Many Faceted Personality

For a time, she undertook part-time study at the Birkbeck Literary and Scientific Institution, where her religious and political activities were to cause alarm. At one point the Institution's governors sought to withhold the publication of her exam results.

Staunch Socialist

For Annie, politics, friendship and love were always closely intertwined. Her decision in favour of Socialism came about through a close relationship with George Bernard Shaw, a struggling young Irish author living in London, and a leading light of the Fabian Society. Annie was impressed by his work and grew very close to him too in the early 1880s. It was Annie who made the first move, by inviting Shaw to live with her. This he refused, but it was Shaw who sponsored Annie to join the Fabian Society. In its early days, the Society was a gathering of people exploring spiritual, rather than political, alternatives to the capitalist system. Annie now began to write for the Fabians. This new commitment - and her relationship with Shaw - deepened the split between Annie and Bradlaugh, who was an individualist and opposed to Socialism of any sort. While he would defend free speech at any cost, he was very cautious about encouraging working-class militancy.

Bloody Sunday

Unemployment was a central issue of the time, and in 1887 some of the London unemployed started to hold protests in Trafalgar Square. Annie agreed to appear as a speaker at a meeting on 13 November. The police tried to stop the assembly. Fighting broke out, and troops were called. Many were hurt, one man died, and hundreds were arrested. Annie offered herself for arrest, but the police refused to take the bait. The events created a great sensation, and became known as Bloody Sunday. Annie was widely blamed - or credited - for it. She threw herself into organising legal aid for the jailed workers and support for their families. Bradlaugh finally broke with her because he felt she should have asked his advice before going ahead with the meeting.

The Unionist

Socialists saw the trade unions as the first real signs of working people's ability to organise and fight for themselves. Until now, trade unions had been for skilled workers - men with a craft that might take years to acquire and which gave them at least a little security. The Socialists wanted to bring both unskilled men and women into unions to fight for better pay and conditions. Her most notable victory in this period was perhaps her involvement in the London matchgirls strike of 1888. Annie was drawn into this first really important battle of the "New Unionism" by Herbert Burrows, a young socialist with whom she was for a time in love. He had made contact with workers at Bryant and May's match factory in Bow, London, who were mainly young women. They were very poorly paid. They were also prey to horrendous industrial illnesses, like the bone-rotting Phossy jaw, which was caused by the chemicals used in match manufacture. Some of the match workers asked for help from Burrows and Annie in setting up a union. Annie met the women and set up a committee, which led the women into a strike for better pay and conditions. The action won enormous public support. Annie led demonstrations by "matchgirls". They were cheered in the streets, and prominent churchmen wrote in their support. In just over a week they forced the firm to improve pay and conditions. Annie then helped them to set up a proper union and a social centre.

At the time, the matchstick industry was an immensely powerful lobby, since electric light was not yet widely available, and matches were essential for lighting candles, oil lamps, gas lights and so on. (Only a few years earlier in 1872, lobbyists from the match industry had persuaded the British government to change its planned tax policy.) Besant's campaign was the first time anyone had successfully challenged the match manufacturers on a major issue, and was seen as a landmark victory of the early years of British Socialism.

Great Liberal Thinker

Annie Besant fought for the causes she thought were right, starting with freedom of thought, women's rights, secularism (she was a leading member of the National Secular Society alongside Charles Bradlaugh), birth control, Fabian socialism and workers' rights. Divorce was unthinkable for Frank, and was not really within the reach of even middle-class people. Annie was to remain Mrs. Besant for the rest of her life. At first, she was able to keep contact with both children and to have Mabel live with her. She got a small allowance from Frank. Once free of Frank Besant and exposed to new currents of thought, Annie began to question not only her long-held religious beliefs but also the whole of conventional thinking. She began to write attacks on the churches and the way they controlled people's lives. In particular she attacked the status of the Church of England as a state-sponsored faith.

Career in Writing

She earned a small weekly wage by writing a column for the National Reformer, the newspaper of the National Secular Society. The Society stood for a secular state: an end to the special status of Christianity. The Society allowed her to act as one of its public speakers. Public lectures were very popular entertainment in Victorian times.

Brilliant Speaker

Annie was a brilliant speaker, and was soon in great demand. Using the railway, she crisscrossed the country, speaking on all of the most important issues of the day, always demanding improvement, reform and freedom. For many years Annie was a friend of the Society's leader, Charles Bradlaugh. It seems that they were never lovers, but their friendship was very close. Bradlaugh, a former seaman, had long been separated from his wife. Annie lived with Bradlaugh and his daughters, and they worked together on many issues. Bradlaugh was an atheist and a republican. He was working to get himself elected as MP for Northampton to gain a better platform for his ideas.

Controversial Book

Besant and Bradlaugh became household names in 1877 when they published a book by the American birth-control campaigner Charles Knowlton. It claimed that working-class families could never be happy until they were able to decide how many children they wanted. It suggested ways to limit the size of their families. The Knowlton book caused great offence to the Churches, but Annie and Bradlaugh proclaimed in the National Reformer: "We intend to publish nothing we do not think we can morally defend. All that we publish we shall defend."

The pair were arrested and put on trial for publishing the Knowlton book. They were found guilty, but released pending appeal. As well as great opposition, Annie and Bradlaugh also received a great deal of support in the Liberal press. Arguments raged back and forth in the letters and comment columns as well as in the courtroom.

For a time, it looked as though they would be sent to prison. The case was thrown out finally only on a technical point: the charges had not been properly drawn up. The scandal lost Annie her children. Frank was able to persuade the court that she was unfit to look after them, and they were handed over to him permanently. Bradlaugh's political prospects were not damaged by the Knowlton scandal. He got himself into Parliament at last in 1881.

Because of his atheism, he refused to swear the oath of loyalty. Although many Christians were shocked by Bradlaugh, others (like the Liberal leader Gladstone) spoke up for freedom of belief. It took more than six years before the whole issue was sorted out (in Bradlaugh's favour) after a series of by-elections and court appearances.

Supporter of Irish Home Rule

Besant built close contacts with the Irish Home Rulers and gave them support in her newspaper columns. These were crucial years, in which the Irish nationalists were forming an alliance with Liberals and Radicals. Annie met the leaders of the movement. In particular, she got to know Michael Davitt, who wanted to mobilise the Irish peasantry through a Land War: a direct struggle against the landowners. She spoke and wrote in favour of Davitt and his Land League many times over the coming decades. However, Bradlaugh's parliamentary work gradually alienated Annie. Women had no part in parliamentary politics. Annie was searching for a real political outlet: politics where her skills as a speaker, writer and organiser could do some real good.

Supporter of Freemasonry

Given Annie Besant's activity in pursuing the rights of women, humanitarian causes, the mysteries and occult teachings, her interest in freemasonry and subsequent leadership and activism comes as no surprise. She pursued freemasonry with equal vigour when it was mentioned to her that there was a masonry that "accepted women as well as men". She saw freemasonry, in particular co-freemasonry, as an extension of her interest in the rights of women and the greater brotherhood of man and saw co-freemasonry as a "movement which practised true brotherhood, in which women and men worked side by side for the perfecting of humanity. She immediately wanted to be admitted to this organisation", known now as The International Order of Co-Freemasonry, Le Droit Humain.

The link was made in 1902 by Francesca Arundale, who accompanied Annie Besant to Paris, along with six friends. "They were all initiated, passed and raised into the first three degrees and Annie returned to England, bearing a Charter and founded there the first Lodge of International Mixed Masonry, Le Droit Humain." "In a very short time, Sister Besant founded new lodges: three in London, three in the south of England, three in the North and North-West; she even organised one in Scotland." Travelling in 1904 with her sisters and brothers she met in Holland, other brethren of a male obedience, who, being interested, collaborated in further expansion of Le Droit Humain. "Annie continued to work with such ardour that soon new lodges were formed Great Britain, South America, Canada, India, Ceylon, Australia and New Zealand. The lodges in all these countries were united under the name of the British Federation." Annie Besant, therefore not only founded the British Federation of Le Droit Humain, of which she was eventually the Most Puissant Grand Commander, she was a major influence in the international growth of the Order.

A Theosophist

Besant was a prolific writer and a powerful orator. In 1889, she was asked to write a review for the *Pall Mall Gazette* on *The Secret Doctrine*, a book by H.P. Blavatsky. After reading it, she sought an interview with its author, meeting Blavatsky in Paris. In this way she was converted to Theosophy. Annie's intellectual journey had always involved a spiritual dimension, a quest for transformation of the whole person. As her interest in Theosophy deepened, she allowed her membership of the Fabian Society to lapse (1890) and broke her links with the Marxists. When Blavatsky died in 1891, Annie was left as one of the leading figures in Theosophy. Her most important public commitment to the faith came in 1893, when she went to present it at the Chicago World Fair.

To India

Soon after becoming a member of the Theosophical Society she went to India for the first time (in 1893). After a dispute in which William Quan Judge, leader of the American section, was accused of falsifying letters from the Masters, the American section split away. The remainder of the Society was then led by Henry Steel Olcott and Besant and is today based in Chennai, India, and is known as the Theosophical Society Adyar. Thereafter she devoted much of her energy not only to the Society, but also to India's freedom and progress. Besant Nagar, a neighbourhood near the Theosophical Society in Chennai, is named in her honour.

A Marxist

During 1884, Annie had developed a very close friendship with Edward Aveling, a young socialist teacher, who lived in her house for a time. Aveling was a scholarly figure and it was he who translated the important works of Marx into English for the first time. Annie seems to have fallen in love with Aveling, but it is not clear that he felt the same way.

He was certainly a great influence on her thinking, and she was a great support to his work. However, Aveling left Annie to live with Eleanor Marx, daughter of Karl Marx. This led to permanent ill-feeling between Annie and Eleanor and probably pushed Annie towards the rival Fabians at that time. Aveling and Eleanor joined the Marxist SDF but they distrusted its leader, Henry Hyndman. Soon they left the SDF to join the Socialist League, a small Marxist splinter group which formed around the artist William Morris.

It seems that Morris played a large part in converting Annie to Marxism, but it was to the SDF, not his Socialist League, that she turned in 1888. She remained a member for a number of years and became one of its best speakers. Strangely, she was still a member of the Fabian Society. Neither she nor anyone else seemed to think the two movements completely incompatible at the time.

Soon after joining the Marxists, Annie stood for election to the London School Board. Because women were not able to take part in parliamentary politics, it is often thought that they did not have any suffrage rights until 1918. In fact, women householders had been brought into the local electorate in 1881, and soon began to make a mark in local politics. Annie drove about with a red ribbon in her hair, speaking at noisy meetings. "No more hungry children," her manifesto proclaimed. She made clear that her Socialism had a feminist side too: "I ask the electors to vote for me, and the non-electors to work for me because women are wanted on the Board and there are too few women candidates." Astonishingly, Annie came out on top of the poll in Tower Hamlets, with over 15,000 votes.

Annie wrote in the National Reformer: "Ten years ago, under a cruel law, Christian bigotry robbed me of my little child. Now the care of the 763,680 children of London is placed partly in my hands." Annie was also closely involved in the struggle for the "Dockers' Tanner". The dockers were poorly paid for hard and dangerous work. They were casual labourers, only taken on for one day at a time. Ben Tillett set up a union for dockers. Annie was crucial in this. She helped Tillett to draw up the union's rules and played an important part in the meetings and agitation which built up the organisation.

Tillett led the dockers in a fight for better wages: sixpence (2½p.) an hour. Annie spoke for the dockers at public meetings and on street corners. Like the matchgirls, the dockers won a lot of public support for their struggle. Even Cardinal Manning, the head of the Roman Catholic Church in England, came out on their side. After a bitter strike, the "dockers' tanner" was won.

3

Significant Writings

[Specimens of Masterpieces]

India and England

Educated India has never desired to throw off her allegiance to the Crown; she has only asked for the self-government enjoyed by the Colonies. Her loyalty is not a change of opinion; it is not an approval of the Arms Act, and the Press Act, and the many badges of racial inferiority branded upon her; she hates these things as she has ever hated them, but, of her own free will, she chooses now to put them on one side. And why? Because she loves England for having aroused her from the sleep of centuries by holding up before her the ideal of liberty, for having sheltered the oppressed of every nation. She rallies to her because England is the mother of free nations; because, if England fell, tyranny would stalk unchecked over prostrate peoples; because England is the most sanely progressive nation on earth, and, with whatever temporary vagaries, her face is steadily set towards the goal of liberty.

India has been inspired politically by the glorious history of England's struggles for freedom. She has read, with breathless interest, how England, step by step, won constitutional liberty; how she curbed her Kings; how she lifted her serfs; how she refused the payment of unjust taxes; how her merchants built up her prosperity; how she educated her masses; how she has widened the sphere of self-government by Act after Act; how her Commons have twice honestly cancelled their own resolutions when they infringed on popular liberty; how she has declared that "taxation without representation is robbery"; how she has freed her press; how she has won full liberty of speech. All this has created the ideals of educated India, and her clear vision has seen the real England through the thick fog of autocracy and bureaucracy which shroud her here.

The danger of teaching English history to boys under an autocracy has been recognised of late years in the efforts to check the teaching, but the check comes too late; it has already inspired educated India, the India which believes in old England, the real England, despite the new angled Anglo-England, and with pathetic intensity believes that if England only knew and understood her grievances all would be redressed. And she is right. How, save in amity with England, how, save with England's help, can she build up the fair fabric of India's liberty, and become that which her voice, her Congress, has persistently demanded, a self-governing nation within the Empire?

The war broke out with a thunderclap, and the Mother of Freedom, waking from her lethargy, sent out her ringing call for help to maintain national honour, international faith. All her admiration for England's past, all her hopes for work with England's future, all her loyalty to a King who had shown her honour and sympathy, all her ingrained feelings of chivalry and truth and faith, brought India springing to her feet, and made her pour out her all for the guarding of the Empire's life - the Empire which is the ark in which all the hopes of the world's freedom are embarked, and which is tossing on the stormy waves of war. India's freedom is in that ark; France, the standard-bearer of ideas, is in that ark; where else can India be?

By her quick answer to the call of the King, India won instantaneous recognition. And now, to make new discord, to re-arouse the sense of injury so magnanimously thrown aside, the strident voices of ungenerous effort to use against India India's magnanimity arise, and thinly veiled dislike of the advocates of liberty endeavours to misrepresent her motives, and to use her loyalty to buttress autocracy.

Does Ireland, in rallying to the Empire, proclaim that in the Penal Laws, in the destruction of her manufactures, in the famine-compelled exile of her once-numerous population, in the suspension of the Habeas Corpus, in the hanging of Emmet, in the imprisonment of Davitt, England ruled her well? Does Russia, in silencing every voice of reproach and rallying round the Tsardom which has knouted, exiled, starved, imprisoned, hanged her noblest sons and daughters, declare that she approves of all these things? Nay. Both nations forget the evils, because loyalty and patriotism, and belief in the splendid immortal soul of England, of Russia, outweigh all transitory wrongs. Oh! let not the fair opportunity of the present union of hearts be flung away by the covert insinuations of those who have tried to build England's rule in India on the ignorance of peasants and the servility of office-seekers, instead of on the rock of the loyalty of free men! Let it be remembered that, under the influence of the spirit of the age, there is no safety for any empire, for any throne, unless it be, like the throne of Britain, in Britain, "broad-based upon the people's will". - New India, October 13, 1914.

England and India

The relations between conquering nations and subject peoples form a question of the present day which may well tax the thought of the most thoughtful, as well as stir the feelings of the most sensitive. How these relations should be carried on, how both conquering nation and subject people may profit by the links that arise between them - on the answer to that problem depends much of the future progress of the world, and I have thought that, with the traditions that are associated with the name of South Place, I might well take up before you this morning the relations which exist between one of the greatest of conquering nations and the greatest of subject peoples, and see how far it is possible to lay down certain lines of thought, which may possibly be of help to you in your own thinking, which may possibly suggest to you ideas which, perchance, otherwise might not have come in your way.

Now, every two nations that come into touch the one with the other should, it is very clear, each have something to learn, each have something to teach, and this is perhaps pre-eminently the case where two such nations as India and England are concerned. Where England has to do with savage peoples her path is comparatively simple; where she has to do with a nation far older than her own civilization, a nation with fixed and most ancient traditions, a nation that was enjoying a high state of civilization long ere the seed of Western civilization was sown - where she has to do with such a people, the relations must needs be complicated and difficult, difficult for both sides to understand, difficult for both sides to make fruitful of good rather than of evil. And I know of no greater service that can be rendered either in this land or in that, than the service of those who try to understand the question and to draw the nations closer together by wisdom instead of driving them further apart by ignorance and by prejudice.

Now it seems to me that with regard to India, the subject may fall quite naturally under three heads: first, the head of religion; then, of education; and then, of political relations, under which latter I include the social conditions of the people. Let me try, then, under these three headings to suggest to you certain ideas as to English relations with India, which may possibly hereafter bear fruit in your minds, if they be worthy to do so.

I said that, when two nations come together, each has something to teach and something to learn, and that is true. So far as religion is concerned, I think India has more to teach than she has to learn. So far as education is concerned, much has to be done on both sides, but on the whole, in most respects, England has more to teach there than to learn. With regard to political conditions, there both nations have much to learn in mutual understanding and in adaptation to this old civilization of India of methods of thought, of rule, of social conditions utterly alien from her own conditions, so that changes, if it be wise to introduce them, must be brought about with the greatest care, the greatest delicacy, after the longest and most careful consideration.

Let us take, then, first, the question of religion, on which I submit to you that India has more to teach than she has to learn; and I say that for this reason, that almost everything which can be learned from Christianity exists also in the eastern faiths, and you have with regard to this to remember in India that you are dealing with a people of various faiths and many schools of thought, some of them exceedingly ancient, deeply philosophic, as well as highly spiritual. Now, seventy per cent of the population of India are Hindûs, belong to one great religion, which includes under that name an immense variety of philosophic schools and sects. For when we speak of Hindûism, we are not speaking of what you might call a simple religion, such as is modern Christianity, though even there you have divisions enough, but of a religion which has always encouraged to the fullest extent the freedom of the intellect, and which recognises nothing as heresy which the intellect of man can grasp, which the thought of man can formulate.

You have under that general name the greatest diversity of thought, and always Hindûism has encouraged that diversity, has not endeavoured to check it. Hindûism is very, very strict in its social polity; it is marvellously wide in its theological, its ethical, its philosophical thought. It includes even on one side the Chãrvaka system, the most complete atheism, as it would here be called; while it includes on the other, forms of the most popular religious thinking that it is possible to conceive. The intellect, then, has ever been free under the scepter of the religion which embraces seventy per cent of the great Indian population.

The majority of the remaining thirty per cent are followers of the great Prophet of Arabia, Muhammad (Pbuh), and amongst them today there are great signs of awakening of thought, there are great signs of revival of deeper philosophical belief. While the majority of them still are, I was almost going to say, plunged in religious bigotry, from western and from eastern standpoints, rather repeating a creed than understanding a philosophy, there is none the less at the present day a very considerable awakening, and a hope that the great faith of Islãm may stand higher in the eyes of the world by knowledge and by power than it has done for many a hundred years in the past. Then, in addition to this - the Hindû with its seventy per cent, the faith of Islãm, which counts some fifty millions of the population - you have Christianity, imported, of course, from the West, not touching the higher classes of the Hindûs at all, but having a considerable following, especially in the South, among the most ignorant, among the most superstitious people; you have the Pãrsi community, a thoughtful, learned and wealthy community, though a very small one, only numbering, I think, some 80,000 people; you have the Jain community, also very wealthy, and having among it a certain number of very learned men, a community whose rites go back to the very early days of Hindû thought and Hindû civilization; and you have in addition to this the warrior nation of the Sikhs, bound together by their devotion to their great Prophet, and forming today a most important part of the fighting strength of the English Empire in India. Buddhism has scarcely any power in India proper. It rules in Burma, and it rules in Ceylon, both, of course, forming part of the Indian Empire, but in India proper it is practically non-existent.

In this way, then, you have a country, including Burma and Ceylon, in which you have clearly marked out some seven different faiths, and you have a ruling nation, Christian in its theory, and entirely unsectarian so far as its rule over the people is concerned; but inevitably under the shadow of that conquering nation there grows up an immense missionary propaganda in India, which is strong, not by its learning, not by the spirituality of its missionaries, but simply from the fact that they belong to the conquering, to the ruling, people, and so have behind them, in the mind of the great mass of the Indians, the weight which comes by the authority of the English Empire, as you may say, backing that particular form of faith. Now it is this condition that you want to understand, if you would deal fairly with the religions question in India.

The most utter impartiality is the rule of the Government, but it is that simple impartiality which may be said to take up the position that all religions are equally indifferent. This is not the kind of spirit that is wanted in a country where religion is the strongest force in life. You need a sympathetic impartiality, not an impartiality of indifference; and it is that in which so far the government has naturally very largely failed. You want in India at the present time a definite recognition of the fact that the religions that are there, and that rule the hearts of the great mass of the people and the minds of the most thoughtful and learned of the nation - that these religions are worthy of the highest respect, and not of mere toleration. You have to realise that the missionary efforts there do an infinity of harm and very little good; that they set religion against religion and faith against faith; whereas what you want in India is the brotherhood of religions, and the respect of men of every faith for the faiths which are not theirs. You need there the teaching and the spirit of Theosophy, which sees every religion as the partial expression of one great truth. The more aggressive one faith shows itself to be, the more it is stirring up religious antagonisms and religious hatreds.

Danger to the Empire lies in the aggressive policy of Christianity, whereby large numbers of men, ignorant of the religions that they attack, treat them with contempt, with scorn, with insult - that is one of the dangers that you have to consider in India, when you remember that in the minds of the people England stands behind the missionary. The Christian missionary converts very, very rarely, in the most exceptional of cases, any man who is educated, any man who is trained in his own faith, any man of what are called the higher and thoughtful castes. He makes his converts among the great mass of the most ignorant of the population; he makes them chiefly in times of famine and of distress; he makes them more largely for social reasons than for reasons which are religious in their nature. By the folly of the Hindûs themselves vast masses of the Indians have been left without religious teachings altogether, have been regarded with contempt, have been looked upon with arrogance. It is among these classes that the Christian missionaries find their converts.

Once such a man is converted to Christianity, he, who before was not allowed to cross the threshold of a Hindû, is admissible as a Christian into the house, because Christianity is the religion of the conquering nation; and you can very well recognise how strong a converting power that has on the ignorant, on the degraded, on the socially oppressed. It is not necessary for me to say much on that here, since here nothing much can be done in this matter. It is rather in India, that one tries to meet that question, pointing out to the educated and the religious how great a danger to their own faith, as well as how great a wrong to humanity, it is to neglect vast portions of the population, and so to drive them, as it were, to find refuge in an alien creed, which at least treats them with decency, if it cannot do much for them in ethical training.

This religious question in India is one that you need to understand, for eastern teaching is everywhere more and more spreading in the West. I could not help being amused the other day by a remark of a disconsolate missionary coming back to America, and declaring that while he was striving to convert people from Hinduism, he found on his return that large numbers of the educated were tainted with the philosophy that in India he was trying to destroy. That is perfectly true. Hindu thought is making its way here in general very much more rapidly than Christianity is making its way in India; and it is touching the flower of the population here, whereas Christianity is only touching the poorest and most ignorant in India.

That is why I said that India had much more to teach than to learn in matters of religion; she has plenty in her own faith which can train and cultivate the masses of her people, but that must be done by Hindû missionaries and not by Christian missionaries. It would be the wisdom of England to look upon all these religions as methods of training, of guiding, of helping the people, and to recognise that the work of the Christian in India is among his own population, is among his own countrymen, is among the Christian communities, and that he should look on his faith as a sister faith among many, and not as unique, to which people of other religions are to be converted. The greatest, perhaps the only serious, danger to English rule in India lies in the religious question, in the bad feelings stirred up by the missionaries, in the difficulties that are caused by their lack of understanding of the people. Theosophy has done much to counteract this danger, and has been striving in India to stimulate the peoples of the various faiths to take up these religious questions for themselves, and by their energy in the teaching of their own religion to cause the spread of religious knowledge which may make each faith strong within its own borders,

Pass from the religious question to the educational, and here a great danger lies immediately in front, a danger which arises largely out of that want of sympathy and that want of understanding which is the chief fault of the English people as a conquering nation, as a ruler in their relations with subject peoples. They try to be just, they try to do their duty, they are industrious, they are hard-working, endeavouring to do the work which is put into their hands. Their weak point lies in the fact that they are very unsympathetic, that they cannot put themselves into the place of others, and that they have a tendency to think they are so immensely superior to others that whatever is good for them is good for everybody else; they fail to understand the traditions and the customs which must exist in an ancient people, a people of high and complicated civilization, and this lack of sympathy has a very great bearing on the question of education.

Practically, Indian education, on the higher line, was started by the wisdom of Lord Macaulay. He began the work of Indian education, and he began it wisely and well. It has been carried on year after year by a long succession of Viceroys, who for the most part have done well with regard to the educational question; but while they have done well, it is perfectly true that there are great and serious faults in the Indian system, faults which need to be corrected and which neutralise much of the value of the education that is given. I have not time to go very fully into these faults; it must suffice to say that memory has been cultivated to the exclusion of the reasoning faculty, and that even when science has been taught, it has been taught by the textbook, and not in the laboratory, it has been taught by memory, and not by experiment. In addition to that there has been a crushing number of examinations, forcing the whole life of the boy as well as of the man, and keeping up a continual strain which has exhausted the pupil ere he has left the University.

It has been forgotten that the Indian student is naturally studious and not playful enough, that his inclination is to work a great deal too hard, that what was wanted was the stimulation to play more than the stimulation to study, that the physical training of the boys was more necessary to be seen to than the intellectual training. The physical training was left out of sight, and though carefully looked after in ancient India it was now neglected. As these differences were overlooked, everything was done to force the intellectual side in an unwise way, by cramming rather than by organic development of study, and as the University degrees were made the only passport to Government employment and to the professions at large, it became a wild desire on the part of the Indian parent to force his boys on as rapidly as possible, with little regard to the kind of education that was given. These faults have been seen by the present Viceroy, and, eager to mend the faults, he sent out a University Commission, which has just made its report. Now the first fault of that Commission was that it had only two representatives of India on it, and the rest Englishmen, and the English members of that Commission were not all acquainted with the nature of the problems of Indian education. They have issued their Report. The Indian judge, who was the Hindû member of that Commission, has issued a minority report, against many of the recommendations made by the majority, consisting of the English members and one Musalmãn.

The very fact that you get a report divided in that racial way ought at once to make our rulers pause, and when you find that many of the recommendations of the majority-report are disapproved by the representative of seventy percent of the population that you are going to teach, it seems as though it might be wise if the Government here would look into the matter a little carefully before it gives its decision. For it is the view of the Indian people, now being expressed in every way possible, that the report of the Commission strikes a heavy blow at Indian education, that much of the great work of the past will be destroyed, and that the education of the future will be placed beyond the reach of large numbers of the people who here dilatory claim it.

To begin with, the education is now made more costly, and by that one word you have its condemnation for India, The fees are everywhere to be raised, so that University education will be practically beyond the reach of those who need it most. It is said that many go to the University who are not fit for it; but the remedy for that is to improve the teaching in your Universities and not to increase the cost of the education; for by high fees you will not exclude the idle and the unworthy rich, but you will exclude great masses of the worthy and industrious poor; and when you remember that it is the Indian tradition that learning and poverty go together, that the man who is learned has no need of wealth, that you find the highest caste the poorest caste, although the most learned - if you could realise that and put yourself in their place, you would understand the agitation which at present is convulsing the most thoughtful people in India, when they see that the Government is going to exclude their sons, the flower of the intellectual population, from all share in education by the high fees which it is going to impose. It is said by the Commission, that scholarships may serve for the poorer classes, but you cannot give scholarships to thousands of that vast population. You can give scholarships to a boy here and there, but you cannot give them to the great mass; the greatest danger is the discontent of the thoughtful, and that is the discontent which is being stirred up at the present time. The truth is, that Lord Curzon, able as he is, has only five years in which to rule, and he is eager to mark his Viceroyalty by some great scheme of change.

But if England be not careful, it will be marked by the saddest monument that ever Viceroy has left behind him, the destruction of the education of a great people, and the shutting out of vast masses of the intellectual from education whereby they might rise to be your helpers in the ruling of their country, but shut out from which they become an element of danger. That is not a thing which it is well to have said by a subject nation of the type of the Indian nation. It is said among the thoughtful people now that this is intended to destroy education, in order that Indians may not have their fair share in the government of their own land. That is the thought which is spreading, that is the motive which they believe lies behind the policy of Lord Curzon. They think he desires to stop education, in order that the Indians may not rise to the higher posts in their own country, and that is a most dangerous idea to spread through the most intellectual, through the most thoughtful classes. I have had letter after letter pleading with me to do something here to prevent this Report from receiving the sanction of the Government; but how difficult is it to do that where the people who give the decision are ignorant themselves, and where they naturally rely on their own agents rather than on what any casual speaker may say.

In the attempt started by the Theosophical Society in India, and carried on by large numbers of the Hindûs themselves, to build up a large Hindû College, we are trying to do the very opposite of some of the things that are being suggested to the Government, and are already doing some of the things they want done. We have put down the fees to the lowest possible point; we are training the lads in the laboratory; we give them less and less instruction in which memory only is cultivated, and in which the reasoning faculties are thrown entirely on one side.

We are teaching them to play games; we are training strong and healthy bodies, and are endeavouring to prevent the great nervous strain involved in study. But if this Commission Report be adopted, much of our work will be destroyed, and the results which we are trying to bring about, and have brought about to some extent, will be utterly wasted, will be impossible to carry on; for the boys that we want to reach, the intelligent, the eager, those who are longing to learn but whose parents are poor, they will be shut utterly out of education, for unless we adopt the Government rate of fees, the Government may close the College and not permit it to carry on its work.

That is the kind of difficulty that has to be dealt with in these educational measures. If you would let Indians guide their own education, if you would give them all that is best in the West, when it is suitable, but not insist that all that is good in England is necessarily good there; if you would try to see things from their own standpoint, if you did not insist on highly paid Englishmen as instructors, instead of educated Indians, you would work at less expense and with more efficiency.

But what is there to be done, when the Government here has the last word, and knows nothing about the conditions; and when the data on which the decisions are made are sent from India by those who are apart from Indian sympathy, data on which the Indians are not consulted, although it is their children whose future is in jeopardy. What is really needed is to make education cheap, widespread, scientific, literary and technical; to change the policy which draws the intelligent Indians only into Government service, and to get them to take up the other lines of work which affect the economic future of their country; to educate them in arts and manufactures; not to leave the direction of industry to people who are of the ruling nation, but to draft into industrial undertakings large numbers of the educated classes - that is the kind of education that is wanted, and the kind of education that England does not give to India, and will not let India give to herself.

Pass from that to the third point I spoke of - the questions touching on politics, including the social and economic conditions of India. It must have struck you, those who have studied the past, that it is very strange that this country - which, when the East India Company went there in the eighteenth century, was one of the richest countries of the world - has now become a country to go a-begging to the world for the mere food to keep its vast population from dying of starvation by millions. The mere fact that there has been such a change in the wealth of the country should surely make those who are responsible for its rule look more closely into the economic conditions, should surely suggest that there is something fundamentally wrong when you have these recurring famines. Six years of famine, practically, India has lately passed through.

It is not due to changes of climate; these have always been there - seasons of drought, seasons of too much rain, seasons of good weather. These are not surely the direct result of English rule! They existed long before England came; they are likely to exist long after we have all passed away. Why is it that these famines recur time after time ? Why is it that such myriads of people are thus doomed to starvation ? Now I have not a word to say as to the efforts that are made by the English when the famine is there, save words of praise. The English officials worked themselves half to death, when the people were dying. But that is not the time when the work is most needed. It is prevention that we want, rather than cure; and the nation that can only deal with famine by relief-works and by charity is not a nation that in the eyes of the world can justify its authority in India. There must be causes that underlie these famines.

It is the duty of the ruling nation to understand these causes, or else to allow the wisest among the Indian population to take these questions into their own hands and act as the Council of the English rulers. Sometimes it is said that the famine is owing to the increase in the population. That is not true. What is called the peace of Britain is not a blessing, if it be the cause of famine. It is easier to the great mass of the people to have wars that kill off some of them quickly, than to have recurring famines that starve them to death after months of agony. The British peace is not a blessing, if it be punctuated by famines in which millions die by starvation. Peace is not a blessing if it kills more people than war, and that is what the peace of England is doing in India, and it is killing them after terrible sufferings, instead of by sword and by fire. It is the cause of these famines that we need to understand. It is a remarkable fact that, where the Indian Princes have been left uninterfered with, the famines have not been so serious.

Everywhere, where a nation lives by agriculture and has to prepare itself for a bad season, it is usual to find out a way of dealing with the natural difficulties suitable to its own spirit. Now that was done in India, and done in a very simple way, although a way that is dead against the modern Political economy. The way was a simple way as in the days of ancient Egypt. We have all read of how when Joseph was the wise minister there, he provided for the years of famine in the years of plenty. That one sentence expresses the Indian way of dealing with famines. When there was plenty, large quantities of the food were stored, and rent and taxes were taken in food these varied with the food raised by the people and therefore they never pressed heavily on the people. When there was much raised the rent and taxes were higher; when the harvest was bad, the King went without his share.

But in the years when he got a very large share, he stored it in granaries. In addition to that, after the people were fed (and the feeding of the people was the first charge), the people themselves stored the year's corn, so that if they had a bad year they could fall back on their own corn. In this way the peasant could make head against one bad season and if there were more than one bad season the Prince came to his aid, by throwing his corn on the market at a price which the people could afford to pay. Now that method of dealing with the famine problem still goes on in some States, such as Kãshmir, because they will not permit their grain to be exported. But the greatest pressure is continually being put on the Mahãrãja of Kãshmir to force him to export his rice, He has been able to hold his own so far, but the resistance to English pressure is a terribly difficult thing for an Indian Prince, and to resist it continually is not possible. Now I know how alien to English thought is that method of dealing with the products of a country; but it is far better to carry that on and save the people from famine, than to insist that the people shall sell their corn in years of plenty and starve in years of scarcity; The people want to store their corn when they have it, to keep it against the bad seasons, instead of having to import it from abroad in time of famine.

And yet, in this very year when famine was threatened, I saw not long ago in a newspaper a telegram advising the recurrence of famine in one part of India, and, in the same paper that contained that telegram, I saw a statement that the first ship loads of Indian wheat had left Bombay. That may be modern political economy, but it is pure idiocy. India if wisely governed may be a paradise, but we have just read that with five fools you can turn a paradise into a hell; and to impose English political economy on India is folly, well-intentioned folly, but folly none the less.

Another great cause of these famines is the way in which the land is now held. In the old days there was a common interest in the land between Princes and people. Now the nobles, the old class of zemindars, have been turned into landlords, and that is a very different thing from the old way of holding land. Then you have insisted on giving to the peasant the right to sell his land, the very last thing that he wants to do, the thing which takes away from him the certainty of food for himself and his children. No peasant in the old days had the right to sell his land, but only to cultivate it. If he needed to borrow at any time, he borrowed on the crop. Now, in order to free the people from debt, they are given the right to sell their mortgaged holdings, and this means the throwing out of an agricultural people on the roads, making them landless, and the holding of the land by moneylenders. That revolution in the land system of India is one of the causes of the recurring famines, the second perhaps of the great causes. The natural result of it is that you put now power into the hands of the money-lender, and you take away from the peasant the shield that always protected him.

The railway system, too, useful as it is, has done an immense amount of harm. It has cleared away the food; it has sent the man with money into the country districts to buy up the produce, which he sends abroad, giving the peasant the rupees that he cannot eat instead of the rice and corn that he can eat.

Even when I first went to India, you could hardly see a peasant woman without silver bangles on her arms and legs. Now large numbers of peasant women wear none; these have been sold during these last years of famine, and to sell these is the last sign of poverty for the Indian peasantry. It is no good giving them money in exchange for their food. They do not know how to deal with it. They are urged to buy English goods of Manchester manufacture, which wear out in a few months, instead of the Indian-made articles which last for many years. You must remember that the Indian peasant washes his clothes every day of his life, and so they need to be of great durability.

Another difficulty is the way in which you have destroyed the manufactures of India - destroyed them partly by flooding the market with cheap, showy, adulterated goods, which have attracted the ignorant people, inducing them to buy what is largely worthless. All the finer manufactures of India are practically destroyed, whereas the makers used to grow rich by selling these to her wealthy men and to foreign countries. Now both the fine and coarse goods are beaten out of the country by the cheap Manchester goods, and the dear fashionable fabrics; even if this had been done fairly it would not be so bad, but the Indian merchants were forced to give up their trade secrets to the agents of English industries. You guard your trade secrets jealously from rivals, but you have forced the Indians to give up theirs, in order that English manufacturers might have the benefit of that knowledge. In this way old trades have been gradually killed out, while the arts of India are very rapidly perishing.

The arts of India depended on the social condition of the country. The artist in India was not a man who lived by competition. As far as he was concerned he did not trade at all. He was always kept as part of the great household, of a noble; his board, his lodging, his clothing, were all secured to him, and he worked at his leisure, and carried out his artistic ideas without difficulty and without struggle. All that class is being killed out in the stress of western competition, and it is not as though something else were put in its place; the thing itself is destroyed, the whole market is destroyed. Now the pressure is falling on the artisan, and he is utterly unable to guard himself against it, and is falling back into the already well-filled agricultural ranks.

These are some of the questions that you have to consider and to understand. You have to understand the question of Indian taxation; you have to understand the question of taking away from India seventeen millions a year to meet Home, i.e., English, charges. You have to consider the expense of your Government in India, the exorbitant salaries that are paid to English officials. You have to realise the financial side of the problem, as well as those that I have dealt with Friends, I have only been able to touch the fringe of a great subject. I have hoped, by packing together a number of these facts, to stir you into study rather than to convince you. For if I had tried to move your feelings I would have done little. I have preferred to point out the difficulties that have to be dealt with, so that you may study them, so that you may investigate them, so that you may form your own opinions upon them.

I do not believe it is possible to do everything at once, but I do think it might be possible to form a band of English experts, who should make these questions their speciality, and who should have weight with the Government over here which deals with India, so that they could advise with wisdom, so that they could point out the most useful path by which improvement could be made. To govern a great country like India by a Parliament over here is practically impossible. It is too clumsy an instrument for the ruling of such a people.

But if you would build up in India a great Council, composed of the wisest and most thoughtful of her own people; if you would take the advice of her best administrators in Indian States, her own sons; if you would place in such a Council her greatest feudatory Chiefs; if such a Council of all that is wisest and noblest in India were gathered round the Viceroy, who should hold his post, not as the reward for political service here, but because he knows and understands India, or, still better, appoint as Viceroy a Prince of the Imperial House; if you would leave him there for a greater space of time, and not make him work in a breakneck hurry to get something done; then there would be a brighter hope on the Indian horizon. This can only be done by understanding Indian feelings and not by ignoring them, by trying to sympathise with Indian customs and not by despising them. Along these lines lies the salvation of India and of England alike, and it is this which I recommend to your most thoughtful consideration.

India and the Future

It may be remembered that in 1889 H. P. Blavatsky wrote that the early years of the next century would see many of the accounts of the nations made up, and verily she was a true prophet in this matter. For one very clear result of the present gigantic war is to bring Asia into new relations with Europe, and to establish her in her old place of power in the shaping of the world's destinies. We sometimes forget that all the old empires of the past were Asian; that India, Persia, Assyria struck the keynote of civilization for thousands of years; and that China, though she did not make so flaming a trace on the world's pages, wrote a self-contained story of rare internal progress and lofty ethics which have maintained her in her sure place among the great civilizations of the world.

Asia has been for centuries a continent to be exploited by the young and virile nations of the West. These started on fresh lines on the younger continent of Europe, the fourth and fifth sub-races spreading westwards, and occupying the lands some of which had but lately emerged from the seas. The great swamps of eastern Europe, as they dried up into habitable soil, furnished a centre for the young fifth sub-race, from which their families emigrated westwards and northwards, to found future nationalities. They naturally forgot their Asian Motherland, as generation succeeded generation; and as they developed their new type of civilization, difficulties of communication kept the two continents isolated from each other, unknowing their relative lines of development. Only, later on, incursions into Europe of hordes of warlike and ferocious warriors from the central parts of Asia made the names of the Huns and others names of terror in Europe.

Then came a new impulse from Asia, which embodied itself in the Saracens, the impulse of chivalry and mysticism, spreading westwards and southwards from Persia. Masonry was enriched from the same source, and these all softened and refined the rougher manners of the West, while Arabia took up the tradition of Greece, enriched and developed it, and brought science to Europe, laying the foundations of the modern world. Not only in religion did Asia teach Europe, though it is true that Asia had the genius of spirituality, and that Europe merely copied and spread, but originated no great religion. In literature, philosophy, science, and art, Asia was the mother of all progress; while as regards tolerance, that true mark of greatness, Akbar was discussing religions among wise men of different faiths while Mary was burning Protestants and Elizabeth executing Roman Catholics. Scarcely for two centuries has Europe been taking the lead, while Asia, sated with great achievements, slept for a while to rest, and let the reins of empire slip from fingers tired of power.

But now Asia is awakening, and Japan first raised her head, and fought her way to high position among the nations of the world, concluding alliance with the mighty Western people whose genius for colonisation and rule was laying deep and firm the foundations of a worldwide empire. Persia stirred uneasily, feeling the breath of liberty, and, though hardly entreated by Russia and Britain, she has her eyes fixed on a fuller national life. And China, that vast, unknown land, that land of far-reaching possibilities, took her fate into her own hands, flung off her empire, established a republic, and is feeling her feet, intent on working out her own salvation.

How could this great wave of new life sweep over Asia and leave untouched the blood in India's veins? She, mightiest, fairest, wisest of all Asian peoples, how should she lie supine, continues to sleep, when lesser nations were stirring? And so has come unrest, and movements of new life, a sense of growing strength and consciousness of national unity. Slowly [60] she has been awaking to self-realisation and measuring her resources, and, quietly learning from the younger nations methods of self-government, has been pursuing the new ways of modern peoples. As a nation, she sprang to her feet at the cry for help that rang across the seas from the little northern island that had taught her the great lesson of liberty, and that found herself confronted by a mighty foe, and she flung her sons into the carnage of war, poured out the blood of her people and the hoarded treasures of her Princes, and proved her worth and her strength on the stricken fields of modern war in Europe. Never again can India, who has fought and died for the common empire side by side with Britain, sink back into the old position of Ma-Bap, and stand with folded hands submissive to the Shaba's nod. When Britain called on India for help, she treated her as an equal, and never again can she, in fairness and in honour, treat the Indian nation as a subject race.

By her sword, drawn for England not against her, India has won her freedom, and the chaplet of liberty has been wrought for her on the fields of Europe, sodden with the outpoured blood of Indians and of Britons. Well, verily, is it for both nations that full national self-consciousness has flowered while the two nations are fighting side by side. There was a time when there was a danger that it might be realised in opposition instead of in union, when South Africa strained India's patience and strength almost to the breaking point. South African oppression did much to awaken the sense of unity in India, but, thanks to all good Powers, Lord Hardinge's sympathy and Mr. V. Gandhi's patience tided India over the danger, and turned anger into gratitude.

All this change and the near approach of self-government in India is making the thoughtful feel the need for preparation, and for pressing on more rapidly the religious, educational, social, and political reforms which are too interlinked and interwoven for separation. - The Theosophist, March 1915.

Memories of the Past

There is probably no man now living in the scientific world who does not regard the theory of physical evolution as beyond dispute; there may be many varieties of opinion with regard to details and methods of evolution, but on the fundamental fact, that forms have proceeded from the homogeneous to the heterogeneous, there is complete harmony of educated opinion. Moreover, the evolutionary idea dominates all departments of thought, and is applied to society as much as to the individual. In history it is used as the master-key wherewith to unlock the problems of the growth of nations, and, in sociology, of the progress of civilizations. The rise, the decay, the fall of races are illuminated by this all-pervading idea, and it is difficult now for anyone to throw himself in thought back into the time when law gave way to miracle, and order was replaced by fortuitous irregularity.

In working up to the hypothesis of evolution small indications were searched for, as much as long successions were observed. Things apparently trifling were placed on record, and phenomena apparently trivial were noted with meticulous care. Above all, any incident which seemed to conflict with a recognised law of nature was minutely observed and repeatedly scrutinised, since it might be the indication of some force as yet undiscovered, of some hidden law working along lines as yet unknown. Every fact was observed and recorded, challenged and discussed, and each contributed something to the great pyramid of reasons which pointed to evolution as the best hypothesis for explanation of the phenomena of nature. Your dog turned round and round on the hearthrug before composing himself to sleep; was he not governed by an unconscious memory from the times when his ancestors thus prepared a comfortable depression in the jungle for their repose? Your cat pressed her forepaws on the ground, pushing outwards repeatedly; was it not an unconscious memory which dominated her from the need of her larger predecessors encircled by the tall grass of the forest hiding-place, to flatten out a sufficient bed for luxurious rest? Slight, in truth, are such indications, and yet withal they make up, in their accumulation, a massive argument in favour of unconscious memories of past lives being wrought into the very fabric of the animal body.

But there is one line of questions, provocative of thought, that has not yet been pursued with industry equal to that bestowed on the investigation of bodily movements and habits. The questions remain unanswered, either by biologist or psychologist. Evolution has traced for us the gradual building of our now complex and highly organised bodies; it has shown them to us evolving, in the long course of millions of years, from a fragment of protoplasm, from a simple cell, through form after form, until their present condition has been reached, thus demonstrating a continuity of forms, advancing into greater perfection as organisms! But so far science has not traced a correlative continuity of consciousness - a golden thread on which the innumerable separated bodies might be threaded — a consciousness inhabiting and functioning through this succession of forms. It has not been able to prove — nay, it has not even recognised' the likelihood of the possibility - that consciousness passes on unbroken from body to body, carrying with it an ever-increasing content, the accumulated harvest of innumerable experiences, transmuted into capacities, into powers.

Scientists have directed our attention to the splendid inheritance that has come down to us from the past. They have shown us how generation after generation has contributed something to the sum of human knowledge, and how cycle after cycle manifests a growth of average humanity in intellectual power, in extent of consciousness, in fineness and beauty of emotion. But if we ask them to explain the conditions of this growth, to describe the passing on of the content of one consciousness to another; if we ask for some method, comparable to the methods observed in the physical world, whereby we may trace this transmission of the treasures of consciousness, may explain how it made its habits and accumulates experiences which it transforms into mental and moral capacities, then science returns us no answers, but fails to show us the means and the methods of the evolution of consciousness in man.

When, in dealing with animals, science points to the so-called inherited instincts, it does not offer any explanation of the means whereby an intangible self-preserving instinct can be transmitted by an animal to its offspring. That there is some purposive and effective action, apart from any possibility of physical experience having been gained as its instigator, performed by the young of an animal, we can observe over and over again. Of the fact there can be no question. The young of animals, immediately after coming into the world, are seen to play some trick whereby they save themselves from some threatening danger. But science does not tell us how this intangible consciousness of danger can be transmitted by the parent, who has not experienced it, to the offspring who has never known it. If the life-preserving instinct is transmissible through the physical body of the parent, how did the parent come to possess it ? If the chicken just out of the shell runs for protection to the mother-hen when the shadow of a hawk hovering above it is seen, science tells us that it is prompted by the life-preserving instinct, the result of the experience of the danger of the hovering hawk, so many having thus perished that the seeking of protection from the bird of prey is transmitted as an instinct. But the difficulty of accepting this explanation lies in the fact that the experience necessary to evolve the instinct can only have been gained by the cocks and hens who were killed by birds of prey; these had no chance thereafter of producing eggs, and so could not transmit their valuable experience, while all the chicks come from eggs belonging to parents who had not experienced the danger, and hence could not have developed the instinct. (I am assuming that the result of such experiences in transmissible as an instinct an assumption which is quite unwarranted.) The only way of making the experiences of slaughtered animals reappear later as a life-preserving instinct is for the record of the experience to be preserved by some means, and transmitted as an instinct to those belonging to the same type.

The Theosophist points to the existence of matter finer than the physical, which vibrates in correspondence with any mood of consciousness in this case the shock of sudden death. That vibration tends to repeat itself, and that tendency remains, and is reinforced by similar experiences of other slaughtered poultry; this, recorded in the "group-soul", passes as a tendency into all the poultry race, and shows itself in the newly hatched chick the moment the danger threatens the new form. Instinct is " unconscious memory", "inherited experience", but, each one who possesses it takes it from a continuing consciousness, from which his separate lower consciousness is derived. How else can it have originated, how else have been transmitted ?

Can it be said that animals learn of danger by the observation of others who perish ? That would not explain the unconscious memory in our newly-hatched chicken, who can have observed nothing. But apart from this, it is clear that animals are curiously slow either to observe, or to learn the application to themselves of the actions, the perils, of others.

How often do we see a motherly hen running along the side of a pond, clucking desperately to her brood of ducklings that have plunged into the water to the manifest discomposure of the non-swimming hen; but she does the same thing brood after brood; she never learns that the ducklings are able to swim and that there is no danger to be apprehended when they plunge into the water. She calls them as vigorously after ten years of experience as she did after the first brood, so that it does not look as if instinct originated in careful observation of petty movements by animals who then transmit the results of their observations to their offspring.

The whole question of the continuity of consciousness — a continuity necessary to explain the evolution of instinct as much as that of intelligence — is insoluble by science, but has been readily solved by religion. All the great religions of the past and present have realised the eternity of the Spirit:

> "God," it is written in a Hebrew Scripture, " created man to be the image of His own Eternity", and in that eternal nature of the Spirit lies the explanation alike of instinct and of intelligence. In the intellect-aspect of this Spirit all the harvests of the experiences of successive lives are stored, and from the treasures of the spiritual memory are sent down assimilated experiences, appearing as instincts, as unconscious memories of past lives, in the newborn form. Every improved form receives as instincts and as innate ideas this wealth of reminiscence: every intellectual and moral faculty is a store of reminiscences, and education is but the awakening of memory.

Thus religion illuminate that which science leaves obscure, and gives us a rational, an intelligible theory of the growth of instinct and of intellect; it shows us a continuity of a consciousness ever increasing in content, embodying itself in forms ever increasing in complexity. The view that man consists not only of bodies in which the working of the law of heredity may be traced, but also is a living consciousness, growing, unfolding, evolving, by the assimilation of the food of experience — this theory is an inevitable pendant to the theory of physical evolution, for the latter remains unintelligible without the former. Special creation, rejected from the physical world, cannot much longer be accepted in the psychical, nor be held to explain satisfactorily the differences between the genius and the dolt, between the congenital saint and the congenital criminal. Unvarying law, the knowledge of which is making man the master of the physical world, must be recognised as prevailing equally in the psychical. The improving bodies must be recognised as instruments to be used for the gaining of further experiences by the ever-unfolding consciousness.

A definite opinion on this, matter can only be gained by personal study, investigation and research. Knowledge of the great truths of nature is not a gift, but a prize to be won by merit. Every human being must form his own opinions by his own strenuous efforts to discover truth, by the exercise of his own reasoning faculties, by the experiences of his own consciousness. Writers who garb their readers in second-hand opinions, as a dealer in second-hand clothes dresses his customers, will never turn out a decently costumed set of thinkers; they will be clad in misfits. But there are lines of research to be followed, experiences to be gone through and analysed, by those who would arrive at truth — research which has led others to knowledge, experiences which have been found fruitful in results. To these a writer may point his readers, and they, if they will, may follow along such lines for themselves.

I think we may find in our consciousness — in our intelligence and our emotional nature — distinct traces from the past which point to the evolution of our consciousness, as the recurrent laryngeal nerve and the embryonic reptilian heart point to the ancestral line of evolution of our body. I think there are memories forming part of our consciousness which justify belief in previous existences, and point the way to a more intelligent understanding of human life.

I think that, by careful observation, we may find memories in ourselves, not only of past events, but of the past training and discipline which have made us what we are, memories which are embedded in, which form even the very fabric of our consciousness, which emerge more clearly as we study them, and become more intelligible the more carefully we observe and analyse them. But for a moment we must pause on the theory of Reincarnation, on the broad principle of consciousness in evolution.

This theory posits a Spirit, a seed or germ of consciousness planted in matter, and ultimately, after long ages of growth, becoming ready to enter an undeveloped human body, connected by its material with three worlds, the worlds of mind, of desire and of action, otherwise called the heavenly, intermediate and physical worlds. In the physical world this growing Spirit gathers experiences of varied kinds, feels pleasures and pains, joys and sorrows, health and illness, successes and disappointments, the many changing conditions which make up our mortal life. He carries these on with him through death, and in the intermediate world experiences the inevitable results of desires which clashed with the laws of nature, reaping in suffering the harvest of his blundering ignorance.

Thus he shapes the beginnings of a conscience, the recognition of an external law of conduct. Passing on to the heavenly world, be builds his mental experiences into mental faculties until, all the food of experience being assimilated, he begins again to hunger, and so returns to earth with the elements of a character, still enveloped in many-folded ignorance, but starting with a little more content of consciousness than he had in his previous life.

Such is his cycle of growth, the passing through the three worlds over and over again, ever accumulating experience, ever transmuting it into power. That cycle is repeated over and over again, until the savage grows into the average man of our time, from the average man, to the man of talent, of noble character; then onwards to the genius, to the saint, to the hero; onwards still to the Perfect Man; onwards yet, through ever-increasing, unimaginable splendours, vanishing into blinding radiance which veils his further progress from our dazzled eyes.

Thus every man builds himself, shapes his own destiny, is verily self-created; no one of us is what we are save as we have wrought out our own being; our future is not imposed on us by an arbitrary will or a soulless necessity, but is ours to fashion, to create. There is nothing we cannot accomplish if we are given time, and time is endless. We, the living consciousnesses, we pass from body to body, and each new body takes the impress made upon it by its tenant, the ever-young and immortal Spirit.

I have spoken of the three stages of the life-cycle, each belonging to a definite world; it must be noted that in the physical stage of the life-period, we are living in all the three worlds, for we are thinking and desiring as well as acting, and our body, the vehicle of consciousness, is triple. We lose the physical part of the body at death, and the desire-part at a later period, and live in the mental body — in which all good thoughts and pure emotions have their habitat — while in the heavenly world. When the heaven life is over, the mental body also disintegrates, and there remains but the spiritual body whereof S. Paul speaks, "eternal in the heavens".. Into that, the lasting clothing of the Spirit, are woven all the pure results of experiences gathered in the lower worlds.

In the building of the new triple body for the new life-cycle in the lower worlds, a new apparatus comes into existence for the use of the spiritual consciousness and the spiritual body; and the latter, retaining within itself the conscious memory of past events, imprints on the lower — its instruments for gathering fresh experience — only the results of the past, as faculties, mental and emotional, with many traces of past experiences which have been outgrown and remain normally in the sub-consciousness. The conscious memory of past events being present only in the spiritual body, the consciousness must be functioning in that in order to "remember"; and such functioning is possible through a system of training and discipline — yoga — which may be studied by anyone who has perseverance, and a certain amount of innate ability for this special kind of work.

But in addition to this there are many unconscious memories, manifesting in faculty, in emotion, in power, traces of the past imprinted on the present, and discoverable by observations on ourselves and others. Hence, memories of the past may be clear and definite, obtained by the practice of yoga, or unconscious but shown by results, and closely allied in many ways to what are called instincts, by which you do certain things, think along certain lines, exercise certain functions, and possess certain knowledge without having consciously acquired it. Among the Greeks, and the ancients generally, much stress was laid upon this form of memory. Plato's phrase: "All knowledge is reminiscence", will be remembered. In the researches of psychology today, many surges of feeling, driving a man to hasty, unpremeditated action, are ascribed to the sub-consciousness, i.e., the consciousness which shows itself in involuntary thoughts, feelings and actions; these come to us out of the far-off past, without our volition or our conscious creation. How do these come, unless there be continuity of consciousness ?

Any who study modern psychology will see how great a part unconscious memory plays in our lives, how it is said to be stronger than our reason, how it conjures up pathetic scenes uncalled-for, how at night it throws us into causeless panics. These, we are told, are due to memories of dangers surrounding savages, who must ever be on the alert to guard themselves against sudden attacks, whether of man or beast, breaking into the hours of repose, killing the men and women as they slept. These past experiences are said to have left records in consciousness, records which lie below the threshold of waking consciousness but are ever present within us. And some say that this is the most important part of our consciousness, though out of sight for the ordinary mind.

We cannot deny to these the name of memory, these experiences out of the past that assert themselves in the present. Study these traces, and see whether they are explicable save by the continuity of consciousness, making the Self of the savage the Self which is yourself today, seeing the persistence of the Individual throughout human evolution, growing, expanding, developing, but a fragment of the eternal "I am".

May we not regard instincts as memories buried in the sub-conscious, influencing our actions, determining our "choices" ? Is not the moral instinct Conscience, a mass of interwoven memories of past experiences, speaking with the authoritative utterance of all instincts, and deciding on "right" and "wrong "without argument, without reasoning? It speaks clearly when we are walking on well-trodden ways, warning us of dangers experienced in the past, and we shun them at sight as the chicken shuns the down rush of the hawk hovering above it.

But as that same chicken has no instinct as regards the rush of a motorcar, so have we no "voice of Conscience" to warn us of the pitfalls in ways hitherto unknown.

Again, innate faculty — what is it but an unconscious memory of subjects mastered in the past ? A subject, literary, scientific, artistic, what we will, is taken up by one person and mastered with extraordinary ease; he seizes at sight the main points in the study, taking it up as new, apparently, but so rapidly grasping it that it is obviously an old subject remembered, not a new subject mastered. A second person, by no means intellectually inferior, is observed to be quite dense along this particular line of study; reads a book on it, but keeps little trace of it in his mind; addresses himself to its understanding, but it evades his grasp. He stumbles along feebly, where the other ran unshackled and at ease. To what can such difference be due save to the unconscious memory which science is beginning to recognise ? One student has known the subject and is merely remembering it; the other takes it up for the first time, and finds it difficult and obscure.

As an example, we may take H. P. Blavatsky's Secret Doctrine, a difficult book; it is said to be obscure, diffuse, the style to be often unattractive, the matter very difficult to follow. I have known some of my friends take up these volumes and study them year after year, men and women, intelligent, quite alert in mind; yet after years of study they cannot grasp its main points nor very often follow its obscure arguments. Let me put against that my own experience of that book. I had not read anything of the subject with which it deals from the standpoint of the Theosophist; it was the first Theosophical book I had read — except The Occult World — and it came into my hands, apparently by chance, given to me to review by Mr. Stead, then Editor of the Pall Mall Gazette. When I began to read that book, I read it right through day after day, and the whole of it was so familiar as I read, that I sat down and wrote a review which anyone may read in the Pall Mall Gazette of, I think, February or March, 1889; and anyone who reads that review will find that I had taken the heart out of the book and presented it intelligently to the ordinary newspaper reader. That certainly was not from any special genius on my part.

If I had been given a book of some other kind, I might have stumbled over it and made nothing of it at all; but as I read I remembered, and the whole philosophy fell into order before me, although to this brain and in this body it came before me for the first time. I allege that in cases like that we have a proof of the accuracy of Plato's idea, mentioned already, that all knowledge is reminiscence; where we have known before we do really remember, and so master without any effort that which another, without a similar experience, may find abstruse, difficult and obscure.

We may apply this to any new subject that anyone may take up. If he has learned it before, he will remember and master the subject easily; if not, taken as a new thing, he must learn step by step, and gradually understand the relation between the phenomena studied, working it out laboriously because unknown.

Let us now apply that same idea of memory to genius, say to musical genius. How can we explain, except by previous knowledge existing as memory, the mystery of a little child who sits down to a piano and with little teaching, or with none, outstrips many who have given years of labour to the art ? It is not only that we marvel over children like the child Mozart in the past, but in our own day we have seen a number of these infant prodigies, the limit of whose power was the smallness of the child hand, and even with that deficient instrument, they showed a mastery of the instrument that left behind those who had studied music for many years. Do we not see in such child genius the mark of past knowledge, of past power of memory, rather than of learning?

Or let us take the Cherniowsky family; three brothers in it have been before the public for eleven years, drawing huge audiences by their wonderful music; the youngest is now only eighteen, the oldest twenty-two; they have not been taught, but have taught themselves, i.e., they have unconsciously remembered. A little sister of theirs, now five years old, already plays the violin, and since she was a baby the violin has been the one instrument she has loved. Why, if she has no memory ?

This precocious genius, this faculty which accomplishes with ease that which others perform with toil and difficulty, is found not only in music. We recall the boy Giotto, on the hillside with his sheep. Nor is it found only in art.

Let us take that marvelous genius, Dr. Brown, who as a little child, when he was only five or six years old, had been able to master dead languages; who, as he grew older, picked up science after science, as other children pick up toys with which they are amused; who carried an ever-increasing burden of knowledge "lightly as a flower" and became one of the most splendid of scientific geniuses, dealing with problems that baffled others but that he easily solved, and standing as a monument of vast constructive scientific power. We find him, according to his father's account, learning at the age when others are but babies, and using those extraordinary powers — memories of the past persisting into the present.

But let us take an altogether other class of memory. We meet someone for the first time. We feel strongly attracted. There is no outward reason for the attraction; we know nothing of his character, of his past; nothing of his ability, of his worth; but an overpowering attraction draws us together, and a life-long, intimate friendship dates from the first meeting, an instantaneous attraction, a recognition of one supremely worthy to be a friend. Many of us have had experiences of that kind. Whence come they ? We may have had an equally strong repulsion, perhaps quite as much outside reason, quite as much apart from experience.

One attracts and we love; the other repels and we shrink away. We have no reason for either love or repulsion. Whence comes it save as a memory from the past? A moment's thought shows how such cases are explained from the standpoint of reincarnation. We have met before, have known each other before. In the case of a sudden attraction, it is the soul recognising an ancient friend and comrade across the veil of flesh, the veil of the new body. In the case of repulsion it is the same soul recognising an ancient enemy, one who wronged us bitterly, or whom we have wronged; the soul warns us of danger, the soul warns us of peril, in contact with that ancient foe, and tries to drag away the unconscious body that does not recognise its enemy, the one whom the soul knows from past experience to be a peril in the present. "Instinct" we say; yes, for, as we have seen, instinct is unconscious, or sub-conscious, memory.

A wise man obeys such attractions and such repulsions; he does not laugh at them as irrational, nor cast them aside as superstition, as folly; he realises that it is far better for him to keep out of the way of the man concerning whom the inner warning has arisen, to obey the repulsion that drives him away from him.

For that repulsion indicates the memory of an ancient wrong, and he is safer out of touch of that man against whom he feels the repulsion.

Do we want to eradicate the past wrong, to get rid of the danger? We can do it better apart than together. If to that man against whom we feel repulsion we send day after day thoughts of pardon and of goodwill; if deliberately, consciously, we send messages of love to the ancient enemy, wishing him good, wishing him well, in spite of the repulsion that we feel, slowly and gradually the pardon and love of the present will erase the memory of the ancient wrong, and later we may meet with indifference, or even may become friends, when, by using the power of thought, we have wiped out the ancient injury and have made instead a bond of brotherhood by thoughts and wishes of good. That is one of the ways we may utilise the unconscious memories coming to us out of our past.

Again, sometimes we find in such a first meeting with an ancient friend that we talk more intimately to the stranger of an hour ago than we talk to brothers or sisters with whom we have been brought up during all our life.

There must be some explanation of those strange psychological happenings, traces — I put it no more strongly than that — worthy of our observation, worthy of our study; for it is these small things in psychology that point the way to discoveries of the problems that confront us in that science. Many of us might add to psychological science by carefully observing, carefully recording, carefully working out, all these instinctive impulses, trying to trace out afterwards the results in the present and in the future, and thus gather together a mass of evidence which may help us to a great extent to understand ourselves.

What is the real explanation of the law of memory of events, and this persistence in consciousness of attraction or repulsion? The explanation lies in that fact of our Constitution; the bodies are new, and can only act in conformity with past experiences by receiving an impulse from the indwelling soul in which the memory of those experiences resides. Just as our children are born with a certain developed conscience, which is a moral instinct, just as the child of the savage has not the conscience that our children possess previous to experience in this life, previous to moral instruction, so is it with these instincts, or memories, of the intelligence, which, like the innate moral instinct that we call conscience, are based on experience in the past, and hence are different in people at different stages of evolution.

A conscience with a long past behind it is far more evolved, far more ready to understand moral differences, than the conscience of a less well evolved neighbour. Conscience is not a miraculous implanting; it is the slow growth of moral instinct, growing out of experience, built by experience, and becoming more and more highly evolved as more and more experience lies behind. And on this all true theories of education must be based. We often deal with children as though they came into our hands to be moulded at our will. Our lack of realisation of the fact that the intelligence of the child, the consciousness of the child, is bringing with it the results of past knowledge, both along intellectual and moral lines, is a fatal blunder in the education of today. It is not a "drawing-out", as the name implies — for the name was given by the wiser people of the past.

Education in these modern days is entirely a pouring in, and therefore it largely fails in its object. When our teachers realise the fact of reincarnation, when they see in a child an entity with memories to be aroused and faculties to be drawn out, then we shall deal with the child as an individual, and not as though children were turned out by the dozen or the score from some mould into which they are supposed to have been poured. Then our education will begin to be individual; we shall study the child before we begin to educate it, instead of educating it without any study of its faculties.

It is only by the recognition of its past that we shall realise that we have in the child a soul full of experience, travelling along his own line. Only when we recognise that, and instead of the class of thirty or forty, we have the small class, where each child is treated individually, only then will education become a reality among us, and the men of the future will grow out of the wiser education thus given to the children. For the subject is profoundly practical when you realise the potencies of daily life.

Much light may be thrown on the question of unconscious memories by the study of memory under trance conditions. All people remember something of their childhood, but all do not know that in the mesmeric trance a person remembers much more than he does in the waking consciousness. Memories of events have sunk below the threshold of the waking consciousness, but they have not been annihilated, when the consciousness of the external world is stilled, that of the internal world can assert itself, as low music, drowned in the rattle of the streets, becomes audible in the stillness of the night. In the depths of our consciousness, the music of the past is ever playing, and when surface agitations are smoothed away, the notes reach our ears. And so in trance we know that which escapes us when awake. But with regard to childhood there is a thread of memory sufficient to enable anyone to feel that he, the mature individual, is identical with the playing and studying child. That thread is lacking where past lives are concerned, and the feeling of identity, which depends on memory, does not arise.

Colonel de Rochas once told me how he had succeeded, with mesmerised patients, in recovering the memory of babyhood, and gave me a number of instances in which he had thus pursued memory back into infantile recesses. Nor is the memory only that of events, for a mesmerised woman, thrown back in memory into childhood and asked to write, wrote her old childish hand. Interested in this investigation, I asked Colonel de Rochas to see if he could pass backward through birth to the previous death, and evoke memory across the gulf which separates life-period from life-period.

Some months later he sent me a number of experiments, since published by him, which had convinced him of the fact of reincarnation. It seems possible that, along this line, proofs may be gradually accumulated, but much testing and repetition will be needed, arid a careful shutting out of all external influences.

There are also cases in which, without the inducing of trance, memories of the past survive, and these are found in the cases of children more often than among grown-up people. The brain of the child, being more plastic and impressionable, is more easily affected by the soul than when it is mature. Let us take a few cases of such memories. There was a little lad who showed considerable talent in drawing and modelling, though otherwise a somewhat dull child. He was taken one day by his mother to the Crystal Palace, and saw the statues ranged along the central avenue. He looked at them very earnestly for a while, and then said to his mother: "O mother, those are the things I used to make". She laughed at him, of course, as foolish people laugh at children, not realising that the unusual should be studied and not ridiculed. I do not mean when you were my mother," he answered. "It was when I had another mother". This was but a sudden flash of memory, awakened by an outside stimulus; but still it has its value.

We may take an instance from India, where memories of the past are more frequently found than in the West, probably because there is not the same predisposition to regard them as ridiculous. This, like the preceding, came to me from the elder person concerned. He had a little nephew, some five or six years of age, and one day, sitting on his uncle's knee, the child began to prattle about his mother in the village, and told of a little stream at the end of his garden, and how, one day when he had been playing and made himself dirty, his mother sent him to wash in the stream; he went in too far and — woke up elsewhere. The uncle's curiosity was aroused, and he coaxed details about the village from the child, and thought he recognised it.

One day he drove with the child through this village, not telling the child anything, but the little boy jumped up excitedly and cried out". Oh I this is my village where I lived, and where I tumbled into the water, and where my mother lived." He told his uncle where to drive to his cottage, and running in, cried to a woman therein as his mother. The woman naturally knew nothing of the child, but asked by the uncle if she had lost a child, she told him that her little son had been drowned in the stream running by the garden. There we have a more definite memory, verified by the elder people concerned.

Not long ago, one of the members of the Theosophical Society, Minister in an Indian State, and a mature man of ability and good judgement, set to work to collect and investigate cases of memory of the past in persons living in his own neighbourhood. He found and recorded several cases, investigating each carefully, and satisfying himself that the memories were real memories which could be tested. One of them I will mention here because it was curious, and came into a court of law. It was a case of a man who bad been killed by a neighbour who was still living in the village. The accusation of murder was brought by the murdered man in his new body! It actually went to trial, and so the thing was investigated, and finally the murder was proved to the satisfaction of the judge. But judgement was reserved on the ground that the man could not bring an action for being murdered, as he was still alive, and the case depended upon his testimony alone; so the whole thing fell through.

Memory of the past can be evolved by gradually sinking down into the depths of consciousness by a process deliberately and patiently practised.

Our mind working in our physical brain is constantly active, and is engaged in observing the world outside the body. On these observations it reflects and reasons, and the whole of our normal mental processes have to do with these daily activities which fill our lives. It is not in this busy region that the memories of the past can be evoked.

Anyone who would unveil these must learn so to control his mind as to be able, at will, to withdraw it from outer objects and from thoughts connected with them, so as to be able to hold the mind still and empty. It must be wide awake, alert, and yet utterly quiet and unoccupied. Then, slowly and gradually, within that mind, emptied of present thought, there arises a fuller, stronger, deeper consciousness, more vivid, more intensely alive, and this is realised as oneself; the mind is seen to be only an instrument of this, a tool to be used at will. When the mind is thus mastered, when it is made subservient to the higher consciousness, then we feel that this new consciousness is the permanent one, in which our past remains as a memory of events and not only as results in faculty.

We find that being quiet in the presence of that higher consciousness, asking it of its past, it will gradually unroll before us the panorama through which it has itself passed, life after life, and thus enable us to review that past and to realise it as our own.

We find ourselves to be that consciousness; we rise out of the passing into the permanent, and look back upon our own long past, as before upon the memory of our childhood. We do not keep its memories always in mind, but can recover them at will. It is not an ever-present memory, but on turning our attention to it we can always find it, and we find in that past others who are the friends of today.

If we find, as people invariably do find, that the people most closely knit to us today have been most closely knit to us in the far-off past also, then one after another we may gather our memories, we may compare them side by side, we may test them by each other's rememberings, as men of mature age remember their schoolfellows and the incidents of their boyhood and compare those memories which are common to them both; in that way we gradually learn how we built up our character, how we have moulded the later lives through which we have passed. That is within the reach of any one of us who will take the trouble.

I grant that it takes years, but it can be done. There is, so far as I know, no other way to the definite recovery of memory. A person may have flashes of memory from time to time, like the boy with the statues; he may get significant dreams occasionally, in which some trace of the past may emerge; but to have it under control, to be able to turn our attention to the past at will and to remember — that needs effort, long, prolonged, patient, persevering; but inasmuch as every one is a living soul, that memory is within every one, and it is within our power to awaken it.

No one need fear that the above practice will weaken the mind, or cause the student to become dreamy or less useful in the "practical world". On the contrary, such mastery of the mind much strengthens mental grasp and mental power, and makes one more effective in the ordinary life of the world. It is not only that strength is gained, but the waste of strength is prevented. The mind does not "race," as does a machine which continues to go without the resistance of the material on which it should work; for when it has nothing useful to do, it stops its activity. Worry is to the mind what racing is to the machine, and it wears the mind out where work does not. To control the mind is to have a keen instrument in good condition, always ready for work. Note how slow many people are in grasping an idea, how confused, how uncertain. An average man who has trained his mind to obedience is more effective than a comparatively clever one who knows naught of such control.

Further, the conviction, which will gradually arise in the student who studies these memories of the past, of the truth of his permanent Self, will revolutionise the whole life, both individual and social. If we know ourselves to be permanent living beings, we become strong where now we are weak, wise where now we are foolish, patient where now we are discontented. Not only does it make us strong as individuals, but when we come to deal with social problems we find ourselves able to solve them. We know how to deal with our criminals, who are only young souls, and instead of degrading them when they come into the grasp of the law, we treat them as children needing education, needing training — not needing the liberty they do not know how to use, but as children to be patiently educated — helping them to evolve more rapidly because they have come into our hands.

We shall treat them with sympathy and not with anger, with gentleness and not with harshness. I do not mean with a foolish sentimentality which would give them a liberty they would only abuse to the harming of society; I mean a steady discipline which will evolve and strengthen, but has in it nothing brutal, nothing needlessly painful, an education for the child souls which will help them to grow.

I have said how this knowledge would affect the education of children. It would also change our politics and sociology, by giving us time to build on a foundation so that the building will be secure.

There is nothing which so changes our view of life as a knowledge of the past of which the present is the outcome, a knowledge how to build so that the building may endure in the future. Because things are dark around us and the prospects of society are gloomy; because there is war where social prosperity demands peace, and hatred where mutual assistance ought to be found; because society is a chaos and not an organism; I find the necessity for pressing this truth of past lives on the attention of the thoughtful, of those willing to study, willing to investigate.

Realising reincarnation as a fact, we can work for brotherhood, work for improvement. We realise that every living human being has a right to an environment where he can develop his abilities and grow to the utmost of the faculties he has brought with him. We understand that society as a whole should be as a father and a mother to all those whom it embrace? as its children; that the most advanced have duties, have responsibilities, which to a great extent they are neglecting today; and that only by understanding, by brotherly love, by willing sacrifice, can we emerge from struggle into peace, from poverty into well-being, from misery and hatred into love and prosperity.

Great Britain and the War

Esterday's telegrams announce the spreading of the European conflagration by the entry of Germany into the war arena. That entry has been signalised by a line of action which, if the telegrams speak truly, is in contravention with the recognised rules of combat. It is true that we are far removed from the chivalrous days of battle, when we had the probably mythic story of Fontenoy, with the English and French regiments facing each other, and the courteous greeting: "Gentlemen of the Guard, fire first". But at least we might expect that neutral territory would not be violated in order to strike at a part of the French frontier guarded by treaty, because bordering on the neutralised State, and that French territory would not be invaded before the German Ambassador had left Paris and before any declaration of war had been made.

We say this with all reserve, for the telegrams may be, and we hope are, misleading, and the very fact that the German invasion of France must drive Great Britain into war with Germany makes us anxious not to judge unjustly. If the telegrams be true, then Germany has behaved most unfairly, and in any case the violation of neutral territory, which is admitted, strikes at the very root of international morality. It is all-important to Germany to strike swiftly, but a message along the wires would have travelled to Paris more quickly than her troops could cross the border.

If this be so, then has "The Day" arrived to which the German officers have long been drinking, and Great Britain and Germany have clinched in the deadly wrestling match for Empire. The double attack on France and England would be consistent with the splendid military organisation over which the War-Lord of Germany presides, and it is but natural that Germany should seek to prevent the despatch of an army corps from England to help in the defence of France by engaging all her attention at home in the prevention of invasion. Great Britain's magnificent fleet is now her protection, and should be fully adequate for its task.

The best service that we can all do is to remain calm and confident, ready to help where help is needed, steadfast in our loyalty to the Empire, suspending our local quarrels in face of the crisis on the issue of which depends the immediate future. India is bound up with Great Britain; we want no German Empire here, with its rough arrogance and military regime. The Indian Princes will be [33] eager to defend the Paramount Power, and it may be worth while for Great Britain to consider what a magnificent fighting force is there, at the disposal of the Empire, and to win their allegiance for centuries to come by showing trust in them now. Everything that can give rise to friction here must be stopped, so that England and India may stand together in defence of the Crown. - New India, August 4, 1914.

Destinies of Nations

In an earlier lecture, I pointed out that certain great ideas, necessary for the evolution of the race, may be said to belong especially to the civilizations of the East, and that those ideas were in danger of being trampled out by the advancing western civilizations. We saw that was a danger to humanity at large, the ideals of both eastern and western civilizations being necessary in the future of the world; and that it became necessary for some definite interference to take place to re-establish the balance of thought. I now want to draw attention to the nature of that interference, to show what lies behind the destinies of nations and what forces guide the current of affairs, so that we may see through the veil of events to the forces that guide them. The great world-drama is not written by the pen of chance, but by the thought of the Logos, guiding His world along the road of evolution. In the course of that evolution many beings are concerned. We have to look on this world as part of a chain of worlds all closely interlinked, all the inhabitants of these different worlds having something to say in those parts of the drama which are being worked out in each. We are all living in three different worlds, and not only in one; and whether in the physical world, or in the next world, the astral, or in the third, the heaven world, the inhabitants are busy with the general conduct of affairs which affect all three. Life becomes enormously more interesting when we recognise that it is shaped not only in the physical world but in other worlds as well, and that when we trace the destinies of nations we find that those destinies stretch backward, and that the working out in the present is largely conditioned by the energies of the past.

Let us look for a moment on the rough plan of the whole. Let me put it as though it were a great drama written by a divine pen. The story of the world, and the various parts of the actors on the stage, are all therein written. What is not laid down is who the actors shall be, and with regard to this a large amount of what is called choice comes in. This drama is the manifestation of certain great ideas in the Divine Mind, ideas written, as it were, in the heavens; for it is suggested in very ancient thought that what we call the signs of the Zodiac have a definite connection with the course of human affairs. Of that, in the broad outline, there is no doubt in the minds of any who have penetrated somewhat behind the veil.

The importance of those starry influences cannot be overestimated; for inasmuch as human beings are related in the composition of their physical and other subtler bodies to the worlds among which they move in space, there must be magnetic relations existing between them and the system of which they form a part, and at certain epochs in the history of evolution there will be one or another dominating influence present in the atmosphere in which men think and act, and they can no more escape that influence than their bodies can escape the influence of the far-off sun. The great drama, then, is the grand plan of human evolution. It is full of parts which are to be played by the nations, but not necessarily by this or that nation; for the nation qualifies itself to play a certain part which may be offered to more than one nation, and one or another may rise to the height of its great opportunity.

Leaving that for a moment, let us ask a question as to the forces which help to adapt players to parts. Is there to be found, in what seems the great chaos of human wills, any guiding force which brings the actor and the part together? You cannot well have a drama vast as the world-process, as evolution, and then a great gap between the Author of so vast a plan and individual players who make up the nations and choose the parts.

How is the right player to be brought into touch with his part in the history of the nation, in the history of individual successive births and deaths? That is the next point to grasp.

Now the vast machinery for bringing together the parts and players is found in the hierarchies of superhuman Intelligences recognised in all the religions of the world, and in the occult teaching on which they are founded. Not one great religion of the past or of the present does not see surrounding the world and mingling in its affairs the vast hierarchies of spiritual Intelligences into whose hands is put the work of bringing together the players and the parts. You will see if you turn to the religions of the nations of the past, how they have recognised these workings as playing a great part in the practical shaping of the destinies of nations. Not one great people of antiquity that did not have its own national "Gods".

The word "Gods", however, as used in the English tongue, is very confusing, for it is applied not only to those great hosts of Intelligences, but also to the Supreme, the Logos, the Author of the drama. Now in the nations that have other religions than the Christian, this confusion does not arise. It is when the Christian is contemplating those whom he calls the " heathen " that the greatest confusion arises, for over the whole of their vast theology he uses the one name "God". And yet he might easily escape that by remembering that his own cosmogony is only a reproduction of the older thoughts of these more ancient peoples. In the East there is one name which is used for these Intelligences - the name "Devas", from the root "div", to "shine" or to "play"; the "shining ones", or the "playing ones", would be the English translation. When Banyan so often used the term "shining ones", he was using a quite eastern phrase, for it is by that name that the East knows this great hierarchy of Intelligence. Among the Christians and Musalmâns, whose religions are drawn largely from the Jewish, the name "Angel" is used, the terms "Angel", "Archangel", "Cherubim", "Seraphim", and so on, being represented in the older faiths either by the word "Deva" or by a word derived there from "God", in the Christian sense, is known by other names, and no confusion arises.

In all the old religions these Devas played an enormous part, and each nation had its own particular set of Devas. The Egyptians regarded certain superhuman Intelligences as their earliest lawgivers and the connection between the human lawgiver, the Divine King, and the Deva is always clearly marked. Every civilization takes its rise in a little group, partly human, partly superhuman, to which it looks back and from which it draws its laws. The Greek had his Demigods or Heroes, and his Gods or Devas. So among the Chinese, the Persians, the Indians, the same idea is found of the nation being founded by the group which contained the human lawgiver and the Deva who worked with him in the building of the nation. Celsus hints that the Beings " to whom was allotted the office of superintending the country which was being legislated for, enacted the laws of each land in cooperation with its legislators. He appears then to indicate that both the country of the Jews, and the nation which inhabits it, are superintended by one or more beings, who cooperated with Moses, and enacted the laws of the Jews" (Origen, Con. Cel. V, xxv).

Now the Divine Kings, the Heroes, passed, but the Deva remains still at the head of each nation, a real existence in the astral and heavenly worlds, with a crowd of less developed intelligences under his guiding hand. And when you come to the Jews, you find that idea very clearly laid down in their scriptures. I pause for a moment upon it, because the sentence I am going to take from the Old Testament, from Deuteronomy, gives exactly the idea which I want to take in considering the working out of a nation's destinies: "When the Most High divided the nations, when He dispersed the sons of Adam, He set the bounds of the people according to the number of the angels of God; and the Lord's portion was his people Jacob (Deut., xxxii, 8, 9, Septuagint). To many modern readers the latter part of that sentence, "the Lord", may sound surprising, for they are accustomed to connect that word with the Supreme God; but we can see from the whole of the sentence that it is the name "Most High" which indicates the Logos, the manifested God, and He ' divides all the nations of the world according to the number of the angels, and to one great angel, "the Lord", He gives Jacob, Israel, as his peculiar portion. Origen, in dealing with this, alludes to the "reasons relating to the arrangement of terrestrial affairs," and points out that in Grecian history "certain of those considered to be Gods are introduced as having contended with each other about the possession of Attica; while in the writings of the Greek poets also some who are called Gods are represented as acknowledging that certain places here are preferred by them before others" (Cau.Cel. V, xxix). And so he points out that after what lie regards as the symbolical dispersion, .at the building of the Tower of Babel, the different nations were given to these groups of celestial beings (Ibid., xxxiv). This idea of "the ministry of angels" is very general among the early Christians; thus we have in Hermas the vision of the building of a tower:

> "And I answering said unto her, These things are very admirable; but, lady, who are those six young men that build ?
>
> "They are, said she, the angels of God, which were first appointed, and to whom the Lord has delivered all his creatures, to frame and build them up, and to rule over them. For by these the building of the tower shall be finished.
>
> "And who are the rest who bring them stones
>
> "They also are the holy angels of the Lord; but the other are more excellent than these. Wherefore when the whole building of the tower shall be finished, they shall all feast together beside the tower, and shall glorify God, because the structure of the tower is finished" (1st Book of Hermas, Vision iii, 43 - 46).

Clement (1st Epistle, xiii, 7) quotes the text above referred to. Also the following remark about Jesus, made by Satan to the Prince of Hell, is noteworthy: "As for me, I tempted him, and stirred up my old people the Jews with zeal and anger against him" (Gospel of Nicodemus, xv, 9). The Jews were under Saturn, or Jehovah, according to Origen. The same idea, is taught among the Musalmâns. They regard the angels as taking a very active part in the affairs of men. And it is hardly necessary to remind you that in the great epic poems of India, the Mahãbhãrata and the Ramãyãna, you find the Devas mingling with the affairs of men, so that when great quarrels are to he decided they manifestly take part in the strife, each struggling for the particular tribe or nation placed in his hands for its evolution. A correspondent, Mr. Tudor Pole, of Bristol, tells me that there is an old Teutonic legend that on New Year's Eve all the "Inner Rulers", the Angels of the nations assemble before the Council of the Gods to receive their orders for the coming year; each has his request to make as to the destiny of his nation during the coming year; the Council arranges the part that each nation shall play during the ensuing year, and the great Lords are consulted. Finally, the Rulers disperse, some with music and joy, some weeping, some in great agony.

In Greece there is much mingling of " Gods" and men, and the Greeks, despite their philosophy, took the matter as real, not as fairy-tale, although the philosophers in Greece, as among the Hindus and Buddhists, did not worship these "Gods". In the 7th Book of the Odyssey we read how "Minerva meets Ulysses, in the likeness of a young maiden bearing a pitcher", and she guides him to the place of Alcinous, a place guarded, in Atlantean fashion, by immortal gold and silver dogs, made by the mind of Vulcan. And so again in many another tale, written when men's minds were less blinded than they are today.

Of course, in modern times this idea has disappeared, and it must seem like a fairy-tale to modern readers when one brings such thoughts into touch with what may seem to them things, so much more real - the strifes of Kings, and the politics of the modern world. And yet behind all these the coordinating forces are still continually at work; and when the time comes for a nation to play a triumphant part in the current history of the world, then, many years before the time of the triumph, there are guided into that nation by the Deva souls which are fitted for its building up and guidance in the coming struggle. And when the time comes for a nation to sink low in the current history of the world, there are guided to incarnation there souls that are weak, undeveloped, cruel, tyrannical, having fitted themselves to fill such actors' parts in the great national drama. Let us keep, then, that theory in mind: the drama on the one side, this great coordinating agency on the other, guiding the self-chosen actors to their appointed parts.

And now let us look at some of the nations themselves, and see how far the destinies that they are working out - fit in with this view of a guiding hand behind the veil. Let us take for one instance the building up of a mighty western empire, so that the great Fifth Race, with its evolution of the concrete mind, might play its part in the drama for the benefit of humanity at large. And let us see, if we can, whether certain definite currents may not be traced which show a plan definitely worked out, and not the mere mingling of the chaotic wills, ambitions, and selfishnesses of nations.

Slowly was prepared this part of a nation to stand high above the nations of the world. The first nation to whom that part was offered was Spain, who had been preparing for it by a very marked and extraordinary evolution. Into her was poured the great flood of learning which linked itself with the dying philosophy of Greece, and drew its rich stores from the Neo-platonic schools; into Southern Spain came the great incursion from Arabia, rich with all the knowledge brought from the mighty schools of Baghdad, which spread over Southern Spain and thence over Europe. To her was sent Columbus, who made it possible for her to spread her conquering troops across, the Atlantic and subject the new world to her imperial sceptre. How did Spain meet that wondrous, opportunity ? In the wake of Columbus came the army, subjecting Mexico and Peru to her sway, and destroying their ancient civilizations, outworn and ready for destruction. She had laid upon her shoulders the task of building up in that new world a civilization based on the solid foundation left there by Atlantis, capable of supporting the structure of the new thought and knowledge. All know how she missed her opportunity; how she drove out from her own country the Moors and Jews, the inheritors of the knowledge, the philosophy, and the science; and how, in the new world, with her greed of gold, she cared nothing for the peoples placed in her hands, but trampled them into the dust. So her part in the drama was taken away and offered to another people.

Another nation became a candidate - a nation which, with many faults, had also many great virtues. England, spreading abroad her race, more and more subjected to her sway land after land. She gained the offer of a world-empire by an act of national righteousness-the liberation of the slaves from bondage, accompanied by the great act of national justice which sacrificed no one class, but placed the burden of the liberation on the whole nation. For that, those who guided her destinies were offered the possibility of world dominion. All the nations that tried to establish themselves in that great land of the East, India, one after another failed, until the English race placed its feet therein.

The story of the placing is not good to read, and many crimes were wrought; yet on the whole the nation tried to do its best and correct the oppressions wrought in India - then so out of reach - as witness her action towards her great proconsul, Warren Hastings, when for his evil deeds she brought him to trial in the face of the world. So, despite many faults, she was allowed to climb higher and higher in the eastern world, partly also because she offered, with her growing colonies and language, the most effective world-instrument for spreading the thought of the East over the civilizations of the West. All know how far that has gone, how all over Northern America, in far-off Australasia, as well as in her own land, eastern thought and philosophy have everywhere penetrated, so that the treasures of Sanskrit learning kept so jealously until the time was ripe for their dispersion, are being spread over the surface of the globe.

Continually, by lessons ever repeated, those Higher Ones, who guide the nation, are striving to impress upon England the lesson that by righteousness alone can a nation be exalted in the long run. And in a critical moment, when luxury was growing too enervating, too selfish, the terrible lesson of South Africa branded on the English conscience the lessons that duty and right must go before luxury. Through the fires of disaster a lesson was taught to England which, may God grant, she has learned for her future guidance.

And then there came the question of what nation should be chosen for the work of lifting up those ideals of the East. India, at this stage of the world's history, could not do the necessary service; she was learning her lessons under a conqueror; but there was a nation in the Far East which had within it the possibility of learning the lesson, and the Devas of the nation began to concern themselves with the attempt to train up in that far-off island a people who should be fit for the mighty task of uplifting eastern thought, of showing that conquest might go on hand in hand with gentleness and self-control, and that a nation might spring into a mighty power without losing its sense of duty. The work began by a change in the education of the people; which might make the nation conscious of itself, and then into the soil thus prepared a group of heroic souls was born.

The Mikado of Japan, a mighty soul, fit to incarnate for that nation its own greatness, fit to use such power that in brief space of years he might transform the nation, put it into new shape, evolve in it unknown forces, and at the same time show out a personality so wonderful that all that nation look to him as Ruler by Divine Right, from whose sacred person flow the powers which in the nation are shown forth, every triumph reflecting new glory on his personality. And round him gathers one great one after another, for the labour of raising up the nation, until at every point of importance you see a statesman, a general, an admiral, fit to lead people from triumph to triumph. A group of strong souls is guided to incarnate there, in order that the nation may fulfil its destiny; for no nation can be great unless at the centre there be an ideal, and a perfect loyalty and self-devotion. It is no mere lip phrase, but voices a feeling deep in the heart of the soldier and of the general, when they thank their Ruler for the victory in the field, and with the eastern devotion say that he is the representative of God amongst them.

Glance at the other nation in the great duel which is being fought in Eastern Asia, and see how strangely Russia, a nation with a great future before her, is being guided through the frightful valley of humiliation. The preparation for that calamitous part in the drama lies in that which has gone before, even within the limits of our own lives. There was a moment, some twenty five or thirty years since, when a wondrous opportunity came in Russia's way. Although ill-judged, there was a noble impulse underneath the freeing of the serfs, and there was a possibility that act might be turned to good purpose for the nation, and raise it higher, instead of leading it well-nigh to destruction as it has done. And then there came, out of many souls born just then among the nobles of Russia, one of the most wonderful things the world has seen - a flinging of themselves out of their own rank down amongst the poor, the ignorant and the downtrodden, a giving of themselves by the lads and the girls of the nobility to the lifting up of the people, not by a far-off charity, but by a wondrous impulse of uttermost self-sacrifice. And how was that met? The divine compassion of those youths and girls was met by the fortress of Peter and Paul, by the mines, and deserts, and snows of Siberia.

Nothing more terrible has been wrought by a government of any people within modern times. And terrible the Nemesis. Driven by despair, their attempts to uplift in all gentleness met with the knout and the underground dungeon, with starvation for the men, with dishonour for the women, what wonder some of them went mad ? What wonder that some of them at last, after years of patience, after cruellest sufferings, answered with the bomb to the knout ? This state of affairs was created in the first place by the bureaucracy, and not by the victims. Thousands upon thousands of those who would have redeemed Russia died on the scaffolds, were slaughtered in those frightful mines, until at last the patience of the Gods grew exhausted, and the time came for the government to learn that governments exist for the helping and not for the crushing of their peoples.

So Russia chose by her past that terrible role which now she is playing on the stage of the world. Against her are all the forces that make for progress; against her from the astral world the myriads that she sent there before their time - all her martyrs, all her victims, are struggling against her. Hence the record of unexampled defeat. And at home, revolution, anarchy, assassination and mutiny are threatening her government fabric from every side, until for Russia at the moment, there is only that valley of the Shadow of Death to be trodden from end to end; and with pain at heart, but with steady hands, her angelic guardians guide her through the defeat and the disaster, willing that their charge should learn her lessons whatever the price she pays. For in those clear eyes the nation's agony for the moment matters little, beside the lessons that through that agony are learned; and until the tyranny itself is crushed, and the rulers of Russia learn their duties to the people, she must still tread the winepress of the divine wrath.

And see how Russia has been prepared for it. Among all her rulers not one strong man; weakness and uncertainty everywhere, changed policy at every moment. Mark the government of him who should be the father, but is the tyrant, of his people - perhaps not a bad man in himself, but utterly unfit for his post. It is part of the destiny of a nation that, when the hour of its doom strikes, nothing but weakness is born into its governing classes, so that those who would not rule aright may lose the power to rule. And on those terrible battlefields of which we have read records in the daily press, is there anything more pathetic than the dauntless courage of the soldiers, and the hopeless incompetence of the officers ? It is not that the soldiers do not fight, but that they are led by men who know not how to lead.

It is thus that nations are guided from above, and into the nation that has to go downwards those are guided who inevitably drag it downwards. The same was the case in Spain - a Child King, and not one able man among the Ministers who could guide it right in the struggle with Cuba and America.

And how are these leaders chosen ? They are chosen by their own lives in the past. A man is found unselfish, brave, and noble, and such a one, in the countless choices of his daily life, is making the choice for the splendid part that hereafter in humanity he shall play. And so with those who are great outside, but have to play a sordid part. By countless selfishnesses and preferring of themselves, by taking ever the lower path instead of the higher, those men choose also their parts in history.

Thus it is that the Occultist looks on human history, and sees preparing around him on every side the men and women who are to be the players of the future in the more prominent parts of the world-drama. For none forces upon us any part, nor imposes upon us special place in the world-drama. We choose for ourselves. We build up ourselves for glory or for shame, and as we build so hereafter shall we inevitably be. Hence it follows that for a nation to be great its citizens must slowly build up greatness in themselves. Hence it is that the greatness that you see now in Japan is a greatness that you can recognise among her ordinary men and women, who are willing to sacrifice all that is dearest for the sake of their country and the glory of their Chief.

And so with England, if she would fill the mighty part which is before her in the near future. She must build up her sons and daughters on heroic models, by placing righteousness above luxury, thought above enjoyment; by choosing the strenuous, the heroic, the self-sacrificing in daily life, and not petty enjoyments, small luxuries, and miserable sensual gratifications, out of rotten bricks no great building can be built, and out of poor material no mighty nation may be shaped. The destinies of nations lie in the homes of which the nations are composed, and noble men, women, and children have in them the promise of the future national greatness. And as we make our conditions better, higher and more evolved souls shall be born amongst us. While we have slums and miserable places we are making habitations for little-evolved souls, whom we draw into the nation. Under the ground the root grows, out of which the flower and the fruit will come, and poor the gardening science which places a rotten root in the ground and expects from it a perfect flower and a splendid fruit. If we would have England great among the nations, and make her destiny an imperial destiny as the servant of humanity at large, we must cultivate the soil of character, plant the sound roots of noble, righteous, simple living, and then the destiny is inevitable, and the nation will be cast for an imperial part in the drama of the world.

India's Age-old Glories

We are to seek for the Indian Ideals which flowered into the National Life.... Because there were so many in India who ever thought of [the] Supreme, therefore did India flower out into a civilization unrivalled in the depth of its Philosophy, the spirituality of its Religion, and in the perfection of its Dharma of orderly and graded Individual and National Life, expressing as none other has ever done that balance, that equilibrium, which is Yoga, that which saved her, when all the contemporaries of her splendid Nationality have been carried away by Time's tremendous rapids, and scattered as wrecks over the far horizon of the boundless Ocean of the Past. She shares their Past, but they do not share her Future, for not theirs the secret of her immortal Youth.

—1925, *Indian* Ideals

The India, I Know

When I think of India. I think of her in the greatness of her past, not in the degradation of her present.... To me she is in very truth the Holy Land, the land whose great philosophy has been the source of all the philosophies of the Western world, the land whose great religion has been the origin of all religions, the mother of spirituality, the cradle of civilization.... I would win your thoughts [to] India unfallen, India as she was in her past, as she shall be in her future mother once more in days to come, as in the days behind us, of art and of knowledge, mother of spiritual life and of true religion. That is the India I know; that is ... the India whose polity was built by King-Initiates, whose religion was moulded by Divine Men; the India which even so late as five thousand years ago felt her fields trodden by the feet of Sri Krishna, which even twenty-four centuries ago heard her cities echoing with the sublime morality of the Buddha; the India which later, when her great wars were over, had her poets who in the *Mahabharata* and in the *Ramayana* gave epic poetry to the world greater than that of Greece; dramatists who in later times still left treasures of beauty that the learned in the West are just beginning to appreciate. That is the India ... which... is to me the Holy Land. For those who, though born for this life in a Western land and clad in a Western body, can yet look back to earlier incarnations in which they drank the milk of spiritual wisdom from the breast of their true mother, they must feel ever the magic of her immemorial past, must dwell ever under the spell of her deathless fascination; for they are bound to India by ail the sacred memories of their past; and with her, too, are bound up all the radiant hopes of their future, a future which they know they will share with her who is their true mother in the soul life.. . .

The uniqueness ... of the Indian civilization . . . consisted in the fact that it was all framed for a spiritual purpose, planned to assist spiritual evolution. The State was framed to a spiritual end;

the family was built on a spiritual basis, the whole daily life was moulded to conduce to spiritual progress. . . . The social life was similarly organised, always for a spiritual end. Take the institution of marriage as you find it... amongst the early Aryan people. You find there side by side husband and wife, united in all the greatest things of life: the man, the priest of his household, the wife the priestess without whom the daily sacrifices could not be performed, and therefore without whom the duties of the household could not be carried on; for the sacred household fire was only kindled by the bride and bridegroom, and without this there was no "household." . . . Every act of life [was] a religious service; the very food . . . was . . . cooked ever as an offering to the Gods, and only secondarily as food for man; hence very largely . . . the abstemiousness of the Hindu nation, all the life of which was to be founded on a spiritual ideal, and not on that of material luxury.. . .

Sleeping she is, and sleeping she will remain, until she turns back to that which inspired the literature of her past, *to* the philosophy and the religion of her greater days. Those only have in them the hope of her future, as they have in them the essence of her past. That is the hope for India that still burns hidden in some few faithful hearts, that hope of the reawakening of India for which some still work and pray. ... Out of that sublime teaching the greatness of her past was evolved. It was when her people thus believed, that India was great.. .. When once more in every Indian household are heard the teachings of the Vedas and the Upanishads; when once more in every Indian household is understood the true meaning of the hymns and of the worship of the Supreme in the hands of the father and the mother of the household — then India will begin to wake from the sleep of centuries, and once more to hold up her head amongst the nations of the world Her civilization — and this is significant — has lasted. None other has lasted, old as hers is old. She is the most ancient of all the Aryan peoples, the mother of all the sub-races of the Aryan nations. She was old when ancient Egypt was young; very old when Assyria and Chaldaea were born. They have passed away and have left no traces save in their pottery and in their ruins. But India is still a people despite the divisions that degrade her, despite the quarrels that deny the brotherhood of her sons; and she remains with the possibility of a nation because of her past, and because even in her present the ancient form remains . . . into which the spirit may again be poured. If her vessels were broken, then the water of life would be spilt in the pouring; the vessels are there, polluted and defiled as they are; they can be cleansed, and the water of spiritual life can still be held in them, ay, and shall be held in them in the days to come.

—Lecture delivered 6 November 1893, *The Birth* of New *India*

Manu — India's Law-giver

Of all the codes of human life that have ever been given to the world, that code which is known by the name of Manu, the great Law-Giver, is the most orderly and the most perfect in its arrangement.

The Manu as Law-Giver moulds the outer civilization whilst the Teacher gives a religious form suitable for the proposed outer polity. Thus the Manu is the great Law-Giver for the Aryan race and His code is contained is the Manu *Smriti,* the Institutes of Manu.

To the Aryan people the Manu gave its lands, its social polity and organisation. He was a Divine King, a mighty Law-Giver, who saw not only with the eyes of matter but with the eyes of spirit and founded a Society on a basis which has lasted for tens of thousands of years and has not yet vanished from the face of the land. . ..

There is nothing more marvellous in ancient history than the way in which every great civilization of the past seems to have been born full-grown and not as an infant. . . . For the earliest civilizations evolved under tutelage and not, as western sociologists have imagined, by the pressure of external necessities. They were ruled by Divine Kings, mighty Initiates who gave laws to their nations and built up Society on the model of the family in which the elders ruled with unquestioned authority and the youngers obeyed with submissive reverence.

It was a perfect socialism under autocratic rule. The well-ordered, well-guided family was then the model to which the State conformed. Each man had his status and his duties, and had no need to claim his rights, all that was due to him being paid as a matter of course....

Now the fundamental ideal in Manu's polity for the Aryan race ... is that of Duty. The fundamental thought of the people of the East has been the thought embodied in that one word Dharma (Duty). Every man has his Duty. But what does Duty mean ? It means the obligations into which every man is born, the obligations which surround him from the moment of his birth. The obligations to the family, the obligations to the community, the obligations to the nation —these are the duties into which every human being comes by the gateway of birth. It is not an arbitrary thing but a natural one. It is not a thing which is created, but it is a thing which comes out of the long course of evolution.

Out of that fundamental idea of Duty comes the thought that the first thing in human life which makes it possible is the fact that obligation is recognised and righteously discharged. Nothing is said about the rights of the individual, for each obtains his rights when all around him discharge their several duties.. ..

Four Great Functions

The Manu of the Fifth Race based His social organisation of the eldest sub-race on a recognition of types . . . known as the Caste System. He guided the souls highly evolved in knowledge and dispassion to take birth as teachers and priests, those highly evolved in power as Kings and warriors, others as merchants and traders, and others as artisans, labourers and servants. The caste system was based entirely on the ideal of Duty: the Duty of the learned to teach; the Duty of the strong to protect; the Duty of the organiser and the distributor of goods to distribute them; and the Duty of the producer to produce. So that we have four great functions coming out in the National life: the Duty of the teacher; the Duty of the protector; the Duty of the organiser and distributor; and the Duty of the producer of wealth. ...

Today we need to hold up again the old ideal; not to force any man to follow it, if he does not see it to be admirable. ... When we are thus able to reform a caste of teachers, a caste of legislators and administrators of justice, a caste of those who organise industry and accumulate wealth, a class of manual labourers who follow a particular craft, or a particular art which is needed for the welfare of the people — all equally honourable and equally necessary, and all equally essential to the nation's welfare; and when the old idea of duty returns and each knows his duty and does it; then shall we again make the golden age, and a happier day shall break upon our earth. For this is what the West is looking for today. It realises its own turmoil. It realises its own dislocation. It realises that constant struggle cannot be the natural and the fitting state of man. It is gradually despairing of the feasibility of its methods, and is looking elsewhere for light. Where should the light come from ? From the East, where the Sun is ever shining, where the laws of the Great Law-Giver were given to all His Aryan children, not only to those who settled in India, but to those who wandered Westward and lost their way to their father's home. —October 1917, *The Ancient Indian Ideal of Duty*

Foundation of the State

Manu's laws are concerned with the inhabitants of a kingdom, their relationships, their offices, their functions, their duties, etc. The Family is the unit: "To be mothers were women created and to be fathers men"; "Let mutual fidelity continue until death; this may be considered as the summary of the highest law for husband and wife." . .. "He only is a perfect man who consists of his wife, himself, and his offspring.... The husband is declared to be one with the wife." ...

To Manu we owe the luminous idea that all human societies, like a family, consist of elders, equals, and youngers, to each of whom special duties should be rendered, reverence to the elders, friendship to the equals, protection to the youngers, and on the due discharge of these, the happiness of all States depends. The State should be founded on the Family, and State obligations are enlarged family obligations. The profound principle which emerges from this fundamental idea that man only becomes man in the family, that Man, the truly *human* being, is, not a separate man, but a husband-wife-child, raises Duty above Rights, obligations above claims; it substitutes mutual helpfulness for competition, the law of sacrifice for the law of the struggle for existence. It is the recognition that man is a social, not an isolated being, and that the State should be moulded in accordance with this natural law ... Modern science reinforced [the] ancient teaching, and thus gave birth to Socialism.

Only in the woman is the old ideal preserved, and her utter sacrifice to husband and son is apt to increase masculine selfishness. None the less, in her self-sacrifice lies the salvation of India. The future welfare of the Indian State depends on the re-establishment of the old ideal of the Family, with its mutual sacrifice, and mutual service, and mutual helpfulness, conditioned, in their form not in their essence, by the "elder, equal, and younger." ...

—1919, *Lectures on Political Science*

Self-governing India

If you go into Indian history at all, you will at once realise that the Nation that built up that history so many thousands of years ago, is a Nation with a typical life of its own. It is capable of steady and constant evolution today. You would realise that so far from the idea of Self-Government being a new idea, which has grown out of contact with Great Britain, which has gradually been adopted by the educated Indians because they have studied English History—you would find, on the contrary, that India was one of the most Self-Governing countries in the world, and that there still remains in village traditions in India the memory of a time when the people truly governed themselves.

And if you study that, not only in the village communal life, but if you study the building up from the village to the ten villages, from the ten villages to the hundred villages, and so on, grade after grade, until you come to the royal power, you would see in that the image of a Nation that was not only capable of Self-Government but that exercised Self-Government; you would realise that Kingship in India, powerful as it was, was powerful because the King was frequently elected by the people; because no great step was taken without the popular approval; because round the King there stood a Council, representing the various grades in the community over which the King was ruling. And you find as you read those old stories that, while the King was mighty, he was the King of a Free State, and you begin to realise that a great deal of the nonsense talked in modern times about India's incapacity for Self-Government *is* nonsense, and grows out of the ignorance of the people, and their utter lack of acquaintance with the past of their own great Nationality.

Moreover, if you study that history, you would find that customs had changed in the most extraordinary way. You would find, when you came to deal with the question of foreign travel, that India was once a great commercial country, manufacturing her own products, and sending them out in her own ships over the whole of the then known world; you would find that there was a great trade carried on with Europe along the borders of the Mediterranean; you would find your sailors sailing over the seas of the then known world, and carrying the products of Indian handicrafts over the whole of that then known civilized world.

—Lecture delivered 1914, *The Birth* of *New India*

Democracy in India

Lord Olivier falls into the common error of thinking that the West had to teach democracy to India. "Centuries of working in Europe and America"? But surely the earliest date in America is the last quarter of the eighteenth century, and in England it is not yet a century old; while democracy is "natural to India." "The East is the parent of municipalities." The "village republics" kept India prosperous, wealthy and free literally for millennia, and lasted up to 1816, with "a school in every village," as Sir Thomas Munro told the House of Commons in 1813. Sir Henry Maine has pointed out these Self-Governing institutions, and de Tocqueville saw in the similar local organisations in the American Colonies the surest foundation of National Liberty.

India's local Governments kept India rich and strong, while Kings and Emperors played about at the top from time to time, and had their little wars while the peasants and craftsmen worked in peace. India wishes to build her own Constitution on the sure foundations of her past, and not to be given a bad copy of British democracy, evolved after feudalism and baronial and royal tyrannies. India kept her Kings in much better order than England did, and the Councils dethroned them when they became too troublesome. As Kautilya said in the fourth century BC, "a King without a Council was like a cart with one wheel." You can only tell what India can be when you know what India has been in the past.

—6 March 1924, *New India*

India's Glorious Cultural Traditions

Lift your eyes to the Universities born on the Indian soil, breathing the Indian air, nourished by Indian traditions. . . . Set the example of the Ashramas and Sangams of the Hindu, the Viharas of the Buddhist, the Madrasahs of the Muslims. . . .

Wander with me for a short space in the forests of the Ashramas, the exquisite gardens of the Viharas, and let us see whether they do not present something that we may learn to utilise.

Three Cultural Heritages

- Vaidic or Hindu (dominant in the ancient period)
- Buddhistic (dominant in the middle period from fifth century BC to AD eleventh century)
- Islamic (dominant in modern period to AD nineteenth century)

Not Mutually Exclusive

These great ages are not mutually exclusive, for Takshashila, the most ancient of the Hindu universities, lasted until its destruction in AD 455. Hindus went to Buddhist monasteries and universities and Buddhists learned from Brahmana Sages. One King might be a Buddhist and his son an orthodox Hindu. Hindu Emperors loaded Buddhist monasteries with rich gifts. Every court had learned men belonging to both religions.

Learning Greatly Honoured

In India the greatest and wisest of her Monarchs found in the promotion of learning their noblest and most beneficent achievement, and saw in the foundation of a University the most enduring memorial of their thrones. Learning in India has ever been regarded as greater than wealth and rank, the fillet of wisdom as more worthy of reverence than the jewelled diadem of Kings.

Nature: the Keynote

In the first two periods the Forest was the fountainhead of civilization. "There, trees and plants, rivers and lakes had ample opportunity to live in close relationship with men. In these forests, though there was human society, . . . there was no jostling.... The Indian mind ... it rendered all the brighter. . . . The current of civilization that flowed from its forests inundated the whole of India." (Rabindranath Tagore)

Even after the forest period, Indian Universities were ever built in scenes of natural beauty, surrounded by lovely gardens, fragrant with blossoms and shady with trees, surrounded by a high wall, with guarded gates where at the "entrance examination" was actually conducted. The site of an insignificant village may sometimes be selected because of its beauty.

Who Became Cultured?

Culture was an innate part of the life of the village, because education in literature and arts and crafts was centred in the Temple and its affiliated schools.

The Universities were attended by the "twice-born," monarchs, nobles, leaders of the great merchant community, who carried their knowledge back to the village hearts of India. Some Universities held from 8,000 to 10,000 students.

The title *Kulapati* was given to him "who had fed, housed and taught 10,000 students."

The sons of poor men earned their tuition by service to the University, or promised to pay their fees later. Some universities were so highly endowed that all tuition and living fees were waived.

Women had opportunities for attaining the highest cultural honours. One Ramachandramha, a poetess of extraordinary powers who could compose with equal facility in eight languages, was accorded the honour of *Kanaka Ratna Abhisheka* (a bath in gold and gems), and by Court assent she occupied the position of "Emperor of Learning."

Subjects of the Curricula

There were Scriptures of Literature, Science, Arts and Crafts, and the practice of Yoga. Much emphasis was laid on the study of medicine and law.

I. The Ancient or Hindu (Vaidic) Age

Centred in Forest.

Discipline—Raja Yoga.

Method—Meditation on a single aphorism until an understanding was reached, the goal being the stimulation of the originality and creative powers of the pupils rather than the injection of well-digested facts.

Not a single pie could the student retain in the great University of Takshashila, thus putting all students on a basis of common democracy.

Subjects Taught

The supreme literature—the *Upanishads* and the *Brahma Sutras.*

All subjects taught had as the ultimate goal—the release of the Self.

> For example, the Classical Dance of India—Bharata Natya—was given with its wealth of symbolism to the Rishi Bharata as another Veda which could be easily understood by all.
>
> As early as the Epic Age, their worship of the great Planetary Devas brought to their discovery the position of the solstitial points and other important astronomical phenomena, which, without the aid of the modern instruments, they fixed to an astonishingly accurate degree.

The orientation to Brahma Vidya or the Supreme Wisdom was evidenced in a dialogue between the Rishi Narada and the Lord Sanat Kumara:

> "O Lord, I have read the Rigveda, the Yajurveda, the Samaveda, fourth the Atharveda, fifth the Itihasa and Purana, Grammar, Rituals, the Science of Numbers, Physics, Chronology, Logic, Polity, Technology, the Sciences cognate to the Vedas, the Science of Bhutas, Archery, Astronomy, the Science of

> Antidotes and the Fine Arts (said by Sri Sankaracharya to be the Science of making essences, dancing, singing, music, architecture, painting, etc.)."

The Lord replied: "All these that you have learnt are merely nominal." *(Chhandogyopanishad)*

Islamic Culture, the Modern Age

Muhammad, the great Prophet of Arabia, set the ink of the scholar above the blood of the martyr and it is well known that the torch of Science was carried aloft by Islam during the period of the dark ages of Europe. The destruction of the Universities and Temple schools by even the greatest fanatics of the tenth century was due to the fact that the followers of the Prophet abhorred images and image-worshippers, though themselves revering learning.

Sultans were ardent patrons of learning. Writes Sultan Feroz (1341-88): "I built many Masjids, Colleges, and Monasteries that the learned and the elders, the devout and the holy, might worship God in these edifices and aid the kind builder by their prayers. The digging of canals, the planting of trees, and the endowing with lands are in accordance with the directions of the Law."

In the height of the Islamic period great toleration for all religions was shown. Libraries of Hindu Shastras were translated by Hindu Pandits for the good of all, the mingling of the cultures developing Hindustani. Akbar's reign (AD 1566-1605) is especially marked for its toleration. "Sufis, doctors, preachers, lawyers, Sunnis, Shias, Brahmanas, Jains, Buddhists, Charbakas, Christians, Jews, Zoroastrians and learned men of every belief "argued on" profound points of science, the curiosities of history, the wonders of nature."

Centred in the Imperial Courts

Method—Study and Discussion

Subjects Taught:

Akbar improved the gradation of the subjects taught, the Curriculum being:

Morality, Arithmetic, Accounts, Agriculture, Geometry, Longimetry, Astronomy. Geomancy, Economics, the Art of

Government, Physics, Logic, Natural Philosophy, Abstract Mathematics, Divinity and History—a graded order from the study of Righteousness to Divinity and Manhood. Progress in the Arts and Crafts—music, painting, architecture—was very noted in Akbar's reign.

Whither India's Glorious Cultural Traditions?

What fed these great Universities of India's Past?

The learning acquired in the village schools in which education began at five or six and was continued in its literary aspect to sixteen, at which time the student either went to the University, or became apprenticed to village craftsmen and agriculturists.

Why has Indian Education Perished?

Indian education did not die when the White Huns destroyed the great University of Takshashila in AD 455.

Indian education did not die when the Muslims with their horror of images destroyed in the eleventh and twelfth centuries both Hindu and Buddhist Universities that contained them.

Indian education did not die in these two great destructions, because universities might come and go, but the village system, the roots and trunk still lived.

Indian education was not meant to die when Britain came to India, for the design which has been partially fulfilled was that the youngest son should disseminate far and wide the glory of the Mother of the Nations of the world.

Indian education perished only when the Village System with its industries, its common ownership in land, and cooperative endeavours, its education in the mother-tongues, was destroyed.

The Renaissance

Indian education can only live when it is again rooted in the very soil of the Indian Village. Restore the Village Panchayat or small Republic—that truest of all democracies, give back to the village its land, and its power to deal with its own internal problems, and again will there grow up generations of young

Indians trained in an education of the hand, the heart, and the head, through which will be expressed the heritage of the Motherland:

> *Creative Spirituality*
>
> Some day from China, at peace and free, we may learn a little more of the ancient history of India, for China sent her countrymen there from time to time, and it is from their writings that we know very much of Indian prosperity under Indian rule.
>
> —18 August 1928, *New India*

Aryan Type Conduct

Character lies at the root of outward conduct as well as at the root of inner aspirations and the nations of the world have each their characters, the groundwork of the national type. These types, taken together, form the Humanity of the age, and constitute its various elements, and in judging the outer social form of any people, it is necessary to understand it as being an expression of national character, slowly moulded from within. Changes may be made which are consonant with the national character, and such grafts will grow and will affect the parent stock to some extent, but grafts of too alien a type will only perish.

The primary Aryan type was of a distinctly marked character, and the feeble remnants that remain of that glorious type bear witness even yet to something of its beauty and its grace. It was a type pre-eminently spiritual, and the social polity that was its natural expression was moulded to give effect to spiritual ideas and to subordinate the lower nature to the higher, so that the nation might be a school of Souls, and the growth and the development of the Soul might be on every hand aided and encouraged. From this past it has resulted in the present that India, even in her present low estate, despite the loss of spiritual life and the almost complete extinction of spiritual fire, yet remains the one country in the world where to put the Soul first, high above all material interests, is not regarded as a madness; the one country where spirituality still hovers in the very atmosphere, and where external surroundings help the Soul to rise instead of fettering it to earth.

But apart from its lofty spirituality, there is another aspect of the Aryan life which, at the present time, is of pressing importance. The Aryan type was one of unbending rectitude, of high morality, and those who would fain see Aryan spirituality again lift its head in the future, will do well to turn their attention now to Aryan virtues, and to try and revive these in the life of the householder.

Out of the spirituality grew reverence to parents, teachers, and elders. Reverence to the gods translated itself in the family and social life into reverence for the parents, who gave and nourished the physical life, for the teacher who gave and nourished the inner life — the second birth — for the aged, whose ripe wisdom served as guide and who handed on the ancient traditions. . . .

From reverence sprang courtesy, respecting others and self-respecting; the gracious courtesy which has stamped itself on the bearing of all classes and, even yet, serves as a pattern of the manners that "are not idle," and that make the wheels of life run smoothly. Then came hospitality, the guest to be honoured as a God, hospitality freehanded and generous-minded, a duty ungrudgingly done; and its sister, charity, so that none might starve while others had enough, not yielded as a legal dole but given gladly, for the householder was the steward of the nation and none of the nation's children must go unfed. Reverence, courtesy, hospitality, charity, these were the social virtues of the Aryan householder that rendered him so gracious a type.

But these would not have availed to build the Aryan character, lovely as they are, had there not been laid as a foundation, the bedrock of Truth. Never might Aryan utter a lie; never might Aryan lips be stained with falsehood. Rigid fidelity to the pledged word, undeviating accuracy, these were taught by sacred precept, by lofty example, and this supreme virtue of Truth—without which all else must wither and perish—so wrought itself into the life of the nation that even now some Indian methods remind us of a time when an Aryan's word was his bond. . . . Would that every Aryan boy would make a vow in his heart to keep truth unstained, for he would by keeping truth do more to serve the nation than if he shone out as a brilliant light in the scholastic, legal, or political worlds !

Courage walks hand-in-hand with truth, and fearlessness was a distinguishing characteristic of the Aryan type; fearlessness, which has tenderness for its other aspect, for only those who hurt none need fear none. Pain inflicted is a prophecy of future pain to be endured, for the Great Law swings unerringly, and to *every* act of wrong brings its need of pain. Therefore is harmlessness the highest Dharma and therefore read we of "the fearless Brahman."

If India is again to hold up her head among nations. India's younger children must begin to lay the foundation in their own lives, of the Aryan type of character. The virtues that I have mentioned were its most pronounced attributes and the revival of these among the Aryan youth would presage the rebuilding of the Nation. Character makes destiny, and Indian destiny depends on Indian character. Here is work for the young whose hearts burn with love for the Motherland, for on the altar of pure morality alone can fall the fire from Heaven which changes the fuel of aspiration' into spiritual flame.

—Article written 9 December 1896, *India*

India the Imperishable

India is a continuum, and her Aryan civilization an unbroken whole. There are invasions and conquests, periods' of strength and weakness, of unity and division, in her aeonian story. But she is always India; always Aryan the MOTHER Imperishable, who has borne uncounted millions from her womb, but at whose own birth no historian can guess, whose death no prophet can foretell. And this it is well to remember in our judgements of today. With an admitted history of nearly 5,000 years, from the commerce between India and Babylon . . . and the proofs of high civilization and wealth then existing; with an admitted literature of least 7,000 years; the period of English rule in India, barely a century and a half, is microscopically small, a tiny ripple on her ocean. Invasions flow and ebb; conquerors come and go; India assimilates what is left of them, is the richer for them, and remains herself. She did without England for millennia, and flourished amazingly; she could do without England for millennia to come; but the two need each other, and will be the better for each other in the near future, and India desires to be linked with England in that future, but on a footing of perfect equality, and on none other. —1915, *A Bird's Eye View* of *India's Past as the Foundation for India's Future.*

Her Nationhood

What is it ... that makes a Nation ? It is, as with other Individuals, a fragment of God Himself, a Jivatma, a living Self, with innate qualities which gradually appear and form its *Character.* Contrast the Indian and the Englishman, and you will see the difference in the National Character: the Indian, spiritual, courteous, polished, keenly intellectual, inclined to philosophy and poetry, with an acute sense of duty, of obligation, to his surroundings; the Englishman, somewhat blunt and abrupt, strong mentality, scientific and practical, public-spirited.

Climate, environment, social customs, all act on physical peculiarities, and through them on character also. A Nation is distinctly an Individual with a Character, and that character depends on the nature of the Spirit at its core, and its gradual unfolding to play its part in humanity as a whole. It draws into itself and assimilates all that is congruous with its inner Self, its Spirit, and it is the Spirit that unites, that harmonises, that evolves the Nationality which embodies it. Anything special may go, only mutilating the National body, but if all goes, the Spirit must find another home. . . .

If India still survives all who were her contemporaries five thousand years ago, it is because the same Spirit lives in her National body as lived in it then; she has passed through many valleys of humiliation, but never has she entered the valley of the shadow of death; she has been invaded, and has assimilated her invaders; her ethnic type, the Aryan, still survives in a minority, though she has wrought into it many others; her ancient language is still living, although it has given birth to many dialects which have become great languages; her Governments have changed their forms, and she has passed through periods of local, but only local, anarchy, and today she is renewing her youth like the phoenix, and from the pyre of temporary subjection she is arising, the same Nation, but purified, enriched, to a future greater than her past. —1918, Lectures on *Political Science*

Her Birthright

To India, rootstock of the mighty Aryan Race, were-; committed those treasures of spiritual wisdom which are held by her for the healing of the Nations, and also the fundamental principles of man in Society, on which alone can be built a civilization which shall endure. She has vindicated her birthright by her long existence as a Nation; contemporary with Babylon the Mighty, she is yet alive and pulsing with new life today. Not in tombs is India to be sought, but in the full glare of modern life.

Nor in mere length of existence is her title to glory, but in the fulfilled treasures of her splendid Past; she was a wealthy trader, sending her ships over the seas, heavy-laden with precious cargo, two thousand years before Harem of Tyre sent to Solomon his cedar trees, and fir trees, and gold; so well cared-for and well irrigated were her lands, that her villagers raised on them two and sometimes three crops a year; mighty were her warriors, her Kings, her statesmen, her republics, kingdoms and empires, and Alexander felt the strength of her free citizens when he was turned back, the ever-victorious, and found the end of his conquests in that strength.

World-famous are not only her philosophers, from whom Plato and Pythagoras sought to learn their wisdom, but also her poets and her dramatists, her artists and her craftsmen, her astronomers, her mathematicians, her architects.

Surely India, with such a past, has some message for the modern world, some spiritual inspiration, some principles of civic polity, which are the secret of her long-continued life.

A Tomorrow of Unrivalled Glory

Under the title of "Educative Work for Home Rule," Dr. Besant's sets forth the greatness of *India and her ancient institutions. In the sixth article* of *this remarkable series, 13 February 1917, "New India," she says:*

> The general impression of India given by such a survey as is afforded by the Arthashastra is of a vast country, presenting many varieties of forms of

> government, making many experiments, discussing with keen interest many political problems, a country throbbing with life and thought, wealthy, happy, free, and prosperous. We realise that her mighty spiritual literature, her philosophy, her epics, grew out of a soil rich in civilization, material and intellectual, as well as spiritual; that India was a land, oldest of living Nations, whose splendid yesterday promises a tomorrow of unrivalled glory.

To Arouse the Indian Will

It is said — I know truly — that the Indian will has been asleep and has not roused itself to carry out its thought, but it also was said by a keen English observer that the reason why the Indian will is sleeping is that there is nothing great enough to rouse it into life, and that is true, for as long as you put before India jewels and gold, rank and titles, those cannot stir the Indian will to rouse itself and carry out that wish, but today there is before India an ideal to rouse that will into mightiest power, because it is the ideal of a mighty Nation that has claimed to itself its own strength to reign. We have been told that, where that will is present, it must achieve its victory; and it is a dream that has inspired and aroused the will — the dream of India one and indivisible, the dream of India mighty among the Nations of the earth once more. The dreamers have seen it and you shall achieve it.

—1917, *New India*

At this Vital Moment

For many long years past I have urged on you, and on those like you in all parts of India, the necessity of a spiritual awakening before the awakening of a material prosperity became possible.... In the past I have sometimes traced for you the steps of India's descent; how from the time of her great spirituality, when the life of the Spirit was seen as the sun in the heavens, how from that time downwards, with the decay of spirituality, went also the decay of the desirable things. And I remember how often I have pressed upon you how first there came the lessening of the spiritual life, then the decay of the original side of intellectual thought, of the creative intelligence, and only when those had gone far down into the twilight, came the slow decay of material prosperity. . . . The awakening, the reviving, of Indian life must follow the order in which the descent has gone. First of all, the reviving of true spirituality, of true religion, of the vital understanding of the profoundest truths of all existence; then, after that had made its way to an appreciable extent, must come the training, the culture, the guidance of the intelligence, so that a wisely planned and wisely guided education might train the future workers of the land. I remember saying to you that when the spiritual life has again become potent, when the educational life has again become pervasive, then only can material prosperity safely return.. . .

In a rightly directed education lies the only way of training for the Motherland citizens who will be worthy of her past and therefore capable of building her future; out of that will arise all the varied activities of a full and rich national life, and we shall see the nation, which India never yet has been, but which India shall be in the days that are dawning... .

To our eyes, looking with purblind vision, we should sometimes be almost inclined to say that events are travelling in India a little more rapidly than is well. For we need for the wise guiding of a material movement men trained from boyhood in religion and in true wisdom, so that the brain may be balanced and calm, the hands strong and steady; for the moment you touch the popular mind and the popular heart you awaken forces that are apt to go beyond the control of wisdom, and it needs a nucleus of wise and steady thinkers in order that a popular movement may find its way aright.

Let us, then, at this moment of immense importance to India's future, consider what ought to be the line most wisely to be followed in the great rush which is coming upon us. ...

We know that. . . . India's Deva-King . . . stands high above the nation and works out, millennium after millennium, the parts which are given to Him for His nation to play in the world's history; these parts have outlined the nation's story through all the difficulties, the dangers, the humiliations of the past.. . . First of all, in order that India might again take her place amongst the nations of the world, mightier even than in the past—a glorious past—there came the spiritual messengers, the messengers who were to revive the varied religions of the land. . . .

—Lecture delivered 1910, The *Birth* of New *India*

Roots of India's National Movement

Before the great National movement, we had a great religious movement, paving the way for more external manifestations. You may go back to the roots of this National movement to those days of Raja Ram Mohun Roy, who was the first great modern Indian leader to arouse the Nation to a sense of the greatness of its past and of the possibilities of its future. He created the Brahma Samaj which later split into two movements, one rather more tending to the lines of western thought than the other. Then there was the Arya Samaj where the great Indian teacher. Dayanand Sarasvati, threw the Nation back upon the Vedas and proclaimed the greatness of the eastern civilization. After that movement came The Theosophical Society, which proclaimed that in the East was the fountain of religious thought and that the great teachers of religion had found in the East their birthplace; and then to complete that cycle of religious evolution, you had the Ramakrishna Mission, with its fiery apostle, Swami Vivekananda, who was great as a religious teacher but no less great as patriot, who struck the note of Indian manhood, of Indian pride, and inspired especially the youth of India to accept self-sacrifice for the sake of the Motherland. Even so hostile a critic as Sir Valentine Chirol honoured me with the statement that when a European woman came to India and said that the West had nothing to teach of religion to the East, she led the people of India to believe that India was superior to Europe, and so even those who are hostile to Indian Nationality confess that in religion lies its root, confess that the Nation was reborn in the bosom of its religion, and that the roots of Nationality are struck deep into the heart of man.

—10 February 1917, New *India*

On Liberty

I crave for every man, whatever be his creed, that his freedom of conscience be held sacred. I ask for every man, whatever be his belief, that he shall not suffer, in civil matters, for his faith or for his want of faith. I demand for every man, whatever be his opinions, that he shall be able to speak out with honest frankness the results of honest thought, without forfeiting his rights as citizen, without destroying his social position, and without troubling his domestic peace. .. .

Liberty is immortal and eternal, and her triumph is sure, however it may be delayed ... and hers is also the triumph of tomorrow if only we who adore her, if only we can be true to ourselves and to each other. But they who love her must work for her, as well as worship her, for labour is the only prayer to Liberty, and devotion the only praise....

—1883, *Civil and Religious Liberty*

I have... learned much of the Divine Plan, and know that Victory is sure, however dark the passing clouds that veil the Sun. As surely as no thickness of earth-born clouds can put out the Sun, so surely can no folly and no crime put out Liberty, though they may delay for a while its rays from falling upon a portion of the globe. —4 November 1925, *New India*

Who is a Patriot?

What does a patriot mean ? It means a man who realises his own country and who loves that country above all else on earth. The patriot is not a man who looks to another country as though it was the centre of the Universe. He must look to his own country, his own people, those who are born on the land on which he himself was born, and the only Indian patriot is the man who loves India first and foremost above every other country.. .. The first thing a man must be loyal to is his own country. . ..

I would ask you to realise that life without liberty is a poor and contemptible thing. But until a man respects himself, until he will not bear an insult, until he is able to hold up his head in the air and declare that he is a man equal to other men on the earth—without such freedom there cannot be greatness either of aspirations or of achievement. And so I would urge on you to think of liberty day after day, meditate on her, long for her. feel her absence as you would feel the absence of the one dearest to you in all the world, that your heart may ever be aching since that liberty is not yours. You should realise that liberty is the one great Devi without whom no country is worth the name of a Nation and, when you feel that, you will have to cry out for it, and then you will be seen by the world as worthy of the freedom you are demanding and liberty will come to your arms.

—17 June 1918, New *India*

A Message to India

[From the President of the Indian National Congress to the People of India:]

Brothers and Sisters—We are living in a time when great changes are being made all over the world. And, as a result, methods are adopted which have the heroic simplicity and directness of the elder times. Our Viceroy, the Representative of our beloved King-Emperor, remembering his Sovereign's words that sympathy was lacking in the Indian administration, has come out from his aloof isolation, and, like an ancient King, is travelling round these immense dominions, to discover for himself what the people want. And with him comes from far-off Britain a special Messenger from the Throne itself, one of His Majesty's Ministers, to bring us the Emperor's Love and Justice: Love, that shall win us to forget what we have suffered; Justice, that shall offer to us the Rights which other Peoples have had to; wrench by force from the fast-closed fists of Sovereigns less wise, and less observant of the high Dharma of a Nation's Ruler.

What does this Justice mean to the highly educated classes of the Indian people? It means that they will have power placed in their hands to carry out the resolutions which they have been passing in the National Congress for three-and-thirty years. They will pass an Elementary Education Bill which, in the words of the Japanese Emperor, will leave no ignorant family in a village, no ignorant member in a family. They will so deal with the tariffs that the bounties given exclusively to India by Nature will bring to her from foreign Nations the wealth she needs to improve her own people, for the advantages given by Nature should fall back upon the people as fertilizing rain on the parched field. They will abolish the coercive legislation which has been invented to crush out expressions of righteous discontent, discontent due to the wrong methods and mistakes inevitable under the rule of a foreign bureaucracy, alien in language, customs, habits, from the people whom they rule. To the highly educated classes, Justice means heavy responsibility and strenuous exertion, with the joy of rendering happy and prosperous the people from whom they have sprung, the relatives in hundreds of thousands of villages in which their ancient families have lived for uncounted generations. "Born of the people, how should they not serve the people ?," for India has no classes, separated from each other by dividing gulfs, such as exist in the West between the noble in the castle and the peasant in the cottage.

What does Justice mean to the active, out-of-door class, the class that, if poor, now goes into the Army and the Police, or, if noble, would go into them if they offered a career to Indians, the inborn warrior class, that is restless and discontented, because its surging energies seek action ? To them, often now the "naughty boys" of families, it opens up a career suited to them, in an Indian Army and Navy and Police, composed of Indians and officered by Indians, in which the bravest and the best disciplined, showing powers of leadership, shall have an open road to the highest posts of command, the very qualities which now cause disturbance being yoked to service of the Motherland, her protectors against foreign aggression, her guardians against disorder within.

What does Justice mean to the merchant class ? It means markets in which wealth shall repay exertion, in which Lakshmi Devi, the Angel of Plenty, shall crown the labours of her servants. The class which guides and coordinates industry, gathering together its products and distributing them over India and over the whole world, which shall welcome into its ranks the shrewd brains and keen insight scattered over India, like jewels embedded in matrices of lesser value—this class shall be the steward and distributor of the wealth of the Nation, the backbone of National prosperity. Into it shall flow of those whose inborn talents fit them for this great branch of National Service, on which, more perhaps than on any other, the general prosperity of Nations ever depends.

What does Justice mean to the huge masses of the people, now toiling without hope, and suffering without relief, the masses who now labour that others may enjoy, who create wealth which they do not share, the producers, whether of food, or of articles of necessary use, or of pleasure ? They see the food stream outwards while their families are left hungry, the products of their hands going to others while their cottages are void of comfort. To them Justice means that the labourers' food and seed for the next sowing shall be the first charges on the crops his toil has raised; that the Panchayat shall be re-established, so that he shall manage his own village business; that the village officials shall again be village servants instead of village tyrants; that he shall have replaced in his village the village school, teaching his boys and girls that they may become more clever and useful in village life; and that any boy or girl cleverer than others may be able to go on to higher schools, a way being opened also from these to the University, less painful and hard than that now existing.

For what is Justice ? It is giving to every man his birthright, and that birthright is Freedom, Swaraj, Home Rule.

Friends, will you work with my colleagues and myself to win this Home Rule, which will make India happy within her own borders, and great among the Nations of the world? Will you not work with us for your own liberty, and for the liberty of your children after you? India is linked with Great Britain by the good Will of God, who would knit East and West together for the welfare of the whole world. The tie is now a tie of force; let us make it a tie of love. But a tie of love can only come when India is free, a willing Partner in the Empire, and not a Dependency. Stand up like men; speak out like men. Then shall your voices, ringing across the ocean, reach Britain, the Mother of free-institutions in the West, and she will greet a sister, India, the Mother of free institutions in the East, who sent out to the West her sons and daughters to build up freedom there, so that now, together, they might build a mighty Commonwealth of Free Nations, and bring happiness to mankind.

—26 December 1917, New *India*

A Message to Britain

[To the Government and Parliament of Great Britain and to the Supreme Government of India As *Britain deals with India, so will the High Gods deal with her.*—July 1915, *The Theosophist*]

The time is a time for grave and weighty decisions, decisions that affect the future not only of Great Britain, India and the Empire, but of the World. The war has reached a critical stage, and plain speech is necessary, alike on the part of Great Britain and of India, if the Empire is to triumph over her enemies, if Liberty is to triumph over Force, Law over Autocracy. In the working of Providence, the destinies of Nations, Great Britain and India have been brought together, and have lived side by side for 160 years. The union has brought both gain and loss to both: gain to India, by being brought into contact with a liberty-loving and progressive western Nation; gain to England by an immense increase of wealth and impetus to commerce; loss to India by the destruction of her power of self-defence, and by her becoming a dependency instead of a number of warlike, wealthy, and independent States; loss to England by the clouding of her principles in the adoption of autocracy, and by the consequent lowering of her status in the world's eyes. The Arms Act of 1878 completed India's subjection and helplessness; and in the moment of the Empire's need, she finds herself in danger of invasion from Central Asia as in the old days, but of Central Asia dominated by Germany, and herself without her old power of self-defence.

Yet the old martial spirit is not dead, as is shown by her soldiers in the present war. Bengal has shown the capacity of her young men for quickly becoming soldiers. And the spirit Bengal has shown exists all over India, even outside the so-called martial races. Can that be called out now for the defence alike of India and the Empire ? Is it too late to evoke the spirit that sprang up in 1914, and was rejected ?

We believe it is not even yet too late; but that which Mr. Lloyd George said of Ireland is equally true of India. We cannot ask young men to fight for principles, the application of which is denied to their own country. A subject race cannot fight for others with the heart and the energy with which a free race can fight for the freedom of itself and others. If India is to make great sacrifices in defence of the Empire, it must be as a partner in the Empire and not as a -Dependency. Let her feel she is fighting for her own freedom as well as for the freedom of others, that she will have her place as a Free Nation in a Commonwealth of Free

Nations under the British Crown; and then she will strain every nerve to stand by England to the last.

For this there must be mutual trust. His Majesty's Government has already promised Responsible Government to India. Let full Responsible Government be established in India within a definite period to be fixed by Statute, and a Bill to that effect be introduced into Parliament at once; let India's leaders be taken into confidence now, and treated as recognised sharers in the perils and triumphs of the struggle; let the Governor-General and the Secretary of State for India say to the leaders of the people what they want; let us all feel that we are one in heart and aim, that we are not servants fighting for our masters, but free men fighting beside free men for a common heritage of Freedom.

Trust Us

We do not want to break our tie with England; we do not want to see it broken by a War into which she entered in defence of Liberty; we detest German tyranny and German methods; the policy of Great Britain has made it impossible for us alone to defend our own frontiers and our own coasts; we do not want to change masters, but to share their freedom, and to live in the happy union of equals, for mutual advantage.

We are ready to make sacrifices; we are ready to fight and work in India as Englishmen and Englishwomen are-fighting and working in England, but it must be for a similar reason; we must work and fight to win liberty, the prize of victory, as they work and fight to keep the liberty they won in past generations. Responsible Government is promised, but the promise is indefinite, hangs floating in the air. Let England-pledge herself definitely to redeem that promise by accepting here, as in Ireland, that which our leaders have asked, in Congress and League assembled; and we will work heart and soul to save Britain, India and the Empire; we will triumph with her, or we will go down with her in a world ruin.. Do not misunderstand us. We shall try to help Britain in any case, for we cannot forget the ties of many years; and we believe that, in the immediate future, liberty stands or falls with the British Empire. But, if Britain refuses us our place in the Empire, we shall try as leading a forlorn hope. Whereas if Britain welcomes us as a Nation whose freedom depends upon the issue of the struggle, we feel sure that we shall win. Only the hope of freedom can arouse popular enthusiasm to the fighting point. Let not the reactionary British politicians prevail at this moment, and thus ruin the Empire. Trust us, and we will not fail you. Be true to us, and we will be true to you. Do not ask us to give everything, while you give nothing, to trust you while you distrust 'us, and try to use us for your own advantage only. Drill us, arm us, officer us with our own countrymen, make us a huge citizen army, and take if you will, the flower of our troops to fight abroad. But let us fight under the - banner of Liberty, for nothing less than the hope of that will nerve our men to fight and our women to sacrifice.

—*The Present Crisis*, published by the Commonwealth Office

We claim liberty, not favour. We claim freedom— not the Goodwill of the Government. Freedom is the right of every human being and without the process of law none should have the power to take it.... Unless a Government is in sympathy with the legitimate aspirations, the legitimate desires of the people, then that Government in the presence of the true Justice of God has no right to govern.

India and Britain

We, who ... have learned to look on the scroll of history as the unrolling of a definite Plan, in which each Race and Sub-Race and Nation plays its own part, cannot but watch the present happenings with intensest interest, as each new event comes into sight, and is seen as a fragment of the great mosaic. In that Plan, as often said, the bringing together of India and Great Britain was for the helping of the world; partly in order that India's priceless treasures of spiritual knowledge might be circulated over all the world in the language that is the most widely spread at the present time, and thus reach and influence the virile but unspiritual younger Nations, springing from the sturdy British stock. Partly also that the Indians, who had so deeply sinned by their divisions, might be driven together by a foreign rule and prepared to make a united Nation. Partly that the literature of Freedom, found nowhere in such splendid form and instinct with such fiery passion as in the tongue of Milton, Burke and Shelley, might reawaken in India her sleeping traditions of intellectual freedom, out of which all other forms of feedom grow, and might drive that mighty force into modern channels, to irrigate the vast extent of Indian life. Through the union of India and Great Britain, at first as ruler and ruled, and then as willing, equal partners in a? world-wide Empire, humanity was to be prepared for the Coming of the World-Teacher, and the foundations of a new civilization were to be laid. —April 1917, *The Theosophist*

For the sake of India, Britain and the Empire, it is necessary that India and Britain should be closely bound together as equal comrades. How many homes in England would today not have been left desolate, if India had been a Self-Governing Dominion, ready to send out her millions to weight the scale of victory for the Allies. How many precious lives would have been saved, how many children would not have been orphaned, if Britain had stood for Liberty within her own Empire, and had not been a house divided' against itself. —April 1918, *The Theosophist*

I have often pointed out in the past, and have just repeated, that Great Britain was peculiarly fitted for her task by her own past history and present Constitution. I may reproduce here that which I wrote in New *India* on March 19th:

Great Britain — which does not include Ireland — is by far the freest country in the world, not only freer than the Central Powers, but freer than the Republic of France and even than the Republic of the United States of America. She has a free Press, and personal liberty is less shackled than in any other land; there is less interference with personal liberty there than anywhere else in the world, and property is safe from executive seizure outside the law. It is because of this that the British throne is safer than any other, and it is because of this that Great Britain was chosen out of the competing European Powers, to bring India into the circle of free World-Powers. East and West, Asia and Europe, can only be brought together in peaceful and harmonious union through Great Britain and India, standing side by side as Free Nations, in close and intimate cooperation. If the primacy of Asia falls either to Japan or China — both Fourth Race Nations — evolution will suffer a serious setback.

Great Britain and India together are the natural leaders of Asia, for the civilizations of eastern Asia have been largely dominated by Indian thought. The Lord Buddha is followed by millions in Japan, China, Tibet and Siam. Japan has long looked to India as to the Mother of her people. The hoary antiquity of China, antedating the birth of the Aryan Race, has been deeply leavened by her thought and culture. The peoples of Persia, Mesopotamia, the Caucasus, Arabia, are all branches of the wide-spreading banyan tree; rooted in India, and those branches have spread over Europe itself, the Kelt and the Teuton finding in the Aryan rootstocks the ancient unity now separated into such wide divergencies. What more fitting than that India and Great Britain, the eldest and the youngest, grey Mother and lusty Daughter, should meet again in the Family Home, and claim their joint Heritage ? May it not be that, in this terrible War, there may be developed by the wondrous alchemy of God a binding material to unite the East and West? —April 1917, The *Theosophist*

Free Indians alone can Defend India

I

What is the right relation of the student to politics ? He should study the principles of politics and economics in relation to the history and present conditions of his own country, but should not apply them in political action while he is *in statu pupillari.* That is what I have said and insisted on for 20 years, and still say. In normal times it is easy to maintain this rule. In abnormal times, such as the present, with the excitement of a World War, the peril of the Empire, the rapidly changing political position of his own country in that Empire, the maintenance of the rule becomes more difficult, and some amount of excitement is inevitable. Now that the Government has called on the elder student population to enrol themselves as members of the Indian Defence Force, to submit themselves to "strict military discipline" so as to be ready to undertake garrison duty if called on, the rule practically becomes inoperative for the recruits.

Young men cannot be expected to make the sacrifice asked for unless they are inspired by a passionate love for their Motherland, such as emptied the Universities of Great Britain. Love for a foreign Empire in which they are a Dependency cannot do it; love for an Empire in which they are a partner will do it. The prospect of the prolongation of a condition of inferiority will not inspire; the love of Liberty and the hope of winning it, and of becoming citizens of an Empire of free Nations will inspire. Let there be no mistake. When Britons want to flatter Indians they call them "fellow-citizens," but both Britons and Indians know perfectly well that Indians are not citizens. Citizens of the Empire live in countries where they have a free press, where they are represented, where they tax themselves, where they cannot be imprisoned without trial, nor their property forfeited without a judicial proceeding. These are elementary rights of citizenship, and they do not exist in India. Therefore Indians are not citizens of the Empire, and if they defend it, it is in the hope of winning freedom and citizenship within it.

Students know all this, and if they—and their elders — are called to perform the citizen's duty of defence, their answer to the call implies that they look for the right of the citizen as the just correlative of the duty. —2 March 1917, *New India*

II

Our very Reasonable Demand is "Give us Home Rule and then you can arm a free and contented India as the strongest bulwark of the Empire." From the British point of view this is probably the strongest argument in favour of Home Rule. For Britain is in deadly need of manpower and has exhausted her own resources; she has wrought a miracle in the number of men she has sent to the battlefields; but she can do little, if anything, further. She must fall back on India, or make an inconclusive peace and prepare for another War—a ghastly prospect. But she dare not arm India until India is free.... A Nation in bondage that is so unreasonable as not to agitate would be unworthy of freedom, would be a nation of cattle, not of human beings. Only liberty befits a Nation of men. —16 February 1918, New *India*

"India alone has the manpower which can effectively maintain the Empire in Asia, and it is a short-sighted, a criminally short-sighted, policy not to build up her strength as a Self-Governing State within the Commonwealth of Free Nations under the British Crown," said Dr. Besant in 1917 . . . *New India*, her journal, quoting the above, adds the prophetic comment: "A few years hence, everyone will see that this is mere common-sense . . . though some solemnly tell us that ' India is defended outside India.' Is anyone really so fatuous as to suppose that if the Germans engineered a thrust through Persia on Baluchistan the victories of the Allies in France would foil that thrust ? Might not such an attempt be made, as in the Punjab, to create a diversion here which would help their situation in Europe ? . . ." —3 April 1918, *New India*

III

Nothing will save India but the Indian valour, willingly coming to the rescue, if contented by the grant of Home 'Rule. The British Empire's fate hinges on the fate of India, and therefore it is but wisdom and prudence to keep India contented by granting Home Rule to her. At present she is treated with distrust, and the Arms Act is but one example of it. That shows that English rulers cannot trust Indians. A rule based on the people's love and confidence needs no Arms Act. India has shown her fervent loyalty; India has saved England when the gallant Indian forces barred the way to Paris. It is they who filled up the gaps in the English army. Let the English Nation know that India is a tremendous reservoir of manpower, far greater than America. The Americans take long to come. Indians are at hand at any time. And is it to the dignity of England to say that it depends upon Americans and not on Indians ? A Home-Ruled India will defend, if needs be, any country in the world with its tremendous manpower, and therefore a Home-Ruled India is necessary for the Empire. It is a matter of life and death for the Empire to arm Indians for defending it. Let this be said in plain words before the English public.

—15 March 1918, *New India*

From Mountain Peaks — a Vision

Principles of World Reconstruction

The Foundation of a Stable Society must be Brotherhood.

The Need of Every Human Being is for Happiness and for conditions favourable to his Evolution.

The Duty of Society is to supply an environment which yields these.

The birth of a human being into an organised Society gives to him a claim, and to Society a duty — the claim of a child on its parents, the duty of the parents to the child. It is this natural and, proper claim of the younger on the elder that has been perverted into the aggressive doctrine of "rights"; animals, children, the sick, the ignorant, the helpless, all these have rights — the right to be kindly used, protected, *nursed*, taught, shielded; the strong, the grownup, have only duties.

Purpose of Organised Society

Is the happiness and the welfare of its members, and where it fails to secure these it stands *ipso facto* condemned. "*Government exists only for the good of the governed.*" So said Pythagoras ... and the phrase has echoed down the centuries, and has become the watchword of those who are seeking the betterment of social conditions.

Theosophical Ideal of the State

As spoken out by Pythagoras:

The Father-Mother of its citizens,

The Protector of all.

The duty of the State, of *organised Society, is to secure to every* one of its *members* at *least the minimum* of *welfare* —of food, clothing, shelter, education, leisure—*which will* enable *each* to develop to the full the faculties *which he brought with him into the world.*

There is no necessity of overwork and absence of leisure, of lack of comfort and the means of enjoyment. Human brains are quite clever enough to plan out a social system in which every citizen should have enough for happy life.

The Only Obstacles are selfishness and want of will.

It Was Done Long Ago under the King-Initiates who ruled in the City of the Golden Gate and in Peru. It was done in the time of King Ramachandra, as may be read in the *Ramayana.* It was done when the Manu ruled in the City of the Bridge.

***The Builders*:** But it must be planned out by wisdom, not by ignorance, and brought about by the love and sacrifice of the higher, and not by the uprising of the lower. Mobs can make revolutions; but they cannot build a State. —1912, Theosophy

Principles of Nation Building

- No past condition of a nation can be reproduced, for a nation cannot retread the path along which it has evolved. Principles can be re-established, but the application of them must be adapted to the new environment.
- A national ideal to be useful must be in harmony with the national character, and must grow out of the national past. It must be a native of the soil, not an exotic.
- Every nation has its own line of evolution, and any attempt to make it follow the line of evolution of another nation would be disastrous, could it be successful; but — as a matter of fact — any such attempt is foredoomed to failure, because it clashes with the World-Plan. The world exists for the evolution of the Soul, and for this evolution varieties of experience are necessary. Races, sub-races, families, nations, like the two sexes, subserve evolution by their differences, and offer the variety of soil and culture which brings out the varied capacities of the Soul. If they were reduced to a dull uniformity, their value as classes in the school wherein the Soul is educated would be lost, and the Soul would have one quality overdeveloped and another undeveloped. —1901, *Theosophical Review*

Principles of the New Order

Basing itself on the study of the past, Theosophy can lay down certain principles, to be worked out into details by the highly educated and experienced. The principles are:

- That Government should be in the hands of the Elders, i.e., the wisest, the most experienced, and the morally best;
- That the possession of ability and of power imposes the duty of service;
- That freedom brings happiness only to the educated and self-controlled and that no one, so long as he is ignorant

and un-selfcontrolled, should have any share in the governing of others, and should only have such freedom as is consistent with the welfare of the community;

- That the life of such a one should be rendered as happy and useful as possible, under discipline until he is fit to "run alone," so that his evolution may be quickened;
- That cooperation, mutual aid, should be substituted for competition, mutual struggle;
- That the fewer resources a man has within himself, the more means of outer enjoyment should be placed within his reach by Society.

The suggestions which follow are the results of my own study of what has been done in the past, and of my own thought on present conditions. They are only suggestions, and many Theosophists might disagree with them. My own wish is to indicate a line of change consonant with Theosophical ideas. Brotherhood imperatively demands fundamental social changes, and the rapid growth of unrest, justified by the conditions of the classes that live by manual labour, will force a change ere long. The only question is whether the change shall be brought about by open-eyed wisdom or by blind suffering. At present, Society is engaged in trying the latter plan.

The Land of a Country should be used to support:

(1) The Ruler, his Councillors, Officials of every grade, the administration of Justice, the maintenance of internal Order and of National Defence;

(2) Religion, Education, Amusement, Pensions, and the care of the Sick;

(3) All who are not included under (1) and (2), and who gain their livelihood by manual labour in production and distribution.

Years of Man's Life

Education, free and universal, should be the only work of the period between seven and twenty-one years of age, so that the youths of both sexes should, on reaching manhood and womanhood, be ready to become dutiful and useful citizens, with their faculties well developed, so that they would be capable of leading an honourable, self-supporting and self-respecting life.

The working life — and all should work in one of the three above-named divisions — should last from twenty-one to fifty years of age, unless a shorter term should be found sufficient for the support of the nation. During the remainder of the life, the citizen should be in receipt of a pension, the result of the accumulated surplus of his working years, and therefore a repayment, not a gift; he should be free to devote himself to any pursuit he pleased.

Production and Distribution should be organised by such men as make the huge fortunes, now becoming so numerous, and after full provision for all concerned in the producing and distributing, the surplus profits should go to (1) and (2), chiefly to the latter.

The Organisation of Industry should be governed by the idea that labour should be rendered as little burdensome as possible by healthy conditions and by the substitution of machinery for human beings in all unpleasant and dangerous work — mining, drainage, and the like; where unpleasant forms of human labour are necessary for the welfare of the community, the hours of labour should be shortened in proportion to the disagreeableness of the task, without any diminution of pay.

The Life of a Scavenger: If the scavenger, for instance, is to lead a human life, as much of his work as can be done by machinery should be thus performed; for the rest his hours should be very short, his pay good — since the health of the community depends on him—and recreation, some refining and educative, some purely amusing, should be readily available within his reach. He is an active hand of Nature, helping her in her constant task of transforming the foul and the dangerous into the nourishment of new life and new beauty. He should be regarded ... not as a drudge but as a co-worker with God. Is it said that he is coarse, repellent ? So much the more shame for us, the refined and attractive, who profit by his work, and have made him what he is by our selfishness, our indifference, and our neglect.

Education: The value of Reincarnation as an explanation of life is untold. It cheers with the proclamation of final success, and ensures the permanence of every fragment, every seed, of good in us, and time enough for the least evolved to flower into perfection.

As Applied to the Child: We see in the child an ego who has come into our care during the time of the growth of his body, to be helped in training it for the purpose for which he has returned to the earth. . . . We seek to draw out of the ego that which he knows, that he may stimulate the germinal mental faculties and so impress the plastic brain. We do not regard the child-body as belonging to us, parents or teachers, but as belonging to the ego, and we see it to be our duty to help him in gaining full possession of it, to work from outside while he works from within, and to follow out any indication given by him as to the best line of study, the easiest road of progress. We give to the child the greatest liberty compatible with his physical, moral, and mental safety, and in everything try to understand and to help, not to coerce.

We must first give a good general education so that all may be able to associate pleasantly in Society by virtue of a common knowledge and a common training; then that specialised education that will fit each for the work he can best do for the State. The Nation must be organised with vocations suited to the people. Until the time again comes when the Devas will cooperate with men by guiding, as they do not do now, the incoming souls to appropriate bodies, we can only know a man's true dharma by the study of the child.

As Applied to the Undeveloped Soul: The congenital criminal is a savage, come to us as to a school, and it is our business to treat him as the intellectual and moral baby which he is, and to restrain the wild beast in him from doing harm.

The Immediate Treatment of *the Criminal,* as he is — we hope, later, to eliminate the type:

Recognition, Segregation, Reclamation: These people, and the almost criminal class above them, are recognisable from birth, and they should be segregated in small special schools, given such elementary education as they can assimilate, be treated kindly and firmly, have many games, and be taught a rough form of manual labour. The teachers in these schools should be volunteers from the higher social classes, willing to teach and play with the boys, and capable of arousing in them a feeling of admiration, attachment, and loyalty, which would evoke obedience. They must be with those who are obviously their superiors if this is to be done.

Happy Labour: From these schools they should be drafted into small colonies, bright, pleasant villages, with shops, playground, music-hall and restaurant, ruled by men of the same type as before; they should have everything to make life pleasant, except freedom to make it mischievous, and miserable; these colonies would supply gangs of labourers for all the rougher kinds of work.... To do right would be made pleasant, while to be rowdy and idle would be made unpleasant; "he that will not work neither shall he eat "is a sound maxim, for food is made by work, and he who, being able, refuses to make it has no claim to it. Checks might be given for each hour's work, exchangeable at the shops and restaurants for the necessaries of life, and the man could do as much or as little as he liked; the equivalent in necessaries and luxuries would be at his own choice.

Beauty Everywhere

From Slums to Gardens: In the light of Theosophy, it is the duty of the elders to plan out, and gradually to construct, towns of decent dwellings with sufficient interspaces, to which should be transplanted the dwellers in the slums, these poison-spots must be pulled down, and the soil, sodden with the filth of generations, should be turned into gardens; the filth will then be changed into trees and flowers, whereas to build new houses on such soil is to invite disease.

The Crying Need: More Beauty must be sought, for it is a necessity of life for all, not a luxury for the few. Beauty refines and cultivates, and reproduces itself in the forms and manners of those who live under its influences. Beauty in dress, in the home, in the town, is a crying need as an evolutionary force.... When people were more surrounded by natural beauty than they are now, the clothes of the people of every class were beautiful, as they still are in the East; it is natural to man to seek to express himself in Beauty; it is only as he becomes far removed from Nature, that he accepts with indifference ugliness in clothes and surroundings. —1912, *Theosophy*

Key is in India

In the Root-Stock exist the germs of all the various qualities of Fifth-Race mankind which become embodied and balanced in our Root-Race. These had to be developed one after another and so the sub-races were dominated by one of these chiefly, and had to develop along those lines and assimilate them together. That is one part of India's great mission towards humanity in the world. The germs of all these sub-races are in her, as the child is in the womb of the mother, and the sub-race comes forth, develops a special quality or capacity through the new sub-race and then reacts upon the Mother. And so her children, spread over the whole western world, are developing their qualities, especially the quality that dominates each. The fourth sub-race is there with its mission of beauty, and the fifth is there with its science of mind, and both can find their key in India from whom they spring, and to whom many of them come back in order to help in the building up of the type of the whole Fifth Race. I cannot go far into that. The whole subject is of profound interest, but if we realise that evolution in the sub-races is for the enriching of the typical Fifth-Race Man, then we shall understand a little more of the way in which migrations go out and some of each come back to the Motherland, and how India is the common Motherland of the whole Aryan, or Fifth, Race.

Work before Us

The Sixth Sub-race will mostly be western. The work here is to build up the great Empire of the Fifth Sub-race by linking together, as I have very often told you in the past, England and India. The two together have been chosen to build a great World-Empire. While that is being built, the younger civilization will grow up under its protection, and the transition to that civilization is the work that the members of The Theosophical Society should take active part in at the present time ... We have to prepare for the future along certain lines of definite work....

The first of these is Education. You must begin by building up the citizens of the civilization, and the citizens are, of course, in the children of today. Education must be founded on Brotherhood, Reincarnation, and Karma, and therefore on the study of the child, finding out what he has brought with him from past experiences as capacity. Do not try to force him into certain definite moulds or grooves, as children are forced today, whether they suit them or not. Find out what suits the child, and do not give him what suits the teacher... . Theosophy lays down the lines of right education. The principles are universal, and the application is national.... Do not mistake me: I do not mean that every one of you must be a teacher; but I mean that every one of you can find no nobler service for the Motherland than helping education. You must help those who can teach, if you cannot teach yourself.

There are other lines of work and there is one which is very badly needed here in India. It is the treatment of the so-called criminal classes . .. The prison system wants absolute reform. The criminals have to be trained, not to be brutalised. The criminals are our brothers. They are younger. Try to lift them up to your own level. True, they have broken their duty to Society, but out of ignorance. The duty of a Theosophist is the duty of an elder brother to the younger. Our criminal system is more brutal than any system which exists in any other civilized country. ... If you exerted yourselves you could reform the system. There is no good in blaming the Government, when you are such a large population, and the rulers a few people. You can impose your will if you care for your brothers in prison, as much as you cared about your brothers in Ootacamund and Coimbatore. You brought us out . . . .

We have to deal with the great problems of capital and labour.... In the new civilization, cooperation is to take the place of competition. Many of you may go to the villages and explain to the people the benefits of cooperation. Much has been done; but little compared with what remains to be done ....

You can choose, each one for yourself, to work in this great world-vineyard, or you can remain idle. Remember that on your choice depends your own future. And on the choice of a majority of you depends the speed of the coming of the new civilization. You can quicken it. You can retard it also. And the choice must be made. —23 January 1918, *New India*

Statecraft

Art of Politics

In Politics as in everything else ... a man needs sound thought to make right action .... If men live from hand to mouth in politics.. . they may often for a momentary gain incur a serious danger, and judging by the things of the moment only may lose the very object that they really desire to obtain ....

I mean by "politics "every form of activity which is carried on in a particular geographical district, under a Government of any kind that rules over that district, no matter what that Government may be called — imperial or local, municipal or parliamentary.... I distinguish political action from voluntary action by the element of force that enters into the Constitution of the former, and the fact that if you want to escape from the scope of the action you must leave the geographical district over which the political government has authority....

No more can you gain an idea of a real Society by taking a man separately, as though he were a marble and Society a heap of marbles with no cohesion in them, you can no more do it and understand Society, than you can tear from the living body one of its organs, and studying the organ by itself, try to understand the working of the whole. For to understand the human body you must study it in life, in the functions, in the working of every part, in every single organ doing a particular work, not for its own gain but for the common good, and the nobler ideal that is spreading amongst men is that we live not to assert our rights but to do our duties, and so to make one mighty Unity where each shall discharge his functions for the common good of all.

Now India is in this remarkable position, that from her own past she brings down the ideal of a system that is essentially founded upon duty ... India is today a strange compound of conflicting theories, of conflicting ideas, is a strange compound of an ancient Nation ruled politically by a modern people, and the two ideas are here face to face.. .. One, the old idea of duty.. . and the other, urged by those who would take as it were the western system completely, transport democracy from America and Great Britain into Indian soil, use the democratic methods, claim the democratic rights, employ here all the democratic organisations; not quite sure whether the soil will suit what is here an exotic, but forced by the necessities of the position to use some of the methods which are familiar in the hands of their rulers....

Therefore, while, for my own part, I stand for the ideal of ancient India, and look on that as a thousandfold loftier than the mushroom civilizations that have grown up in later days, none the less am I bound to admit that we must deal with the country as we have it, and that where you are pushed into western methods, you must adapt your own methods somewhat, so as to meet the new conditions, so as to deal with the new ways of thought.

The Thinker

. . . There are three great ways of influencing human life and human conduct: the first and the greatest of all is the work of the Thinker, who by himself alone, face to face with the problems of life, uses all the powers that he has, and looking out into air which is unbeclouded by the dust raised in the strifes of parties, deals with principle instead of detail, deals with essence instead of form, the Thinker, he who gives out to the world some mighty thought. . . . Action is but for a day, thought is everlasting in its generating energy; and therefore the greatest among the sons of men, nature's most imperial children, are the Thinkers....

The Teacher

Then from the sphere of thought there comes down a great idea into the sphere of discussion;... it passes from the brain of the Thinker to the lips of the teacher; and the teacher going out amongst his fellowmen and gathering masses of the people together, uses all his power of brain, all his imaginative ability, all his skill of golden tongue and % deftness of oratorical presentment, to popularise among these masses of the people that thought which was born in the brain of the Thinker.. . .

The Politician

Then comes the third stage—action.... The great thought is to become bread for the hungry, and drink for the thirsty, and shelter for the homeless, and defence for the oppressed. There is the work of the politician, there is the work of the actor. He applies to practice that which the Thinker has thought, which the teacher has uttered, and he brings it down into the practical life of man, and makes the common lot happier and better by applying to the ordinary daily life the great thoughts and the teachings that have gone before. . . .

There should be no quarrel between the politician and the teacher, no quarrel between the politician and the Thinker. . .. Each is wanted by the other. The Thinker is like the head, and without the head the body could not act; the politician is like the hands, and without the hands you could not have action, though the brain should plan.. .. But there should be no confusion between the functions. The Thinker weakens his power if he mixes himself up with the strifes of political parties.. . . Nor should the teacher be a politician; for the teacher is to put the ideal before the eyes of men. No ideal can at once be put into complete practice, no ideal can be carried uninjured through the struggles of a legislative assembly; for there the principle has to be whittled away, has to be subjected to compromise, has to be narrowed down. . .. Compromise is a necessary part of political action and you cannot avoid it. ... Statesmanship is skilful compromise.. .. Therefore, I say, the teacher should never be a politician. Let him set up the ideal which politicians are to work towards; let him stand aloof, holding up the picture which is to attract the hearts of men.... The work of the politician [is] to make the ideal ultimately realisable by going towards it. Step by step he must work in the right direction, and the ideal must be held up steadily, in order that the final direction may not be lost in the necessarily devious walking ....

Some of you are politicians. How are you going to choose your lines of advance ? Has it ever struck you that the current of thought in a nation is that which is seen in the hopes, the aspirations, the longings of the young. . . . Therefore I say, watch the young, for what moves them is a movement of the future, and if you want to legislate on lines that will last, see what is most touching the hearts of the young ones; for there is the future life of the people, there is what it will desire.. . .

The duties of the politician are what were in olden days the duties of the Kshatriya, the great caste in the old days that had all these political duties in hand, . . . that had this charge in the State, and was bound to administer it for the common good.

We find the politician limited. He may make a good law, but if the people are bad the good law is useless. He may make an improvement in outside shape, but if the people are unworthy of it the old evils return despite the new shape he has made. Therefore is it that you need the teacher; therefore is it that you need the *Thinker;* and only where they are at work in a nation, making noble ideals that purify the heart, only there will the politician be successful and the progress of the nation be secured ....

What has Theosophy to do with politics ? I say that it has everything to do with them. It has to build up a State of which Brotherhood shall be the foundation; in which the rule should be accepted that every child born into a civilized Nation has a right to be surrounded by the conditions that enable him to develop to the utmost every faculty that he brings with him into the world. Until that is the rule of a State, there is no true civilization. There lies, then, the duty of a Theosophist: He has to deal with politics in order that a Nation may flourish. The question of the Liberty of a people — do you call that politics or not? I call it politics, because to me "politics "means the organised life of a Nation. It is not party politics, it is not a question of this man up and the other man down; it is not a question of quarrelling between different detailed views and methods; but the Liberty of a Nation is a point that no one, who feels the duty of a religious man to his Nation, can ever possibly put aside on any pretext. ... The great reason why a Nation should be Free and Self-Governing is that because without these a man is not a man: he is only a half-man ....

The duty of a Theosophist here is to help in the liberation of India — not of The Theosophical Society, because our Society is international, everywhere, and you cannot ask a Russian Theosophist to help in the liberation of India. I speak only of the Indian Theosophists and Theosophists who are residents here. The duty is not imposed upon them by The Society, but by the principles of Theosophy. *There* lies the duty of the true Theosophist — a human duty, a National duty, a duty which comes from service to the Motherland, which none has a right to forbid. Your individual influence on the lesser political movements will be valuable, because it should be guided by the wisdom you have gained amongst us, and by the application of those great laws of Karma, Reincarnation, and Brotherhood — the only sure foundation for the continued life of any Nation ....

—1895, *The Place* of *Politics in the Life* of a *Nation*

Lesson in Statecraft

During the short space of three years in the Indian political field. Dr. Besant secured that which has not since been achieved— the union of the dominant Hindu and Muslim elements and the union of the conflicting Congress elements. Forgotten were differences. India alone was remembered.

Mr. Jinnah then worked for a "United India." Hindus spoke from the Muslim League platform and Muslims from the Congress platform, their two Congresses having concurrent gatherings.

If any one doubts that Dr. Besant was the uniting force between the Hindu and Muslim communities, the tribute of the Hon. Syed Ali Nabi, the last speaker before the fateful "Self-Determination" resolution was put to vote in the 1917 Conference of the All-India Muslim League, will make the position clear.

"I should be untrue to myself, untrue to the Muslim community, untrue to the community at large if I failed at the moment to publicly acknowledge the services rendered by that great and sincere lover of India, Mrs. Annie Besant, who was mainly instrumental in bringing about the spirit of unity between the two great communities." The reporter here inserts the words "long and continued applause." The speaker concluded: "It was she who made that union possible and we cannot be sufficiently grateful to her."

"It was Dr. Besant's efforts with the great leaders, Gopal Krishna Gokhale and Bal Gangadhar Tilak, at Poona in 1914, and ever since, which brought about the happy union, whose full significance has been *seen* and felt at Lucknow .. . which has closed the gulf of nine long years. *New India* has been instrumental in bringing the two Parties in the Congress together, so that today there are no Moderates and Extremists, but all Nationalists, the majority of whom have seen the wisdom of Mrs. Besant's contentions." —3 January 1917, Editorial New *India*

"So the Home Rulers have at last captured both the Congress and the League. Glory to Mrs. Besant ! Her bitter persecution has not gone in vain. Practically the whole of the educated Indian community has caught the cry of Home Rule in right earnest, first raised by this illustrious lady. Even moderate Congressmen, who did not see things eye to eye with her, have become converts to her views." —Amrita Bazar *Patrika*

How was this miracle accomplished, a miracle that all today would see repeated ? Dr. Besant herself reveals the secret:

> "Nothing is too great a sacrifice if it secures a united front."

Of the deliberations of the historic Calcutta Congress in 1917 Dr. Besant tells a story that might well be called "A Lesson in Statesmanship":

> "The Committees of the Congress and the Muslim League met for some hours, and were profoundly interesting. On all the main principles the representatives of both bodies were thoroughly at one, a few very minor points of difference having been settled at Calcutta. The difference was on the details of the representation of the two communities in the Legislative Councils of the future, and the interest lay in the thorough threshing out of every aspect of the question, the grasp of principles and of details, the statesmanlike willingness to come to a common agreement, and the admirable spirit of sacrifice and the good feeling manifested' by almost every member of the two parties. If proof were wanted of the capacity of the Indians to govern themselves

> it was found in that Chamber; both parties made sacrifices, the Muslims in Bengal, the Hindus in the United Provinces. With the utmost patience, a *via media* was sought, almost found, lost again, again acquired, until finally complete agreement was reached, and Hindus and Muslims stood shoulder to shoulder, heart to heart. All honour to the leaders of both communities alike, for both realised that Indian unity was the supreme necessity, and, refusing to yield to the clamour outside among the more ignorant of both communities, they resolutely led the way to union. Posterity will bless them for their patriotism and their courage. How ringing were the cheers which later on welcomed the Muslim leaders to the Congress platform, and those which welcomed the Congress leaders to the Muslim League platform. The representatives of India in both Halls passionately acclaimed the union, and the joint scheme is now accepted by a United India, to be presented to the British Nation as the demand of a Nation awake to its own needs, and conscious of its own strength."

Home Rule Involves a Home to Rule

Listen, Brothers !

The Home Rule League has been established to carry out the following Objects:

- To secure Home Rule for India through all law-abiding and constitutional activity.
- To maintain the connection with Great Britain, by becoming a free Nation within the British Empire, under the Imperial Crown of His Majesty the King-Emperor, George V, and his successors.
- To support and strengthen the National Congress, which has laboured for thirty years to lay the foundations of Indian Self-Government.
- To carry on a continuous educative propaganda on the necessity of Home Rule for India.

Home Rule means the Government of the People by the People.

Home Rule means the right of the People to send their Representatives to make laws for the People, and to levy taxes on the People. Subjection to laws not made by the Representatives of the People is Tyranny. The levying of taxes not approved of by the Representatives of the People is Robbery. Thus has England proclaimed, and she has enforced these principles in her own Government, so that no one now denies them. Home Rule in England has carried out these principles. Home Rule in India will also carry them out.

Home Rule means the Education of the People, free and compulsory for every child.

Home Rule means the cooperation of all to ensure a happy and prosperous life for every citizen of the State; the creation of conditions which will enable every child born into the Nation to develop all the faculties he or she brings with him or her into the world, so that each may grow to the full stature of the manhood or womanhood of which he or she is capable.

Home Rule means that every grownup person shall have a share in choosing the persons who shall represent him in the Village Panchayat, the Taluq Board, the District Board, the Provincial Legislative Council and the Supreme Legislative Council. This will not all come at once. Every Village resident householder will at first have a vote in the Village Panchayat; probably there will be a small property or educational qualification for the franchise for the higher Boards and Councils. There will be no advantages or disadvantages attached to caste, creed, or colour.

Home Rule means that white and coloured people will be equal before the law and in practice; that judicial officers and their courts will be stationary, not peripatetic during the trial of a case; that the collector of revenue will not be a judicial officer also; that the judicial officer will not also be an executive officer.

Home Rule means that Indians will manage their own affairs, but foreign and international affairs, like Peace and War, will be managed by a Council of the Commonwealth, to which India will send some of her own men like the other free Nations belonging to it.

Home Rule means that the C.I.D. will no longer be allowed to meddle with political matters, to harass harmless people; to terrorise the law-abiding. It will be confined to its legitimate duty of hunting criminals, not patriots.

Home Rule means that the Police will be the servants of the People, not their masters, will be feared by the bad citizen not by the good, and will have a pay sufficient to live upon without taking from the poor.

Home Rule means Home Defence; it means that, being free to manage your own land, you will also have to defend and protect your own land. You will not be able to depend upon a foreign Army for safety, but you must maintain your own Citizen Army, and you must keep order within the Motherland, as well as guard her borders.

You will be a Free Nation in a Free Commonwealth. You will be men, not serfs; citizens, not dependents.

Annie Besant

President, National Congress, 1917-1918.

President, *All-India* Home Rule League, 1917-1918.

— 8 May 1918, *New India*

What Does India Want?

[Dr. Annie Besant's Charter of India's Liberties: framed in the hearts of her people]

To be free in India, as the Englishman is free in England;

To be governed by her own men, freely elected by herself;

To make and break ministries at her will;

To carry arms, to have her own army, her own navy, her own volunteers;

To levy her own taxes, to make her own budgets;

To educate her own people;

To irrigate her own lands, to mine her own ores, to mint her own coins;

To be a Sovereign Nation within her own borders owning the Paramount Power of the Imperial Crown, and sending her sons to the Imperial Council;

Britain and India hand in hand, but an India free as is her Right.

Fundamental Civic Rights and Duties

(The essence of ideas and principles voiced by Dr. Annie Besant in her famous Commonwealth of *India Bill, (read in the House* of *Commons 1925-6) and elsewhere, with the addition* of *Article D contributed by Dr. George 5. Arundale).*

(A) Every citizen, human and subhuman, shall be represented, directly or indirectly, in governmental councils and assemblages, and his interests protected.

[The Right of Democracy. By Proportional Representation, this Article could be accomplished, a method which with common electorates still ensures that every minority shall have a full percentage representation in all governmental councils, the Council Chamber thus becoming a true mirror of the Nation's every interest.]

(B) Every citizen shall have his say in Government to and only to, the limits of his understanding and capacity to govern.

[The Aristocracy of the Wise fulfilled by Graded Franchise]

(C) Each citizen shall have the duty and the right to contribute to the welfare of the nation.

(D) Every citizen shall be recognised as an integral part of the State with due, simple, and dignified civic ceremonies at appropriate times.

(E) All persons in the Commonwealth shall have the right to free elementary practical education, to medical attention and care, and to self-supporting work, or, if unable to work for a living, to a minimum subsistence allowance, and such rights shall be enforceable so soon *as finances are available,* and due arrangements shall have been made by the competent authority.

(F) The liberty of a person, his dwelling and property are inviolable, and no person shall be deprived of liberty, nor dwelling, nor shall his property be entered, sequestered, or confiscated, save in accordance with law and by duly constituted Courts of Law.

(G) Freedom of conscience and the free profession and practice of religion are, subject to public order or morality, hereby guaranteed to every person.

(H) The right of free expression of opinion, as well as the right to assemble peaceably and without arms, and to form associations or unions, is hereby guaranteed for purposes not opposed to public order or morality, or the law relating to defamation.

(I) All persons shall have an equal right to the use of roads, Courts of Justice, and all other places of business or resort dedicated to the public, provided they do not disturb public order or disobey any lawful notice issued by a competent authority.

(J) All persons residing within the Commonwealth whether permanently or temporarily are equal before the Law, and no distinction of Court or Judge shall be made between one class of person and another with respect to similar legal matters or offences. Every man shall have the right to a trial by a Jury of his peers.

(K) There shall be no disqualification or disability on the ground only of sex, caste, race, or creed.

(L) Within this Constitution, each unit of government from Village Council or Panchayat upwards shall be self-contained and democratic in all that concerns only itself, the residuary powers to be transferred to the next higher unit, finally resting in the Commonwealth itself. A unit ceases to be so self-contained when its citizens make protest to a higher unit that their constitutional rights are being ignored.

[Dr. Besant's principle of de-centralisation with the ultimate unit as the Village Panchayat.

The word "democratic "implies that the executive of each unit shall be responsible to and elected as representatives of the people.

The word "self-contained "implies a return to the public ownership of land, each village controlling the land immediately around it.]

(M) Linguistic Areas should be the bases of the Legislative Assemblies.

Let us remember that "the East is the parent of Municipalities", and set a world-example. I know that this cannot be perfectly done until we are free from foreign rule; but let us, while we fight for the latter, awaken the souls of our cities.

— 23 November 1928, *New India*

> "I am glad to see that your proceedings were conducted in Tamil. What will Englishmen think if they have to have a knowledge of German to do political work in their country ? In the Supreme Council, you may have a vernacular and a common language, English or Hindi. Your linguistic areas should be the bases of the Legislative Assemblies."
>
> —(Dr. Besant) 21-1-18, *New India*

Evolution of an Indian Self-government

In this pause, wherein internal controversy is silenced, while the thunder of guns rolls over the battlefields where Nations are at death-grips; in this hour of waiting, while the destinies of Empires are flung into the scales of War; we, in India, have time for earnest thinking, for solemn preparation, for that serious constructive work, *on* which the immediate future of India depends. The Leader [Gopal Krishna Gokhale] whose departure has set our hearts a-bleeding, had his mind set on this problem when he was shadowed by the wings of death. In my last visit to his Poona home, most of the hours of which were spent with him, this was one of the subjects which we discussed. ... He, too, saw that the present time was apt for such discussion among thinkers, so that when the War was over, India might be ready to take her rightful place in the Empire.

In the West, Democracy has taken on a form which has been shaped in the strife of classes; and the masses of the people, a true proletariat, landless and ignorant, with no possession save their naked labour, which they must sell or starve, have naturally seen their power in their numbers, and every struggle has been a struggle.. . [which] has ended in an enlarged franchise, a franchise extorted by riot and fear of increasing riot... Thus, finally, Democracy voiced its demand as Universal Suffrage and the elimination of all "fancy franchises "that sought to give weight to aught but numbers, and "one man, one vote "became the watchword — the counting of heads.

In India, nothing of this kind of struggle has been known in her long history. Village Government she had, and the idea and the capacity for carrying out the idea have never quite disappeared from the village folk. Above the village came the group of ten villages, and the groups of ten villages formed the larger group of 100 villages, and so onwards up to the Council of the King. The political arrangement was not based on voting, but rather on a representation of organic units, linked into an organisation for the promotion of general wellbeing, rather than for the possession of power as against others, either for offence or defence. Life and comfort were the objects of the social State rather than power. The first charge on the peasant's harvest was the food for himself and his family until the next harvest came round; the next charge was the seed-corn, requisite for the sowing of that harvest; after that came the claim of the Ruler.

Out of a past so different, a different type of Self-Government may be expected to arise, and nothing would be more unlikely to prove successful than a bestowal on the peasantry of a voting power through which they should decide the fate of Governments.

Here we come to the question which we ought to discuss Do we want here a replica of English Self-Government, in the form which England, with the wide extension of the Suffrage, is discovering to be unworkable ? ... Why should we plunge into this road which will land us, as it has landed England, in a bog? Devolution is an awkward process; evolution is natural and easy. Shall we not try to evolve?

The Villages

The village is the unit, and there suffrage may be universal — the fathers and mothers of the village, above the age of 21 years, form a natural electorate, and they elect the Village Council, dealing with village questions, with matters known to all, on which all can form opinions. That the voter should understand, and be capable of forming an opinion on, the questions which his representative is going to decide is a *sine qua non,* if Democracy is to be aught but chaos. The Village Council, the revived, modernised, improved Panchayat, would deal with all matters wherein the village is self-contained — sanitation, hygiene, village cooperation, wells, irrigation, tree-planting, elementary schools — though here comes a link with the outside — workshops, disputes, suits up to a certain value, internal roads, etc. Meanwhile, a knowledge of the three R's and of some geography — geography of the district, at least — should be necessary for membership in the Village Council, but knowledge of village life and village needs is a more important qualification.

The Towns

In the towns, there should be a group of Ward Councils, in which universal suffrage should equally be the rule, the electors being over the age of 21; and the Ward Councils should be responsible for the smaller matters now so much neglected, elementary schools, scavenging, sanitation, prevention of the adulteration of foodstuffs, street water-standards, troughs for horses and draught-cattle, etc.

District Councils

Taluq Boards in the country and Municipalities in the towns below a certain population would be the second grade of Councils, and these should be elected by the first-grade Councils, and by all men and women in the area who had reached a certain standard of education, and had attained a certain age, say 25. They should have charge of secondary and high schools, model farms, technical institutes, markets, electric-power installations, and such part of the administration of roads, lighting, etc. as may be handed over to them by the District Boards, and should form a kind of court of appeal when any wrong or lapse of duty occurred in the Village Councils.

District Boards and Municipalities of towns above a certain population would form Councils of the third grade. These again would be elected by the Councils of the second grade, and by all men and women over the age of 30, who had reached a certain educational standard. Roads, local railways, colleges — including agricultural and technical as well as arts and sciences — the general supervision and fixing of localities for large markets, agricultural and technical shows, etc., the fixing of the proportion of money to be raised by local taxation in each subdivision, would be some of their duties.

Provincial and National Parliaments

Above these come the Provincial Parliaments to be elected by Councils of the third grade and by all men and women over 35, who have reached a certain educational standard. The provincial University or Universities, provincial railways, and all the larger concerns of provincial life would come under their administration.

Above these would be the National Parliament, controlling all National affairs, post, railways, army, navy, etc. The electorate there would be the Provincial Parliaments, and men and women over 40, of University or equivalent educational standard.

Thus might complete Self-Government come about, built from below upwards into a secure and stately edifice.

The Judiciary

The administration of Justice is not here dealt with; the appointment of Judges of all ranks should probably come from above downwards, in order to secure independence of the immediate local authority, always a menace to the Bench. We have seen in the United States the degradation of Justice which has arisen from bringing the Judiciary under popular control.

Qualifications and Disqualifications

The qualifications of members of Councils of each grade should be generally:

- Knowledge — proportionate to the Council, entrance to which is sought, the educational qualification being higher than that of the electors;

- High moral character;
- Experience of administration in a lower grade Council, or some public body, large business concern, or equivalent;
- Age.

Conviction of an offence involving moral turpitude should be a disqualification either for the exercise of the franchise or for membership in a Council. Whether this should be for a term of years, or for life, is a matter for consideration, and might form part of the sentence.

While conviction should be a disqualification, high moral character should be a necessary qualification. It is sometimes said that a man's private life is no concern of the State, and it is true that anything like a moral inquisition is detestable. But a man's neighbours, his community, know his general character, and respect or distrust him according to their knowledge. His bearing among his fellows, his uprightness, his honour, his candour, his magnanimity, all these are known, and win public trust. No amount of anonymous abuse or journalistic malice permanently shake public confidence in a person whose character is unblemished, though they may cause a wave of prejudice... . S. Paul once asked as to a Bishop: if a man cannot rule his own household, how should he rule the Church of God ?—and the argument is valid. If a man is untrustworthy in his private life, how shall he be trusted in public affairs ? A man is a unit, and he cannot be divided into watertight compartments.

Some experience in administration is needed before large public affairs can be well dealt with. A man must not experiment with public business on a large scale without experience on a smaller.

As regards age, we may tentatively place it at five years above the minimum age of the elector; but it may be that this should not be laid down at all. A wise youngster is better than an old fool, and minds and souls do not match bodies in their age.

Such is a very rough outline of a scheme, intended only to serve as a basis for discussion. I believe that this question should be brought before all political organisations of this country, and should be thoroughly debated from every point of view. Thus only can a satisfactory and workable plan be arrived at, each stage being taken up and worked out in practice as the foundation for the next. The Village Councils should be instituted at once; the Constitution of the present Taluq Boards should be reformed immediately and that of District Boards should quickly follow, both being made entirely elective. Then, when the War is over, steps should be taken to establish Provincial Autonomy, and the time for the establishment of a National Parliament fixed.

Dealing only with India, I have not touched on the Imperial Parliament, above all the Self-Governing units, federated into an Empire. The post, army, and navy, spoken of above, would link on to the Imperial organisation.

—19 March 1915, *The Commonwealth*

Preparing the Foundations

India must immediately address herself to the preparation needed and her sons must shoulder local responsibilities which are the practical training for National Self-Government... for the foundations must be laid deep and strong for an edifice which is to be crowned with a National Parliament. England and the Self-Governing Colonies already have these; we have them partially, feeble and but half alive. Our first task is to supply them where lacking, and to organise them fully, the next to vitalise them where they exist, so that the Legislative Councils and the Provincial Governments may be supplied with all the local information needed for due administrative action by what are really the beginnings of Provincial Parliaments — information as to needs to be supplied, grievances to be redressed, local peculiarities and customs to be taken into account.

Only with such effective bodies below it, each efficiently performing its own work, can the central body properly discharge its duties. No longer must Indians look to the Government to initiate and to guide, they must themselves take the initiative and propose the necessary changes, giving the information which will guide the Government in the administration of the central funds, and the co-ordination of the various local bodies.

Now for this preliminary work of preparing the foundations of Self-Government, we must look to the District Conferences already existing.... Religious, educational, social, political, workers are all uniting to form one National Movement, a Movement which, gathering force as it proceeds, will gradually become irresistible, absorbing into itself all the highest and best elements to be found in India, including the best in the English official class, who honestly desire to help India to Self-Government.... There should be, as the next step, established in each area the four departments of the National work, a department controlling religious endowments, and adapting their use to the needs of the time, a department controlling educational institutions, a department organising industries, agriculture, trading associations, local administrative and judicial affairs and reforming social customs, a department dealing with civil and political matters and preparing legislation.

These should form the central fourfold Sabha, working in a defined area — a village, a group of villages, a district, etc. In the fundamental unit, the village, this central Sabha—one Committee with the four sub-committees — should be at once established, *i.e.*, a village should have its Council, its Panchayat — to use the old term — with the four departments, each controlling its share of the local activities, and reporting its detailed work to the Council as a whole, which would assign to each its share of the available funds. Such a Village Council would be able, at any moment, to supply detailed information as to its village, its industries, its education, its roads, its sanitation, its agriculture, its needs, its surplus of any kind.

Above this would come a similar Council for a group of villages, which would see to communications between villages, cooperation between them for the sharing of agricultural and other machinery (lighting, grinding, etc.), the breeding of cattle, etc., the gathering of surplus products and their forwarding to a common centre, the supply of necessary materials for industry and agriculture (cotton, silk, manures, etc.); remunerative prices, hospital accommodation, model farm, technical elementary school, and anything else better done by a group than by a village. Next the District Council on the same lines, dealing with all that demands higher intelligence for organisation, central stores for collection and distribution, higher schools, literary and technical; here, probably, would come the supervision of the religious endowments of the whole district, and their administration in the way most conducive to the welfare of the community — its temples, its schools, its poor, all coming within this distribution. Here would be collected and classified all the records concerning the district, ready for the information of the Provincial Parliament, enabling a wise distribution of Provincial funds.

The preliminary machinery for the establishment of these graded Councils should at once be taken in hand, and for the beginning of this we must look to the educated men of the towns, who gather in the District Conference and could map out the District and assign the local workers. The Cooperative Movement may serve as model, for it was started and nourished by these men, and they still' initiate each additional centre. These pioneers retire as soon as the village can walk alone, and start a similar organisation in another village. One or more such men would, by consultation with the villagers, establish the first Village Council, which later would be elected by the householders.

The number would be decided by the amount of work to be done. The next higher unit, the group, would probably be elected by the Village Councils, the next higher by the Group Councils. The outline of this should be discussed' and decided by a joint meeting of the District Conferences. Thus would be builded up a graded organisation, until the Provincial Parliament is reached, and these are unified by the National Parliament. Thus would Self-Government be established throughout the land, and India would be ready to take her place in a Federal Empire, and to send her -representatives to the imperial Parliament. .. .

This organisation must be begun in the centre, and spread thence over the Presidency, while the general idea of the territorial organisation for Self-Government should be sanctioned by Congress for the whole of India and committed by it to its District Committees, for the local discussion through their Conferences, allied with the Social and Theosophical.

— 10 and 17 April 1914, The Commonwealth

What is a Nation?

Refuting the constant argument that India is not a nation, Dr. Annie Besant discusses the various factors that are supposed to constitute a Nation, i.e., geographical area, unity of language, unity of religion, unity of race and demonstrates that Nationhood has its roots in a tar deeper source:

> *Geographical area* ... is clearly an exceedingly superficial definition, because the boundaries of the so-called Nations are from time to time changed. Much of the geographical area of a Nation might disappear, and yet the Nation might remain.

Unity of Race: . .. Every Nation in the modern world . .. is built of various racial constituents. Other Nations have invaded it, or it has invaded other Nations. In the course of long periods of time and gradually, the various Nations have blended together and have taken on common characteristics. You may, in some ways, look upon races as constituent parts of a Nation... The more constituents that have entered into a Nation and blended together, the richer and the greater ... the whole Nation. [Dr. Besant *then* traces the various elements that make *up the English Nation* and the American Nation, as great in diversification as the various types *in* India.] Most certainly it is not necessary to have unity of race in order to have an intense love of country, a strong feeling of patriotism.

Unity of Language: *While emphasising the* importance of a common *language, such as Sanskrit or Arabic, Dr. Besant points out:*

> In America, people talk in the Finnish, Italian, German, and Russian languages. Language need not, therefore, be a great bar to Nationality, if language is taught reasonably; and if in India it were possible to use one form of writing, then the question of communication would be very easily solved.

Unity of Religion: Do religious differences divide India so hopelessly that she cannot be called a Nation ? The antagonism between Hindus and Muhammadans, where it is still unhappily found, is nothing like the antagonism that existed until 1829 between Roman Catholics and Protestants in England and Ireland. When Akbar the Tolerant was ruling in India, he had Hindus as his Commander-in-Chief and Finance Minister. Then Roman Catholics were burning Protestants, and a few years later, Protestants were starving and pressing Roman Catholics to a slow death. I have not heard of such horrors between Hindus and Musalmans.

Roots of Nationhood

A Nation does not depend on unity of race, unity of language, or unity of religion. It depends on the fact that a Nation, like a man, is the building up of a complicated body which is inhabited by a higher life — a life that is divine. Just as each one of you is a Jivatma — a portion of the Self of Ishvara — that moulds your character, shapes your destiny, and is an impulse for your evolution, so it is with the life of a Nation: a Nation is an individual of a higher order. The spirit of a Nation is a fragment of Ishvara, comes direct from God Himself, and according to the peculiarities embodied in that fragment, are the characteristics of the Nation which is built up thereby. No two individuals are alike, and, similarly, no two Nations are alike. It is the totality of all Nations that builds up Humanity — the human reflection of Ishvara Himself. Each has its own individuality. That which makes the richness of the National Life of India is its marvellous literature, its history, its religion, its science—and all these are so highly evolved because the Nation is so ancient a Nation. During the early life of a Nation, religion is an essential for the binding together of the individuals who make the Nation. India was born, as it were, in the womb of Hinduism, and her body was for long shaped by that religion. Religion is a binding force, and India has had a longer binding together by religion than any other Nation in the world, as she is the oldest of the living Nations.

India-to-be: Always a Nation at her Heart

Over and over again, conquest has swept over her, and other religions have now their place here. But India has ever assimilated her conquerors and turned them into Indians, so that a Muhammadan is as proud of his Indian Motherland as a Hindu is. And she shall ever remain herself and not another. No other

Nation shall impress its seal upon her; no other mint shall coin her with its own stamp; no other religion shall dominate the hearts of her people; no other philosophy or science shall come to regulate her life or conduct, it shall only come to enrich and not to destroy. That is India's future built up by many trials, strengthened by many struggles, made enduring by many sufferings, by long patience and the overcoming of difficulties, and that India, the Sacred Motherland, shall survive in the future, as she has lived in the past—the mightiest of all the Nations that God has made, and always a Nation at her heart.

—21 February 1917, New India

Our Ideal of Empire

What shall be our Ideal of Empire? Shall it not be a Federation of free peoples under One Monarch, a Federation too strong to be attacked, too united to be afraid ? Shall it not exist for the good of the whole world, for the helping of backward peoples, for the spreading of knowledge and happiness, for the upholding of justice, for the protection of the weak ? Shall not all its citizens have the whole Empire for their Motherland, and all its peoples as their family ? Shall not the clamour for Rights be stilled, and the strong voice of Duty be the arbiter alike for peoples and for individuals ? Shall not goodness be encouraged, and evil made difficult ? Shall not all religions be honoured, and none be privileged ? Shall not Righteousness and Wisdom alone hold authority, and Character be the road to Power? Let us make such an Ideal our Ideal of Empire, and then shall it bring blessing to the whole world. —April 1913, *Young Citizen*

A World Citizen

A Theosophist must be a citizen of the world at the same time that he is a citizen of his own country; he must love all other Nations, he must try to draw them together. ... He must be a peacemaker outside his Nation and also within it — within the Nation, drawing the communities together into one; outside the Nation, trying to draw Nations into a Brotherhood, so that there may be no more war, none of the misery through which the world is passing today.

Therefore, in your life outside your Nation, do nothing to increase the spirit of hate, even towards those who are our enemies in the physical world today; remember that they also are our human brothers, separated now by a gulf of blood and of misery; but love can build bridges across the gulf and look forward to a future where the Nations shall be once more at one.. .. You cannot go wrong in love; you are sure to go wrong in hate; hating dulls the intellect and hardens the heart. Take due care that, in this terrible strife, in your struggle also in your own Nation for constitutional liberty, you remember also your duty to Humanity, that you work by love and not by hatred, that you try to raise all and not to degrade any. Let us draw our bonds together, let us approach each other, and not repel each other; for only thus will the Will of God be done, and the Brotherhood of Humanity be realised in our world. —1917, *Duties of the Theosophist*

Aristocratic Socialism

[Telling a "Fairy Tale "of an Ancient State which was built on the idea that he who had most should sacrifice for those who had least, Dr. Besant puts forth "certain lines of reorganisation "which, she modestly states, "are well worthy of consideration and discussion ":]

The Village Unit: A small area should be the unit of administration—a village, a township, any small area that may be named, so long as it is small.

The Elders: The people in that area should have the right to elect those who are to guide; but only people over a certain age, or with a certain definite experience of life—the "elders" in the old sense of the term. It should be their right to choose those who immediately should guide their little polity, so that the administration of the small area may be always under the control of the people who have to live in it.

The Head of *the Council* of the area should be chosen out of those elected by the people living therein, but chosen by the authority immediately above it. That has not been tried for many thousands of years, but it is a sound system....

Ever-widening Authority

The whole life of the people as regards agriculture, crafts, amusements, libraries and sanatoriums, should be in the hands of these local councils; so that the life of the unit in each State should be self-contained to a very great extent. The next area would be the area in which many of these were gathered together into a single organisation, say a Province.

All the primary councils would advise the Province Council, and only those would have the right to rule in that larger organisation, who had proved themselves good rulers in the smaller organisation below—not fresh from ignorance, but partly trained, would be the rulers of this next greater area, and their chief, again selected by the authority next above.

A Parliament of the Nation, which should guide national affairs, would be chosen again only by and from those who had shown themselves efficient in provincial politics. And international affairs I would not give to the ordinary Parliament at all, but to the ruler of the State, the Monarch, and to the men old in knowledge and experience, the best of the Nation, who should be round him as his council; to the hands of that body only should international politics be trusted.

Keynote of Statecraft

The general idea is that each man should have power according to his knowledge and capacity. None should be without some share, but the power that he has should be limited to his knowledge, experience and capacity; and only those should rule the Nation who have won their spurs in good administration of national affairs. In this way, we should restore to the State something of the knowledge that it wants, and we should take away from the State the danger of allowing a mass of ignorant electors—who are really fighting to elect a man who will look after their mines, their drains, their local interest, matters they understand—to upset international arrangements, and possibly plunge us into war — or worse, into dishonour. Those are the general principles which might be worked out, and might be applied to modern days.

And the keynote is that of my fairy tale: "From every man according to his capacity; to every man according to his needs."

A democratic Socialism, controlled by majority votes, guided by numbers, can never succeed; a truly aristocratic Socialism, controlled by duty, guided by wisdom, is the next step upwards in civilization.

Aristocratic Democracy

The problem of the moment is how to find the best man, and then to put him in the seat of power. If you say: "What do you mean by best?" I answer: "I mean the wisest, the most strong-willed, the most resolute, the most unselfish." Those are the qualifications of the Ruler, and without those qualifications in the Ruler, no happiness is possible for the State. ... I have not heard one reformer in India suggest that power should be given to the illiterate millions of this country. When they talk of "democracy "they mean the rule of the educated class. It is not democracy which they want, though they talk of democracy, but a far more rational system of Government. Whither is real democracy leading the West today ?... Is it aught but chaos ? Is it aught but ignorance? Triumphant numbers having their foolish way, till unorganised force is crushed by organised force. There you see the fruit of making ignorance strong and wisdom weak; of counting heads, however empty; of thinking that multiplication of nothing makes something. The nations are trying democracy in the West; beware how you try it here. That is not the way of progress; it is not the way of prosperity.

Now our ideal of Brotherhood applied to Government claims power for the wise and not for the ignorant; places lawmaking in the hands of those who understand the complex problems of industry, and not in the hands of those, who only know the needs of the household, or perhaps the needs of the town. The people have a right to happiness, % but they can never get it for themselves by physical force, . by legal violence, and by competition; they must be guided to it by knowledge, by those who understand . .. When organisation is unselfish, instead of selfish, then this labour problem will be solved and not till then. Now how to find the best ? That is the problem. Everyone of us who studies must try to solve this problem.... But you will not solve it until you realise the hopelessness of the present line of ruling—or not ruling—and accept the Ideal that the best should govern.... There lies much of the work of Theosophy where it is dealing with the problems of Government. Oppose all that would level down, but help all that would, level up. Do not allow the culture and refinement of ages, gathered by toil and pain, by the long struggles of generations, to be overwhelmed in one mass of ruin by the ignorant; and the foolish, as has happened so many times before... To these problems of Government ... bring the power of a great Ideal ... It is thought that builds nations as well as individuals; that which the thinker conceives, that which the prophet declares, that which the poet sings, that becomes *the* life of a nation, and is worked out in social organisation.

—1912, The *Ideals* of Theosophy

To Students: India's Good must Come First!

I hear that you are being asked to pass a resolution at' Youth and at Students' Conferences in favour of the Independence of the Motherland. I most earnestly pray you to leave that question to men and women who are self-dependent and have the right to work for India's Independence, if they decide to take the risk of carrying on such a propaganda, being convinced that it is necessary for the welfare of their country. Many elders, like Deshabandhu C. R. Das, whose patriotism none can deny, regard membership in a Federation of Free and equal Nations as a higher ideal than isolation. But you are not yet in a position to make that choice. You are dependent on your families, many of whom have made great sacrifices to send you and to keep you at School or College. Some have mortgaged their family properties; others stint themselves even in necessaries, in order to give you a good education, and they look to you for support to them in their old age.

What right have you, while dependent on others, and as yet inexperienced as to the consequences of hasty political action, to risk the whole future of your life, without any power even to defend yourselves ? You are in the condition of pupilage, liable to fines your parents would have to pay, or to expulsion, if your superiors are harsh, thus ruining your future life, your future career, on which your families largely depend. If you are expelled, those who incited you do not help you. When some such students went for help to Mr. Gandhi he merely told them that they had made a sacrifice. And, after all, what could he do for hundreds? [1] Study, think, prepare yourselves for your future as citizens of an India that will be free. But do not plunge now into a struggle for which you are unready and, by your condition, unfit.

Annie Besant

30 January 1929, *New India*

To Madras Students: To you, Dear Sons and Grandsons, I have a word to say: you love me, I know, and you will listen to me. You have seen a great struggle going on, in which by steadfast persistence in constitutional agitation, your elders have won our release and have given us back to your service. During the last few weeks, you have been growing impatient, naturally enough, for the time seemed long. But I earnestly pray you not to step outside the lines on which we have all been long agreed, nor to rush into action, which is not your duty. As Sir Subramania advised you, memorialise for the withdrawal of Order 559, but do not call outside meetings, for those mean political action, which we all, and you yourselves, have recognised as not students' work. The question of National dress can be arranged without meetings.

India's good must come first, with you as with us. We have serious work to do, preparing for Mr. Montagu's visit and winning his assent to the proposals of Hindus, Musalmans and all patriotic Indians. Help us in this, by not trying to force subsidiary matters, and by thus playing into the hands of those who are opposed to India's freedom. I know you will do this, for this struggle is for the Motherland, and you, the Sons of India, will make her cause your own.

Annie Besant

—22 September 1917, New *India*, (the first issue after her release from internment and arrival in Madras.)

Industry and Economics

Nation's Prosperity

That the Government of India should be in Indian hands is all-important, because whatever may be done by other professions and arts for the helping of the greatness of India, it must always be in the hands of the mercantile community, on whom a nation's prosperity must lie. It is especially vital, therefore, to the merchants of India that they should obtain political power before the great problems of peace arise, in which the questions that affect you most, the questions of the natural products of the soil, of their manufactured exports and imports, of the relation between the raw products and manufactures, will have to be dealt with by the merchant community. For, you must remember that you will be thrown against the strongest mercantile interests in the world, and one great object that they at present -have, is, if possible, to make India a place where raw products will be produced which shall be carried out of the country for manufacture elsewhere. That has been long attempted, but it has now been clearly stated to be the object by a very powerful mercantile combination which is -forming in London in connection with the merchants here.

The idea is that if they can persuade you to allow all the raw products to be exported and not to trouble you with their manufacture and to make you buy them back from the foreign merchants instead of utilising your own resources for the prosperity of yourselves and the country, then you will find that India will go downwards among the nations of the world. You must have control over finance. Financial autonomy is absolutely necessary for the welfare and prosperity of the whole country. It is only on you as a mercantile community that the prosperity of the country depends. You cannot separate them from each other. And inasmuch as your community is a religious community, also inasmuch as you desire religious education and realise that the gaining of wealth is one of the three objects of human life as laid down in the Shastras, then you also see that the gaining of wealth is in order that you may be helpers of the Nation and supporters of the people's good, as the stewards of the wealth that you rightly acquire. If then you can help the rest of the country in gaining that political liberty without which the physical liberty is impossible, then in helping yourselves you will be of invaluable service to the country.

There is an awakening of the mercantile community in every part of the country, although in Madras we are in the background because we are dominated by the English trade; as you know that merchants of Madras are not as independent as merchants in many other parts of India, and many of them who are [thought] to be masters in their business are simply acting as agents of foreign merchants for their enrichment. Taking the whole country, there is an awakening in the mercantile community. This is one of the vital signs which proves that India as a whole will soon have Home Rule. And if you here in Madura, powerful, wealthy and influential as you are, will throw yourselves on the side of political liberty, so that you may have prosperity for the country, control in your own household, management of your affairs, and if you also favour the National Education which will be an education designed to help the Indians to prosper, to teach them what they need to know, not only to fill the learned professions, as they are called, and the Government Service, but more and more to be able to hold their own in the great commercial competition of the world, then Home Rule on one side and National Education on the other will *be* like the two wings wherewith the bird rises in the air. Both are wanted and both must be had if India has to come forward. Then the great bird of India will rise high in the atmosphere and will be as it was of old the admiration and splendour of the world. (Cheers.) —17 April 1918, *New India*

Wanted a Radical Programme

What is wanted is not just a constructive programme, theoretically perfect and comprehensive; but one which is sufficiently radical to make an appreciable change in the lives of the masses of the people and, at the same time, one for which adequate funds can immediately be found. The Karachi resolution fails in this latter respect; for the items relating to the Congress economic programme will cost a few hundred crores per year. There has been no adequate thought bestowed on this vital aspect by the framers of the resolution. India will have to depend on increasing her National prosperity, and the taxpaying capacities of her people, if Swaraj is to be made a blessing to the masses. The difficulty of the problem will not only be that the process must of necessity be a gradual one; but India is a peculiar country in her economic structure. The desperate poverty of her people is an obvious and striking fact. What is not so obvious is that such wealth as there is, is in the hands of a small section which escapes with a light burden of taxation, in comparison with the load imposed on the poor. The readjustment of taxation on an equitable basis will be the biggest problem of the next few years.

—30 July 1931, *New India*

On Taxation

The whole system of laying taxes on the necessaries of life is radically vicious in principle. To tax the necessaries of life is to sap the strength and to shorten the life of those men and those women on whose strength and whose life the prosperity of the country depends; it is to enfeeble the growing generation; it is to make the children pale and stunted; it is in fact, to undermine the Constitution of the wealth-producers. To tax food is to tax life itself, instead of taxing incomes; it is a financial system which is, at once, cruel and suicidal. As a matter of fact, taxes taken off food have not decreased the revenue, and when this policy of taxing food shall have become a thing of the past, then a healthier and more strongly-framed nation will bear with ease all the necessary burdens of the State. Indirect taxation is also bad, because it implies a number of small taxes (some of which are scarcely worth the cost of collecting), and thus necessitates the employment of a numerous staff of officials, whereas one large direct tax would be more easily gathered in.

It is also bad, because with indirect taxation, it is almost impossible for a man to know what he really does pay towards the support of the State. It is right and just that every citizen in a free country should consciously contribute to the maintenance of the Government which he has himself placed over him; but when he knows exactly what he is paying, he will probably think it worth while to examine into the national expenditure, and to insist on a wise economy in the public service. I do not mean the kind of economy which is so relished by Governments, the economy which dismisses skilled workmen, whose work is needed, while it retains sinecures for personages in high places; but I mean that just and wise economy which gives good pay for honest work, but which refuses to pay dukes, earls, even Princes, for doing nothing. This great problem of fair and equal taxation ought to be thoroughly studied and thought over by every citizen; few infringements on equal liberty are so fraught with harm and misery as are those which pass almost unnoticed under the head of "collection of the revenue"; few reforms are so urgently needed as a reform of our financial system, and a fair adjustment of the burdens of taxation....

On Land Ownership

With our great and increasing population it is absolutely necessary that all cultivable land should be under cultivation. To hold uncultivated land which is capable of producing bread and meat is a crime against the State.... Then instead of sending the cream of our peasantry abroad, to seek in foreign countries the land which is fenced in from them at home; instead of driving them to seek from the stranger the work which is denied to them in the country of their birth; we should keep Englishmen in England to make England strong and rich, and give land to the labour which is starving for work, and labour to the land which is barren for the lack of it. "Land to labour, and labour to land "ought to be our battle-cry, and should be the motto engraven on our shield .. .

Land, like air, and like all other natural gifts, cannot rightly be held as private property. The only property which can justly be claimed in land is the improvement wrought in the soil. When a man has put labour or money into the land he farms, then he *has* a right to the advantages which accrue from his toil and from his invested capital.... It is the farmers and the labourers who have a right to life-tenancy in the soil, or, more exactly, to a tenancy lasting as long as they continue to improve it. The farmer, whose money is put into the land — the labourer, whose strength enriches the soil these are the men who ought to be the landowners of England.... Sacred rights of property! But what of the more sacred rights of human life ? The life of the poor is more holy than the property of the rich, and famished men and women more worthy of care than the acres of the nobleman. If these vast estates are fenced in from us by parchment fences, so that we cannot throw them open to labour, so that we cannot make the desert places golden with corn, and rich with sheep and oxen; if these vast estates are fenced in from us by parchment fences, then I say that the plough must go through the parchment, in order that the people may have bread.... —1883, *Civil and Religious Liberty*

Ancient Method of Famine Alleviation

Everywhere, where a nation lives by agriculture and has to prepare itself for a bad season, it is usual to find out a way of dealing with the natural difficulties suitable to its own spirit. Now that was done in India, and done in a very simple way, although a way that is dead against the modern "political economy." The way was a simple way in the days of ancient Egypt. We have all read of how, when Joseph was the wise minister there, he *provided for the years* of famine in the years of plenty. That one sentence expresses the Indian way of dealing with famines. When there was plenty, large quantities of the food were stored, and rent and taxes were taken in food; these varied with the food raised by the people, and therefore they never pressed heavily on the people. When there was much raised, the rent and taxes were higher; when the harvest was bad the King went without his share. But in the years when he got a very large share he stored it in granaries. In addition to that, after the people were fed (and the feeding of the people was the first charge), the people themselves stored the year's corn, so that if they had a bad year they could fall back on their own corn. In this way the peasant could make head against one bad season, and if there were more than one bad season the Prince came to his aid, by throwing his corn on the market at a price which the people could afford to pay.

Now that method of dealing with the famine problem still goes on in some States, such as Kashmir, because they will not permit their grain to be exported. But the greatest pressure is continually being put on the Maharajah of Kashmir to force him to export his rice. He has been able to hold his own so far, but the resistance of English pressure is a terribly difficult thing for an Indian Prince, and to resist it continually is not possible.... It is far better to ... save the people from famine, than to insist that the people shall sell their corn in years of plenty and starve in years of scarcity... And yet in this very year when famine was threatened, I saw not long ago in a newspaper a telegram advising the recurrence of famine in one part of India, and in the same paper that contained that telegram I saw a statement that the first shiploads of Indian wheat had left Bombay. That may be modern political economy, but it is pure idiocy....

Another great cause of these famines is the way in which the land is now held. In the old days there was a common interest in the land between Princes and people. Now the nobles, the old class of zamindars, have been turned into landlords, and that is a very different thing from the old way of holding land. Then you have insisted on giving the peasant the right to sell his land, the very last thing that he wants to do, the thing which takes away from him the certainty of food for himself and his children. No peasant in the old days had the right to sell his land, but only to cultivate it. If he needed to borrow at any time he borrowed on the crop. Now, in order to free the people from debt, they are given the right to sell their mortgaged holdings, and this means the throwing out of an agricultural people on the roads, making them landless, and the holding of the land by moneylenders. .. . You put ... power in the hands of the moneylender, and you take away from the peasant the shield that always protected him.

The railway system, too, useful as it is, has done an immense amount of harm. It has cleared away the food; it has sent the man with money into the country districts to buy up the produce which he sends abroad, giving the peasant the rupees that he cannot eat instead of the rice and corn that he can eat. Even when I first went to India you could hardly see a peasant woman without silver bangles on her arms and legs. Now large numbers of peasant women wear none; these have been sold during these last years of famine, and to sell these is the last sign of poverty for the Indian peasantry. It is no good giving them money in exchange for their food. They do not know how to deal with it. Another difficulty is... all the finer manufactures of India are practically destroyed, whereas the makers used to grow rich by selling these to her wealthy men and to foreign countries. . .. The Indian merchants were forced to give up their trade secrets.... In this way the old trades have been gradually killed out, while the arts of India are very rapidly perishing. The arts of India depended on the social condition of the country. The artist in India was not a man who lived by competition. As far as he was concerned he did not trade at all. He was always kept as part of the great household of a noble; his board, his lodging, his clothing, were all secured to him, and he worked at his leisure and carried out his artistic ideas without difficulty and without struggle. All that class is being killed out in the stress of western competition, and it is not as though something else were put in its place; the thing itself is destroyed, the whole market is destroyed. Now the pressure is falling on the artisan, and he is utterly unable to guard himself against it, and is falling back into the already well-filled agricultural ranks.... —5 October 1902, England and India

Labour Movement in India

I know the suffering that people went through in England, I know what long hours of labour meant: men went to work before their children were out of their beds and did not get back until their children had gone to sleep. Father and children scarcely knew each other and husband and wife never saw each other except by lamplight. The only way we could hold meetings was to go down to the place at 12 o'clock at night and then men wearied after long hours of labour would gather in an open street or even under the snow and there was no hour at which they could gather except the midnight hour when they ought to have been asleep.

It is these things which made the bitterness in England between class and class. It is better in India that these conditions do not arise, better that there is no enmity between class and class, because employers have to deal with labourers who are gentler, far more reasonable than men in the days of the terrible conditions in England. Here they ask so little, they are so easily pacified. Surely then it ought to be possible here to begin the labour movement. You should not go through that terrible time of trouble, starvation and misery that the men went through in England; you should not have here the conditions that have prevailed in England, you should not make slums like the slums of the manufacturing cities. You should begin on a human level and not on the level of one who would wrench everything from his employee with the resultant bitter resentment that he is starved into unwilling submission.

It is for that we have made a Labour Board trying to bring employers and employees together, because when a dispute begins, bring the men face to face, let them sit round a table, not the employer sitting comfortably on his chair and the men standing outside at the door, but as brothers discussing, as men mutually respecting each other, the difficulties that have arisen. Strike and lockout are both methods of war, they are not means of brotherhood. Very often some sort of explanation will suffice to make friendship where there is danger of quarrel. In England they have come to the conclusion—not everywhere—but the wisest and most thoughtful—that every dispute that arises should be submitted to an arbitration board, that instead of strike, instead of lockout—those outworn weapons of the employers and the employed, they should bring their grievances, put them before men chosen equally on both sides, and one chosen by both sides *as* the central and final arbiter and then the whole thing should be threshed out and conclusion come to without anger on either side. . . .

The point that I would put to you is: support the men in uniting, advise them and help them to make their union strong. Then they can put their case to the best among them and he can speak to the employer. Instead of an organised mob, you have a definite associated band to represent what the men want. Without unions in every trade it is impossible for the men alone depending on their wages to stand up against their employer, and no good employer dislikes a union. I hope to see here in Madras every trade with its union. As Mr. Wadia can tell you, one of the first things I suggested was a Union in our printing-office, so that it would be convenient to have the definite wish of the men employed put before us. We have a Union there, and it is so much more comfortable for everyone who does not want to oppress.

You know the fable of the bundle of sticks. Numbers make men strong. You can learn by the lessons that have been learnt in the countries of the West. The other day a great employer of labour put it frankly that he realises that short labour and good wages were for the employer a condition of success. Let us try to acquaint the people with the elementary conditions of effective and useful labour.

And meanwhile I would earnestly ask you to help your brothers a little so as to prevent starvation during the time which must necessarily be taken up in arbitration. As long as a man is hungry, as long as a woman is starving, as long as children are crying out for food, so long every meal we eat should be bitter in our mouths. We are one people, one blood, brothers and sisters—every one of us no matter what our work may be, what our social rank may be. Those who can sympathise with their brothers are worthy of the best gifts that God can give.

—16 December 1918, New *India*

To Lift the Submerged

And our beloved Theosophical Society, what of it in the coming year? In my Presidential Address I have tried to sketch in outline the mighty task which is set before it. It has to permeate the mental atmosphere with Theosophical ideas so that in every department of life in the New Civilization, these thoughts may inspire and guide. Education must be recast; penology reformed; labour must be raised from drudgery to creative joy; the submerged in every Nation must no longer remain the disinherited; Society must no longer hold a differing standard in sex morality for men and women. We have studied to no purpose unless we can bring the fruits of our study for the feeding of humanity, and justify our teaching by our lives. —January 1918, *The Theosophist*

It is not enough that we have learned something of the great Wisdom, and that our own lives are lighted by the glory of that light. It is no true light for us, unless through us it shines out upon the world. And the great evils of the world we must strive to remedy; and if we give the lead the world will follow.

—November 1927, *The Theosophist*

Three things you must remember as guiding principles, when you deal with social matters. Karma must never be forgotten. Reincarnation must never be forgotten. Brotherhood must never be forgotten. Let us apply those principles first to the large numbers of our people here whom we call the submerged classes... "*Submerged*" is my word. I do not like *depressed;* it sounds so dull, so sad, so miserable. I prefer *submerged.* They are down below the surface of happy society, and we have to lift them up. There lies the first great Indian duty of service....

Every nation from the far-off past has been built upon that mass of suffering humanity.. . . They have fallen because they were built against Brotherhood. . . . What is it that has saved India — India that traded with Babylon, that traded with Persia, that traded with Egypt, that traded with Rome ? The one thing that has saved her is that she has never quite lost sight of the great principle of Brotherhood, for, as Manu taught, let the Shudra be the younger son in the household—a member of the family and not outside the family pale. And although India has sinned grievously in this matter, she has not sinned unto death;,.. through many sufferings she has paid the debt of her National Karma, and she has finally expiated the debt by being made the servant of another Nation, and thus has paid to the uttermost the debt that she owed to the karma that she had made.. ..

Now our duty is to lift our submerged brethren on to the level of National Consciousness, so that they may know themselves as part of a living Nation.... We look down on these submerged men and women, but we are standing on their shoulders, and they keep us out of the mire in which otherwise our feet would be plunged.... Their hands keep our civilization clean by doing all those lower functions which we should have to do for ourselves were it not for them .... No class can rise until self-respect begins, and how can a man, always treated with contempt from childhood, respect himself ? .... The higher is responsible for the lower, as the elder brother is responsible for the bringing up of the younger. These are our younger brothers and sisters. . .. We *are* more below the Highest than they are below us. We share a common flesh and blood. Shall we not see the Self in the Chandala and honour the One Life in the embodiment of the Pariah ? That is the duty of the Theosophist to the submerged classes—to begin with those he meets in his daily life, to say a kind word, to answer a salute.... I would ask you in your personal dealings to introduce the affectionate human factor that teaches a man to respect himself by showing respect first to him.... They are brothers—younger brothers, yes, that I grant — but the younger brother is more kindly treated than the elder. If anybody goes short in a household, it is not the baby that goes short—it is always the elders. Apply that to our social life. ... Respect is the first step, then education, then training in trade or profession, giving them every opportunity of rising....

It all comes back to Brotherhood... so long as our younger brothers, so long as our lower classes, are not tenderly cared for, trained and nurtured, so long our Society cannot take its place in the comity of Nations. More is. expected from you than from the younger Nations of the West. In a kind of rough-and-tumble way they have claimed their citizenship, but you are an ancient people; you have thousands of years behind you; God expects more from you than He expects from the western Nations and He is calling on you to take your place as leaders in the civilization of the world. India is destined to take the highest place in the advancing ranks of Nations, and I hope and pray, as I have hoped through all my Theosophical life, that England and India may go forward hand in hand as the leaders of the highest civilization in the East and West together.

I hope that the wisdom of the East may permeate the rougher mind of the West, that the spirituality of the East, no longer dreamy but practical, as it was in the old days of India, may show that the spiritual man is not a sluggard, is not a dreamer, is not a visionary, but is the greatest force in the world for the uplift of Nations and for the uplift of man; and this is because I know something of what India is. I do not pretend to know her thoroughly—for who shall know the Mother of Nations, the Mother of civilizations, with her thousands and tens of thousands of years behind her ? But I know her by twenty-three years of loving life among her people. I know her by my own incarnated past, and by the love of India, that makes me reckon nothing worth having in comparison with her service. I know her, I love her, I worship her, as I know and love and worship no other country on the surface of the earth, and therefore I would fain see her what she can be, what she is in reality, what she must be in the lives of the men and women born of her; and because I believe that Theosophy is but your own Para-Vidya come back to you in a modern phase, therefore I call on every Theosophist—whether a member of The Society or not — to yoke himself to the service of Indian society and put it in the place in which it ought to be —an example, a model, which Vaivasvata Manu gave for the great Aryan Race, and which will be perfected in you, if you will add your ancient knowledge to the modern thought of the world in which we are.

—1917, *The Duties of a Theosophist*

Caste

Caste... is real as long as you have quality present in the caste, marking it out as distinct, but ... it becomes unreal the moment quality has disappeared, and you find merely the outside characteristic of birth and not the inner characteristic of qualities. ... There is no caste, it is written over and over again, unless birth and quality go together. Take the famous passages in the *Mahabharata* with which you must all be familiar, that a Brahmana who shows the qualities of a Shudra is a Shudra and not a Brahmana; that the Shudra who shows the quality of a Brahmana is a Brahmana and not a Shudra.. . .

There was no such thing known in ancient India as caste by itself — Varna. Varna and Ashrama always go together .. . and that is a point more important than you may realise. The Guru had as pupils twice-born boys; he had pupils of the three twice-born castes; they were all his pupils from the time of the giving of the sacred thread.. .. They ate together; no distinction of caste was known while the pupil was in the house of the Guru ... So no caste during their boyhood made a dividing line between the pupils of the same Guru.. .. When the boy was to be married ... began the Grihastha Ashrama, the household life [where] caste was recognised, for children were to be born, and hereditary race to be preserved.... When the household life was over, then came the Vanaprastha, where again caste disappeared, and finally Sannyasa, where obviously no caste showed itself.... Where children were not concerned, caste was ignored. Even in the household life it was not so rigid as it is now. What does Manu say ? You may take food from the servant of your own house, from your own ploughman; why ? Because the taking of food in the old days was based on a principle. Where the life was clean, where men and women led a pure and decent life, where you knew your own servant's life and knew it to be well and decently lived, there you could take food from him; for it is true that the magnetism of the man affects the food, and so has much to do with the building up of a pure body. But in your modern way of having Brahmanas for your cooks, you do not think of his life but of his birth. You would rather take food from a profligate Brahmana than from a decent Shudra. There is no reason nor sense in that; it is not the old law but a modern prejudice, and where you have prejudice instead of reason, then it is time for a custom to come to an end. . .

I would rather take food with a man who in his body belongs to a low caste but in his mind is pure, than I would sit down and take food from the hands of one who is nominally pure and whom I know to be stained with ambition, and to be soiled with lack of truth and honour in daily life. . . .

By a slow change in hundreds and thousands of years, the duties of the Caste have been forgotten. The Brahman has sought for power and wealth. The Kshattriya has sought to do the teaching work of the Brahman. The Vaishya has forgotten his duty and has wanted to take up the work of the Kshattriya, and the Shudra has claimed the right to take the duties of the twice-born. No caste is content to do its own duty, but everyone claims to do the duties of everybody else. . .. The beginning of this degradation lies on the caste that ought to be the noblest, that ought to be the highest, that ought to be the purest, and the degradation began when first the Brahman coveted wealth, and desired physical authority, when he took the wealth that belonged to the Vaishya, the rule that belonged to the Kshattriya, and was dissatisfied with his spiritual knowledge, and was discontented with his spiritual authority. ... So ... a confusion of castes has arisen, and with that confusion what Arjuna prophesied — degradation of the nation and the gradual lowering of the whole of the national Life. Side by side with that spiritual degradation, there is the maintenance of an outer rigidity which gives privilege without discharge of duty.... No man is fully a Brahman unless the Brahman Soul has a Brahman body, and unless the Brahman body has in it the Brahman Soul....

—18 and 25 September 1914, *The Commonwealth*

To Brahmans

I believe in the reality of Brahmanhood I who know that there is a Brahman caste in reality, which is a living and working power in human life today, tell you that just because I honour the real Brahman, do I look with sorrow and shame on many a nominal Brahman that I see around me; for, so says the Law, those that cannot teach are not Brahmans. ... If India is to be helped . .. some few at least must lead the Brahman life, in order to make it possible that the caste may be kept alive for happier times, to serve as the vessels into which spiritual life may hereafter be poured... .

You have a choice between two ways of change.... There are two ways in which privilege disappears: one when the people, who no longer respect the privilege-holders are angry with these privileges which outrage their sense of justice; and if it goes too far you get a great uprising like the French Revolution and the privileged aristocracy perish by violence and are lost in the midst of the nation. Or you may have the wonderful action of the privileged class in Japan, as privileged as any of the Brahmana caste here, who, called on for their country's sake, stripped off every privilege they held and threw them at the feet of the Motherland, in order that she might become free and great. Their privileges were even greater than the Brahmana privileges here. They might strike down a man in the street who they thought insulted them, striking him down with the sword which they alone might wear. None could say them nay, none could arrest or save; and yet that warrior caste, proud with the pride of warriors, flung all aside and stepped down amongst the people, content to justify their warrior spirit in the war against Russia, where those very Japanese who had thrown away their privileges showed their Kshattriya spirit, lived on the battlefield in defence of their country.

Which way will you take, you of the great Brahmana caste ? Will you wait until the surging wave of prejudice and anger, rising higher, higher, and higher, sweeps you all away against your will ? Or will you perform that noblest of all acts—sacrifice your privileges for the sake of freedom, for the sake of the greatness of the Motherland, stretching out your hands to all without exception, and calling on all to share with you in the redemption of the land?

Oh! I have had a vision, which I hope is not only a dream, of this mighty caste, which in the past has given to India all that she has of greatest in her literature, in her arts, of you, the natural leaders of the people by your high education, by your brilliant intelligence, by your power of speech—I have had a vision of your mighty caste going forward to the feet of India, the Mother, talcing off the coronet of privilege from your own heads and laying it down in sacrifice at her feet. I have dreamt that this great act of National sacrifice, once accomplished, splendidly performed, India the Mother would stretch out her hand in blessing, and would say to her children who had made the sacrifice: "Go back to your people, and take your rightful place again as leaders still in India. Give to them your splendid intellect, give to them your wonderful eloquence, give to them the power of your past and the influence of your names, crowned no longer with the crown of privilege but with the deathless crown of self-sacrifice."

That is the vision which I have seen, that the dream which I hope will prove true. Then the Brahmanas, having stepped down, will be raised up by the love of a grateful people, who will follow leaders who are leaders of quality, and not merely by the accident of birth.

—1895, *India* and 1913, in 27 November 1918, *New India*

Foreign Travel: You need the education of foreign travel in order to play your future part in this World-Empire into which you are entering.... You cannot grow up to it, if you keep a social organisation which is out of touch with the whole of the social order of the civilized world. You have to eat with other people, and you have to meet them on an equal footing; you have to associate with men and women on a footing of social equality. You have to realise that you are a Nation among Nations, and that you cannot have a social organisation apart from ail the rest of the civilized world, and separate yourself socially from the people with whom you are to share the direction and the government ... of the Empire at large.

—18 and 25 September 1914, *The Commonwealth*

Intermarriage: But there is one point I would ask you 'not to forget when you are dealing with the question of intermarriage. Race is a reality, and you cannot ignore it... Race *is* important; it is important in the plant, in the animal, and it is also important in the man; and you must recognise the law of heredity, although you may say that it is no longer carried out under the name of caste. General avoidance of intermarriage is vital for a Nation's future .. .

There lies before you this path of reform to tread or not as you will. Every Nation is given its opportunity, but none can force it to tread the upward path. You have to modify your caste; you have to take foreign travel as a matter of course; you have to educate your women; you have to educate the masses of your people; you have to do away with child-marriage. These great reforms you have to bring about. The Nation's life depends on them; and remember that the Indian Nation does not live for itself alone; it is a type unique among all the Nations of the world. It knows how to join spirituality to intellect, intellect to physical prosperity, and so to build up the Nation on all sides....

One thing you must remember; that none outside yourselves can make India what she ought to be. No tongue of a foreigner can build India. It is Indians themselves must build their Nation, and they alone can make India what she ought to be, what she shall be in the days to come. No Government, no power, no friendship, no amount of eloquence, can make a Nation. It is the men and women of the Nation only who can build it.

—18 and 25 September 1914, *The Commonwealth*

You see the line of thought: namely, not to abolish but to make real; not to get rid of, but to reform; so that, as in the old days, there may be bodies fitted for the incarnation of the higher Souls, parents leading the life of Brahmans, not only in the food and the outer observances of the caste....

Then let learned men come together to take common counsel for the common good, and little by little, step by step, bringing back the Spirit into Indian life and into Indian religion, giving honour where it is due, honouring the Brahman if he be pure and communicates his spiritual wisdom and is able to teach; honouring Caste not in its name only but in its reality, not the outer show but the inner life. Thus in the centuries that lie in front of us, shall be undone the evil work that has been done, and the Nation shall be raised as a whole. That is the work that lies before us. That is the work in which I ask you to take me as your helper; for the life which came from India is given back to India for service, and I sacrifice it to the helping of our race. —1895, *India*

Widow-remarriage

In trying to remove an obvious evil, entailing much suffering, an eager reformer is often apt to make changes without considering their bearing on other matters than the one at which he is aiming, and thus, in removing one limited evil, he brings about others of a more serious and sweeping character. This is especially the case when the reform touches the bases of the social fabric, and where these are concerned, the greatest care and circumspection are needed, lest, in endeavouring to knock off excrescences, we bring down the whole fabric.

In discussing widow-remarriage we must have in view the Hindu ideal of marriage in its bearing on Society, and must consider how far such remarriage would affect wifehood in general, with all that the wife means to the home and the State.. .. Hinduism presents man and woman as complementary halves of a single whole, each supplying what the other lacks. It regards the marriage union as applying to-all parts of the nature, and as passing therefore unchanged into the worlds beyond death, unmarred by the loss of the physical body. It considers husband and wife as spiritually one, even as they are physically united, and it fosters so-intense a love and devotion in the wife to the husband that the ideal Hindu wife could not dream of a transference of that affection to another. I doubt if any ordinary Hindu wife would tolerate it for a moment. This love to the husband is interwoven with the very fibre of the Hindu woman's life; it comes out in the plea of Savitri to Yama, by which she victoriously wrested her husband from the noose of death: he had promised her sons; then he must restore the husband who could alone make that promise effective. Death admitted the cogency of the plea, and restored the husband to the faithful wife. "Mayst thou be as Savitri." must no longer be said to the young wife, if a second man may draw her to his bosom. And surely it is worthy of consideration whether this intensity of love, with all it implies, is to be eradicated from the hearts of Hindu women, by reducing marriage from a sacrament to a contract.

This closeness and sacredness of family ties may render partly intelligible the horror felt by Hindus — men and women alike, about the idea of widow-marriage. The maiden given in marriage becomes a member of the family to which her husband belongs; she bears children into it and becomes to them an incarnate Goddess, presiding in the sanctuary of the home. The husband dies, but she is still a part of him, daughter of his parents, mother of his children, a stone in the family house; shall she be wrenched out thence to be built into another household, loosening all the other stones, shattering the family altar ? . . . It is sacrilege, it is adultery, it makes marriage a commercial contract, a union of bodies only, as well as disintegrating the sacred life of the family, which is the dearest pride of the Hindu. It may be said that this view is not enforced on men; they may remarry. That is so, for the man in remarrying does not dislocate the family, but only brings into it another member. No tie is broken either to ancestors or to children; all remains intact... . Nor does it apply to the marriage of virgin-widows, that have been betrothed or wedded in childhood and have never passed into the family circle of the new home. . . .

Many, however, do not advocate the remarriage of widows in general, but only of virgin-widows, and they urge the injustice of shutting out many young girls, many of them mere children, from all the sweetness of wifehood and motherhood.... Let us admit to the full that such a lot is generally sad as compared with that of the happy wife and mother; but let us see whether widow-remarriage would avert it, or only transfer it to other shoulders.

In this relation we have to face the fact that there are more marriageable women than marriageable men. Boys die in greater numbers than girls. .. . We do not then solve the problem of the sad lot of solitary women by permitting virgin-widows to remarry. Every widow remarried means one unmarried girl the more. We only transfer the solitariness from the widow to the maid.

Secondly, the large number of virgin-widows is due to child-marriage, and the number would be far more wisely checked by preventing premature marriage than by remarrying widows. The higher death-rate among the boys disappears after 14 years of age... . This change, necessary if India is not to perish by racial decay, will save large numbers of girls from widowhood, and will abolish child-widowhood entirely.

Thirdly, the lot of widows may be changed by making them the willing helpers of their sex, by training them as teachers and as nurses, and by thus making widowhood a consecration to the service of humanity. In the West, tens of thousands of women willingly embrace the celibate life, in order to devote themselves to intercessory prayer and meditation, or to serve as nurses of the sick poor, as educators of the young, as guardians of helpless orphans and the friendless aged. How many good works in India are crippled for lack of such a class, and Indian girls are taught, and Indian orphans are cared for, by Christian women, because none of their own faith are available for such charitable duties. Here is a vast field of noble labour, of peaceful and happy usefulness for any Indian widows whose hands are not already filled with helpful service in their own homes. Society cannot exist without the service of self-abnegating women, who are free from immediate personal ties. Widowhood is a call to such service, and lives thus passed have the sweetest consolations for the loss of husband's and of children's love. . . .

I have two women in my mind now, exquisite types of gentle dignity and serenity, with faces divinely pure and compassionate. [But] the lot of the child-widow is hard, as things are.. .. Taking the ordinary run of Hindu girls they are not fit for this selfless life of ministration, and they fret sometimes against the enforced austerity for which they are not ripe. The Hindu ideal of marriage is pitched too high for the modern Hindu, man or woman, and with the failure of marriage, remarriage becomes less disastrous....

It may be asked whether the Hindu type of womanhood is one that it is desirable to spread among Western nations. The answer may bluntly be made that such spreading is impossible. That delicate, gracious, sweet, and tender type, with its gentle courtesy, its serene dignity, could not endure in the rush of western life and the self-assertiveness of western civilization.

One might as well picture Savitri in a divorce court, or Sita suing the cobbler for damages in a libel suit. Leave the Hindu woman untouched by Western thought and do not destroy a type which, just because it is unique, would leave less full by its disappearance the chord of humanity. We have women enough who are brilliantly intellectual and competent; let us leave unmarred the one type which is the incarnation of spiritual beauty.

—3 June 1896 and 1903, Articles in *The Birth of New India*

Polygamy without Responsibility

[Ever did Dr. Besant strive for a better understanding between civilizations. Much has been made in the West of the fact that within the Eastern civilization under certain circumstances polygamy is practised. While strongly upholding the glorious Indian ideal of a marriage-tie that exists even beyond death, she yet contrasts the legalised polygamy of the East with the irresponsible polygamy of the West.]

The true and righteous sex-relation between one man and one woman is preached as an ideal in some countries, but is generally practised in none. Islam permits polygamy; Christendom forbids but winks at it, provided that no *legal* tie exists with more than one. There is pretended monogamy in the West, but there is really polygamy without responsibility. The "mistress "is cast off when the man is weary of her and sinks gradually to be the "woman of the streets," for the first lover has no responsibility for her future, and she is a hundred times worse off than the sheltered wife and mother in the polygamous home. ... It is better for a woman, happier for a woman, more respectable for a woman, to live in... polygamy, united to one man only, with the legitimate child in her arms, and surrounded with respect, than to be seduced, cast out into the streets — perhaps with an illegitimate child outside the pale of law — unsheltered and uncared for, to become the victim of any passer-by night after night, rendered incapable of motherhood, despised of all.

It is good for Society that monogamy should be held up as an ideal, for its public recognition as right and the inner shame connected with resort to prostitution are purifying forces; but monogamy is not practised where there is one legal wife and hidden non-legalised sexual relations. The recognised polygamy of the East degrades the social conscience more than the unrecognised polygamy of the West — "hypocrisy is a homage vice pays to virtue" — but the happiness and dignity of the woman suffer less under the first than under the second.

—1912, Islam *in the Light* of Theosophy

Brahmacharya

One of the customs of ancient India which has perished and needs to be re-established is that of Bralimacharya during the student life. In the old days a boy was given into the hands of his teacher, or Guru, when he was from five to seven years old, or sometimes later. From that day forward he lived in his teacher's house, serving him and studying under him, the period of study being nine, eighteen, or thirty-six years, or until he had mastered his studies, and sometimes even lasting throughout the life.... During the whole of this period the student was under the obligation of absolute chastity. Only after he had kept the rule of studentship, had left his teacher, and had returned home, might he marry. It was well recognised that the excitement and preoccupations inseparable from marriage were destructive of the single-minded devotion to study which is necessary for its due effect on character.. . . Over-early parentage is as ruinous physiologically as it is injurious mentally.

The effects of the modern system of early marriages are visible on every side in India. Her students are tired when they should be in the first flush of vigorous manhood, and at the age when they should be doing their best work— from 40 to 60—they are old men.... It is no answer to this to quote individual cases of strength; it is the slow sinking of the general average which is a Nation's signal flag of national peril. And even where men are strong, there is generally noticeable in them a dislike of exertion, a wish for physical inaction, which speak eloquently of the lack of vitality in the system. ... Boys who wish to have a healthy, vigorous manhood and a healthy old age, must be Brahmacharins during their student-life. And this does not mean only that they must not marry, but also that they must be pure in thought and act. Secret vice is a thousand-fold worse than premature marriage, and is far more fatal to health. It means lassitude, destruction of nerve and brain power, disease, and miserable old age.... For your own sake, and for India's sake, my young brothers, be pure, be pure.

—1901, *Central Hindu College Magazine*

Value of Young Men's Associations

[Dr. Besant *founded the Young Men's Indian Association in Madras and always took a deep interest in it.*]

In India . . . lads crowd into large towns to attend High Schools and Colleges; they live where they can, they eat as they can. Crowded in backyards, sometimes in the upper stories of houses of ill-fame, thousands of them live neglected, without any of the nobler influences of home, without opportunities of relaxation and amusement save at the peril of health and morals; too often they are led astray by those who need them as tools; their readiness to sacrifice themselves, their eager enthusiasms are played upon, and their noblest feelings are distorted and degraded.

For such lads a Young Men's Association means a helper, a friend, a saviour. It brings them into touch with elder men of high ideals and of pure life, who are still young enough to sympathise, yet old enough to advise; it places before them good examples of patriotism, of service of the Motherland, of daily self-sacrifice, and stirs them to emulation while insensibly leading them away from evil. It gives them -friends who are worthy of confidence, leaders who inspire to enthusiasm, and thus disciplines emotion without chilling it, and trains it to serve, not only to shout.

Self-control, courtesy, helpfulness, flourish in such an atmosphere, and unconsciously youthful ambitions are purified and youthful hopes flower into deeds. It is impossible to overestimate the value of the association with the coming generation of true, brave, and unselfish elders. These youths who will be the citizens of tomorrow and hold the destiny of India in their hands—these are here, ready, eager, to set their feet on the path of Service. God grant that all who have set their hands to this great work may so inspire them by high example that Madras, and gradually all India, may rise to a noble ideal of patriotism and of public life.

Another side of these Associations is that they offer recreation of an attractive kind in pure surroundings. A gymnasium should always be established as soon as possible, and fitted up with suitable apparatus. Some officer should be found to act as drillmaster, and a trained Indian athlete to teach the indigenous exercises in addition to the Western methods; there is nothing so good as the former for developing every muscle in the body and increasing chest capacity; for this, breathing exercises must not be forgotten. At the Central Hindu College we had these exercises in addition to games, and the effect on the health and growth of the boys was striking.

There should be recreation-rooms for suitable games, as well as a reading-room for ephemeral literature and a good library for study and quiet reading. Music should not be forgotten, while lectures and debates should also find their place.. ..

These associations should by no means be confined to students. The young men who have left college or school, who are employed in Government or other offices and banks, clerks who are educated but poor, — all these will find a home in such Associations. The field is wide; the harvest is ripe; many labourers have come forward. All patriotic and wide-minded men, who work for the future, should be ready to help in the Madras centre, if residents here, or to found and guide similar Associations all over India.

—20 February 1914, *The Commonwealth*

Resurrection of Indian Women

In discussing the question of the position of Indian women, it is sometimes, indeed generally, forgotten that their exclusion from the life of the Nation as such, and their confinement to home interests, are of very modern growth in India. We need not go back to the far-off days of Savitri, in order to prove that a girl might wander about outside her home, and might fall in love before her parents had chosen her future husband. Nor to the time of Damayanti to show that a maiden might select her own husband.... We have heard of these so often that they scarcely now make any impression on our minds. When we read that of old two paths were open to the woman as to the man, the path of Brahmacharya and the knowledge of Brahman, and the path of the householder, of the wife and mother, it affects us not—it was so long ago.

But there is no break in the glorious history of Indian womanhood down to the time when English education made a new culture for the man in which the woman did not share, carrying him away from her into a new world of interests from which she was shut out. Indian history is studded with the names of Indian women who were warriors, Queens, rulers, patriots, scholars. The names of Padmavati of Chitor, the gallant wife of Bhimsi, of Mirabai, the poetess of Marwar and Mewar,. . do not these shine out as stars in India's sky ? They lived and died for the Motherland, and saw naught unwomanly in any service which she needed and which they could render.

Gradually the woman was pushed out of her place in India's life save as mother, as wife, as head of her household. Within the house none has disputed her sovereignty, but she ceased to be the counsellor of her husband in his public life and national interests; thus has the whole country been the loser, for woman's viewpoint is not identical with that of the man, but differs as the two eyes differ.... The axes of vision are different though correlated, and make for fuller vision than one eye can compass by itself.... The Nation with one eye blinded cannot see nor judge aright. Man and woman are not identical, but the one is the complement of the other as the two eyes of the human being, the two wings of the bird. National life is impoverished, is crippled, deprived of its feminine element.

But of late there has been an awakening of women, touched by the wide sweep of National consciousness, and feeling their modern exclusion from all humanity outside the home. The wrongs wrought in South Africa on Indians brought the Indian women there to face, as of old, the dangers which were faced by their men. Women went to gaol as men went, aye and died from the hardships suffered. Then women in the Motherland arose, stung into action by the sufferings of the exiles, and women's meetings called for justice, so that men and women together marched in one army against wrong—and won. The degradation, foul and monstrous, inflicted on Indian women in Fiji as indentured labourers, called on their sisters in the Motherland for help; again they moved, sent a deputation to the Viceroy and succeeded in gaining a promise that indentured slavery should cease. A third great victory was won in the internment struggle—nine women's meetings and women's processions played a remarkable part in the agitation.

Meanwhile efforts to win higher education were steadily carried on, and progress was made. Qualified women teachers, women doctors, began to appear. Handicapped by the evil custom of child marriage and child motherhood, women yet strove for education, and Mr. Karve's bold stand for widow education, widow marriage, finally for a Woman's University, played a fine part in the struggle. Girl undergraduates and graduates attended Government Universities and distinguished themselves in the examinations. A woman poet, Sarojini Devi, showed an easy mastery of English melody that no masculine Indian has rivalled. Toru Dutt might have held her own had not death cut short her promise. Shrimati Sarojini's rare eloquence alike in English and in Urdu is making her a power in the political field of India.

Everywhere, as we look around us, we see the glorious arising of Indian Womanhood, the promise of a near and sure victory for Liberty. For Woman is the Shakti, the Divine Power, and, without her, Man cannot reach the fullness of Life. Partner, not subject; comrade, not rival; complement, not antagonist; helper, not burden—such is Woman to Man. With her Freedom, India shall become free. The subjection of the Motherland and of the Mother must end together. For Man and Woman are the halves of a Perfect Whole, and by their united strength shall India enter into her Kingdom. —22 February 1919, New *India*

The Shakti

No Nation is made of men alone. The wives of a Nation give courage to their husbands, the mothers of a Nation train the generation that will inherit our work in freedom, in self-respect, in nobility of character. No bird can fly with one wing: no Nation can rise with only one sex taking part in the National life. We are not identical, we have differences, but in the differences, complementary and not antagonistic, lies the perfection of humanity... .

It is quite natural that here, in India, women should advance beside their men, for India has had many capable women Indian Rulers, sometimes in their own right, sometimes as Regents for their minor sons, and this has continued down to our own time....

There is no Deva without his Devi. You cannot have the spirit without the matter which it inspires and which embodies it....

Moreover, from the Hindu point of view, the Shakti, the active Power of God, is feminine, and in all troubles and distresses all the Shining Ones cry to the Shakti for deliverance, and where the masculine fails, the feminine triumphs, and drives away the Evil, and restores the throne to Good. ... And the woman is Her Representative on earth, the Mother, holiest and sweetest of names....

The Shakti is the true power of Deva and in the help of the representatives of the Shakti will lie the certain triumph of India in the Nation and in the Indian home; and so it is that we go forward full of courage.

—27 September 1917, New *India* and September 1918, *Theosophist*

Religion

Regenerating Energy

To whatever land we may go, through whatever country we may pass, we have still Humanity as "the great orphan "crying for the Spirit, striving after Light, after spiritual unity, striving to find in the many exoteric religions the one Spiritual Truth which alone can satisfy the soul.... In this land there is more hope of a spiritual revival, and if a spiritual revival here there may be, then it will pour outwards to all the four corners of the world. For spirituality is more easily awakened in India than elsewhere. The spiritual heart here is only sleeping, whereas in some other lands it has scarcely yet come to birth; for you must remember that in this land is the birthplace of every religion, and that from India outwards, religions have made their way. Therefore it is that the soul of our Mother India is so important for the future of the world, and therefore it is that the materialism of India is so fatal. For it is here alone that lies the hope that man has been looking for spiritual life; for, in truth, unless the life of the Spirit come in this land, by reviving here, then the hope is baseless that spirituality is to spread over the world.... If you cannot revive spirituality in India through *Hinduism,* if you cannot thus reach India, then there is nothing else you can hope to do.. .. If this shall again become a living thing, India shall herself live; and, with the revival, all the sleeping truths of other religions shall look again towards their Indian Mother, and make her once again the spiritual teacher of the world.. ..

There is one thing that is eating the heart out of India, and that is modern materialism. There is one thing which is poisoning the mind of India, and that is the kind of science which is the teacher of materialism and works against Spirituality in the mind. How should I be able to tell you of the moral regeneration of India unless first I can strike at that which is piercing her heart and sucking out her very life-blood. So, as I have been trained in the science of the West, trained in the knowledge of the physical Universe, which is so much used to make men believe that nothing but the physical remains — I take for my first subject, this undermining of materialism by science, and I attack it with the weapons that were once used to build it up. ...

It is from the Supreme Will that forms emanate and build the Universe. And you may understand that this power of the Supreme is more manifest in the power of the mind than the powers of the body, and that true activity is shown not in running about from place to place, held in the bonds of physical facts, but in quiet thinking, in the use of the imagination and the will. Therefore the Yogi sitting apart, with body absolutely still, with eyes closed, and mouth not communicating with other men, if he be a Yogi indeed, a Yogi in heart not only in dress, he has an inner life, a spiritual life and he may do more than the man of action by his thoughts, by his meditations, by the forces which are going; out from him. On these more than on the work of politicians may turn the life of the nation.

Nor is this work only for the Yogi. Every one of you is sending out thoughts that, passing into the astral atmosphere, will take form, and thence affect the lives of men and in their totality the Nation's future. If only every one of you would give one brief quarter of an hour's thought each morning to the future of India and send out earnest wishes for her welfare, hopes for her revival, aspirations for her spiritual greatness, believe me you would make a force that would raise the nation and would mould her future. Your thoughts would gather together, modelling, as it were, an ideal India that should take shape in the external world; your prayers would gather together and ascend to the Feet of Mahadeva, whence would flow forth a regenerating energy that would manifest itself in teachers, in leaders, in guides of the people, who could move the hearts of men, and unite them into one mighty Unity. Such is your power over the future, such the service you may render India, for in thought is the power of the Supreme, and it is man's, because "Thou art Brahman."

—1895, *Materialism Undermined by Science*

Gift of the East

Three Great Ideals

- The world is under a *divine governance,* invisible worlds mingle in the affairs of men, with the inevitable corollary of "the ideal of the *responsibility* of *the rulers for the ruled.*"
- The Ideal of Duty or *Dharma* rather than Rights or Privileges dominating each man in his respective sphere of activity, with the corollary of the *relativity* of *morality.*
- *Simplicity and Renunciation — hence Comradeship*:

  "That simplicity of material life which lays stress on knowledge, character, service, instead of on wealth," and hence brings about "a recognition of a common human life" and through likeness of daily life and refinement, a comradeship between rich and poor, class and class.

Dr. Besant sees a true aristocracy as "the custodian of stately manners, dignified bearing, artistic culture, simple or splendid living, according to the seemliness of the occasion, the ever-present example of 'good taste.'"

Destinies of Nations

A Nation that would fill a mighty part in the near future must

Build up her sons and daughters on heroic models

By placing righteousness above luxury, thought above enjoyment,

By choosing the strenuous, the heroic, the self-sacrificing in daily life, and not petty enjoyments, small luxuries, and miserable sensual gratifications.

If our nation is to achieve its destiny as *the servant* of *humanity at large.*

We must cultivate the soil of character and plant the sound roots of noble, righteous, simple living. —*The East and the West*

Listen, Brothers! Let us Think about Truth

It is said in the Veda: "Brahman is Truth." Now you know that your life, the life of your body by which you move about, by which you hear, see, smell, taste, touch, is part of the life of Brahman, it is Divine Life, by whatever name you worship God. He is everywhere, in everything, and so is in you. The life of your feelings, by which you enjoy and suffer, by which you are happy and miserable, by which you love your father and mother, your brother and sister, your wife and child, your friends, is part of that same life of Brahman. The life of your mind, by which you think, and remember, and judge, and direct your actions, is part of that same life of Brahman.

It follows from this, that if your life is part of that larger life, the one life, and if that life is Truth, you must be true in your body, your feelings, your mind. You must act truth, you must feel truth, you must think truth, in one phrase, you must Live Truth.

This is what your forefathers did. You remember how Harishchandra gave up his kingdom, let himself, his wife and his child be sold into slavery, became the keeper of a burning-ghat, and would not even take his owner's wood to burn the dead body of his son, because he would not forsake Truth, by breaking his promise. You remember how King Bali, having promised the Divine Dwarf—not knowing him to be Divine—the ground he could cover with three steps, seeing two steps cover earth and sky, offered his own breast for the third, and refused to break his promise even though commended to break it by his Guru.

You remember how Shri Krishna raised from the dead a child, using the Power of Truth to revive it, the command coming from lips which "had never spoken a lie, even in jest." By Truth, we can conquer everything: "Truth alone prevails, not falsehood," it is written. Truth is Fearlessness; Truth is strength; Truth is Fortitude; Truth is Endurance; Truth is Patience; Truth is Might. Where Truth is, there is Victory. Ancient history tells us that Indians were, of old, remarkable for their truthfulness; in the eighteenth century, the same thing was remarked by an Englishman, Colonel Philpotts. Truth has been the National characteristic from time-immemorial, and therefore invasion and conquest and foreign' rule have not been able to destroy the National life of India. So long as Truth remains in the life of a Nation, that Nation cannot be destroyed, for the Eternal Life dwells therein.. . . Let everyone who reads this make up his mind to follow Truth at all hazards, no matter whither she may lead them. Let Truth be our spear and sword, Truth our shield and armour. Though she slay us, yet let us trust in her. She will crown us with victory in the end. By Truth we shall win Home Rule.

Annie Besant

President, National Congress

President, *All-India* Home *Rule League*

—2 May 1918, *New India*

Special Religious Duty

The special work that we have to do for Religion ... is to proclaim with all the energy that we can the unity of religions, to live it as well as to speak it; for what is true Religion, of which all religions are only the outer forms ? It-is the realisation of the Oneness; that we are one with God, and therefore we are one with every child of God, with every son of man. That is our special religious duty today: not only to say it, but to live it; not only to talk about it, but to practise it; that the Hindu and the Musalman shall join hands as sons of a common Father; that the Brahmana and the Pariah shall join hands as sons of one God; that whatever we have of larger possessions, whether it be of knowledge or of anything else, we shall share them with those who are poorest in the things of which we have the most; to realise that Brotherhood does not only go upwards seeking equality with our superiors, but it goes downwards to lift up our inferiors until they stand on the same level as that on which we stand ourselves. That, then, is our great duty — the unity of all religions, the unity of men.

The last duty that I want to lay stress upon is one which is essentially Hindu, but has been in modern days forgotten: namely, that there is nothing, nothing in all our activities, which can be separated from religion. It was said of the old Hindu that he slept religion, ate religion, thought religion, lived religion.... That is true, and that must come back, not only to the Hindu but to every religious mind. In the West they have a Sunday—the "Lord's Day": one day in the week belongs to the Lord, and to whom do all the other days belong ? "This book is sacred, and all the others profane; this thing is religious, everything else is secular." To believe and to live that, is to eat the heart out of every human activity. If in God we live, move, and have our being, if God dwells in your heart and in mine, what can you and do that is not divine activity, and that ought not to be penetrated by the spirit of Religion ? You are religious in the temple; you must be religious in the marketplace. You are religious in the puja room; you must be religious in the court: as vakil, pleading; as judge, giving judgement; as doctor, healing; as soldier, fighting; as merchant, trading. You must be religious right through, or else you have no true religion. Nothing is outside Religion. They say: "Mrs. Besant is a religious teacher; she must have nothing to do with politics." But I assure you that just because Mrs. Besant is a religious teacher, therefore she has everything to do with politics.

—December 1916, Theosophical Convention

Religion and Patriotism

Only during the last centuries have Patriotism and Religion been divided, by the claim of one religion — first the Christian, then the Muhammadan—to be world-embracing. Disregarding all national boundaries, these religions built walls which were not coterminous with the limits of the nations, and violently wrenched apart the twin-sisters who had dwelt so long in peace within each national area. With this claim of uniqueness and universality has arisen the fierce spirit of bigotry and fanaticism, until the Indian Muhammadan feels more akin to his brother Muslim of Turkey than to his Indian-born brother who is a Hindu, and the Indian Christian feels more patriotism for Christian England than for Hindu and Muhammadan India.

This is the real difficulty; we have a Pan-Islam and a Pan-Christendom, dragging Indians away from India, and making the centre of their life extra-national. Thus are religions made agents for national disruption, and religious exclusiveness destroys love of country. It is the exclusiveness that is the enemy and not

Religion. Therefore must the warring religions learn their unity, and when they feel themselves to be one, they will strengthen, not weaken, Patriotism.

The lesson will be learned in India first, and through India in the world, because here alone are all the great religions found living side by side. They must be reconciled, in one of two ways. An attempt may be made to deaden religious feeling, to get rid of warmth, energy, devotion, to slay the love of the Hindu for Hinduism, of the Musalman for Islam, of the Parsi for Zoroastrianism, of the Christian for Christianity; were this possible—but it is not possible—we should have a nation of corpses, not of living men... .

The second way is to see in each religion a branch of a single tree; to act on the saying of Shri Krishna: "On whatever road a man approaches me, on that road do I welcome him, for all roads are mine "; of Muhammad the Prophet: "We make no differences between prophets "; of the Sufis: "The ways to God are as many as the breaths of the children of men." ... What matters it that one worships in a temple and the other in a mosque, if both are Indians and serving a single nation ?

As there is one God with many names, there is one India with many sub-races and families. Why should Bangla Hindu and Bangla Muhammadan behave as though their interests were opposed, when they both are born of one India, are sons of one Motherland ? There is no religion which can be cast out of the nation's household. We may think of Christianity as the religion of the white races, and hence foreign. But in the south-west of India there are Christian towns and villages dating from the second or third century of the Christian era, and thus have an Indian life of over 1600 years.

They cannot be ostracized, or treated as stepchildren in the house of the Mother. And indeed, a nation is the richer, not the poorer, by varieties of thought and not one jewel should be grudged its place in the necklet that adorns the Mother, whose most ancient possession is the jewel of the religion of the Universal Self. As many peoples must blend here into One Nation, so many religions must blend into the One Religion.

From Nationality to Humanity

Religion is essential to patriotism, because nothing else destroys the separative tendency in men, and prevents the disintegration of bodies of workers by continual subdivisions. Religion alone teaches man to feel his unity with his fellows, and leads him to sacrifice the smaller to the larger Self. Unless the isolation brought about by antagonistic self-interests can be destroyed by religion, nationality will ever remain a dream. It is religion which has ever bound individuals into a tribe, and tribes into a nation. With the revival of religion in India has come the spread of a sense of brotherhood, of unity, of nationality. With the growth of religion, nationality has grown. With this more and more will come the spirit of self-sacrifice, the spirit that sacrifices itself as a part to the whole, the only spirit that can make a nation. Love of family grows into love of village; love of village into love of district; love of district into love of province; love of province into love of nation. Ay, and love of nation shall grow into love of Humanity, and all religions blend one day in a Universal Religion.

But as the various religions are still needed, and the next step is to see them as branches of One Religion, so various nations are still needed, and the next step is to see them as branches of Humanity, so that we may love all and hate none. At our stage of evolution, patriotism, love of one nation is a necessity, for each nation has to develop its own characteristics, in order that Humanity may show forth a manysided perfection. A man who is not a patriot, unless he be a great Rishi or Sage, will be no true lover of Humanity. The man who has not evolved the smaller loves cannot really feel the larger.

The indifferent husband and father is not the material out of which the good citizen is made; it is the man who is the good householder who is also the good citizen. The man who neglects the sanitary arrangements of his own house will not attend to those of the Municipality; and how shall the man who neglects the lighting, and draining, and paving, of his own town, be trusted with the affairs of the Province; and how shall he who cares nothing for the welfare of his Province, be trusted with the affairs of the Nation ? How shall he who fails in the small, succeed in the great?

The good father expands into the good citizen; the good citizen into the good provincial leader; the good provincial leader into the good national leader, and these, perchance in future lives, to the leaders of Humanity. The great lovers of Humanity love it with a passion such as that with which a mother loves her first-born son. Never, then, let a man fear that love to his Motherland will prevent him from loving Humanity. It is the road thereto; the heart expands as it is exercised.

Ungrudging love of the Motherland is, then, the thing needed. *Vande Mataram;* worship the Mother. But let it be remembered that while patriotism is the flower, service is the fruit, and patriotism must grow into service.

As men of every faith unite in social, civil, and political work they will bring the spirit of religion into all, and work with love and knowledge. Then shall India show the world that a Nation may embrace all varieties of thought, and only be the richer for the variety, and from India shall spread that spirit of knowledge and love which shall blend all nations into one Brotherhood of Humanity, and merge all religions in the Wisdom.

—June 1907, Religion *and Patriotism*

Your Mother, India is Appealing

India can never again be great, save as she is religious; India can never again be great, save as she gains the Spirituality that she has lost. If she can win that back, then behind it will come all other things, intellectual power, and material wealth, and all the lower things that enter into the growth of national life. But one charge has she received from the Highest; one duty that, undischarged, weighs her down to the ground but, that discharged, will lift her again a light and beacon in the eyes of men, and that is to be the safeguard, above all things, of religion and truth, and to wed spiritual philosophy to the devotion of a noble religion. If that great work is taken up and carried out, everything' else will follow in its train; if it is sought after, all other things that are good will come to you as its inevitable successors.

Your Mother, India, is appealing day by day and year by year. Often I think that, during these years of the Kaliyuga, she has gone away into some far-off region to wait thereuntil her children call her back; for how shall she. Mother and Guru of the world, from whose past have grown the world's philosophies, the world's religions, the world's sublimest teachings—how shall she come and dwell in a land-that forgets religion and philosophy, and plays with the toys of children instead of realising the aims of men ? She often bows in worship to the Great Ones who watch, far off, on the Himalayan peaks, all the pitfalls in the way of the child they love.... I seem to think that India, our Mother, is standing there in the midst of this circle of the Rishis, waiting for the time when she can descend again and illuminate the child she loves.

And what shall bring her ? What brings the mother hastening homeward? The thought that her children are crying for her in her absence.. .. Sometimes I think that India, the Mother, is only waiting patiently, contentedly enough in the wisdom of her mother's love, seeing her children playing in the streets with the toys and follies of the little child; waiting till hunger for spiritual knowledge and thirst for spiritual teachings shall send the children clamouring home with the cry for mother on their lips. I hear in my dreams that cry rising from the Indian land; I see in my dreams child after child weary of the play in the street, and thinking of turning homeward where the mother's arms are waiting. Looking upwards, I see on her face a smile, the smile of mother's love waiting to welcome her truants home again. I know that soon there will rise from the whole of India the one mighty cry:

> "O India our Mother; Mother and Guru of the world,
>
> Come back amongst us once again! Come home!"
>
> —1900, *India*

In the White Light of India, a Nation

I feel strongly ... that only on the basis of religion can a true Nationality be built up—Religion itself which gives the sense of human dignity joined to the sense of human duty, and the self-respect of India could never have arisen as it has arisen today, had not the philosophies and the religions of the past re-won their empire over the Indian heart; and the virtues that the great religions typify, all of which we find in this sacred land, are virtues that we need for the building of our Nation.

Shall we not learn from Hinduism to see the one Self in all, and to know that in men of every caste, of every class, to see the Self equally dwelling is to touch the central truth of that most ancient faith ? Shall we not learn from Zoroastrianism the necessity for National purity, from Buddhism and Jainism the need for wisdom and right thinking ? Shall we not learn from Islam that great lesson of true democracy which Islam above all other religions of the world exemplified in the life and teachings of the great Prophet ? Shall we not add to these the courage of the Sikh and so make perfect the virtues of a great National life ? And shall we not realise that Christianity brings also the great jewel of sacrifice and its lesson ?

Thus,. . looking at all the religions of the world as rays of the one Light, these religions shall join together to make the white Light of India a Nation, nothing left out, nothing excluded, learning from each other and trying to admire and serve each other.

And so, on that foundation, building up the great life of the Nation, we will recognise the truth . .. that England has revived the faith in her own love of liberty which, it was thought, was becoming a doubtful thing in many an Indian heart. With the West represented by England and the East represented by India, we have the mightiest combination that the earth can show, each necessary to the other. —27 September 1917, *New India*

One important section of the Plan is the Union of Great Britain and India as Free and Equal Nations in the greats. Federation of Free Nations which will form the splendid Indo-British Commonwealth, linking Asia and Europe together in amity, and embracing the Dominions which ring the globe.

It will join all the Religions which are followed within the Nations into a spiritual Union, which shall know no rivalries save those of Service, no bond save that of Love, in which all are recognised as ways which lead to the One without a second, the Universal FATHER, who "hath made of one blood all the Nations upon earth." In the New Age the Unity of Religions will be recognised, and religious Peace will reign instead of religious wars. —March 1923, *Theosophist*

Culture

Secret of India's Immortal Youth

What is that secret ? It lay hidden in her Education and her Culture, or rather in the Ideals which created these; for the Idea is prior to the form, and if today men think that her strength is dissipated, her energy outworn, it is because she has for a moment—for what is a century and a half but a moment in her millennial life ?—sold her birthright, as her Mother's first-born child, for a mess of western pottage. Let her turn again to her Ideals, and she shall renew her strength. For Ideals are the generating Life which unfolds through many incarnations, embodies itself in many a successive form, but remains ever true to type. We, who believe in India's Immortality, do not need to reproduce the bodies, the forms, of the past, but we need that life, the life of the Mother Immortal, shall embody itself in new forms, but that it shall be Her Life, and not another's.

Let us distinguish between Education and Culture: Education is the drawing out and training of inborn capacities and powers—brought over from former lives and developed in the Svargic or Deva world.... Culture is the result on the mind of certain forms of Knowledge, and is based on these; but it differs from Education in that it is not the drawing out and training of faculty, but is the result of the exercise of faculties on subjects which arouse sympathetic emotion and imagination, broadening the mind, eliminating personal, local and racial prejudices, acquiring an understanding of human nature in its many aspects, and contacting the life-side rather than the form-side of creatures; hence the quick internal response to other lives, and the intuition of the unity of life beneath the diversity of life-expressions.... literature and Art are the instruments of Culture.

Science and the "clear cold light" of reason are the area and the guide of Education. The Life in Nature and the intellectual intuition, which recognises truth by its harmony with its own nature –– "whose nature is Knowledge" — are the area and the guide of Culture. If these are completely separated during the plastic period of youth, Science tends to hardness, and, in overspecialisation, to narrow-mindedness and intolerance; Culture tends, when exaggerated, to false sentiment and fastidiousness in non-essentials. The training of the instruments of knowledge and the storing of the memory with facts is the work of Education by others in youth, and their application to the facts and conditions is the self-education which continues during life.

Culture in youth consists in the unconscious development and refinement of passions into emotions amid beautiful surroundings, for the contacts with beautiful objects and the evoking and the control of the emotions in response to them, and the moulding of these by Literature and Art develop the discrimination which is an element in self-culture, the critical faculty which manifests as a balanced judgement, not as mere fault-finding, and lends poise, dignity, and gentleness to the attitude towards life... . Beauty was an essential feature of the Indian Ideal of Education and Culture.. . .

In the Ancient System of India, Education and Culture were self-controlled... The University was the Temple of Learning, and the learned were its only Hierophants. When Learning visited Royalty, when a Wise One entered a Court, even Sri Krishna descended from His throne and bowed at the feet of the Sage...

The revival and advance of true Indian Art Ideals, in the renaissance identified with that gifted family of true Artists, the Tagores, .. nurses in its bosom the rightful Infant Heir of the heritage of India's Art Ideals in the Past, the Infant who, in the future, in the maturity of India's Art Ideals, shall give to the world the priceless gift of an Art which shall redeem it alike from materialism and superstition, and shall make the life of the Nation and the life of the individual' full of Beauty, in the cottage as well as in the palace, for Art, as I have often times said, must be no longer a luxury for the rich but the daily bread of the poor. That is part of India's Dharma.

For Beauty diversified into the Arts is the true refiner and uplifter of Humanity, for it is the instrument of Culture, the broadener of the heart, the purifying Fire which burns up all prejudices, all pettiness, all coarseness. Without it, true Democracy is impossible, equality of social intercourse an empty dream. Art is the international language, in which mind can speak to mind, heart to heart, where lips are dumb. Painting, Sculpture, Architecture, Music, these need no translations, they speak the universal Mother-tongue. Centuries do not age them. Custom does not stale them. Boundaries do not exist for them. Their message is for every country, for every tongue. Art will permeate the whole atmosphere of the New Civilization which is on the threshold. Religion and Art have ever been twin-angels. Let us follow them as they point to the East, where the fair Dawn Maidens are tinting our earth-born clouds with their rose-tipped fingers,, to welcome the Rising Sun of India, as He leaps across the horizon, and floods our world with the glory of His Unveiled Face.

—1925, *Indian Ideals* (Kamala Lectures)

Indian Ideals of Art

In seeking the Ideals of India, most ancient of Nations, we naturally turn to the Ancient Way of Knowing, and seek in the Universal the Ideal of Beauty, the origin of all beautiful things. In the Supreme Self we find the triple aspect Sat, Chit, Ananda: Being, Cognition, Will. To which of these should we relate Beauty ? I submit that it is a Composite of the three: of Being as Becoming, of Cognition as the awareness, the recognition, of things considered by the observer as beautiful, of Will which, as desire, seeks to appropriate these as happiness-giving. . . .

The third aspect in the Supreme Ishvara as in all Ishvaras, in Becoming, is a manifestation of Beauty in all His works— His *Activity* is Beauty. The Ancient Wisdom declares this omnipresent fact, whether it comes down from 'old Egypt in the symbolical form of Freemasonry, or revels in natural beauty, due to the embodiment of Devas, in the Vaidic hymns; and this is equally though less poetically asserted by Modern Science in its microscopical researches, when it finds that, let its vision be extended to embrace the minutest forms yet reached, they are ever beautiful, and exquisitely finished by the Divine Artificer of our world. It is in the Philosophy of Hindu India that her Ideals of Beauty are firmly rooted, and in Art, as in all manifestations of the Divine Life, it is Cosmic Ideation, the Creative Activity of the Divine Thought, which—bodying itself forth in subtlest matter in which Sattva, Harmony, predominates over Tamas and Rajas —

imposes Beauty: the inter-harmonious relation between all parts of every form, that is the essential characteristic of every Type-Idea, or Arche-type, whence all special forms belonging to that Arche-type are generated. . .. Take with this the Greek idea of the Supreme Divinity, as the Good, the Beautiful, and the True, and you have in "the Beautiful" the abstract Idea, of which the essence, the Real, the Eternal, is Beauty, whence all beautiful particulars, concrete things, emanate, come forth, as though it were an aroma, which gives its fragrance to many objects, making each sweet with its touch. If the view of Plato and the Indian view are put side by side, they will be found to be practically identical.... To Plato, Universals were Real, were true Being; particulars share, as it were, are derived from, the Realities... . Beauty has Real Being, and all beautiful things have this quality, which makes them Beautiful; they do not exist as Beautiful by Human thought, but by Divine Ideation. The universe lives and moves "according to God," as Plato taught, and all beautiful things are as veils through which Eternal Beauty shines... .

We might then say that, as the Life of Ishvara is immanent in everything in His universe, so the aspect of His Life which is Beauty is immanent in all beautiful things.. ..

We can make our definition of Art: It is an attempt to bring down within the vision of ordinary mortals some of the Divine Beauty of which the Artist catches glimpses; he strives to translate these into colours, sounds, sculptures, poems, and other literature, reproducing in others through his special art the pleasurable emotion aroused in himself by his glimpses of supernal Beauty, sensed by the Ego. . . .

For all True Art, as all True Science, comes from Above, through mortals of our race who have risen above the crowd by memory and imagination—imagination based on memory, not memory of physical happiness, but of the Ego, when in some rapt moment of ecstasy, freed from physical limitations, he touches illuminated reach of wondrous manifestation, lit by the Light which is from Above.

Take Music and Architecture, and you will understand the feeling which made Goethe describe some great religious Cathedral as "frozen music "; listen to some true melody, and let yourself drift away from its waves, and see an exquisite fairy structure rise before your closed eyes, reproducing the melody which bore you into a subtler world, wherein sounds build forms, and gracious temples rise around you, built by the music which Devas use to erect in lines of light those shining fanes. ...

When we remember that Beauty is clothed in the matter in which Sattva, Harmony, predominates, it is easy to see why music, the very embodiment of Harmony, is the highest of the arts, and is so much in evidence in religious services. It aids meditation, soothes the restless mind into serenity, and exalts the feeling of Bhakti.

Nataraja dancing, as in the wondrous figure in the heart of the great Temple of Chidambaram, shakes from His Damru the sounds which built worlds, for creation is the activity of the High Gods, whose laughter falls in golden rain of benedictions on Their Work, and all the Sons of God surround it, shouting for joy... .

Priest of the Beautiful

Art. . is the vision, or the intuition, of the Beauty Aspect of the Self. The Artist sees more, intuits more, than the man of the world. It is this which makes him the Priest of the Beautiful, the mediator between blind men and the Divine Aspect which is Beauty, the Revealer of the Hidden Beauty, so often hidden by unrealities.. ..

The artist is great or small by the greatness or smallness of his Ego, not by the deftness of his hands. No perfection of technique can avail if naught comes through it; it is but as a tinkling cymbal. Plato, with his clear vision of the relation between the outer and the inner worlds, said that you could foretell the outbreak of a revolution by the change of the people's taste in music. Art belongs to the life-side of Nature, and hence the type of a Nation's Art is a "key-signature," a "mind-signature," of the Nation's inner life. Frivolous music attracts the "butterfly mind." The fierce "ca ira" set the French crowd singing it into a wild whirling dance through the streets in the days of the Revolution, and it came back during the days of the Commune....

How opposite is the effect of sacred Indian music, how closely is it allied to Nature, and how accurately it sings itself into her moods. The raga of the morning freshness cannot be used in the evening hour, for music is Nature's moods intellectualised and made articulate in the world of Buddhi.... It builds and shatters, it creates and destroys; hence its enormous power over a crowd, where it is in harmony with their dominant emotion, and raising it to the -nth power, it tosses them about as it will.... Beauty [is] the manifestation of Being in all creative work of Ishvara during the period of His Activity, and hence the infinite number of beautiful things which bear Beauty as His hallmark, the signature of the Divine Artist.

The Being is Beauty; the beautiful particulars are in a continual flux of Becoming, on the wheel of births and deaths. Art is the creative activity of Man, his heritage from his "Father-in-Heaven," and his duty, as animated by the One Life, is to make himself, in all his creative activities, a co-worker with the Supreme Artist, a centre of Beauty, and a creator of beautiful actions. Ugliness, dirt, unseemly behaviour, coarse words, rough speech, clumsy actions, are all offences against the law of Nature, which is, as Goethe said, the Garment by which we see God. ... Man can be Nature's best co-worker ... [in her] ceaseless efforts to eradicate the ugly and to restore Beauty.... He can quicken the Becoming, and guide it in the best way. ...

Let us make our cities beautiful; above all, let us make our Schools beautiful. Let us surround the children with beauty and joy; and they shall grow into harmonious relations with each other. Let us bring Art to the Schools, the Colleges, the Universities, as of old, and the Arts and Crafts to our Villages. Let us wear the graceful and suitable raiment of the East, not the ugly and inartistic raiment of the West. Let each of us be a messenger of Beauty, in our language, our manners, our courtesy. All this Beauty is hidden in the Indian heart, in the Indian customs; why do you hide it away, as if ashamed of it, instead of reforming those who bring uglier ways from abroad ? Your dharma, as Indians, is to spread Beauty around you, and not allow yourselves to be distorted into ugliness.

—1925, *Indian Ideals*

Release through Music

Why does music exercise so great an influence over the passions and the emotions of man ? Why is it that religion has ever found in music one of its strongest helpers, one of its most inspiring agencies ? Why is it that.. music.. is found to be most useful . . to enable the mind to rise from the physical plane, and to soar upwards into the higher regions of consciousness ?

Both in Chinese and Hebrew music, as in Hindu, the intervals between the notes are much less than in western. A chromatic scale in the West gives the limits on a western piano; in the East, many notes are interposed, and the gradations are so fine as to be indistinguishable to a western ear until it is trained to hear them; hence Indian musicians are often accused of being "flat," "out of tune," by the western stranger, while they are producing thrills of joy among their compatriots, sheer gasps of pleasure over the exquisitely fine gradations produced by the skilled voice or fingers. The Indian ear by long heredity has been evolved to appreciate these minute gradations of sound, as the eye of the Kashmiri and Persian weavers has been evolved to perceive nuances of colour to which other eyes are blind. I presume that the Indian ear has thus become a more finely organised sound-receiver than the European. . . .

There is another fundamental difference between eastern and western music; eastern music is a succession of notes, a melody, while western music consists of notes played simultaneously, and yielding harmony. The one, as it rises, becomes more subtly divided, more ethereal and elusive; the other, as it rises, becomes more massive, more splendid in complexity or blended sounds. ...

In the West. . there are Niagara cascades of sounds, whirlpools and rapids of chords, storms of thunderous instrumental clashings, and then finally, when the breath is well-nigh strangled in the rushing waves of sounds, one is flung panting on to a flower-sprinkled meadow of peace, and a melody exquisite, celestial, sweet, breathes a harmony more tender and serene than eastern music knows. Another marked thing in western music is that it stirs the passions, sometimes masters the intellect, but it does not touch the spiritual notes, which often thrill the nerves to a pleasure that touches pain in its keenness, well-known in Indian music. And I have sometimes noticed that where the Indian music is appealing to the passion of love, where the songs are love-songs, even then they tend to pass beyond the passional;into the emotional, from the coarser to the subtler forms of the master-desire. The music stirs the more delicate shades of love, the finer chords, the unsatisfied yearning of it, the ever-frustrated longing for utter identity, so that it is not an appeal to passion but rather of lifting passion into emotion purifying and refining, with an ever elusive suggestion of the underlying meanings of the physical, of the regions where Spirit is the lover, where God is the beloved.

There is a well-known use of music for the rousing of passion, alike in East and West, the use which is made of it in war. We read in the *Bhagavad-Gita* of the use of the conch by the leaders in the great battle, sending out the conch-note like a lion's roar, and how the mighty sounds enheartened the combatants, ringing across the embattled hosts in challenge and reply.. . .

I have not found in western music, however, strong and ennobling as it is, that peculiar and elusive power which in Hindu music predisposes to the higher forms of meditation by which, as its own sounds sink into silence for the entranced mind and heart, the consciousness slips away from the body, leaving it cradled in the melody, and passes into the higher regions. There are delicate notes given out by the instruments which thrill softly out and cause subtlest vibrations in the higher bodies, till all sounds are left behind and spirit is set free. Those single delicate notes seem to have a power greater than any chord; the chord raises passion or emotion; these single notes thrill to spiritual ecstasy; the one predisposes to activity, the other to quiescence, to contemplation, to peace. This seems to me to be the greatest service that music can do to religion. For the difficulty met with in meditation is very largely a difficulty caused by the subtle body. Accustomed to respond continually to impacts from without, this body is ever vibrating and ever changing its vibrations. These vibrations bring about continual changes in consciousness, and these again react on the body. Religious music checks these movements, imposes its own vibrations on the body, and instead of the jangle that is noise there are the rhythmical vibrations of the music. Gradually the whole body is calmed, and held to these steady vibrations, and the calm is answered by the steadiness of the consciousness, responsive to its rhythmically vibrating vehicle. Thus by music can the subtle body be made a help to the steadying of consciousness instead of being, as it usually is, a hindrance. This calming and steadying, then, is one of the services that music can render to meditation.

There is another, when we use the specialised form of music known as a mantra. A mantra is a sequence of sounds arranged so as to bring about a definite result. The mantras has its Devata and this Devata belongs to one of the Hierarchies, each one of which has its own musical note, and the sequence is arranged in harmony with this. When the subtle body is made to vibrate according to this sequence, it is vibrating with the vibrations of the Devata, and thus is more susceptible to his influence, more open to receive impressions from him.

A mantra brings about mechanically with little difficulty a condition which is hard to reach in any other way, thus shortening the time of preparation and leaving more strength of mind and will for the proper work of meditation. Only the mantra must be accurately chanted or recited. Full effect must be given to every note, whether sung aloud or within; the right sequence, the right cadence, must be employed. Every sequence, every cadence, has its own vibratory effect, and if you change these you change the effect: for the laws of sound are as inviolable as any other law of nature. . . .

As the earthly mantras aid in harmonising us, we are going towards the chanting of that final mantra which shall be ours when the Spirit realises its freedom, and thus reaches the true liberation, the true moksha, the mantra which shall make our bodies impervious to the jangling noises of earth. Music will help you, if you choose it well; music will hinder you, if you use it to stimulate the lower instead of the higher in you. Knit religion to music, and music to religion, and then music will become more inspired, and religion more beautiful, until the highest music and the most spiritual religion will be the atmosphere in which you can most freely breathe. —7 March 1908, *Religion and Music*

Hindu gods in Art

There is one matter on which—considering how much of Indian Art is Hindu—it is necessary to touch, and that is the way in which Hindu Art in the olden times treated Devas and Divine Men.. ..

In the innumerable images of the three-aspected Ishvara, Brahma, Vishnu, and Mahadeva, their Shaktis, as those of the Devas and Devis of the various worlds of living beings, the Hindus of the early period set the method of representation which became traditional in the religion. Beauty of Face and Form is not sought for in Divine Images; the task of due representation is recognised as impossible. The Images represent powers, qualities, symbols signalising incidents; or they are seated on special animals, Siva on Nandi, the Bull; Vishnu on Garuda, the Eagle; Brahma on Hansa, the Swan, and so on. They are meant to be used in worship, and to fix the attention of the worshipper on the qualities of the Object of his adoration. Rich and varied is Hindu symbology, rich and varied as the Powers in Nature which the symbols represent. The Hindu faces philosophically and equally all the phenomena of Nature, terrible or agreeable; they are all emanated from the One Love and work out His beneficent purposes, since there is but One Life, and he shares it with all that live.

—1925, *Indian Ideals*

India's Unique Genius

Come to the East, and stand in front of a dim but all-alluring image of a range of the Himalayan snows. How wonderful they are. They draw you towards them; you are there among them; you are in that rare, tense atmosphere which takes you to its bosom, and you feel the chill as the mist enwraps you, and you are all alone, one with the eternal snows, with the mighty strength of the mountain which has become yourself. Alone ? Are you so sure ? Your eyes rest on the snow on that great peak, which draws your very life away,'yet leaves you more living for the draining. Through the mist, through the snow, through the mountain itself, there slowly emanates from them a Face—surely a Face? Yes ! there are the profound all-seeing Eyes, the calm broad forehead, like a cliff, arising above the brows—and in those Eyes all the strength of the mountain, all the magic of the snows, all the depth of the over-arching sky. It is Mahadeva! It is Siva, the Beloved ! It is the Beauty Eternal, the Youth. Immortal. It is not man lifted into Godhead, but God out-gazing at you through the mask of a human face. Oh! wonderful illusion of a great Artist, who can so suggest the Indescribable as not to jar either the memory or the imagination of a devotee.

On a much lower plane is a difference I have remarked in the average Indian Artist, when he draws or paints a portrait, and his fellow-artist in the West. He does not have "sittings." He watches his subject when engaged in his various pursuits; presumably he notices expressions and stores them in his retentive memory; finally, he produces a *likeness,* of which the actual technique may be good or bad, according to his training, but it conveys something of the character of the subject, and is alive.. . .

A similar peculiarity is seen in the eastern animal drawings and paintings; they are alive, they are moving, they are full of vivid energy; the flying bird, the bounding deer, the galloping horse, live on the canvas. One imagines that the artist has watched the creature he portrays, and, again, has stored up the images in his memory, whence he projects a composite which expresses the creature as *we see it*.. . .

A true Indian painter ... studies the natural object he is going to paint. He goes away and meditates on it. He is able to bring through more of the Divine thought embodied in it than you and I can see in that natural object, and so to add to our knowledge of God by showing the powers of the Self shining out through the forms He has created;., That is the Indian genius and the Indian way. —1925, Indian *Ideals,* and 12 January 1918, *New India*

Fertilizing Charity

It is not that there is not money enough in the country. I know it is said that India is poor; so she is, in a sense, poor, that is, as regards the masses of her people. But not too poor to build colleges and schools for your children while you are able to maintain, as you are doing, large crowds of men as mendicants, in the full strength of vigorous life, who are innocent of all sacred learning, innocent of' the light, who have nothing of the Sannyasi but the cloth that covers them, and who are yet fed and sheltered by the crore. India is not poor so long as your Chettiars and Banias can give lakhs upon lakhs of rupees for the restoration of ancient temples and the gilding of their pinnacles. You do not need to increase your charities; that is not wanted; but oh! if you would only turn them into channels that fertilize instead of channels that corrupt, India would have wealth enough to educate her sons and daughters, and to make possible a new life in the future.

I do not speak against the restoration of temples. That is well. It is well that man should worship, rightly, nobly and rationally.. . But I do speak against the mere restoration that leaves the priesthood ignorant and profligate. I do speak against the restoration of a temple where no school lives under its shadow, and where children are not taught by those whose duty it is to teach—less gilding on the pinnacles of temples, and more gilding of learning in the hearts of boys and girls. And if you would still keep your temples in order, but spend some of the money that is wasted on vast crowds of idle mendicants on the education of your children, how rapidly would India rise in the scale of nations, and how quickly she would claim her right place among the peoples of the world.. . .

Begin at the Right End

I urged upon you the formation of Educational Boards in every district of India. Now Government has nothing to do with that. You do not need to ask for Government permission or authority. You have only to gather a few of your cleverest men and Princes together and make them into an Educational Board for a definitely outlined area. What is wanted is not Government help. It is your work. What is wanted is self-devotion, energy, initiative, the willingness to go through years of drudgery, for only in that way can true education be built up. This has not yet been acted on. The idea, when spoken about anywhere, causes a good deal of cheering, but only in a few places has there been any real earnest work, even in starting an Indian school. [Referring to the protests that had followed the passing of the Education Act.] Such protests are necessary, but they should be followed by action, for thought that is not followed by action acts like a gangrene in the human mind. Better remain silent, better not even think, if you are not prepared to act; . . . for in the higher spheres, as you know, thought produces action; down here, thought, and especially talk, without action does not get a nation very far along the line of progress. So all the energy flows out in the talk, and nothing is done. ... I am glad [the Act] has passed, because it has— I hope it has — given the impulse which will make men take the education of their children into their own hands.

But now, how ? By beginning at the right end and not at the wrong. First, by making your Educational Boards all over the country; next by creating colleges and Universities, and most of all making such a public opinion, especially among the Indian Princes, the great merchants, and employers of labour, as shall induce them to recognise the degrees given by the Indian Universities as valid credentials for those who are seeking employment. Until you have done that, you have done nothing. It is no good even making a University, unless you have made a body of people who are prepared to take its graduates when they have taken their degrees, and thus open to them means of livelihood. It is no good beginning with boys. You must 'begin with men.. . .

What you should do in Madras, and do at once, is to begin the formation of a great organisation of leading, wealthy, influential people, who will give employment to your boys, if need be, when the pinch comes, and Government refuses to recognise your colleges or Universities. I believe in Indian Universities for Indians, where Indian degrees shall be given in Arts, and Science, and in Industries that are useful for the national unfolding.

— 1910, *India's Awakening*

India Must not Lose her Heritage

In the East the rationale of the education of the child has a sound philosophical and natural basis. The child comes into the hands of the teacher with a character which it is the teacher's duty to mould according to the child's tastes and tendencies. A child is not an empty bucket into which education is to pour a large number of facts to be poured out again in an examination-room.

The wise way of teaching a child is to have a playroom instead of a schoolroom which carries with it an uncomfortable idea. A child learns by play in happiness and in joyfulness what he used to learn with difficulty and struggle and sometimes with pain in school.

The senses in a child are very much alive. The sensible thing is to cultivate the sense-organs at a time when they are most active, keen, and receptive of impressions. Obviously, in the whole plan of teaching, the vernacular must be the medium of instruction. To teach facts to a child in a foreign language is so absurd that no one but a person in a lunatic asylum would think of it. In no country except India and Poland is education carried on in a foreign language. Teaching facts to a child in a foreign tongue injures the brain of the child. The difficulty in making the change is not with the teachers but with the parents and guardians of boys. It is a most foolish system of education whereby a boy learns facts without understanding the relationship of those facts to life. A foreign tongue cannot appeal to the feelings of a boy as his mother-tongue can. English may be taught to Indian boys as a second language, but you do not want the English of Chaucer or Addison.

In India too much has been made of examinations. The test of a boy who has been in school for several years, and has been four years in a college, is his knowledge, and the only test of that knowledge is gained by keeping a record of his study. A boy's teachers are the best judges of his capacity and not some stray man who comes from another place and sets conundrums. A much wiser course would be if boys were examined by their own teachers according to a standard set by someone from outside. The whole plan of education up to the time of examinations in India is wrong.

There might be examinations in a very limited way, but the years of training should weigh more than the few hours in the examination room.. ..

Spiritual nature is innate in Indians and what they want are manly, virile qualities, initiative, quick judgement, prompt determination, and, above all, courage to face opposition, to endure, strive, and persevere, and such qualities are not encouraged in any Government or missionary institutions of today.

Another thing for which we want National Education is to inculcate feelings of patriotism among Indian boys, pride in their country, pride in their mighty civilization, pride in the antiquity of their race, and pride in the glory won in the past. Patriotism is not popular and an Indian boy is not allowed to exercise independent thinking; he is to think only of the blessings of British Rule. Indians must teach history to their boys as it is and not as Englishmen write it. If they really thought of the future of India as that future ought to be, they would not allow their boys to be twisted and distorted as they are today.

India has a priceless heritage that she must not lose for the sake of the world at large. At this time we are standing on the threshold of a change which will revolutionise the life of the country, and by the training we ought to be giving in our schools today will the India of the future be shaped and made great among the Nations. Indian boys are not being prepared now to bear the weight of responsibility which will devolve on them as citizens of their country. They are being brought up as if they were always to remain as slaves and were not free men and free citizens.... I hope that the education that is given to Indian sons and daughters on National lines will make them worthy of the India that will soon come amongst us. Nothing is more glorious than that there should be springing up in India schools where patriotism is the atmosphere and devotion to the Motherland is the ideal of service.... — 26 March 1918, *New India*

How to Rebuild the Nation?

The East India Company Rule gradually reduced India to extreme poverty, and poverty is the mother of ignorance. From a literate and religious Nation, the admiration of the world, India slowly became illiterate and sceptical, and thus lost her high place among the Nations.

A Master has remarked that India degenerated slowly and must also slowly regain her position. The greater the reason for beginning the climbing at once. With what shall we begin ? I think with the education of the young, before their inborn tendencies have been distorted by foreign ways. Free and compulsory education must be started under Indian control, and in the Indian tongue spoken in the home; in this all the early education must be given. No foreign language should be used as the medium for teaching in primary education. This free and compulsory education must be established without further delay, and primary education must, as said, be given in the vernacular of the children. No self-governing Nation uses a foreign language as the medium of teaching in primary education.

Before the British ruled India, her people were an educated people, and travellers from neighbouring countries came to see her marvels. The reports of these travellers bear testimony to the respect felt for her people and to the fact that there was "a school in every village "as late as 1813. A foreign Government naturally prefers that its subjects should remain ignorant; for an ignorant people may riot when their sufferings become intolerable in any part of the country, but they cannot combine to break the foreign yoke. A revolution of hunger is but a series of temporary riots, and these are inevitably crushed by a well-fed, healthy, and well-disciplined army. The fear of such a catastrophe in India has haunted me like a nightmare for years. Our first duty, then, should be to take over primary education and rebuild it on National lines; also a few striking sayings of the great religious Teachers should be used to open and to close the schools. Let us give the highest of *each* religion as representing it best. The little *Universal Text-Book* of *Religion* is very useful for this object.

There is a great teaching which has been put most forcibly in Christianity: "He that is greatest is he that doth serve." "Behold ! "said the Christ, "I am among you as he that serveth." We might fairly urge that Service should be the leading characteristic of a truly National Education. —20 August 1931, New *India*

Commonwealth of Brotherhood

To Britons in London, Dr. Besant said: Now of Great Britain, I ask: What is her place in the Plan ? Great Britain has a possibility before her, and a power of accomplishing that possibility, which are not so great in any other Nation in the world ... The tendencies everywhere are not only towards Union within the Nation, but of Union of larger Nations as we go on in evolution... Now Britain has the opportunity to make a mighty Empire— Empire I call it for a moment, for its name has been Empire hitherto... Britain's opportunity is hers, because all round the world there are Free Nations that have sprung from her, that you call the Self-Governing Dominions, and other lands that have been acquired largely by the help of their own people, and which you call Dependencies or Colonies; they, all that huge possibility of all those varied Nations, not only of white people but of coloured, not only of western Nations but of eastern, not only of Europe but of Asia, are awaiting federation. Think what it means if, for the first time in the world, a Power as strong as you admittedly are today, instead of relying on strength, tries to seek for and to do justice. Instead of trying to tyrannise over others, open to them the gates of Freedom, and say to all the Nations that make up this great Empire: "Come and form with us not an Empire, but a great Commonwealth of Free Nations; not a white Commonwealth, but a Commonwealth into which men of every race, of every colour, of every ancestry, of every creed, of every tradition and custom, shall come willingly as free members." Ah! If Britain can do that, then she will do her part in the Great Plan. That is her place; that is her opportunity. No other Nation with dominions so widespread and so varied can build up that mighty Commonwealth of Brotherhood, of all the races of every faith, of every colour, of every line of thought. Have you the strength to do it ? I believe you have. Have you the love to do it ? I hope you have.

That is your place in the Plan; take it or leave it. It is your decision, your right to say what you will do. But if you can do it, if you *will* do it, if you will *encourage* Freedom and not try to hold her back, if you will welcome her everywhere where your power extends; if you will help, strengthen, inspire, lead, but let the Nations take their Freedom and be your brothers and not your subjects—then you will do more than build a mighty Commonwealth; you will build a Model, which the world shall copy; you will build a Temple, which shall become the model for the Temple of Humanity; within your own power you will make

Freedom extend everywhere over your Dominions, and thus set an example that other Nations shall follow; for you will *never* reach true Internationalism until the Nations have recognised their Brotherhood, and have willingly joined together in bonds of Love, of Amity, and of Freedom.

—July 1921, *Britain's Place in the Great Plan*

Coming Aryan Empire

Two views of India's future have been put forward: one that India is effete and is passing into decay, to vanish as Babylonia and Egypt have vanished; the other, that she has a future greater than her past, and is destined to rise to a peak of dazzling glory, the Heart of the greatest Empire that the world has yet seen. It is the second of these two views that I have been doing my best to popularise as an inspiring ideal during the last seventeen years, and it was for the helping of the realisation of this Ideal that I joined hands with others to found our beloved Central Hindu College.

The evolution of Humanity is guided by a mighty Brotherhood of Sages—of Rishis, as They are called in India—who constantly watch over it, choosing Their agents; sending them hither and thither; mingling the blood of races to produce new combinations; building up Empires—by sending into birth in the chosen centres egos of advanced evolution—spiritual, intellectual, moral; pulling them down again, when their use is over, by withdrawing these egos and sending into them egos of low evolution; preparing for a foreseen end for hundreds of thousands of years; working out the details of a mighty plan committed to Their charge. From time to time, when it suits Their purpose, They divulge a fragment of Their plan, that it may win conscious cooperation from the willing and the devoted. The present is such a time and a corner of the veil has been lifted.

Through much tribulation has India been guided for some five thousand years, in order that by conquests, colonisations, wars, tumults, and manifold grindings of the divine Wheel, various races and sub-races might be mingled in the blood of her children, to enrich the current of her life. Long long ago a mighty Atlantean civilization ruled in India, while, in a huge Empire, with its centre at Shamballa, the Aryan Root- -Race grew and multiplied under its Manu and His lieutenants the Divine Kings, while He prepared and sent forth its subraces to occupy and subdue the near and further West. Over it He watched, improving and refining, until—the dispersing work over—He sent it southwards gradually to occupy the land destined to be the cradle of the future Aryan Empire, carrying with it the tradition of a past Golden Age. Some mighty intellects He sent to India to take birth in it, to build its literature, and from time to time, some lofty ego to inspire its spiritual life. Then He sent these intellectual giants to take birth elsewhere, in other branches of His Aryan Race, to develop manysided capacities, to grow in different soils prepared to evolve definite characteristics; wherever they went, the nation in which they incarnated became the crest of the evolutionary wave.

Differentiation had done its work, and the time for reintegration began to dawn. Messenger after messenger was sent to the West, in order to permeate its turbulent civilizations with the higher spiritual ideas; splendid intellects were sent thither to lead it onwards to heights of scientific knowledge and artistic achievement. In the nineteenth century the time had come for "a more sympathetic mutual understanding between East and West," between the elder and younger Branches of the Aryan family, and for this The Theosophical Society was founded; it was sent to bring to the West the forgotten spiritual knowledge of the East; to lead it to drink at the long-sealed Aryan wells; it was sent to recall to the East the memory of its own treasures, to revive Aryan ideals, and to bring to it the accumulated treasures of western learning, to knit together its warring elements into a single nation, and above all to blend into one the eldest and the youngest children of the Aryan Race, the Indians and the English.

On this union, close, brotherly, indissoluble, the future Empire depends. And it is inevitable; Those who strive against it will be eliminated, for the will of the great Father must be wrought out. The rebellious, the haters, the inciters to strife, will be scattered among other nations, among nations backward in evolution, where their unpleasant peculiarities may work less harm. When the union is accomplished, when the field is ready, then Vaivas-vata Manu will send hither the master intellects of humanity, to raise the people composed of the best elements of His race to a dazzling height of glory, and the great Aryan Empire will stand revealed.

—October 1910, *Central Hindu College Magazine*

O 'India ! Awake ! Arise !

O India ! O Perfect Nation !

O India that shall be !

How long till Thou take station ?

How long ere thralls live free ?

How long ere all Thy Soul

Be one with all Thy sea ?

O People of India, whom I have striven for more than half a century to serve, is it not time to stop wasting your strength on fragments of bondage, instead of breaking that bondage once for all, meeting Britons as their equals, not as their inferiors, and clasping hands of friendship—God grant it be not too late!—for the helping of the world?

Let all else wait. This equal alliance is necessary for the sake of the Peace of the World. This alliance concluded, East and West, Asia and Europe, will march together, side by side, for the helping of Humanity. —1 May 1930, *New India*

Consecration

Turn inwards and say: "My body, my tongue, my brain, my mind, I consecrate for the service of the Motherland," and go and serve her. Surely none can resist the demand of a united Nation. You must be united in your demand. .. Freedom comes from God. He has the right to give it, but no Nation can give it to another.

You were so mighty in your past even in the days of comparative degradation by assimilating all that the conquerors brought to the conquered people. Mother India swallowed them all to make them of her own flesh and of her own blood. We know no differences now between Muslim, Hindu, Parsi, Christian, and Jew. All those who belong to the various sects of Hinduism are our brethren and we are all common worshippers in the Temple of our Mother, and, like the Temple of Jagannath at Puri, which knows no difference in worship, that Mother knows no division among the children of her heart and womb.

Let us leave this sacred place, sacred because it is the Temple of Liberty, carrying India in our hearts, in our lips, and in our brains, so that when we meet again, we shall be on the road to freedom, a freedom that is worthy when a Nation demands it, and when a Nation demands it and when a Nation takes it, it shall lead you to a height that even ancient India was not able to touch. For you are stronger even than that ancient India and the measure of the greatness of your past is not even the measure of the height of your future.

— From the closing of the Congress Presidential Address, 1917, for the first time reprinted from 1 January 1918, New *India.*

In Indian Hands

The most important point from the standpoint of National Education is that education must be in Indian hands and under Indian control, because you will be able to judge the character you desire to develop in your boys and girls better than any *one* else can do. So you will notice that in the Board of National Education it is Indians who fill it, with the only exception of myself and Mr. Arundale, and the moment somebody else is ready to take our place, both of us will be willing to clear out.

—12 March 1918, *New India*

India is Herself

National Education must meet the National temperament at every point and develop the National character. India is not to become a lesser—nor even a greater—England but to evolve into a mightier India. British ideals are good for Britain, but it is India's ideals that are good for India. We do not want echoes nor monotones; we want a choral melody of Nations, mirroring the varied qualities of Nature and of God. Shall Nature show but a single colour, and trees, and flowers, and mountains, and sky, wear but a single hue? Harmonious variety and not monotony is the mark of perfection.

Away with all apologies for India, with all deprecatory explanations of India's ways, and customs, and traditions. India is Herself, and needs not to be justified, for verily God has evolved no greater, no more exquisite Nationality than India's among all the broken reflections of His own Perfect Beauty.

—9 April 1918, New *India*

Citizenship

Creating India's Leaders

To the Youth of India: It is but repeating truisms to say that the Destiny of a Nation is folded within its youth, as is the flower within the close embrace of the sepals that sheathe the bud. That which you are thinking today, the Nation will think tomorrow. That your characters, bold or timid, noble or base, generous or sordid, chivalrous or mean, pure or unclean, will show out in the characters of the Nation's citizens, a few years hence. That you are creating those characters now,. shaping them out of the materials you brought with you to your present bodies; for what a man thinks upon, that he becomes. Your thoughts in past lives created the character you brought with you into the world; your thoughts in the past of this life have moulded it year by year into its present form; your present thoughts are creating the character of your manhood, shaping the citizens who shall be India, when we, the elders, shall have passed away. India gave you birth, she is your Mother; yet you shall recreate her as your daughter, in the years to come. In the great chain of life, in which each generation is a golden link, every link is supported by those that are before it, every link supports those that are after it. These are, indeed, but truisms, but they are truisms that live, and should guide and inspire.. .. Young India, then, means the youth of the Nation, rising above all divisions, forgetting all ancient animosities, with its watchword, *United India,* with its banner on which is inscribed: Worship the Motherland, Vande *Mataram*... .

First Rigorous Training

To send men to fight without training, without discipline, without knowledge, would be sending them as sheep to the slaughterhouse. And, gentlemen, in the service of the Motherland, in the service of the Goddess Liberty, do you suppose that you can enlist and go straight into the noblest and holiest of struggles, the struggles which create National Self-Rule, which set free a Nation, without serving as National Recruits, without undergoing the preparatory discipline which alone makes citizenship possible, the training which develops the youth into the man, the man into the citizen of a free country ? Do you feel in the flush of the hot enthusiasm which leads you to enlist in the Service of the Motherland, that you want to act to act at once ? So feels the recruit. But he has to pass through the hard training which alone can make a soldier, worthy to wear the uniform of his country.

Does it chill your enthusiasm when you are told that National Service begins with rigorous training ? If so, your enthusiasm is only like a fire of twigs that blazes up furiously with much crackling and then dies down. The only enthusiasm worthy of a Patriot is that which remains white-hot under difficulties, under drudgery, under discipline. Do not venture to profane the Altar of the Motherland with a fire that dies down under the breath of disciplined training. The only enthusiasm useful in the cause of Liberty, is like the tempered steel; it has been purified in the furnace of discipline, hammered on the anvil of knowledge, poured red hot into the ice-cold water of drudgery, until it has a strength that naught can break, a resilience that naught can overstrain, a keenness that naught can resist, a flexibility that naught can escape. Only when your characters are like tempered steel will you be worthy to go *on* active service. .. .

To Become Soldiers of Freedom

You, the students of today, boys in school, young men in college, are to go out into a New India, an India that is rising out of Other-Rule into Self-Rule, like Lakshmi out of the ocean churned by the Suras and Asuras. That New India will be shaped, guided, developed by you, and by thousands like you, all over the land. Among the students in schools and colleges today, among you, are the future statesmen, the future leaders, the future generals, the future admirals, the future merchant Princes, the future scientists, the future rulers of India. Nay among you are also the future members of the Imperial Council, the Council which shall control the destinies of a mighty Empire, which is to be a blessing or a curse to the whole world—a blessing if guided by noble, unselfish, pious, righteous statesmen, a curse if guided by the base, the selfish, the materialistic, and the bad. ...

Now that things are changing, you must change with them, and you must bear in your youth the training of the free. For in the maturity of your manhood, you will be responsible for India's peace, India's order, India's progress; with the glory, you must take also the responsibility of Freedom. And Freedom is a Goddess beautiful but austere; she is the armed Warrior, strong and unstained. The Heroes who follow her are mighty men, not weaklings, and she needs for her service men, and not drones.

Without preparation some of you would rush into action, raw recruits into the firing-line, more dangerous to their own army then to the army of the foe. Many of you do not realise how serious a thing is political action, how far-reaching are political movements, how interdependent the parts of the complex body of a Nation, how rashness means ruin, and folly spells catastrophe, and blunders slip insensibly into crimes. In politics men play with human lives, with the prosperity of Nations, with the plenty or starvation of Peoples, with the safety or destruction of homes, with the happiness or misery of millions of men, women, and children. If Temples of stone are held to be holy, are guarded from the foot of the profane, shall any unclean and unfit enter the Temple that is built of human lives, that is consecrate to the service of Humanity ? Would you enter it in manhood, you who are students ?

Sowing of the Seed

You are constituted of four important elements; your body, the instrument of your actions; your emotions, the root of your happiness or sorrow, your virtues and vices; your mind, the builder of your character and the director of activity; your Self, the Spirit, the Inner Ruler Immortal, the broken rays of whose perfection are what we call down here the Good, the Beautiful, and the True.

The body, the emotions, the mind, form the Field, which you, the Spirit, must till and cultivate, where the seeds of a noble harvest must be sown....

Now you must train your body for the sake of the 'Motherland; it is hers, and she has need of strong, vigorous, enduring bodies, hard in muscle and steady in nerve. Soft, flabby, fat, lazy bodies are not bodies for freemen; they are only fit for slaves. And remember that youth is the only time for making a strong and vigorous body. . . .

The emotions of youths are strong and apt to carry them away. Yet if you would serve the Motherland in the future, you must learn self-control, you must encourage right emotion, and starve out wrong by turning away from it. You need to cultivate courage and endurance, kindness and 'helpfulness, truth and generosity.

You must show reverence to all that is worthy of it: to God, to your parents, to your teachers. You must protect the weak, show tenderness to the aged, be courteous to the poor, to all below you in rank. Never speak a rough word to one whose position renders impossible a rough retort, and never cringe to a superior. Never lie, either from fear or greed, nor play the hypocrite to please... Play well the great game of life...

If you would serve the Motherland well, you must study hard and deeply. Remember that education does not mean storing the memory with facts; it means drawing out the faculties of the mind, and bringing them under control, so that you can address them to any question, and deaf efficiently and adequately with the problems of life as they present themselves. You need to cultivate observation, accuracy, discrimination, the power of classification, the seeing of things in true proportion — that is, the perception of values, and of the relation of one object to another.

Thinking is the establishment of relations. You must cultivate attention, both alert and sustained, for concentration is only formal and developed attention, and without concentration-no mastery of great questions is possible.... But whatever you study, remember to do it for the Mother's sake, and that dedication of all to Her, of ail as the preparation for Her Service, shall make all drudgery fascinating, and gild the dullest study with the promise of future use. Body, emotions, mind, all are consecrate to Her, are held in trust for Her Service.

One-self

What shall I say of this, your very Self ? The religions of the world have all one aim—the Realisation of the Self, the Knowledge of God. Their outward rites and ceremonies are intended for the training of the body, to overcome its sloth, to teach temperance in all things, to make it a useful servant, not a tyrannical master. Their moral precepts are directed to the training of the emotions to the loftiest end. Their metaphysics and philosophies aim at the highest development of the intellect. But the essence of Religion is Unity, the Realisation of the One God, within and without, flowering into the Brotherhood of all that lives.

In India, all the great religions find a home, and some say that religious differences must ever prevent the growth of a true Nationality. Ill do they think, who thus assert. The details of religions vary, and the unspiritual fight over non-essentials. But the heart of Religion is one—the Love of God and Man... Let a common pride replace religious jealousies all over India.

Recruit Manoeuvres

I have spoken much of the training which should fill the student's days; but what of his touch with the outer world ? Our recruit learns to dig trenches, to march, to manoeuvre, to fire. How else should he become ready for the battlefield ? And so with you. You should take interest in the political questions of the day, read them in the papers, debate on them in your debating societies; if possible, as in the Central Hindu College, make a Parliament, where you *can* learn the forms of Legislative Assemblies, learn to argue cogently, to bear opposition with good temper, to be sound in your logic, accurate in your facts, clear in your exposition. Or have a Union, like those of Oxford and Cambridge, where Gladstone and others won their first laurels.

Your opinions will often be crude, one-sided, exaggerated; how can they be aught else in the beginning ? Better to have them crude now, than when you go out into public life, when the crudity will affect the lives of others. These discussions will force you to study, if you are not to make yourselves ridiculous. If you have fluency, a facile tongue, take care that your knowledge outruns your speech, not your speech your knowledge, and do not let your fluency tempt you to hide ignorance with words. Oratory should cover a plenum, not a vacuum, and for its support it needs constant study; it must be uplifted by the pillars of Wisdom and Strength; not by Beauty alone.

And let your debates deal with questions of details, the formation and work of Panchayats and Local Boards; with sanitation and hygiene, urban and rural; with the establishment of village schools, with curricula, elementary, secondary, technical; with the uplift of the submerged classes; the questions of mendicancy, charity, cooperation, and the like. You will need all this when your college work is over.

To a Young Prince: the Ideal of Kingship

Does it seem strange in these democratic days to hold up the Ideal of Kingship? But human beings are much the same, whatever be their label, and one of the deepest longings of the human heart is to find and follow a true leader.

We "needs must love the highest when we see it," and the strongest Democrat is loyal to his Leader, if the Leader be worthy of loyalty. The pity is the Leader and the Ruler are not now always found in one and the same person, and the "Hero as King "is not always one with the wearer of the royal robe; it is likely that one outcome of the present anarchy in western Nations will be to prove that ignorance cannot rule, whether embodied in a mob or in an autocrat, that folly, whether in purple or in fustian, spells ruin. Democracy will probably work out some way of finding a Nation's best, and placing them in the seats of power; for superior wisdom and character are the only true credentials of authority. Eugenics justifies the value of breed, of race purity, of physical type. But the essentials of breed have been disregarded in princely and noble houses, and descent loses value where the factors which should mark it have long been disregarded. Birth and *Dharma* together preserve the purity of descent, and where the second has been neglected the value of the first disappears. Princely by birth, see to it that your character is princely, and that the inner life corresponds to the outer label.

—18 February 1932, New *India*, From "Advice to a Prince"

Scouting

[A Message Dated 7 March 1929]

If I had a dozen sons—I have only one—I would send them all into the Scout Movement, as soon as they could enter its lowest grade. And I would send the daughters into the Girl Guides, under similar conditions, to begin at the beginning. Now do you think that I could say anything stronger than that, as a recommendation to you, who read this, in the way of advice as to joining the Scouts or the Guides, according as you are a boy or a girl?

If you are wondering why I write so strongly, I will tell you why I do. It is because I have seen Cubs, and Scouts, and Rovers, and I know what a useful lot they are, as boys and as men. And so also with the girls.

They are good citizens of their country, ready to work for it; ready to live for it; ready to die for it. That is the idea conveyed by the word "citizen." It means a man who is fit to live in a city; in other words—a man who is fit to live in Society, fit to live among a group of other people.

We put this in another way in our Scout pledge. We promise to "do a good turn every day." As you know, a good turn is some helpful act, for which you are not paid in any way, except by love which cannot be bought or sold. And you promise on your Honour. Honour leads you to do good things without being made to do them. It is the Voice of God within you, bidding you to do some good act which you are not ordered to do by someone who has the right to give an order to you.

You see why you should do a thing that you feel, inside you, that you ought to do. That inner feeling is God's Voice speaking inside you; and if you do it, you will become a good and noble man, and help your Nation to hold up her head among the Nations of the world.

And so Good be with you, Brothers, for I, though in a woman's body, am your Brother Scout.

Perhaps you may like to know that I took the Scout's pledge from our Chief Scout, Sir Robert Baden-Powell, here in Madras, at a big Scout Rally.

[Dr. Besant also received from his hands later the Silver Wolf, one of the highest honours conferred by the Chief Scout upon those who had rendered great service to the Scout Movement.]

Find Your Hero

To Serve is the crown of human life. The fortunate ones, eager to *serve,* find one to whom they can render service, and joyfully enrol themselves as helpers. To each Young Citizen I would say: Look around you for some one who is greater than yourself, who, to some extent, embodies that which you fain would be. Hero-worship is uplifting and' inspiring, it purifies the heart, ennobles the character, and stimulates the energy.

Serve your Hero in every way you can, and pay him that truest flattery which is imitation. Joyfully will he help you to find *one* greater than himself and for your practice with him, will increase your capacity for service. Work well done with the lower is the passport to higher Service, and each rising presages the one beyond. Happy are they who have found their Master and their work. Happy are they also who are still seeking, for they who seek shall find. —March 1913, *The Young Citizen*

A Young Man's Duty to his Country

I cannot hope to sum up better your duty than with the thought of the vow taken by the youth of Athens:

> "We will never bring disgrace to this our city by any act of dishonesty or cowardice, nor ever desert our suffering comrades in the ranks. We will fight for the ideals and the sacred things of the city, both alone and with many. We will revere and obey the city's laws and do our best to invite a like respect and reverence in those above us who are prone to annul or set them at naught. We will strive unceasingly to quicken the public sense of civic duty. We will transmit the city not only not less, but greater, better, and more beautiful than it was when transmitted to us."

[Dr. *Besant made* of the New *India Office practically a recruiting bureau tor the Defence* of *India Force, appealing to those over 18 years* of *age to take advantage* of *the special opportunity to defend their Motherland."*]

That opportunity must not pass ungrasped, unseized. We have been talking for years and years about the right of Indians to defend their country, about their right to carry arms, about their claim to be drilled and trained, so as to be able to guard their own land and the Empire. Now, the Defence of India Force is meant for the defence of this country, and it would be a scandal and shame if, when the opportunity is given, those who had talked so loudly should shrink back from putting their words into action. That is the reason why I make, and shall continue to make an appeal. I know that it means throwing back for a time the Home Rule propaganda, and the loss of our best workers in the political field, but that does not count in a moment like this.... India cannot hold back without shaming herself in the face of the world. Inasmuch as the younger men are ever the most enthusiastic, the most ready to sacrifice, I urge that all of you who can do it, and whose parents consent—and most of them I know will—should come forward and be trained, learn military discipline, learn to use the rifle and the gun, and remember that you will be able hereafter as men to serve your country as you never could do, if you were a disarmed and helpless mob. ... You are not asked to go outside the country, but you are asked to be ready to defend your own country, and to set free the trained soldiers who will be ready to go to the front. Do not let such an opportunity be missed.... —13 February 1917, *New India*

Volunteer Defence Corps

It is very desirable that Home Rulers everywhere in India-should take counsel on the question of the Defence of the Motherland, and of their duty in connection therewith-Disarmed as Indians have been for 40 years, and unreasonable as it is under such conditions to ask them suddenly to-become the bulwark of the Empire in Asia, they must yet prepare themselves for the natural duty of men, to protect their own country from invasion and to preserve internal order.

From time immemorial there have existed in the hills and jungles of India, wild tribes who have lived mainly by hunting and foraging. They did no particular harm when the population was armed, save when they profited by any local invasion, or foray, and they joyfully took part in any looting that might be going on. Raids on villages they sometimes-made, but they were not a source of more than temporary annoyance. They still descend and plunder from time to time, knowing that the villagers are now defenceless, save for the sticks which they ply lustily on occasion, but which are a poor defence against firearms.

The Government in some parts of the country is now calling on the police to volunteer for the Army, and the response is very largely made. As this process continues, the police force will become more and more depleted, until at last it is no longer competent to preserve internal order. Towns will be largely at the mercy of the criminal classes, and rural districts at the mercy of dacoits.

Ought we to remain quiescent, looking on indifferently, and making no preparations for the preservation of our homes from attack ? Surely it would be more reasonable to enrol ourselves as Volunteers for the preservation of civic order, and to organise a band in every ward or other division of our cities, who should be ready to act at once, if occasion should arise. We cannot wait until, as at Mussoorie, the whole European police force and all but three of the Indian force have volunteered for the front, We can drill and learn to obey promptly, and though we cannot have arms, a policeman's truncheon is enough to disperse an ordinary mob, where men act together, and obey the word of command. Each man in the force should know his central station, and the area with which he would be concerned if called on. He should learn the signal which summons him to his centre, and know the quickest way to reach it. Bands of young men should be trained in patrol duty, as indeed some are already training themselves in neighbourhoods where tendencies towards looting have appeared, and the formation of such bands is urgently necessary in rural districts.

These citizen police forces would form nuclei for the Citizen Army, which will be evolved by the pressure of circumstances, however unwilling the Government may be to initiate, or even approve of, such a step. Moreover, more definite steps may be taken in this direction, and will, we hope, be taken by the Home Rule Council.

In Bombay, the Home Rule League has a well-drilled Volunteer Corps; they wear uniform, and, consisting as the corps does, of stalwart young men, they present a very smart and soldier-like appearance. The Corps was organised to help in the general work of the Branch, and to serve it in all ways required.

This Corps could easily be sufficiently enlarged to provide bodies of well-drilled men for the preservation of internal order, should need arise. And it might also form a very strong nucleus for a division of the Citizen Army. Such Corps of Volunteers should be formed everywhere.

Volunteering is the only way. Men must earn their livelihood and give their spare time to drilling and training. We have no funds for paid soldiers; we must follow the British Territorial plan. Now is the hour for sacrifice to the Motherland. Let those who love Her respond. —29 June 1918, New *India*

True Patriot

"To Indian Youth: I shall give up the Home Rule Movement if you do not come forward to defend your home. If you want Home Rule, be prepared to defend your home. Had it not been for my age, I would have been the first to volunteer. You cannot reasonably say that the ruling will be done by you, and the fighting for you by Europeans or Japanese in the matter of home defence..."

Those words [said Dr. Besant in addressing a recruiting meeting] came from Mr. Tilak the very day after he had received the order of Sir Michael O'Dwyer forbidding him to enter the Punjab I mention that, because it shows the spirit in which all patriots should act. We have many grievances against our local Governments, but this is the time not to dwell upon them, but to forget them. When there is a call to the defence of the Motherland, all grievances must be thrown aside, and it is the test of Indian patriotism how many will come forward to enrol.. . Over and over again it has been said that those who desire to rule their country must be prepared to defend their country, and that is true. It is idle to claim to play a citizen's part in the ruling, unless you are willing to play a citizen's part in the defending... Nor if you can afford it, should the question of pay come into your minds. It is the honour of serving the Motherland, the honour of being one of the defenders of the country, making yourselves ready for the time when other Nations shall no-longer say that India is unable to defend herself. —22 February 1917, *New India*

While early enthusiasm has been completely killed out by the difficulties put in the way. . . this is no reason why men of the right age should hold back [commented Dr. Besant at a public meeting in Trichinopoly, 27 May 1917 on the recruiting of men for the Home Defence Force]. Enthusiasm that blazes for a moment and then dies down is not the enthusiasm that will make our Nation great. It is like a flame of straw, it is not *true* patriotism, not the real love of country, and not the devotion to the Motherland. Granting the conditions are unfavourable, it does not matter to young men if they have difficulties. They should think it not as a call to the 'Government but as a call of the Motherland. ...

I will feel very discouraged about the political work unless this recruiting work comes out gloriously. Let no official be allowed to hinder our work. If you do not subscribe to the War Loan it does not matter. Men are better than money and more useful to the Motherland.... Men are needed, brave and gallant men out of which stuff the Nation is made. I would ask you to put aside all discouragement and think of the Mother.... I have no son, no grandson to give, but I give my life *to* India, and if persons give all they have, they cannot give anything more.

I am risking far more for India than any of you will do who join the Volunteer Force. I am risking—I know—the likelihood of imprisonment and bankruptcy. What do I care, what is life worth except for India's sake ? What is suffering worth if it finds India's freedom ? Russia's freedom has been made by Russian young men and young women who went to the scaffold and exile in order that they might redeem their Motherland from tyranny. They did not count the price or cost but gave themselves freely at the feet of the Motherland.

Young men, lay your youth, your strong muscles, your brave hearts, [at her feet]—it is not much to give for so short a time, but she will take it. Go to her great altar and vow your lives to her. Give her everything you have to give, she will take it up and bless it, and your poor gift shall be turned into gold and jewel, for the touch of the Motherland makes all sacred. Do not let the world say that India's children are unworthy of their past, that India's sons are today cowards where once they were heroes. Show as far as you can in this paltry opportunity that you are willing to do all you can, and then the high Gods will give you greater opportunities. They will open for you wider ways and more splendid chances than those given today—the poor three months asked of you in the Indian Defence Force, and then you shall have shown your earnestness and have the right to ask in future years greater gifts for you to give her, and the power that is only rightly used by those who know how to sacrifice and how to pay.

—28 May 1917, *New India*

Reservoir of Power

For all who are Theosophists the destiny of India looms large in their Theosophical horizon. It is "the land of my Master." as H.P.B. told us. It is also the land of the other Great Ones, since among the many nations of the world today it is the land where there is an Inner Peace in the life of the people which reflects the great Peace within Them. It is a land that is old and yet full of youth; a land of hoary traditions, yet emerging out of them to build herself into a new and mighty Nation. When India achieves her destiny, the charm which the peoples of the West already find in India will be increased an hundredfold.

For throughout the ages, from the thousands of shrines in this land, from every banyan tree and bo-tree at whose foot a saint has meditated, there has radiated a network of magnetism whose influence is felt as the charm of India. But largely, even now, these centres of magnetism are unreleased and have not spent their full vigour, and generation after generation each shrine and temple has become the reservoir of mighty forces awaiting the great day of the Coming of the Lord. ... Many are the whispers in this land of mystery from rock and tree, from forest and shrine; for ages they have whispered of the great Day to be, and now these whispers have changed to a chant of triumph. For what the high Gods decree, no puny human will may thwart, and where the Hand of the Highest on Earth is upraised in protection and benediction, there all opposition dies away, for His Will is victory and triumph.

—August 1907, *The Theosophist*

Master Builder

I believe in the Plan ... and part of that Plan was to bring the English traders to India for a good that was seen in the then far-off future. The preparation has been going on for long, but.. the end is sure. The end is sure because there is a Plan, because the Divine Architect has drawn that Plan, because this ancient country has the right to express herself and to be as free in her own country as you are in yours. That is the goal which we are striving for—many of us, I think, most of us would hope that the goal may be reached in peace and not in struggle, so that India and England may remain friends and comrades, friends and comrades on an equal footing. No other friendship or comradeship is any longer possible.... 1 look forward not with hope only, but with a feeling of certainty that which has been foreseen shall be accomplished ere many years have passed ....

A Master-Builder wants many builders for his helping . . . Only by free choice between the good and the evil . . the better and the worse . . . between every vice and every virtue, can man grow in the image of the Master-Builder, the Divine Architect of the world in which we live.

There you will find the answer to many problems. The day shall come, far off but growing ever nearer with every year that passes, when man shall truly be in the image of God, with his will free as the Divine Will is free, but by himself determined to Good.

—18 August 1928, New *India*

Centre of a World Commonwealth

Benjamin Disraeli, who became Premier of Great Britain, Lord Beaconsfield, was a man eastern in heart, though he dominated a typical western Nation, a man revelling in the splendour of an eastern imagination, and with his mind ever steeped in the poetry and glamour of the East. When he won for the British Monarch, in the teeth of British prejudice and democratic feeling, the splendid title of Emperor of India, he argued for the adding of the Imperial to the Royal Crown, and he said that in the changes among Nations Asia again might have her turn in Empire, and that it might be that the centre of the Empire might shift from the unruly West to the loyal East, when the Monarch of the Empire might be enthroned in the great continent of India, instead of in the little Island of the northern seas.

A splendid ideal, a glorious possibility; but let such possibility be the parent of duty... Those Nations only are worthy of freedom whose citizens have conquered passion and have achieved self-control. Only among such citizens, only in an India peopled by such men, could the centre of the Empire be established.

—29 February 1908, *The East and the West*

Queen Mother

Let those who know not the Indian spirit say what they will, misrepresent as they choose. Let us who work for the Mother forget everything save her cause, and do not make the fight for liberty more difficult by desire to resent insults, levelled after all at the personality which cannot touch the Spirit, which cannot soil the real life. And so with brave hearts but gentle hearts as well, let us go onwards together to the victory which Ishvara will give to His people, for the days of Indian subjection are over and the days of her suffering are accomplished (cheers). The discrowned Queen is coming to her own, and let the Mother, when she comes among her children, find love in their hearts, courage in their actions, that we may be worthy to welcome to her throne that mightiest and holiest of Nations — the Indian people.

—24 September 1917, *New India*

Not for ever shall the birthplace of the two mightiest religions known on earth sit mourning as a widow, bereft of God's divinest gift, the gift of Liberty. For her, too, and that ere long, shall the voices of her Rishis and her Devas ring out the trumpet-call: "Arise ! Shine ! Thy Light has come! For the Glory of the Lord has risen upon thee." —25 December 1918, New *India*

Will the Year now born. 1918, bring us Peace ? God grant it. Yet only if the coming of Peace would mean true blessing to the world, and not a breathing space to recover for fiercer war. For if Might could triumph over Right, and the rod of oppression could *remain* unbroken, whether in East or West, then were Peace a deadlier curse than war.

What has the New Year hidden in his bosom for our India ? Does he hold the sure and certain promise of the Freedom that we strive for ? Is it the rising of the Sun of Liberty that is painting the fair rose of dawn on our horizon?

—January 1918, *The Theosophist*

Temple of Humanity

Nobody can say that the Allies have wholly triumphed. There is a state of turmoil and unrest which is persisting throughout Europe. Nor can that end, unless India comes to her place.

The next stage of the Plan is the building up of a free Commonwealth of Nations in which India plays her equal part. That is why the English came here and others had to go away; and the one Nation that is free in her institutions in her own island, if not free in her practice outside her own island, is the English Nation, chosen to come here and blend with the Indian Nation in the building up now of the World Empire, to be really a World Commonwealth, not a World Empire which was to rule by force, but a World Federation which was to govern by love and in peace. That is the ideal towards which some of us are trying to work, towards which the Manu is working, and He asks for cooperation from His elder children here, to bring together East and West, not for themselves alone but for the future good of the world; to draw them together, not losing their characteristics but harmoniously blending them for the helping of future generations, with the great spiritual ideals of India and the great material and scientific progress of Britain.

These two are to be the main constituents of this Commonwealth, which is to be the model of the World Commonwealth of the future. It is a model on a small scale of internationalism — the British race consisting of different Nations scattered all over the world, drawn into equal partnership, equal Commonwealth of mutual service, of mutual love, of mutual help, and not of tyranny on the one side and of subjection on the other. That is the great building which Vaivasvata Manu is trying to bring about, against the clashing Wills of men and against all the strivings of the ignorant and, far worse against those Powers of Darkness who are ever the opponents of the Brothers of Light.

You have heard of Asuras and you know that in the long run even Asuras are compelled to cooperate with the Divine Will. All that they can do is to resist the speed of progress. Asuras cannot stop the chariot of God which rolls along the track of evolution, but they can delay it, retard it, and inflict greater pain and suffering upon men.

It is on the men in India that the great burden of that choice is falling today. India is now divided into two great: camps and two only: one camp marked by love and the other by hate, one camp marked by love of liberty and the other by desire to tyrannise, one marked by cooperation and the other by antagonism. It is for you to choose which of these camps you will strengthen. I cannot say to you, members of The Theosophical Society: "Join that camp, join this camp," but I can say to you as Theosophists, to you as members of The Theosophical Society, that for forty-five years this teaching has been in the world and you ought to know more about it than the outer world. The outer-world may be moved by temporary injuries, carried away by wrongs inflicted and sufferings endured, but you, students of the Wisdom, ought to realise that behind all these outside things, the Inner Government of the world is ruling and ultimately must have Its way, in one of two ways, by destruction or by evolution: yours is the choice.

If you find a movement marked by hatred, if you find a movement marked' by tyranny over the opinions of others, by trying to force-people along lines that some of them may adopt, if you find those means are means of compulsion, of tyranny, of social ostracism, of spreading hatred in India and dividing her more than she had ever been divided before, I tell you, no matter who may lead it, no matter who may join it, that is a movement of Brothers of the Shadow and leads to destruction. Those are the marks that show what they are. The Lords of Light sent our

Society for this great crisis, to save the Indian Motherland. Every movement They instigate is moved by love, every movement.

They instigate is moved by drawing together, by cooperating for the common end, for the common purpose, and for common work; and as the mark of the sixth sub-race is to make a union and not to combat further, to work hand in hand and not strike each other, therefore, in this great critical moment of transition, the decision has come to the Mother and to her children scattered over the far wide world to choose. Will you follow the teachings of your ancient Rishis? Will you reform abuses, but keep the central treasure in your hands in which there is the spiritualisation of the world ? You alone can save the world from going down into the gulf of materialism; India alone, with her glorious past, with her religion which contains everything that every later religion has given to a portion of the Race—India, the Mother, has the right to spiritualise the world, and with spirituality to bring back to the world intellectual greatness, to bring back to it all the beauty of devotion as well as the splendour of the mind. The centre of the conflict is transferred from Europe to Asia. India is the heart of Asia, and on the decision of India the whole immediate future depends.

—December 1920, *The Great Plan*

4

Significant Speeches

East and West - the Destinies of Nations

In this "East and West", and in another lecture entitled "The destinies of Nations" which follows hereafter, I propose to deal with the making of history in a way that seems to me to give much deeper interest than one can find in studying it in the ordinary historical textbooks. Here we shall take a more general view, while, in the succeeding lecture, we shall specialise. We shall consider the premises which underlie the present conflict in the Far East, and the broad results which flow from the triumphs in arms of Japan. For we have before our eyes a great object-lesson, and in this twentieth century, as H. P. Blavatsky told us, some of the outstanding accounts between eastern and western nations are to be settled.

Because of this, I wish to bring some thoughtful minds towards a deeper view of the actions of the men who play great parts in the world-drama we call history, so that instead of looking at the events of ordinary life among the nations as though they were really guided by rulers and statesmen, we may learn to understand that the drama of the nations has an Author who writes it, and that the actors play the parts for which they have prepared themselves in the past; the players are actors in, and not creators of, the world's history.

Now, in order to set forth this view of life, and to render intelligible part of the argument that I desire to submit, I must define what I mean here by " ideals". I mean the dominant ideas expressed in civilizations, being shaped and moulded according to the dominant ideas or ideals, the views as to life-values, that rule in the minds of the nation concerned. And I say "eastern" and " western " ideals, because the differences between these, and their utility in the evolution of humanity at large, must be understood if we would rightly follow the acts of the world-drama. And we need to understand that in the present condition of affairs then is a distinct weighing down of a balance that had grown too light and was threatening to kick the beam, so that humanity was menaced by a loss of ideals vital for its full development. It is not that I want to put the ideals of the East and West in antithesis.

Rather I want to show that both are necessary in the great evolution of humanity, and that there was a danger of late years that the eastern ideals might perish. That humanity might not thus be deprived of part of its ideal wealth, it became necessary to redress the balance between East and West, between Europe and Asia. That redressal could only take place by checking the conquering march of Europe, and giving back to Asia some of its ancient independence. So that looking at the present struggle, whether our sympathies go with the one nation or with the other, it is wise that we should understand the deeper issues concerned, and read with eyes of wisdom rather than with eyes of passion the pages of history now being unrolled before us.

I have said I do not want to put these two ideals in conflict. None the less, to some extent, that conflict has been inevitable; and it is, I think, the part of a student of the Divine Wisdom to try to feel peace amid combats, and to fix his eyes steadily on the goal to be arrived at, so that he may not be whirled off his feet by the turmoil of the moment. If we look back over the nineteenth century we shall notice that more and more the West has been dominating the East - by conquest primarily, but to an immense extent by the spread of western thought and civilization following in the wake of conquest. We have seen in eastern lands that the old ideals tended to disappear. That they did not make their way largely in Europe would have been of small import; but that they should be menaced with death on the soil of their birth was a true peril to humanity. As western arms and commerce spread, western thought among eastern nations began to claim predominance, the more readily and the more dangerously that it was associated with the conquering sword, with the growth of military power. Some of the conquests in the East were very definite in their nature, as that of India, by Britain ; others less above board, but none the less effective.

And Europe grew more and more to regard Asia as her natural inheritance, so that Asian policy was to be directed, Asian interests were to be controlled, not for the benefit of Asian peoples but for the enrichment of Europe. This was done largely under the guise of commercial interests; but the commercial interests were the commercial interests of the West, seeking to discover for itself new markets and further expansion. No one asked, when questions of the open port, and so on, were discussed, whether the eastern nation concerned would benefit in its commerce by the intrusion of western rivalry; no one asked whether eastern industries could meet without peril of destruction the rough shock of western competition; no one ever dreamed of considering, in the many debates that have taken place in the Parliaments of Europe in connection with Asian affairs, whether these nations of the East would be the better, the happier, the wealthier, for the forcing upon them of goods for which they did not ask.

All that was considered was the question of the market for Europe, and the European countries quarrelled among themselves for advantages among eastern peoples. The commercial contest was not between Europe and Asia, but between European nations planted on Eastern soil without the consent of the natural owners of the land. Wars even were begun in order to force the open market on Asian nations, wars often started by peoples who closed their own markets against the goods of the foreigner. All the considerations that here are regarded as binding were entirely disregarded in dealing with the eastern peoples, and China, for instance, was to be compelled to admit into her land foreign goods she did, not require, and even detested, while, on the other hand most of the western nations guarded themselves by protective duties and legislation against the competition of Chinese goods and of Chinese labour. The whole current of affairs meant the complete subordination of the East to the West, and that carried with it the perishing of the eastern, and the substitution for them of western, ideals.

Now this substitution of ideals has made but small way at the present time. Of course, in India, to some extent you find a substitution of western ideals among a certain class of the population. A number of English-educated youths among the Indians have accepted enthusiastically the ideals that are current in the West, but the vast masses of the Indian people are thereby unaffected. Not only the agricultural and artisan population, but the population rich with the culture of eastern thought and literature, remain unaffected. But then we must remember that the affected classes are the most energetic, those with the most power of influencing the activity of the country, if not its thought. So that they weigh heavier than they count. The numbers are comparatively small, but the weight behind those numbers of power of thought, quick intelligence, keen enthusiasm, these weigh heavily in the scale.

In China and Japan things have been somewhat different. Japan has the advantage England also has, of being an island empire. That enabled her to keep within her own borders, at the same time that she might bring into them anything she chose from western lands. The westernising of Japan at one time appeared almost complete, and it was this triumph of western ideals that made the redressal of the balance absolutely necessary. For with the complete westernising of Japan would have come a great reaction upon other eastern nations, and Japan, drawing as she did - as was well pointed out by one of her leading writers - all her ideals of life from India, would have been a powerful factor in the westernising of Asia, had she abandoned completely those ideals.

China, affected on her sea boards, was not at all affected in her inland parts. There she preserved her old teachings and her old morality, butt there was a question, in the descent of an armed empire on her coasts, whether it would be possible for her to retain that isolation when Europe was practically bordering her country with colonies under European rule. The time was critical. Those who guide human destinies saw that the eastern ideals were in danger of being trampled out, and that the West would only listen to lessons enforced by the mailed hand. It was necessary to change the balance, and it is changing under our eyes.

Now what are these Eastern ideals regarded as so important by the great Intelligences that guide the destinies of nations? One leading eastern ideal is that the world is under a divine governance, that the destinies of nations are guided from the invisible world. In eastern lands the unseen worlds always play an immense part in the drama of human life, whether in the form of ancestor-worship so largely prevailing in Japan, or in that same form, one of the great ruling creeds of China; whether in a modified form of that same idea in the daily sacrifices to the Pitris in India, or in the form of the recognition of non-human Intelligences, such as in the West are spoken of as Angels or Archangels. There is thus acknowledged to be a most powerful, constant, and directive action playing on the world of men from superhuman Intelligences that do not belong to the human evolution.

That belief is universal in the West. It is not a mere lip belief; it is an active, working belief recognised in ordinary life. If over in the West some public men, discussing some question of public policy, talked about the influences of Angels as one of the things with which politicians had to reckon, you can imagine the kind of comments that would be passed in the journals on the following morning; but in the East that is natural; the work of the Devas, as Indians call the Angels, is part of the recognised work of the world, and every nation has its ruler in the unseen world, guiding the rulers on the physical plane. How utterly different is the attitude to life among peoples who thus regard superhuman Intelligences as constantly intermingling in human affairs. We find the belief very much, of course, among the Jews of old, where they speak of the Angels of the nations.

We find allusions to them in the canonical Scriptures, sometimes veiled under the name of Jehovah, or Elohim - translated into the singular form God, though plural in the Hebrew - the Hebrew not meaning by that at all the supreme God of the universe, but the tribal national Deity, such a one as we should call an

Archangel at the present time. And that this is so is obvious when we find that in the battle fought by Israel against opposing forces, he was able to drive out the inhabitants of the hills but not the inhabitants of the plains, because they had chariots of iron, and the one who was able to conquer the hill-men but not the plain-men was the "Lord"; yet surely it was not the universal Deity who was thwarted in His attempts by the mere possession by His opponents of chariots of iron.

And so among the early Christian Fathers, especially in Origin, you will find many allusions to the national Angels that belong to particular peoples and not to the universe at large. It is true that in modern days in the western world the name of God is very often invoked in national strifes, and each nation claims that help as belonging specially to itself. But I heard the other day of a little boy making a remark that seemed to me to show a truer insight into the relation of God to man than many of the statements made by rulers and by statesmen, when they claim the success of their arms as proofs of the divine favour of the Lord of all.

For, hearing his elders discussing the war now going on, and hearing a difference of opinion as to whether God was on the side of the Japanese or Russians, he struck in with his young voice and said: "I do not think God fights either for the Japanese or Russians; nor do I think He would fight for us if we went to war, although of course we should ask Him to do it; for God is against no nation, but He is for every one." That the divine government is carried on by these various subordinate agencies, who often struggle among themselves as men on the physical plane also struggle, is a view interwoven into the very fibre of eastern thought, although it has vanished from the West. .And that ideal of the invisible worlds mingling;in the affairs of men was one that had to be saved.

This view of a divine governance moulds the eastern idea of human government; it is always thought to be drawn from above and not from below. The idea that a King rules by the voice of the people rather than by divine authority is only just making its way into eastern thought among nations influenced by western ideas. The result of the view that he who sits upon the throne rules by divine appointment and not by human suffrage has been that all through the East the responsibility of the higher for the welfare of the lower has been a definite, established thought. You find it through all the literature, although it is perishing now. Confucius, asked by a King why thieves were so prevalent in his land, remarked: "If you, O King, lived honestly and justly, there would be no thieves within your realm". So again, through all the old laws of India, you find the King, the governor, the ruler, right down to the pettiest village official, held responsible for the happiness, health, prosperity, of the people whom they ruled. Hence the difficulty very, often in the elder days of finding any one who would take office as governor of a district, of a town, or of a village. Strictly held accountable, by the ruling hierarchy right up to the King himself, for the happiness of the ruled, the place was not a bed of roses, and there was less satisfaction to pride than demand on time and industry.

For, great as was the power of the King in eastern lands, there was one thing that ever stood behind his throne, administered by invisible rulers. That something is denoted by the word Danda, and it is translated "punishment" by Max Müller in his translation of the Institutes of Manu. But I believe the true translation would be the word "Justice," or "Law", rather than "punishment" - Justice regarded as a Deva ruling Kings more sternly than peoples, so that where the King went against Justice, Justice cut him off. So you have the famous warning, that you may read, coming from the lips of a Hindu statesman to a young monarch, where he is warned to dread above all else the cries of the weak. "Weakness", says the dying statesman, " is the worst foe of Kings. The curse of the weak, the tears of the weak, destroy the throne of the oppressor." And that thought goes through all the old theories of government in the East; so that even today, in India, if there be famine, plague, pestilence, it is the government that is blamed for it by the masses of the people.

The old idea there is that every national misfortune is the fault of the rulers who have neglected their duty, and not the fault of the ruled. Such an idea is utterly outside the range of thought of a western thinker or statesman; and yet, for the safety of the Indian Empire, it is necessary to understand the thought of the Indian people, and not merely the thought of the West, and to deal with that thought as it spreads through the minds of the vast masses of the uninstructed population, uninstructed in western ways, but not uninstructed in their own traditions.

Let us pass from that view to the next great ideal that we find in the East, growing naturally out of this ideal of the responsibility of the rulers for the ruled: the idea of Duty. The word "duty" does not carry with it the force of the Sanskrit word "Dharma" which means far more than that. It means the law of all his past, whereby the man is incarnated into the place for which his evolution fits him; the law which, placing him there, surrounds him with all the necessary duties, by the discharge of which his next stage in evolution will be made. All that is contained in the Indian word "Dharma". Coming into the world, then, with the past behind us, we are guided into improper environments. In the duties imposed upon a man by that environment lies his best path of evolution. If he follow them well for the progress of the soul; if he disregard them, progress for him becomes impossible.

Hence the social and political ideal of eastern nations is built on duty, to take the narrower word. The ideal here, of course, is "rights". A man has certain rights with which he is born; that idea made the American Revolution, and later the French, and still later became the basic thought of the political and economical writers of the early days of the nineteenth century; but that idea of rights has no existence in the East. It has its place in evolution, but it is an ideal of combat, of competition, absolutely necessary, with all its undesirable accompaniments, as a stage in the progress of humanity; but it is the very antithesis of the eastern ideal, which sees a man surrounded by duties and is practically blind to his rights. No man following an eastern ideal says: "It is my right to have so and so". Duty, yes, duty to all around, to inferiors, to equals, and to superiors, but always duty, and no excuse for broken duty because another has broken his duty to oneself. Hence arises an entirely different attitude towards life; hence the ease of ruling eastern peoples. Now I am not arguing for the one or the other ideal, but only trying to make us all realise the profound difference between the two, and the value to the world of that ideal of duty, that it should not wholly pass away from the minds of men. What it can do embodied in a nation, we have seen in the triumphs of Japan.

Out of that ideal, again, grows another thought: the relative character of all morality. A man born into a certain environment of duty finds his proper morality in the discharge of the duties imposed upon him by his environment. Hence his morality will vary with his position, with his stage in evolution. No eastern sage or thinker dreams of laying down one common moral ideal for all; that is a purely western fancy, and does not on the whole work very well. In the East the fighting caste will have its own set of duties and its own morality; the caste of teachers will have its own, duties and its morality, very different from the humility of the fighter; the merchant caste will have its own duties and its own morality; and the peasant and the artisan will have - their own moral code and duties.

The servant has his special code, with comparatively few duties to be found within it - obedience, honesty, and good service - but those to be thoroughly discharged. Outside that, what would be willed wrong is not regarded as wrong for him. The other parts of moral codes will find their accomplishment in lives yet to be lived. There is no hurry. We need not try to compass universal perfection in a single life - the most impossible of all impossible tasks. If we learn the duties belonging to our stage and do them well, our progress is secure. Hence the moral code will vary with every stage. I will take a common example. A man out in India surrenders everything, has become what in the West would be called a monk of the most extreme type of poverty. He owns nothing; he has given his life for service of the world, and those who guide the world will direct that life. His only to give. He has no further care for his own life.

With that view of absolute surrender goes also the duty of absolute harmlessness. He must not touch a life sharing the world with him. The venomous snake must go unslain, the tiger go unharmed. He must not use any power of the surrendered life to defend it against the attack of any other creature; for if the serpent or the tiger come to him and slay, it comes as a messenger from behind the veil to tell him that his service in that body is over. But the same rule does not apply to the householder, to the man who has children to guard, servants to protect, animals who are part of his household. He, being the guardian of the younger, more helpless lives, must stand between them and peril, and it is as much his duty to slay the intruding serpent, if it menaces them, as it is the duty of the Sannyãsin to let it pass unharmed. Hence arises much confusion in the western mind in reading eastern books, because they read, as binding upon all, ideals which in the East are related to their proper stage of evolution - a doctrine that in the West finds small acceptance. And naturally so, among modern Christian people, because the Sermon on the Mount is thrown broadcast as the moral ideal, but that ideal of non-resistance applied to the ordinary man of the world is impossible, and therefore disregarded.

When a man like Tolstoy applies it all round, people say that he is a "crank". Certainly he is very unwise. No State could live on such a foundation, false alike for the citizen and the thief, true only for the Saint. The late Archbishop of Peterborough said that, a nation founded on the Sermon on the Mount would very soon go to pieces. But then is it not a pity to put the Sermon on the Mount as binding on all Christian men ? For the result is that, inasmuch as they know it to be impossible for them, it leads them to profess a belief with the lips which does not guide the life. The view of the relativity of morality, is another of the valuable eastern ideals which then, may have something to do and to say in the West.

The last great ideal of wide spreading importance that I can deal with here is the ideal of what is now called the " simple life," and of voluntary poverty. There must be in a nation some standard of social position. Among most of the western nations, coining down from feudal times, the standard of social position has been a standard of birth. Of late years that has become largely mingled with a standard of money, partly because great wealth often received the title which placed its owner among those whose titles came to them by long descent, and partly because, with the growing luxury of the time, wealth weighed more and more heavily us a social distinction. The result of that is widely to be seen in the vulgarising of society, in the loss of noble manners, stately and dignified. A man making a vast fortune has not, as a rule, time, leisure, or taste for the culture of the more delicate mental faculties, and those graces that go with a culture that has come down through centuries. And so gradually, in the western world, a new standard asserts itself against the standard of birth: the standard of great wealth. Society is adapting itself to the new conditions; no future Tennyson will write about:

> that repose
>
> That stamps the caste of Vere de Vere.

The manners of the great lady of the past are indeed past, and loud voice, noisy laughter, familiar gestures, have taken the place of the soft tone, the low musical In laughter, the courteous but stately bearing of the leaders of society, when a golden key did not open all doors. And the change means much, for

> Manners are not idle, but the fruit
>
> Of loyal nature and of noble mind

An aristocracy should he the custodian of stately manners, dignified bearing, artistic culture, simple or splendid living, according to the seemliness of the occasion, the ever-present example of " good taste ". It is now only too well symbolised by the motorcar, rushing headlong, careless of life and limb, screaming its right of way discordantly, rattling noisily and panting furiously, regardless of all comfort but its own, scattering dust and evil smell on all behind it.

Now in the East, wealth has never been regarded as the standard of social' consideration; on the contrary, the gathering of wealth was the work of the third caste, not of the second nor of the highest. The warrior and the teaching castes had not the duty of gathering and holding wealth. The warrior had to be generous and splendid. You may still find in India an immense display of wealth in rulers and Princes on State occasions; but go into their houses when no great ceremony is going on, mingle with them in their domestic life, and you will find there a simple life - splendour for the ceremony of the rank, simplicity for the service in the home. And when from the warrior caste with its public splendour you pass on to the class of learning, then wealth is marked as a disgrace, not as reason for pride. "The wealth of a teacher is his learning", it is written. And social consideration you must remember, has gone to the teacher, not to the millionaire, so that the millionaire and the Prince alike bow down at the feet of the half naked but learned man. That gives an entirely different standard of social life, and it works effectively even now, with all the changes that have come over Indian life. The ordinary round of living, so much alike in the different classes, draws these different classes together in a way that is never dreamed of in the West. You send for a man in India to sell you a shawl. He comes into your room and sits down on a carpet near you. He plays with your children; he talks with you as friend with friend, until the coolie comes along with the shawls for you to choose from. He would never dream of taking what is here called a liberty; he is too well-mannered.

To meet you in that way is not taking a liberty, but the recognition of a common human life. And so right through; and inasmuch as the clothing and the food are very much alike in the different classes, save where western influence has spread, there is not the same bitterness and jealousy as you find in the West, where the life of the poor is compulsorily simple, and the life of the rich luxurious and complicated. Both alike in their home will wear but a single cloth - finer in one case than in the other, but still the simple common garment worn in similar fashion; both sit down to their meals in similar ways, and the difference of the meals is not so great as you might think. These forces it is which make the general refinement of the people to be noticed in India. You may meet a man who is but a labourer, but his manners will be the manners of a gentleman.

A gentleman gives a play in his house, and any one may walk in from the street and share the amusement; part of the hall is kept for the invited guests; the uninvited crowd outside this, perfectly well-mannered and content. You find refinement there, because the standard for all is so much alike in those outward things. To live luxuriously means to live in the western way, and among the bulk of the people it is rather a reproach than a praise, although there is a growing desire to imitate, which is threatening largely to corrupt the old simplicity of the Indian life.

Now that simplicity of material life which lays stress on knowledge, character, service, instead of on wealth, how well it would be for western nations if that also made its way to some extent among them ! The frightful competition, the multiplication of endless articles of luxury, the crowding of houses with useless furniture, and the heaping on that furniture of still more useless knickknacks, so that when you go into a room it is more like a bazaar than a room - all these things you see on every side do not tend to beauty but only to ostentation. It is the vulgarising of the whole of the peoples, and the dragging them down to a lower plane of life. It means increasing competition, increasing struggle.

It means the growing poorer of the poor, while the wealthy become wealthier; for it means the turning of labour into useless channels, the multiplication of new wants and the devisal of new objects to meet those wants, until all life grows complex and overburdened. And while I would not ask that every life should be as simple as the best Indian life, I do say that it would be well for England, and well for all the western nations, if those who alone can do it - the wealthy and the highly placed, especially the highly placed, even more than the wealthy - followed a noble simplicity and a dignified beauty of life, which would encourage true art but discourage idle show, and replace ostentation by beauty, and undue luxury by simplicity.

Now, to come back to my starting-point. Those ideals of the East were in danger of perishing. Humanity cannot afford to let them die. Western energy, western initiative, western willingness to bear responsibility, are all good for eastern life; but the West has also much to learn from the East as well as much to teach, and the danger was lest the growing power of the West in the East should kill out those great ideals which change men's attitude to the world and to life as a whole. And if the balance is being redressed today, if on land and sea an eastern nation is conquering a western, it is because the West will only learn to respect where armed force can hold its own against the West, and eastern ideals have no chance of anything save contempt and despisal until they are lifted on high in a hand that can wield the sword, and show itself as strong on the field of battle as it is in the realm of mind.

Europe and India

Even in a question seemingly remote from India — the *building* of a *United States of Europe, Dr. Besant saw India's release as a vital factor. In a lecture given 2 October 1927 on a Federation* of *European States, she said:*

> Soon I am going back to India, to strive there to increase the movement for India's freedom. That has

> a great part in this future, because as long as India is outside, a subject Nation, a War of colour may break out at any moment — the most disastrous War to which any civilization can be exposed. Before we can look for the United States of Europe we must make friends with our coloured brothers everywhere; and India is the one place where that is at once possible, because she is within the Realm of what should be the great British Commonwealth of Free Nations instead of an Empire ruling over a subject people.. . . — *The Future* of *Europe*

A Lesson in Commonwealth Building

To govern a great country like India by a Parliament over here [in England] is practically impossible. It is too clumsy an instrument for the ruling of such people. But if you would, build up in India a great Council, composed of the wisest and most thoughtful of her own people; if you would take the advice of her best administrators in Indian States, her own sons; if you would place in such a Council her greatest feudatory Chiefs; if such a Council of all that is wisest and noblest in India were gathered round the Viceroy, who should hold his post, not as the reward for political service here, but because he knows and understands India, or, still better, appoint as Viceroy a Prince of the Imperial House; if you would leave him there for a greater space of time and not make him work in a breakneck hurry to get something done; then there would be a brighter hope on the Indian horizon. This can only be done by understanding Indian feelings and not by ignoring them, by trying to sympathise with Indian customs and not by despising them. Along these lines lies the salvation of India and of England alike, and it is this which I recommend to your most thoughtful consideration.— Lecture delivered 1902, *Speeches and Writings of Annie Besant*

Case for India

[The Presidential Address Delivered by Annie Besant at the Thirty-Second Indian National Congress Held at Calcutta 26th December 1917]

Fellow-delegates and Friends,

Everyone who has preceded me in this Chair has rendered his thanks in fitting terms for the gift which is truly said to be the highest that India has it in her power to bestow. It is the sign of her fullest love, trust, and approval, and the one whom she seats in that chair is, for his year of service, her chosen leader. But if my predecessors found fitting words for their gratitude, in what words can I voice mine, whose debt to you is so overwhelmingly greater than theirs? For the first time in Congress history, you have chosen as your President one who, when your choice was made, was under the heavy ban of Government displeasure, and who lay interned as a person dangerous to public safety.

While I was humiliated, you crowned me with honour; while I was slandered, you believed in my integrity and good faith; while I was crushed under the heel of bureaucratic power, you acclaimed me as your leader; while I was silenced and unable to defend myself, you defended me, and won for me release. I was proud to serve in lowliest fashion, but you lifted me up and placed me before the world as your chosen representative. I have no words with which to thank you, no eloquence with which to repay my debt.

My deeds must speak for me, for words are too poor. I turn your gift into service to the Motherland; I consecrate my life anew to her in worship by action. All that I have and am, I lay on the Altar of the Mother, and together we shall cry, more by service than by words:

Vande Mataram.

There is, perhaps, one value in your election of me in this crisis of India's destiny, seeing that I have not the privilege to be Indian-born, but come from that little island in the northern seas which has been, in the West, the builder-up of free institutions. The Aryan emigrants, who spread over the lands of Europe, carried with them the seeds of liberty sown in their blood in their Asian cradle-land. Western historians trace the self-rule of the Saxon villages to their earlier prototypes in the East, and see the growth of English liberty as up-springing from the Aryan root of the free and self-contained village communities.

Its growth was crippled by Norman feudalism there, as its millennia-nourished security here was smothered by the East

India Company. But in England it burst its shackles and nurtured a liberty-loving people and a free Commons' House. Here, it similarly bourgeoned out into the Congress activities, and more recently into those of the Muslim League, now together blossoming into Home Rule for India. The England of Milton, Cromwell, Sydney, Burke, Paine, Shelley, Wilberforce, Gladstone; the England that sheltered Mazzini, Kossuth, Kropotkin, Stepniak, and that welcomed Garibaldi; the England that is the enemy of tyranny, the foe of autocracy, the lover of freedom, that is the England I would fain here represent to you today. Today, when India stands erect, no suppliant people, but a Nation, self-conscious, self-respecting, determined to be free; when she stretches out her hand to Britain and offers friendship not subservience; cooperation not obedience; today let me: western-born but in spirit eastern, cradled in England but Indian by choice and adoption: let me stand as the symbol of union between Great Britain and India: a union of hearts and free choice, not of compulsion: and therefore of a tie which cannot be broken, a tie of love and of mutual helpfulness, beneficial to both Nations and blessed by God.

Ideal of Duty

We have met together this evening in order to celebrate the anniversary — a double anniversary, I may say — the annual meeting of the Srinivasa Mandirani on the one side and the anniversary of Sri Ramanuja on the other. Especially is it my duty to urge upon you tonight that sympathy, that help — both pecuniary and moral — which an institution like the Srinivasa Mandiram has a right to expect from a public so intelligent and so wealthy as that of Bangalore and Mysore. You have here in your midst an Institution of a kind that links together the religion of your ancestors with methods of work which meet the needs of the present day. Around the Temple, as in older days, various useful activities are gathered. You have heard from the report of the gatherings of ladies — educational and social — that form part of the work of the Institution: you have heard of the Orphanage—too little supported unfortunately —which seeks to train to useful manhood, some of the children who are left, without the help of fathers and mothers, to the mercy of the world; and this, with the Library—one of the most important instruments of adult education, with the Reading Boom, open as you have heard, to thousands and used both for amusement and instruction — with all these gathered round a Hindu Temple, sorely there ought not to be need to plead with any words for this.

It should plead for itself, by its utility and its beneficence, and yet it seems as though the work in itself was not sufficiently eloquent to move the hearts and to open the purses of those amidst whom and for whose benefit it, is carried on. It is for that reason that I have been asked to come here and see whether spoken words may do what silent work does not seem strong enough to bring about. And I would fain win your sympathy and cooperation, and ask you that this work which has been going on amongst you for some six-and-twenty years, should not be allowed to languish for want of the support to which it has a righteous claim. Quite truly, in the report, it was said that religion and the secular work of life ought not to be separated one from the other. You can no more separate religion from life than you can separate the spirit from the body and expect the body to remain alive.

The religion of a people is the source of life, out of which must inevitably flow everything that is useful and beneficial to the community; and if there be one religion in the world which has the right to call upon its children for support and help, it is that ancient religion — the Sanathana Dharma — to which the vast majority in this ancient country belong. This ancient religion, the religion of Hinduism, has the noble end and aim which 1 have just named — the Sanathana Dharma — the teaching of the ancient Dharma that is of value today, not only to India, as some might imagine, but to the whole of the modern world. There are difficulties confronting the nations today, alike in the East and in the West. There are problems clamouring for solution in every civilized country and on the solution of these problems the whole future of modern civilization depends.

Among all the religions of the world, there is none which has so bound up in itself the private life of the individual with the public life of the nation and the State, as the religion of the Sanathana Dharma, which has laid down at once a polity and a social organisation of which the foundations are eternally true, and which only needs today new applications to meet the new needs of life. I want, if I can, this evening very briefly to show you how an Institution such as you have here, based on the fundamental ideas of the Sanathana Dharma, trying to apply itself to modern needs, is one which is really based on truth not only here, but everywhere else; and just in proportion as you of this ancient faith can realise its value and live its truth, so the whole world will look to India for guidance, so the whole world will become grateful to India as the preserver of the life of religion. I am not specially concerned with the small details of the Sanathana Dharma. It is the broad outlines that I want to remind you of, in order that you may realise the answer which they contain to the pressing needs of our day. First of all you will notice — when you compare the fundamental idea of the Sanathana Dharma with that of modern Western life — that two ideals are held up by the one and by the other, of which the Eastern is the idea of *duty*, and the Western that of *rights*. Now, on the difference between those two fundamental conceptions of human organisation, of national life, the whole of the future will turn.

As you know, the fundamental thought of the people of the East has been the thought embodied in that one word *Dharma*. Every man has his Dharma. But what does Dharma mean? It means the obligations, into which every man is born, the obligations which surround him from the moment of his birth. The obligations to the family, the obligations to the community, the obligations to the nation, these are the *Dharma* into which every human being comes by the gateway of birth. It is not an arbitrary thing but a natural one. It is not a thing which is created, but it is a thing which comes out of the long course of evolution. And out of that fundamental idea of Dharma comes the thought that the first thing in human life which makes it possible is the fact that obligation is recognised and righteously discharged.

When the baby is born into the family helpless, unable to feed itself, lying there without strength, without ability, naked, feeble, what is it that preserves the life of the babe ? It is the duty of the mother and of the father, the duty of the elder to the younger, the sense of obligation which surrounds, helps, guards and preserves the babe through the years of childhood and of youth; out of that discharge of duty to the child grows the obligation of the child to the family and the community. The elders guard the child in infancy. The child in its manhood must repay the obligations in its turn. Thus you come to the idea of Manu of the debts which every man is bound to pay; the debt to the *Devas* for giving him the whole of the natural advantages, the whole of the gifts of nature by which alone life is possible; the debt to the ancestors whose labours he has inherited, and by the fruits of whose progress his life is rendered possible today; his debt to the human beings around him; to the animals below him; his debt to the Sages of the past, all these he cornea into; they make the obligations into which he is born, which he must pay back by the useful life of the man the father and the citizen. Out of that idea of human duty, oat of that recognition of human obligation, out of the realisation that we are beings on whom duty has a claim — out of that grows the stability and the orderly progress of human society.

Now, in the West, another idea grew up which is really less than two centuries old — it is the idea that the human being is not a part of an organisation but is an isolated individual, that he stands alone and apart, and that the fact of birth clothes him with certain rights. The "declaration of the rights of man," the famous historical episode, sums up in a single statement that modern idea of human and national life. According to that, society is not based on a common obligation; it is based on the inherent right? of the individual which he may enforce by any means in his power. Law is only binding, because people have accepted it and consented to it, and not because it is based on nature and expresses the Divine Will. Kings, according to this, rule not by the grace of God, but only by the acceptance of the people.

Everything is based on the idea of the right of the individual, which he only yields partially in order that he may enjoy the remainder the more fully. His interests are antagonistic to the interests of others, instead of being common and universally binding upon all. This idea has grown and spread during the last 150 years. The result has been continual struggle, disturbance and difficulty. The assembly of the notion is no longer the representative of the nation as a whole, but merely of a body of interests, one conflicting with the other. The members of the modern Houses of Legislature do not represent the common interests of the whole nation, and so, you have the modern struggle, the modern turmoil, the modern quarrels and the danger of the dissolution of the modern civilization.

But, strangely enough, there has come in the West a reinforcement of the Eastern ideal. Science has grown up and science has studied nature. Instead of manufacturing paper; Constitutions and imaginary rights of man, science has declared that human beings, like all other things, are the result of evolution, and that individuality is subordinate to the common good, and the benefit of a party is subordinate to the good of the whole. Science is again declaring that society is an organism, and not a body of people based on an imaginary contract. Science is declaring, again, one life, us religion has always been declaring it; and just as Hinduism has proclaimed the one Life, the universal Spirit, and *therefore* the solidarity of man, so is modern science declaring one life and one consciousness in all, and, therefore, that society is a growing organism, in which everyone has duties growing out of his life in the social unity. Thus, from the West is coming the reinforcement of the ancient theory of Dharma of the East and it is for the East to proclaim now the predominance, the superiority of an organisation that demands from every man discharge of duty, and to realise that on that discharge alone, the whole wellbeing of society depends But that is not the only vitalising influence which the Sanathana Dharma exercises on the world. It proclaims also the necessity of *Order.*

There again Western Science is beginning to strengthen the Eastern religion. Science also proclaims Law and Order as the essential conditions of progress. Science has discovered that only' by order is it possible for humanity to evolve. Of all the codes of human life that have ever been given to the world, that code which is known by the name of Manu — the great Law-giver — is the most orderly and the most perfect in its arrangement. Here is another gift that you have in your hands to give to the Western world.

After the idea of Dharma, what are the next ideas that come forward in the Hindu polity? The next idea is that all mankind is divided into two enormous groups: one walking on the path of pursuit, the *Pravritti Marga* — the path of going forth; and the other, that of those who are turning their faces homeward, that are treading the *Nivritti Marga.* How does this apply to human life? It shows us that the ordinary life of man, the common life of every day is but a part of the divinely ordained evolution by which the progress of humanity is governed; and on the path of going forth, the *Pravritti Marga,* are laid down the rightful objects of all human effort. First comes the Dharma that I have spoken of, the duty that guides and limits; and then *Artha* — possessions in the widest sense, all that the world has to give and all that man is able to possess.

Man, according to Hindu Dharma is not to be an ascetic while he is treading the *Pravritti Marga.* He is told on the contrary, that the enjoyments of possessions, the gathering of wealth progress in worldly matters, all belong rightfully and usefully to that path of pursuit. Those who know the Hindu Dharma will realise that this is so, and that, in modern India, much confusion has arisen, with the result that this teaching is for the most part forgotten. Modern India has talked too much of the path of return — the *Nivritti Marga* — quite forgetting that, that is the path for the few, while the path of forthgoing is the path for the many. They forget that Manu laid down for his children, the pursuit of possessions and the enjoyment of pleasure *Artha* and *Kama* are the objects of the path of pursuit limited and guided by Dharma. How much more wise was the ancient Lawgiver than are many of our modern teachers, those who would have every man an ascetic, those who declare that renunciation is the only rightful path of human life.

Manu, the Lawgiver, is the wisest of the Divine rulers of man, and Manu realised that, for national prosperity, effort and enjoyment were needed; that it was right that those who Were evolving should evolve their faculties by effort and by enjoyment, and so possessions and pleasure were made part of the path of foregoing. And the great masses of the people were pointed to that as the path by which progress was to be made. Only when a man has trodden that path, only when he has developed high intelligence; only when he has developed unselfishness and the pure love of God, then he is ready to turn his face homeward and tread the path of renunciation. Then it is that *Bhakti,* the love of God, takes the place of *Kama*— the love of the objects of desire.

Then it is that the *Siddhis,* and the powers that they give, take the place of the worldly possessions, which are to be used only for the benefit of man and not for the gain of the possessor. Then it is that, instead of the outward law of Dharma imposing duty from without, there comes *Mukti,* the freedom of the Self-made manifest, who needs no law from without, he cause he realises his divinity, and, forsaking all Dharma, be becomes one with the Supreme Being, and the Divine Will is his. Such is the course of human life according to Manu, balanced, rational and useful for all. No asceticism, premature and therefore useless, but the full development of faculties; only when these have been developed may come the turning home, the treading of the path to liberation. Step by step, in orderly and progressive fashion, Manu bids man tread the path of human life.

The last of the great principles given by Manu for the evolution of man is what is called the *Varnashrama; varna,* the stage of the human soul, the ego, the division of men into classes according to their characteristics; and *ashrama,* the stages of the individual life through which each should repeatedly pass.

Now, much is said for and against caste— something in its favour by those who know the turmoil of classes in the West, something against it by those in India who feel its barriers rather than its value, and resent the privileges claimed by some became duty has been forgotten by these while only privileges are claimed. And yet, rightly looked at, that four-fold division brings a detailed answer to the problems of human life aforementioned. What is the first problem that is pressing on every nation ?' That of the education of the young. There is not an assembly in the world from the Parliament of Great Britain to the Legislative Council of the Viceroy down to the smallest Municipality that has to guide the welfare of a part of the community — there is not one that is not standing puzzled and bewildered before the great problem of the education of the people. How should that be solved ? There is one way — though no public leader yet has suggested it — that has within it the power of solution, and that is by the recognition of real castes and among them the caste of teachers. Your Dharma as Brahmanas — those of you who are Brahmanas — is not the gatherings of wealth and the holding of places of power; but the gathering of knowledge and the imparting of that knowledge to the people. If the Brahmanas would only do that duty as Brahmanas, then there would be no educational problems in India today. But the Brahmanas, instead of doing their duty by imparting instruction, are busy in administering justice — which is properly the function of the Kshatriya; they are busy gathering wealth — which is properly the duty of the Vaishya.

Worldly men rebel against the Brahmana because he has forgotten his duty and no longer fills his proper position in the State. If we had true Brahmanas in India, all educational problems would be solved; for there would be Brahmanas in every village and every village would have its teachers, and then education would be given as duty, as in the older time, and not for money as at present. You may say: "This a very fine idea, but how are you going to persuade your Brahmana caste to give up all power and make itself available to promote the welfare of the people ?" I don't expect to get it from the grown up men, those who are middle-aged and mature, those who ate old and Hardened by the life of the world; and I am sure no words of mine would move them to have recourse to the path of renunciation which is the path of the Brahmana.

But I have hope in the younger men of India, who are growing up today in schools and colleges. I have hope in those sons of: India, who are vowing themselves to the public weal, and are ready to labour for the public good. I believe that we shall see growing up a new Brahmana caste, a caste which will be known by quality more than by birth, and by characteristics more than by outward marks, a class that will see the glory of sacrifice, a class that will realise the happiness of renunciation; these young men, full of enthusiasm, full of passionate devotion, who have in them the passion of self-devotion, which ought to be the mark of a Brahmana, in these is my hope, and i believe that we shall find actually growing up in India an order of young men who, between the time when College life ends and the householders' life begins, will give themselves up to some years of service to the welfare of the nation, and give that service to the masses of the people in order to elevate, guide and inspire them It is on the young men of India that I place my hope for the redemption of the masses of India from ignorance and degradation.

And *so*, when it is realised that the problems of Government, the problems of legislation, the problems of the administration of justice, the problems of the Army and of the Navy, and of the Police, are all problems that belong to the old Mann's ideal of the Kshatriya Caste; when it is realised that the Kshatriyas are the defenders and guardians of the nation, that it is on them that the burden of guiding the nation should fall as a matter of duty; then we shall have growing up a caste of Kshatriyas, educated for their work, and capable of performing it most efficiently. Then we shall see disappearing all discontent, arising from the oppression of the people by any of those who carry on the nation's working to day. For instance, let me speak of the Police. These are fundamentally a part of the great Kshatriya caste by their office. We know bow many complaints are made in India against men taken from the lower grades of society, who are invested with authority they are constantly tempted to misuse.

If we realise that, for public service, training in youth is necessary; if we realise that those who are to take the varied Offices in the State, even the lowest of them, should be trained for those Offices in youth; if it were understood that, when a man joins the Police he should have been trained for his responsibilities previously; if it is only realised that he should have been trained here as the Police are trained in England; if it were only realised that for purposes of public service, he should be the friend of the common people; how different would be the feelings of people in India towards the Police and how willing would be the help given by the ordinary citizen whenever he was asked for it the name of Law? It is when you realise the functions necessary for the wellbeing of a community, that you realise the wisdom of the ancient Lawgiver. How be made the functions separate in order that each class might discharge the same well! The teacher was one class; the warrior, the protector, another; the merchant, a third class, the makers of wealth, in order that thereby the nation as a whole might prosper.

Looking for a moment at modern India, such a sketch as I am giving to you now seems an impossible Utopia. But nothing is impossible; for thought creates action, and that which a man thinks inevitably comes to pass. We want to hold up the old ideal;

not to force any man to follow it, if he does not see it to be admirable. We hold it up, that all men may see it. It will gradually dominate the public mind and bring about its realisation. When we are able to reform a caste of teachers, a caste of legislators and administrators of justice, a caste of those who organise industry and accumulate wealth, a class of manual labourers who follow a particular craft or a particular art which is needed for the welfare of the people—all equally honourable and equally necessary, and all equally essential to the nation's welfare; and when the old idea of duty returns and each knows his duty and does it; then shall we again make the golden age, and a happier day shall break upon, our earth.

For this is what the West is looking for today. It realises its own turmoil. It realises its own dislocation. It realises that constant struggle cannot he the natural and the titling state of man. It is gradually despairing of the feasibility *of* its methods, and is looking elsewhere for light. Where should the light come from ? From the East, where the sun is ever shining, where the laws of the Great Lawgiver were given to all his Aryan children, not only to those who settled in India, but to those who wandered Westward and lost their way to their father's home. So, here in India, this ideal can again be restored, adapted to modern ways, flexible, as it was in the older time. If, as in the past, men's qualities were regarded as well as their family, then family would take its rightful place as one of the factors in human evolution, which is largely dependent on physical heredity; but today the Ego that comes into any particular body is often unsuitable; because Dharma has been neglected, there is confusion of caste today.

Because the higher castes have not done their duty, physical heredity is no longer a guide to caste as it was in the older days, and yet physical heredity is a law of nature and cannot wisely be ignored in natural life Sometimes, men wonder how all the sub-castes have sprung up. They have often sprung up by natural differentiation in the quality of the physical body which follows a special occupation of brain or hand. There is no caste in England, but you find that in Lancashire, the spinners and weavers of cotton cloths have grown up so much in families, that employers of labour give larger wages to a boy or girl coming from a weaving family than they will give to a similar boy or girl coming from some part of the country, where weaving is not a hereditary occupation That is the way in which nature works. That is the justification of family trades. Only it has grown far too rigid here in India, and intermarriage and interdining are forbidden between sub-castes. This is of course one of the things that will have to disappear; for though physical heredity give variety to the community as a whole, yet it is not necessary constantly to intermarry too closely and thus weaken that strength which you desire la maintain.

Complicated are the questions of national life, and complicated are the problems to be dealt with. But it is in that ancient Law, in the Sanathan Dharma, that answers to the modern problems are to be found. But remember that, according to Manu himself, when circumstances change, the old principles are to be adapted to those changed conditions; for which reason customs should be kept flexible, instead of being inflexible as they are in the India of today. Much lies in the hands of educators of the young. All those who follow the ancient rules should bring up the young to work for the reform of India, to make her what she should be, flexible, elastic, adapting herself to the needs of modern life; but in all they should hold firm to the fundamental principles, for they are the conditions of national prosperity. They hold, as I said, the solution of national problems.

Now, at the end, to go back to the place from which I started.

It is your duty as Hindus, as citizens, to help every effort in your midst which is based on the old principles and try to adapt them to the changed conditions of human life. Stretch out your hand ID help to all efforts for human improvement; strengthen those of your fellow-citizens whom you find able to guide the young and help the old along the path that combines modern progress with the ancient wisdom. And among those efforts, do not forget that we have gathered this evening in order that we may help and strengthen the hands of your fellow citizen in the noble work that he is carrying on, thus making it possible to gather together here the orphans that ore helpless so that they may be guided and disciplined in their early life. Join together in the work which will bring credit and glory to your country and do not let it be said of the town of Bangalore, that when there is a good thing in its midst it is allowed to starve; if it is allowed to perish and then rebuilt, much labour and difficulty will be required to do that which, comparatively easily, might have been carried to success by a little timely and united effort.

Speech at Manchester, UK

When we recognise that unity of all living things, then at once arises the question - how can we support this life of ours with least injury to the lives around us; how can we prevent our own life adding to the suffering of the world in which we live?

We find amongst animals, as amongst men, power of feeling pleasure, power of feeling pain; we see them moved by love and by hate; we see them feeling terror and attraction; we recognise in them powers of sensation closely akin to our own, and while we transcend them immensely in intellect, yet, in mere passionel characteristics our natures and the animals' are closely allied. We know that when they feel terror, that terror means suffering. We know that when a wound is inflicted, that wound means pain to them. We know that threats bring to them suffering; they have a feeling of shrinking, of fear, of absence of friendly relations, and at once we begin to see that in our relations to the animal kingdom a duty arises which all thoughtful and compassionate minds should recognise - the duty that because we are stronger in mind than the animals, we are or ought to be their guardians and helpers, not their tyrants and oppressors, and we have no right to cause them suffering and terror merely for the gratification of the palate, merely for an added luxury to our own lives.

. . there is one other thought closely allied to this. What of our duties to our fellow-men? And here I appeal particularly to my own sex, because women are supposed to be rather the standard in the community of refinement, of gentleness, of compassion, of tenderness, of purity. But no one can eat the flesh of a slaughtered animal without having used the hand of a man as slaughterer. Suppose that we had to kill for ourselves the creatures whose bodies we would fain have upon our table, is there one woman in a hundred who would go to the slaughterhouse to slay the bullock, the calf, the sheep or the pig? . . . But if we could not do it, nor see it done; if we are so refined that we cannot allow close contact between ourselves and the butchers who furnish this food; if we feel that they are so coarsened by their trade that their very bodies are made repulsive by the constant contact of the blood with which they must be continually besmirched; if we recognise the physical coarseness which results inevitably from such contact, dare we call ourselves refined if we purchase our refinement by the brutalisation of others, and demand that some should be brutal in order that we may eat the results of their brutality? We are not free from the brutalising results of that trade simply because we take no direct part in it.

Indian Commerce

In opening the National College of *Commerce, Madras, Dr. Besant said:*

It is the belief of those who are working in this movement for National Education that the Indian ideal of civilization is the highest that the world has yet known, that in the recognition of knowledge as greater than wealth you have the proclamation of the true nobility of mind, that when knowledge, wedded to emotion and recognising the unity of the race, becomes wisdom, then it is that you have enshrined in the civilization the hope of the coming world.

We see breaking down among us in western lands the civilization which is founded essentially on combat. We shall see arising with its leadership in the East the civilization which is founded on unity and not on struggle, which realises that men are brothers more than they are rivals, that they are helpers more than they are combatants, and that while the law of the struggle of the survival of the fittest is the law of evolution for the brute, the law of self-sacrifice is the law of evolution for the man. It is one of our objects to maintain the great ideal that man becomes more and more human as he becomes a helper and server of his fellow-creatures and his country, that the greatest virtue of human life is to help those who are weaker than yourselves, and that the glory of life lies in service and not in rule. That has always-been the ideal in India, and ... in the past of India that rule has been supreme. .. . Although in India, among its many different forms of Government, you do find "absolute monarchy," yet the word *absolute* is much out of place, because above the monarchy there was always Dharma, the divine law, and that law, if the monarch failed in his duty, destroyed both himself and his house. ...

In other parts of India, where the monarch was surrounded by a council, those who are represented by the commercial ranks of today were the most numerous among the councillors of the monarch. According to ancient code it was not the Brahmana who ruled; he was the teacher and not the ruler. The direct ruler was the Kshattriya and the majority of his councillors were drawn from the Vaishya caste; and rightly, because in the hands of the council lay the guidance of the State: because it was among those who had to do with the commercial and industrial welfare of the Nation that the King's councillors were most rightly and naturally found. So, you realise that in the past organisation of India you can learn lessons for the organisation of today.

In this College of Commerce we shall have growing up as we hope, not the clerks in government offices, not those who are struggling for that poor and difficult livelihood, but those who are able to guide the commerce and industry of India, so that India shall make her mark among the Nations of the world. By knowledge, careful detailed knowledge alone, can the merchant community take its right place among the Nations of our modern world. They must know the history of the Nations, they must know the theories of the State, they must realise the laws of economics, science, and apply them to their own country. To learn to be great merchants is to master the Science of Nations as regards the supply and demand for all that makes life healthy, happy, and beautiful. It was to the merchant class of old that all the other orders looked for sustenance and help, and their marvellous charity has overflowed the whole of the land and still exists to render fertile the desert places.. . . We may hope that here we shall train up men of whom India will be proud in the future as great leaders in commerce and trade.

If you remember that in the older days no Indian merchant was asked for any receipt, that his word was his bond, that in the banks, nothing like what we have as the legal receipt of modern times was demanded — so high was commercial honour — you will realise that in the commerce of today India has a lesson to teach to the world, to show that the gaining of money does not mean anything unscrupulous, anything dishonourable, any taking undue advantage of the weaker, for the Indian ideal of commerce was high and noble: it was based upon truth; it was covered with honesty, clothed in honesty as a garment; and I hope that the young men who are coming here will bring back the ancient spirit into the struggles of modern life.

Our object then is to give the best that at present can be given to strengthen the eastern civilization and to keep its characteristic features, and for this particular College to help forward above all others the commerce, the industry, the trade, the many occupations on all of which depends the material progress of the country. In doing this it is no selfish work to which our students are called, for it is theirs to show that in all matters that make the greatness of human life, India has more lessons to teach than India has to learn, and progress in her own civilization means the lifting of the civilizations of the world on to a higher level. For India is a supremely spiritual Nation, and, as such, she cannot rise for herself alone; she must raise up with her the other Nations of the world, so that all must become more spiritual and nobler, because India takes her own place in the forefront of the world's civilization. Much has been lost to the world by the partial submergence of Indian ideals. Ours is to raise those ideals again in the face of the world, so that all may realise how much the Motherland has to give, and how she will enrich the world, even the western world that has impoverished her so sorely.

I would ask you for your sympathy, for kindly thought does much and in the beginning of a movement, it begins like a tiny seed but hopes to grow into a great banyan tree, with its branches spread over the whole of the land, with its roots struck deep in the soil and the heart of the Motherland.

—11 July 1918, *New India*

Social Life

Manu on the Need for Change

It is necessary in the course of evolution that every living religion shall adapt itself to the change of the conditions of the times in which it finds itself. A religion which cannot adapt itself is one whose work is practically over... . There is nothing which is clearer and plainer, when we study the history of India, than that from time to time great changes have come over her civilization, that she has been able to % assimilate new thought and new ideas without losing her own fundamental type.... In the closing words of the *Institutes* of *Manu,...* the great Law-Giver, conscious of the changes which inevitably would be brought about in the course of millennia, advised that when the times had changed, and those laws were no longer useful for the community, a council of learned men should be gathered together, who should make the changes which were necessary for the welfare of the people. . . .

The difficulty of anyone who speaks about Social Reform today is that it is taken for granted that the present views are orthodox, that they are the traditions and views of Indians coming out of the past, whereas they are really modern, and not orthodox restrictions. In the old times there were continual changes, the Nation suiting itself to the conditions of the times and not permitting itself to be bound in the fetters which modem ignorance has put around the limbs of modern Hindus.

—Lecture delivered 1914

Eastern Age-old Hygiene

Superstition can only be destroyed by knowledge, not by abuse. Theosophy gave that knowledge. It laid stress on the things in religion which were based on natural laws, and so justified very often some old custom that otherwise would have died away.. . Europe is rediscovering some of these very laws and scientific men are beginning to insist on the careful rules of hygiene and sanitation that our Manu had taught thousands of years ago. ... Some modern Hindus, not knowing either the ancient scriptures or modern science, scoff at these observances. Why, they say, insist on the Brahmanic superstition that the Brahmana alone should draw water from the village well, and pour it into the village pots brought for filling? And yet an English, Inspector travelling through these Provinces said that the custom checked disease, for you could take care of the one vessel and see that it was clean, whereas if any vessel, brought perhaps from a dirty house, were dipped into the well, the water would be made foul, disease would spread, and health be injured. It is silly to throw away these hygienic rules when Europe is rediscovering them. I know only one man in the West who is as careful as a Brahmana, and he is a doctor. He washes his hands before he eats, and when asked the reason, he answers: "Microbes." Such rules of caring for food-vessels are not superstition; they are good hygiene; we have been blamed for justifying them, but the more you disregard them the more disease will spread. And so with many other customs and ceremonies called superstitions by the ignorant.

—December 1909, The Theosophical Convention

Protection of Children

It is sometimes said that the position of women in a country marks the level of civilization to which the country has risen; but it seems to me that the position of the child even more marks the state of the community, and that where the children are not carefully nurtured and protected, there the nation cannot expect either the blessing of God or the respect of man.... The King is the father of every fatherless child, and the helpless and the suffering look to him for rescue and for compassion.... To the strong belong only Duties, to the weak alone belong Rights. Men and women have duties; children and animals have rights in every civilized community—the right to be protected, the right to be guarded, the right to be fed and clothed and shielded. If the tears of the little children, the groans of oppressed animals, if these ascend to God, they rot the foundation of a State and make hopeless the future of a nation. . .. Well is it written in a great Scripture of the Hindus that it is the sorrow of the weak that undermines the thrones of Kings.... Every one of mature age should be a father and a mother to the fatherless and the motherless of the community... .

I find cases here of young girls pledged in their girlhood, ere they knew the world, to the ruin of their womanhood in their maturity. .. . For nearly twenty years in this land I have worked and lived in public life and in home life with the educated Indians of the land; and I know I am speaking for them when I say that this shameful traffic is no part of Hindu civilization, and that Hindus are the first to desire that these little girls should be saved from the degradation that is implied in the word *Devadasis*—servants of God—prostituted to the vilest uses of human passion. It is those who belong to Hinduism who must take this shame away and sweep it from our Indian land.... Is it not written that the wife is the Goddess of the household, the Light of the home ? Every child who is ... pledged to shame might be a happy mother, and might be the light of husband and children in some respected Hindu home. Do you say that your own daughters are safe ? I tell you that every daughter bom of Hindu parents is your child, and you are bound to save and to protect her.... Public opinion must speak strongly; because there are so many matters that laws have to deal with, and unless they are supported by the public voice they are likely to be put aside....

Boys and girls are sent out into the street to beg, not for their own support—though that is sad and shameful enough — but in order to keep lazy elders, who out of the begging by the children make their miserable livelihood. ... Take the other cases where little girls, sent out to beg, pass well nigh inevitably into a life of shame.... These children when they are taken from the street can only be changed by education and by love. There is not one boy, however turbulent, in whom there is not the instinct of hero-worship which you should utilise for his salvation. If you take a so-called bad boy, shut him up in a house where he has no freedom, give him tasks and punish him when he fails, that boy will grow into a criminal and will be a curse to the community. Rather let some of the young among you — young, rich and idle — come forward and enrol yourselves as men who will look after these troublesome boys, who will play with them — and play better than they do — and so become heroes in their sight.

Draw out the love of the boy; there is no boy who has no love in his heart. Do not threaten the boy, do not punish him, but coax him and give him prizes, show him things that attract him, and then you will win him back. That is a splendid work, a work which each of you can do; but the danger is when each of you say: "It is not my duty; others will do it." So long as one child walks the Madras streets, helpless and miserable, so long as one boy causes terror to his neighbourhood, so long it is your duty and mine to bring forward the help that those helpless ones have a right to demand at our hands. It is thus that some of us have learnt the meaning of religion.

It is not religion simply to go to church or mosque or temple. That is good, but it is not the heart of religion. It is religion to help the little children; it is religion to wipe away the tears of the sorrowful; to nurse the sick; to comfort the afflicted; to make the world a better and a happier place, because you *are* living in it. In vain do you mark your foreheads, and in vain you wear the green turban of Mecca, which shows that you have been on pilgrimage to that holy post. The true religion is the serving of the helpless, and thus alone can man testify his faith in the eyes of God and man alike.... Sure am I of this, that as you help the helpless, so will stronger help come down to your own homes and lives. Oh! we are always ready to stretch out empty hands to God and the Angels above us; but full hands must be stretched out to those below us, otherwise the hands held upwards will ever remain unfilled, the cries unanswered from on high.

—Lecture delivered February 1913, *The Birth* of New *India*

Kindness to Younger Indian Citizens

I notice . .. the cruel hobbling which is used sometimes in the tying up of animals which are to be prevented from straying from the fields in which they are grazing, the hobbling especially of cattle that are driven along the roads I do not of course deny .. . that some form of restraint is necessary in order either to keep the animals within due bounds, or in some cases to prevent them from injuring passers-by on the roads. We know well enough here in India that the bull and the cow by the custom of thousands of years have been regarded as sacred animals, and the result of that is, for the most part, that they wander harmlessly and unfettered through the roads and through the streets.

In Banaras, where is my oldest Indian home, while walking through those narrow streets, we constantly have to push gently aside some bull that is let loose and that walks along the road taking grain at any shop he passes at his will, for none would deny to the Bull of Mahadeva that nourishment which his hunger craves; and a strange result is shown there in the feeling of the man to the bull and the bull to the man. A friend of mine was walking along waving carelessly a heavy stick, and a bull put down his head ready to charge. A shopkeeper called out: "Put down the stick, and the bull will not touch you." He at once dropped it and the bull walked quietly by. I mentioned this for a specific reason. The bull in western lands is a dangerous animal' and is always kept under restraint; but here he is allowed to wander freely at his will. Hence, when we see the creatures passing along the road with the head hobbled to the foot, so that every step of the animal is a difficult one, we may assume that generally the animal is dangerous and is thus hobbled for the sake of passers-by. But that is no reason why the hobbling should be cruel, and why every step should be made painful. The creature must be prevented from harming the human beings whom he passes without being practically tortured as he makes his way along the road.

I should like to draw .. attention ... to another point. . .. The donkey is an animal which is here very largely used for the carrying of burdens. There are two points with regard to that which it is the duty of every one of us to try to change: The first is the overloading, which is sometimes so extreme that if you walk behind the animal, generally very small in India, you will see those delicate legs bending under the weight of the burden that is being carried. The second thing is the way of loading.... We need some-clever person who will invent some way of loading the donkey which will not inflict constant pain; for if we look we see that the strap, which passes across behind to steady the load, is constantly cutting through the skin into the flesh. If you ask why this is done, you will be told: "Because the load does not balance." Then it is the duty of some inventive person ... to invent some kind of saddle or pad which will secure the load on the animal's back without mutilating it, as it is practically mutilated at the present time. . ..

In the West and in the East animals are looked upon differently. The Englishman treats his animals exceptionally well — the favourite dog, the favourite cat, and the favourite horse. These are practically members of the Englishman's home. The children play with them—sometimes a little too roughly, and then they are always tenderly rebuked. But many an Indian may say: "Yes, that is all very well, but you eat animals. How can you tell us that you love them ? "That is why I say that we need to try to understand each other The nations of the West, like the Aryans when they came first to India, are as a rule meat-eating nations, but they are just as tenderhearted to the animals in touch with them as those of the East, who would think it a sin to slay an animal... .

You will often find an Englishman sitting up all night by a sick horse or dog, nursing it as he would one of his own race, and trying to keep the life in it and to relieve it from pain... You will find that the Society for the Prevention of Cruelty to Animals is asking .. for a lethal chamber to be made for the painless killing of pariah dcgs. There again you have different lines of thinking, and sometimes they cause great mistake and misjudgement. The Englishman will say: "The Indian is cruel; he will not put a suffering animal out of its pain." The Indian answers: "You are cruel. What right have you to take away the life that you are not able to give." These are the differences between the two civilizations, and it is the duty of those who are living side by side to take the best of each and not to misjudge each other. . . .

Take one point which is not unimportant, and here I especially address my English brothers. In these large towns you will very often find that the animals used for draught purposes are miserable skeletons of cattle or they are mere apologies for cattle or horses, drawing their loads painfully along the streets. You say: "How cruel to underfeed and drive these wretched animals ! "But I say: "Yes, but look at the drivers also, and you will often find the ribs of the drivers as visible as those of the bullock or of the horse." Another point is that the carters are not always responsible for the overloading of the carts; and if the carters do not take these carts and keep the appointed time for the delivery of the load, they will be dismissed or fined, or punished in some way; so they flog the helpless animals in order that they may not lose the bread for wife and child. I am not saying this in order to stop any action which would check the underfeeding or ill-using. I say this only in order that you may remember sometimes the pitiful condition of the human beings, and not be too hard on man while you are trying to help the animal.. ..

Education is always better than punishment. Much of the cruelty is thoughtless. I have seen a man thrash a bullock and then, a few minutes afterwards, go up to it, and pat it, and give it food out of his hand. You will never succeed in stopping cruelty in this country, or in any other land, until every member of the community realises his duty to the animals that serve the community. Understand that to stop cruelty it is not enough to give to the Society Rs. 50 and then feel your conscience clear. It is the daily duty of each of you, whenever you see an act of cruelty, to stop and remonstrate with the man who has done it, and try to persuade him rather than threaten him.... If you are threatening, if you hold up the rod of the law, then the brain becomes bewildered and the heart terrified, then the argument and reasoning fail to move the culprit.. ..

There is not one person .. . who has it not as a religious and moral duty upon him to stop cruelty wherever he sees it. If you are determined it shall not be, cases of cruelty will no longer be found in this city. The fault is not so much with the ignorant foolish people who strike the animals they are driving. The fault is with us, with you and with me, who see an animal tortured and pass by on the other side, leaving the animal to suffer unregarded and uncared for. The man who is cruel needs to be helped *as* well as the animal who suffers. It is far worse to inflict cruelty than to suffer it and the man who tortures is an object of greater compassion even than the tortured animal. Indignation makes people forget that. But never yet was an evil cured by art evil. If you go in an angry mood yourself to rebuke an angry man, what does he say in his heart ? "You are angry, and I am angry and we use the same means to show the same feeling." But if you go up to him as a friend and brother, if you say to him: "My brother, that animal you are torturing has the same life as you and shares your own nature "; if you plead in this way instead of threatening, if you explain instead of menacing, then you have won a human heart as well as saved an animal, and the man will be tender in the future. Whereas if you attack him, he-will strike the animal again when you are out of sight and he is no longer afraid. There lies our path.

In a little Society we Theosophists have for the Protection of Animals, every member takes a pledge every morning that he will stop, or do his best to stop, any act of cruelty towards animals which he sees during the day. It is not necessary to enter a Society in order to make that promise to yourself, and to carry it out. But why should we do it ? We should do it not only because there is but One Life, and because that Life is wronged in every animal that is hurt. Not only because those who injure animals are injuring their Lord, but also because the whole level of a community depends on the human qualities that are developed in it; and compassion to the weak and the helpless is the quality that separates the man from the brute.. . .

You can do anything with an animal if you are good to it anything with an animal if you are kind. If you will not treat it as an infant soul put in your hand to care for, then you have no right to come into touch with this younger generation who, in the future, will stand where you are standing, and whose evolution you are delaying by cruelty or harshness. With terror you can do nothing either with the child or with the animal; but with love you can do everything. But love means patience, and we are more apt to be irritable than patient.

One other point I will venture to put to you although . .. it is going outside the line of ordinary thinking: Every man has around him a certain protective coating that keeps him safe from the many lives around, which might be hostile to himself. He walks, as it were, angel-guarded as long as he breathes the life of love, the love that is divine and 'makes all creatures friendly. But if you do a cruel thing to an animal, or slay an animal, you attach that animal to yourself by the link of fear and hatred. The animal cannot by itself do much. One animal's feelings are not much in this great world. You have done more by that act of cruelty; you have broken through the covering which keeps you safe from the evils around you. You have opened the door by your cruel act, and through that open door all the animal suffering in the world can pierce you; the one becomes a channel through which the whole can pour into you and affect you for evil. You will not believe it; I do not suppose most of you will; but you will remember it, and sometimes you may think of it.

And so I would ask you, friends, ... to go out as messengers of mercy, as messengers of love. Let every one, man or woman, feel his or her own duty, feel his or her personal responsibility; if you will check every act of cruelty you see, explain the wickedness of it and the harm it carries with it, then ... a year hence .. . your city will have become a city of love instead of one of much preventable suffering, and then you will feel that you are leading the higher life and are channels of mercy and not of suffering to the animal world.

—16 March 1910, *On the Prevention* of *Cruelty to Animals*

To Help the Miserable Myriads

Every competitive civilization has, as its base, a mass of poverty-stricken people on whose bowed-down shoulders the happier classes stand. In England some twenty or more years ago, they formed one-tenth of the population; that must now, I think, have been diminished by free and compulsory education. In India they form one-sixth of the population, and the country cannot rise into full National life until these are redeemed from their servitude and their disabilities are swept away. Every earlier civilization has perished, dragged down into the waters of the past by the weight of its submerged classes.

—1917, Theosophical Presidential Address

Therefore Fight, O' Arjuna

Courage, fearlessness, splendid generosity, throwing away of life in the defence of the weak and in the discharging of one's duties—that is the Dharma of the Kshattriya. His duty is to protect what is given him in charge against all aggression from without. It may cost him life, but never mind that. He must do his duty. To protect, to guard, that is his work. His strength is to be a barrier between the weak and the oppressive, between the helpless and those who would trample them under foot. Right for him the following of war and the struggle in the jungle with the wild beast. Because you do not understand what evolution is, and what the law of growth, you stand aghast at the horrors of war. But the great Rishis, who made this order, knew that a weak soul can never attain perfection. You cannot get strength without courage, and firmness and courage cannot be got without the facing of danger, and the readiness to throw away life when duty demands the sacrifice.

Our sentimental, weak-kneed, pseudo-moralist shrinks from that teaching. But he forgets that in *every* nation there are souls that need that training, and whose further evolution depends upon their success in attaining it. I appeal again to Bhishma, the incarnation of Dharma, and I remember what he said, that it is the duty of the Kshattriya to slay thousands of his enemies, if his duty in protection lies in that direction. War is terrible, fighting is shocking, our hearts revolt from it and we shrink before the anguish of mutilated and mangled bodies. To a great extent this is because we are utterly deluded by form. The one use of the body is to enable the life within it to evolve. But the moment it has learned all that body can give it, let the body break away, and' let the soul go free to take a new body that will enable it to manifest higher powers.... Does not the soul require a new body for its higher growth ? Let then the body go. This is the hard lesson the Kshattriya learns, and so he throws away his bodily life, and, in this throwing away, his soul gains the power of self-sacrifice, he learns endurance, fortitude, courage, resource, devotion to an ideal, loyalty to a cause, and he pays his body gladly as the price for these, the immortal soul rising triumphant and preparing for a nobler life.

Brethren, You are given a great opportunity which, rightly utilised, may carry you far. Learn through the present turmoil in India to distinguish the Real from the unreal, the underlying Truth from the veil of passing phenomena. The spiritual life is not disturbed by combat, if the combatant be free from hatred and anger, indifferent to success and failure, peaceful in the midst of strife, calm though surrounded by tumult, fighting for the Right, which is already conqueror in the higher world. Was not the great Scripture of the *Bhagavad-Gita* given "in the midst between two armies "? Was it not given by the yellow-robed Yogi to His disciple, and was He not in a high state of consciousness during the giving, while His strong hand was on the reins of the eager white warhorses, ready to plunge into the fray ? Did He not utter as the refrain of His matchless discourse: "Therefore fight, O Arjuna!" ? Will any dare to call the Lord of Yoga unspiritual, because He bade His beloved disciple engage in the strife which had been forced upon Him ? Therefore stand up, O children of Manu, followers of our great Warrior Master, the Rajput Chief of the

Morya clan, resolute to defend our righteous cause. "Taking as equal pleasure and pain, gain and loss, victory and defeat, gird yourselves for the battle; thus shall ye not incur sin." Ours in India is the glorious privilege of standing by . . . our true Leaders, in the day of reproach and imputed dishonour. I congratulate you, I congratulate myself, that we are found worthy to defend Their cause. —1912, *Presidential Address*

India of Tomorrow

It is not the right way now to tread only in the footprints of the past, simply to reintroduce what has been. Your duty is to be inspired by the same spirit that made the past great, and in that spirit to shape the form suitable for the India of tomorrow.. .. Trust to life, to the living spirit. We were not there to guide the life, when it made the glorious past. Life can be trusted, for it is divinely guided, and all we have to do is to cooperate with it... Study life's tendencies and work with them, but it is life that builds, not men... If a form does not succeed it will be broken; and you should be glad in the breaking of the useless form, as you should be glad in the form that means success. Failure often means winning, and it needs dozens, nay hundreds, of attempts before the perfect masterpiece shines out in full. Trust life; that is the great lesson for these days of change, for change is coming, change from every side. Those changes that are good will endure, and you must be very patient while they are in the making. Be full of hope and full of courage....

There is a new form to be built here, a form to be which has never yet been built, and that is India herself as one nation. As one nation, she exists in the world of mind. *As* one nation, she has never yet existed on the physical plane, but the day of her birth is near. Many States and Kings have been, many Maharajas, Rajas, and sometimes one Raja, great beyond his fellows, has held a wide imperial sway. But never yet has there been one India from North to South, from East to West. But she is coming. That one India, when she comes, will have her head crowned, with the Himalayas, and her feet will be bathed in the waters that wash the shores of Tuticorin; she will stretch out her right hand to Burma and Assam, and her left hand to Kathiawar and Baluchistan.

That India has to be born. How ? First, by believing in her with a strenuous faith, for faith is a mighty power; and then by thinking of her and aspiring after her as an ideal. For what a man thinks becomes actual in practice. And never yet was a nation born that did not begin in the spirit, pass to the heart and the mind, and then take an outer form in the world of men. That India, the sound of her feet is on the mountains, and soon the rising eastern sun shall glow upon her forehead. Already she is born in the mind of men.

I am an Indian

But let your thought for unity be potent and resolute; learn to drop sectarian divisions; learn to drop provincial divisions and animosities; leave off saying: "I am a Madrasi; I am a Punjabi; I am a Bengali; I am an upcountry man "; leave all that behind and teach your boys and girls to say, "I am an Indian." Out of the mouths of the children thus speaking shall be born the India of tomorrow. Many religions will grow within her: not only her own parent religion, but others too will be woven into her being. Hindu and Musalman must join hands, for both are Indians. Hindus, Musalmans, Parsis, Christians, must join hands, for all are Indians. In the India of the future, all men of every faith must join. If India is to be the spiritual light of the future, in her must be focussed the light that comes from every faith, until in the prism of India they are all united into the one light which shall flood with sunlight the world, and all lights shall blend in the Divine Wisdom. That is our work.

My Brothers, I am now talking to you, but this thing will not be made by talking. It is made by living. I would not dare to speak to you and offer you counsel if I did not strive to live that which I advise. Day by day, week by week, month by month, I strive to shape my life on the noble models which may serve the land, and in serving India will serve Humanity; for greater than any land is Humanity, and greater than any one people is the Race of whom all peoples are but branches; and if we have such hopes of future India, it is because we believe that her coming will be a new light to the world.... If India's humiliation has been, in a very real sense, the riches of the world—for this has been the means of spreading India's thoughts in the most widely-spoken tongue of the world; to the North and South, East and West, all round the habitable globe — what shall it be for Humanity when India herself in her new glory is bom into the world ?

India, from whose lips, in this land of the Rishis, came the religion that uplifts and spiritualises, the philosophy that illumines and the science that trains; India, from whose mind, throughout the world of mind, came those great systems of thought which are now recognised as the noblest products of the human intellect; India, whose feet once passed through many States, and made every one of them fertile, prosperous, and wealthy; India, who was perfect in spirit and mind; when that India is born into the full vision of the eyes of men, perfect in body, is it too much to say that her coming will be as life from the dead ? That is the glorious goal, for which we work; that is the splendid hope, that cheers our labour; that is the sublime aspiration, that rises perpetually to the ears of the Devas. For India's coming means the spiritualising of humanity; India's thinking means the lifting of thought on to a higher level; India's prosperity shall be the justification of religion, the justification of philosophy, as part of the life of a nation; and the world shall be redeemed from materialism, because India is awake.

—Lecture delivered 1910, in *The Birth* of *New India*

Aim at progress, my sons. Strive to make India's future worthy of her ancient greatness. Outgrow your fathers in knowledge, outstrip your elders in devotion. For the days of India's greatness are by no means over; her future shall be mightier than her mighty past. India shall wield a power greater than the Imperial, if only her people will realise her true strength and utilise it, leading a life in which Spirit shall guide and love shall inspire. Then indeed shall she be immortal. But if she deserts that ideal, and strives only for material gains, then shall she surely die, as all her contemporaries of the past have died....

—1911, *Central Hindu College*

India's future lies not in political greatness; India's future is as a spiritual nation, as the teacher of the world in spiritual truth... And so, looking forward and hoping, we see her awaking from the sleep of centuries, taking up again her ancient faith, taking up again her ancient religion, her ancient philosophy, her ancient literature; taking up again her place as evolver of the inner man, as teacher of the possibilities of the human soul, as leader of the way towards union with the higher nature, and, therefore, towards the higher and grander race that in days to come shall tread upon our earth. For the future is not with the things of the body; it is with the things of the soul.

The body perishes, but the soul is immortal. Civilizations rise and fail, but the spirit of man endureth for ever. Like that from which it springs, it is indivisible and immortal, unborn and undying, taking body after body as a garment and throwing them aside when they are worn and done with. That is the mission of India to the world, that teaching is the claim of India to the love and to the homage of mankind. And the ' day shall surely come when sleeping India shall awake and rise again amongst the people, and rise, not to lead them along the road of material domination, but along the road of spiritual triumph to union at last with the Supreme Goal.

—Lecture delivered, 6 November 1893

India's Mission among Nations

Every person, every race, every nation, has its own particular keynote which it brings to the general chord of life and of humanity. .. India .. struck the note of spiritual greatness, of pure devotion to a spiritual ideal, of worship that asked only to become what it adored, of the gathering of spiritual knowledge.. . This spirituality of India has, then, been her contribution to the world's progress, and it has manifested itself in the dual aspect of wisdom and devotion. Jnana and Bhakti. Thus she has wedded philosophy and religion and shown them both as aspects of spirituality, the noblest religion enshrined in the sublimest philosophy. Not without significance it is that in the great temple at Madura, the worshipper must stop and pay homage to Ganesha ere he can pass onward to the shrine of Shiva, for Mahadeva, the great God, must be offered wisdom as well as love by His devotee, if the devotee would pass into the innermost recess and pay his homage to the lotus-feet of Maha-yogi, the source of wisdom as of love.

And it is the perpetual affirmation of spirituality as the highest good that is India's mission to the world. As her past glory resulted from her spiritual knowledge and devotion, so must her future be based on the revival and re-proclamation of the same. Her genius is for religion and not for politics, and her most gifted children are needed as spiritual teachers, not as competing candidates in the political arena. Let lesser nations and lesser men fight for conquest, for place, and for power; these gimcracks are toys for children, and the children should be left to quarrel over them. India is the one country in the world in which it is still easy to be religious, in which the atmosphere of the land and the psychic currents are not yet wholly penetrated with materiality. If religion perish here, it will perish everywhere, and in India's hand is laid the sacred charge of keeping alight the torch of spirit amid the fogs and storms of increasing materialism. If the torch drops from her hands, its flame will be trampled out by the feet of hurrying; multitudes, eager for worldly good, and India, bereft of spirituality, will have no future, but will pass on into the darkness, as Greece and Rome have passed.

—Lecture delivered 6 November 1893, The Birth of New *India*

India's Destiny — World Saviour

This first offshoot of the great Aryan Race had settled in the northern parts of India. It had there served as the model, the world-model, for a nation. That was its function. A religion, embracing the heights and depths of human thought, able to teach the ryot in his field, able to teach the philosopher and the metaphysician in his secluded study, a world-embracing religion, had been proclaimed through the lips of the Rishis of this first offshoot of the Race. Not only a religion, but also a polity, an economic and social order, planned by the wisdom of a Manu, ruled at first by the Manu Himself. Not only a religion and a polity, but also the shaping of the individual life on the wisest lines—the successive Varnas, the successive Ashramas; the stages of life, in the long life of the individual, were marked in the castes, and each caste life of the embodied Jivatma reproduced in its main principles, in the individual life, the Ashramas through which a man passed between birth and death. Thus perfectly thought out, thus marvellously planned, this infant civilization was given to the Race as a world-model, to show what might be done where Wisdom ruled and Love inspired.

The word spoken out by that ancient model was the word Dharma—Duty, Fitness, Right Order. Gradually, like all things human, it deteriorated, and grew weaker and weaker. It had done its work, in building up for the world a model, from which the younger nations of the world might take what parts they could, and build them into their own civilizations.

Another function, grander, diviner, more wonderful, was now to come to the sacred Eastern Land, and it was to prepare it for that function that Shri Krishna wrought out the change. India, that had been a world-model of ordered duty in her divinely-moulded peoples, was in the far-off future—which to His divine eyes was not distant, for what is distance to the Deity to whom past and future are but one eternal present?—to serve not *as world-model but as World-Saviour;* that is the key to the later events. No nation may come to such high office save by treading the valley of the shadow of death, and by drinking to the very dregs the bitter cup of humiliation; for that Shri Krishna came—to make it possible, and to make it inevitable.

No hands less loving than those of an Avatara might start the Indian nation on the path, the bitter path of humiliation and of suffering. And this dominates—as you will see if you read His life-story carefully—this dominates His policy right through. He never swerves, He never changes. All His work, into which He throws His matchless power, is guided by this farsighted, unswerving, changeless, will. The changeless will is there, in whatever veil of maya He may, for the time, enwrap Himself. He wills to shape this land, this race, to be a World-Saviour. What does the shaping mean? It means' first humiliation; and has not India passed through humiliation after humiliation ? Who can look back to her as she existed in the splendour of her past, and see her, Empress of the worlds of spirit and of mind, with her triple crown of spiritual knowledge, of intellectual power, and of prosperity unbounded, and then, looking around today, see her discrowned, without tears, tears of the very heart, more like to drops of blood? And yet, the Lord of Love on Kurukshetra made that very destiny possible which today we see; nay, made it inevitable. He broke into pieces the hard wall of steel, wrought of the swords of her Kshattriya caste; He slew them by their own sharp swords, this, the mighty Lord of All, for He had come as time of doom:

> Time am I, laying desolate the world,
>
> Made manifest on earth to slay mankind;
>
> Not one of all these warriors ranged for strife Escapeth death.

The hour had struck; the swords of the Kshattriyas shivered against each other in fratricidal strife. The bodies of the Kshattriyas were left corpses on the plain of Kurukshetra. The struggle for a kingdom resulted in the dissolution of two kingdoms and modern India was born. The forehead with the triple crown was cast down into the dust, so that the destroying waves of invasion might sweep over her time after time. Alexander came, and swept over the northern lands, and his armies rolled back again to Greece, enriched with eastern thought. Still bitterer the passion, still more cruel the humiliation, when wave after wave of the northern Asian nations, from Mongolia, from Turkestan, holding the fiercest form of the faith of Islam, the Islam of the sword not of the pen, rolled over her and strove to overwhelm the faith of the Hindu people, and the Mughal throne was set up on the very site where Yudhisthira had reigned. Later still, one European nation after another played with the dice of war and commerce for the ruling of India. Her embankments were gone. No warriors or armaments, however heroic, were strong enough to stem the flood; the waves of the ocean of invasion swept from coast to coast and submerged the whole. It was the hour of her passion, of her crucifixion among the nations.

Lifted high upon her cross of pain, jeered at and mocked, derided and scorned, her robes of beauty the spoil of the contemptuous soldiery, she has hung there dying, these many hundred years. But when you have told of the humiliation and the passion, of the crucifixion and the wounding, you have told only half the story of a World-Saviour; for after the passion comes the resurrection, as inevitably as day follows night. And if you look with clear-eyed vision, unblinded by the tears provoked by that story of the humiliation and the passion, you will see that as each wave of conquest swept over the land, it fertilized the land, it did not really destroy it. And each wave, on rolling back, carried back with it something wherewith to fertilize its own land, and left in India some new thought, some fresh idea, some treasure to enrich her ever-growing thought. A destructive flood it seemed, when you looked at it from the outer side of invasion. A fertilizing flood it was known to be, looked at from the inner side, like the Nile that floods Egypt so that all the land seems drowned, but on that flood the crops of the coming season depend.

For does not the Avatara guide the world ? And out of seeming evil. He brings unceasing good. And because He loves, and is wise as well as loving, with unswerving hands He guides His chosen through the valley of misery and the hell of humiliation, in order that, purified by suffering and enriched by the experience gathered from many nations who came to mingle with her own, the World-Saviour might arise glorious on the morning of resurrection, to shed new light over the whole world, instead of the light being shed on one nation only.

Such was the meaning of the coming of Shri Krishna, and such the work that the Avatara saw before Him, and with unchanging will steadfastly carried out. But herein lies for us another lesson, for we observe that in carrying out the end, He never forgot or failed to use the means which Right Order demanded at the time. Do you remember how, before the battle-day dawned, Shri Krishna went to the court of the King Dhritarashtra, and how with His matchless eloquence, His golden tongue, He pleaded there for peace ? You remember how He called Duryodhana, how against his obstinacy He matched His patience, and against his mad folly His own sweet wisdom; how mild His words, how tactful His suggestions; nay, when all else had failed, even a partial unveiling of His form as Ishvara, in order that He might strive to the uttermost to carry conviction to the hearts opposed to Him and bent on fatal war. So many efforts for peace, and yet He knew that war was inevitable. . Such striving after the unattainable, such endeavourings to bring about things which would have frustrated His own mission. How strange that seems to our purblind eyes. But how necessary, and how wise when we begin to see. For although He knew that those efforts would fail in the purpose of the moment, though He knew that war was inevitable and Himself willed that war, and was resolute to bring it about, none the less He knew that duty must be performed, and it was His duty as patriot and as statesman to strive for peace with every human power He possessed.

He knew in His divine wisdom that the value of effort does not lie in the immediate success, as success may be counted by you and me; that efforts, directed to noble ends, are never lost, but are an ever-accumulating force, and that the future success could not work itself out correctly and perfectly, if one of those efforts were lacking, if one of those struggles were not made. He knew the secret of all action. He knew that right action is not wrought by the wise for the immediate and apparent fruit of action; that right action ought always to be performed, even though inevitable failure waits to meet it, and He well knew that all those efforts of His were forces, energies, necessary to bring about the ultimate result in what is still to us the far-off future. Those efforts for peace made by Shri Krishna, frustrated as they seemed to be at the time by the wilfulness of Duryodhana, those efforts are part of the energies that are making for peace universal in the future, when the need for the lessons of war will be over, and the white wings of peace will brood over a world at rest.

—December 1905, *Convention Lectures*

Indian Womanhood

Where true knowledge is added to inborn devotion, the Indian woman is incomparable. On all hands it is admitted that no country can rise high among the Nations of the world, unless its men and its women work together for its uplift; differences may arise as to the fashion of the cooperation, and various communities have seen the question from different viewpoints; but that a high type of womanhood is as necessary for the National welfare as a high type of manhood, that is granted on all hands. The position of women in Modern India is abnormal and transitional, due chiefly to the fact that, during the last century, two civilizations have been living side by side in the land, and that the men have, by force of circumstances, been largely moulded by the one, while the women have continued to be shaped by the other. The women continue to be wholly eastern, while the men are largely western, and so the old cooperation is lacking. The man has lost his sympathy in religion with the woman, while the woman has lost her sympathy in public life with the man, leaving both the poorer for the double loss; religious life has been narrowed by the loss of intellectuality; public life has been coarsened by the loss of idealism. India is divided in the forum and in the home; instead of a double-aspected unity, she has become two separate units, and however loving may be the units, they are twain, not one.

But while the woman remains eastern, she is not eastern of the older type. She has lost her knowledge while retaining her devotion; she has lost her share in public life while retaining her authority in the home. It is clear from the recent, as well as from the ancient, records of India that the modern woman is a dwarfed and mutilated copy of the ancient model. The ideal women of ancient India were cast in heroic mould. Damayanti was consulted by the ministers and nobles of her husband's kingdom, and appealed to against his folly.... when the King had forgotten his duty;.... Sita remained fearless, although alone and surrounded by enemies, and, pressed too far to repeated self-justification, went away in quiet dignity; Gargi faced great Sages in argument, and out-argued the greatest; Kunti was the brave adviser of her sons; Gandhari entered a council of warriors and chiefs to rebuke her arrogant son. And they left their successors behind them in the heroic women of Rajputana and Maharashtra; women who aided their husbands in council, if need be, fought beside them in the field, sat on the gadi as Regents, held the sceptre as Queens.

Who has forgotten Tara Bai... of Thoda, the skilled warrior;.... and Chand Bibi, ... the defender of Ahmednagar;... and Ahalya Bai,.... the peasant-born, the great ruler of Indore,... the last living on into the opening nineteenth century, and leaving behind her a flourishing kingdom, admirably administered ? It is the coming of "English Education" that has made the gulf that has dwarfed and exiled the woman from fullness of life, and has -hardened and rendered less effective and less patriotic the man. For woman is man's inspirer to greatness, and sacrifices acceptable to the Gods cannot be rendered where she is not.

For India's uplift, then, her daughters must come out from their seclusion, and take back their place in the common life, out of which they have slipped during the last %century, to the sore detriment of the Motherland. They do not need to copy the western women, forced by economic conditions to become man's rivals in the struggle •for existence, to the great injury of the children born of them, whose vitality is lessened by antenatal hardships .. . But neither man nor woman should be artificially restricted; each should unfold their respective capacities to the full, nor be shut out of any field by law or custom. What a human being *can* do, that he may do, provided that he injures none.

Woman must be educated; that is her fundamental need; the treasures of philosophy, literature, science, art, must be thrown open to her as to man. There should be no storehouses of knowledge, locked by the key of sex. The 'Woman Sage is wanted as well as the Woman Saint, and women's wisdom as well as men's is needed to dig deeply and build strongly the foundations of the New India, the India of the Free. For her, Religion must be philosophic and scientific and Science must again become the handmaid of Religion.

She will apply to practice the truths she learns far better than men are applying them, for she is the born administrator as man is the born legislator.

The tendency of women to put into practice the truths she has learned is one of her marked characteristics. She is less of a theorist than is man, and is far more practical. Her instinct is to apply knowledge to conduct, rather than to remain content with it as an intellectual possession. And in this application she is not daunted either by difficulties or by the necessity of making sacrifices. Sacrifice is so essentially a part of her daily life as a wife, a mother, a mistress of her household, that she does not calculate it as does a man. It comes to her by habit, and the good of her unit, the family, so dominates her mind that it never strikes her to-put her individual comfort in conflict with her devotion to those she loves. When that is extended to the country, when she makes the larger interests her own, the same-characteristic comes out.

During the patriotic resistance of Bengal to the ill-advised Partition sprung upon it by Lord Curzon—now happily undone by the gracious act of the King-Emperor—the women of Bengal took a very active part, and one of their manifestations shews this characteristic very forcibly, The brother of Swami Vivekananda, the Editor of the Yugantar, was sent to prison.. There was a large gathering of Bengal ladies to show sympathy with his mother, and their sympathy took the form not of condolence, but of congratulation.

Few realise the immense strength now latent in Indian Womanhood, ready to be aroused when they again interest themselves in public life. The agitation in Bengal against the Partition would very likely have died down, had it not been for the women, for the mothers. The Bengali and the Maharashtra women are the most highly-educated women in India — not always in reading and writing, though these also *are* more general than elsewhere, but in that true culture which grows out of a knowledge of literature, and out of that, inevitably, National pride. India's uplift will come speedily, when her daughters put to it their delicate, but strong, hands.

For India's uplift, the woman must have an open field, unfettered hands, and unimpeded activity. The two sexes were not evolved that one should enslave the other, but that they should utilise for fuller life the differences which pertain to sex. Womanhood as well as manhood must be consecrate to the Motherland, for in their union lie the strength, the stability, the freedom of India. — 16 July 1915, *New India*

5

Select Letters

TO W. Q. Judge

Mr. Judge challenged me to give my opinion on this letter, but — acting within his right as Editor — excluded from the columns of the *Path* my answer to his challenge. Not only so, but he reverses my answer — and this is outside his right as Editor — by saying that I allege the message to be non-genuine, "and thus walks beside Col. Olcott in abuse of H. P. B." In my answer I said very distinctly: "I do not regard the letter as genuine, *but I have never attributed it to H.P.B.*" (italics in article), and I went on to give my reasons, drawn almost entirely from H.P.B.'s own writings, for not regarding the letter as authentic. I do not complain that Mr. Judge should suppress my answer, nor that he should convey to his readers' minds the opposite of my statement about H.P.B.; for I know that it is necessary to his position that I should be represented as attacking my dear friend and teacher, and that those who do not see my own words should be confirmed in their belief in this industriously-propagated delusion.

The publication of the letter, if it should be regarded as from H. P. B., may do some harm to the Theosophical Society in India, and will certainly injure her memory, as it is in flagrant contradiction with her definite and published teachings. The recipients of it wisely kept it to themselves, and thus little harm was done by it, beyond the shutting out of the Theosophical Society of a few men who would have been useful members. The gentleman who sent it to Mr. Judge is much distressed at the use that has been made of it, and the best that can now be done to repair the mischief is to publish Mr. Judge's own letters about it, which will show how anxious he was a short time ago that it should not be regarded as anti-Brahmanical.

His second letter is an admirable one, and puts the matters in question in a very clear light. In the third, two points are interesting; one, that in January, 1894, Mr. Judge frankly stated that he was not in a position to ask as to the genuineness of the letter, and the second, his statement that the channel through which a message comes may distort the intended meaning of it — a view which, from the context, was intended to depreciate this particular message, and which, taken in conjunction with Mr. Judge's present declaration that the message came through H. P. B., seems to put him in the position taken by Col. Olcott, and for which he so bitterly attacks the latter.

Annie Besant

[For background on Annie Besant's 4-page Reply to W. Q. Judge's Nov. 1894 E.S.T. circular, see: *The Theosophical Movement 1875-1950*, Chapter XVI, especially pp. 241-246; and Henry S. Olcott's *Old Diary Leaves*, Volume V, Chapter XIX, "Mr. Judge Denounces Mrs. Besant," especially pp. 252-260. — BAO Editor.]

I received yesterday, December 18th, from Mr. W. Q. Judge, a circular dated from New York, 3rd November, 1894. I had previously received, on November 14th, in Australia, a curt telegram from Mr. Judge informing me that he had notified the School that he was sole Head of the E.S.T. with control of everything by "Master's Orders." I did not reply to the telegram, as it said the notification to the School was made, and there was nothing for me to do until I knew what notification had been issued. All the further information I had was contained in telegrams to the Australian papers, stating that I was expelled by Mr. Judge from the Theosophical Society in consequence of the exposures in *The Westminster Gazette*. The public disgrace seriously interfered with the end of my Australian work, but it fortunately came nearly at the end of the tour; fortunately also it came ere I left Australia; and there reached me telegrams and letters from our Lodges promising fullest support and unanimous loyalty.

I make the following comments on the circular sent to me, and I add certain statements that the members may judge with both circulars before them. I deeply regret the delay in communicating with you, but Mr. Judge issued the circular when I was in New Zealand, and it only reached my hands yesterday afternoon. I post this today to catch the London mail. That the time chosen gave Mr. Judge three months for action while my mouth was closed, is therefore no fault of mine.

- I do not know if the statements as to Mr. Judge's part in the foundation of the E.S.T. are or are not true. H.P.B. never mentioned to sme the alleged facts, except the one that Mr. Judge had not taken the ordinary pledge, he being already pledged.
- The statements as to the I.G. and myself are misleading, because incomplete. I complete them. H.P.B. did, when I left her, give me a sealed statement, constituting me Chief Secretary of the I.G. and Recorder of the Teachings. She also wrote to Mr. Judge stating that I was her "Successor," when she had to leave us, and Mr. Judge read that extract to our little group at Avenue Road when he came over after her death, as constituting — with her statements as to himself — the basis for the future arrangements. (On this matter of H.P.B.'s wishes as to the work I may be able to tell you more presently, but I cannot delay this circular.) Her dying gift to me was the ring she always wore — of which she had given me a duplicate in 1889. Ere leaving for America I asked her if I might discuss the I.G. Instructions with Mr. Judge; she answered: No, not unless he took the I.G. pledge. When he came to London after her death I told him this, and the first of the spurious "messages" was the assent to his question if he might enter the I.G. without taking the pledge. It seemed to all of us natural and right that he should come in, and we joyfully welcomed him. The Instructions of H.P.B. to

the I.G. were written down by each member, and these notes were handed to George Mead and myself, we always writing them down promptly, and H.P.B. often looking over the completed version, so as to ensure accuracy. There are other papers of teaching left in my hands by H.P.B. and in her own writing.

- On my own value or worthlessness (pp 3, 4) I have naught to say, beyond what I was bidden by H.P.B. to assert (else would I be silent) that I am a disciple of her Master, and know him independently of her, I add, without her permission, that her blessed hand opened to me the path to His Feet.

- pp. 5-9. The "plot," so far as I know, is the purest delusion. What is said of Mr. Chakravati I know to be false, and I can but feel the profoundest pity and sorrow for him who uses the holy name of the Master to cover such a charge. Believing in Karma as I do, compassion renders anger impossible. The statements about myself are untrue, but they matter but little.

- The statement on p. 9 as to "inside facts" is to me a little surprising. At the beginning of February, 1894, Mr. Judge wrote to me, saying the time had come for me to be the sole head of the E.S.T. and rejoicing in my closer touch with the Masters; a little later, on the 12th February, I had a peremptory telegram from Mr. Judge, sent to me *through Mr. Chakravati*, bidding me issue notice to the School that I took it over. I did not act on either letter or telegram, and shortly after Mr. Judge, having meanwhile received my letter telling him that I knew he had deceived me, telegraphed again, cancelling the telegram I had received on February 12th.

- As to East and West, I follow H.P.B. Her Master is an Indian, Master K.H. is an Indian, her writings show her love for India, she named her School the *Eastern* School. Ere she died, she approved my seeking in India the help of which I was to be deprived by her approaching death, and that help came to me as she said. The importance put by the Masters on India may be seen in what Master K.H.

> writes on it in the letters quoted in *The Occult World*. The Eastern Occultism that was good enough for her is good enough for me. But I will be no party to setting West against East, nor East against West; the Great Lodge works for Humanity; IT seeks to bind men together, not to stir up racial passions; IT includes Masters of different nationalities. What to us are these battle cries of divided hosts? From the Supreme Self flow all human souls; the Egos are embodied wherever their Karma leads them; not for us the heresy of separateness; from the Diamond Soul all colours flash.

The "E.S.T. Order" on page 12 I reject. I shall pursue my work quietly, with such of the council left by H.P.B. as think it right to work with me. Mr. Judge thinks it right to rend the School in twain, and I can only go on steadily as I have learned. We have come to the parting of the ways. I recognise no authority in Mr. Judge. Not from his hands did I receive my work; not into his hands may I surrender it.

And, now, brothers and sisters, you must choose your road, grievous as the choice must be to you. Mr. Judge casts me aside, breaks the last tie between us that remained. Read carefully his circular, and if your intuition tells you that it breathes the compassion which judges not a brother, the all-embracing love that draws all men together, the chivalrous honour that seeks no advantage over the absent; then follow your intuition, and obey what to you is the Master's holy voice; to such I say: "Brothers, go in peace, and may the infinite mercy of the Great Lodge guide into the path of Truth all who seek to tread it through the Maya of the physical and psychic planes."

To you who will stand where H.P.B. left us together and work with me, I have also a word to say: "Remember the ancient rule: 'Hatred ceaseth not by hatred at any time: hatred ceaseth by love.'" Follow peace and charity; attack none; blame none; impute no evil motives; cast not back reproaches. There are now two Schools not one in outer organisation; but what if our love, that is not bounded by outer organisation, should nourish a seed of unity and preserve it alive for happier times? Let us put all our energy into the work, let us love and serve the Masters and pray

Them that if we blunder in our service the involuntary fault may speedily be shown to us by pain. The Good Law sweeps on unerringly; let us rest on Them in whom it is embodied.

Annie Besant

Business Notice

This circular is sent to all members of the E.S.T. in both Divisions. Members in Europe must, within a week of their receipt of it, notify the Corresponding Secretary, 19, Avenue Road, London, N.W., whether they remain with me or go after Mr. Judge. Members in India and Australia must, posting their letters within one week of their receipt of it, notify me, addressing Mrs. Annie Besant, Banaras City, India, N.W.P. Those who do not answer will be struck off the register, but will be restored, if they write within one month of receipt of this circular.

Members in America must notify the Corresponding Secretary as above, if they wish to work with me; otherwise it will be taken for granted that they follow Mr. Judge. No member can belong to both Schools.

Annie Besant

Colombo, Ceylon,

December 19th, 1894.

Letter to Editor, Pall Mall Gazette

Sir,

In the controversy that has arisen in your columns between Mr. G. Bernard Shaw and Mr. H.M. Hyndman, the original point or dispute has disappeared. Mr. Shaw originally stated that "modern Socialism is not based on Marx's theory of value." Mr. Hyndman, after a personal reference not in the best possible taste, asked who had "abandoned Marxist theories, economical and political" — a totally different issue, cleverly substituted for the original one. Will you permit me to give one only of the many reasons why some Socialists do not found on Marx's theory of value? Marx speaks of "value," "exchange value," and "use value" in the opening pages of the "Capital." He defines "value" as a "common substance" present in products of human labour, human labour being regarded "in the abstract." This "common substance" is the "same unsubstantial reality in each" product, "a mere congelation of homogeneous human labour." It is obvious to any one familiar with the controversies of the Middle Ages, that Marx has entered the region of pure metaphysics, and metaphysics, moreover, of a discredited kind. His "common substance" is one of the old realities, analogous to the tabularity which is present in all tables. Marx, however, is clumsy in his use of his medieval weapon; to speak of a "substance" as an "unsubstantial reality" would have horrified the acute metaphysicians whose phrases he borrowed. We are then told that "a use value or useful article" has "value only because human labour in the abstract has been embodied or materialised in it"; so that use value is value as before defined plus utility of the product.

Having grasped this conception, the student of Marx is startled to learn, two pages later, that "a thing can be a use value without having value," as air, &c. (but why call this Use value, when value is absent?) and that "lastly, nothing can have value without being an object of utility," because "if the thing is useless so is the labour contained in it; the labour does not count as labour, and therefore creates no value." Now as we have already been told that the "labour" which "creates" "value" is "labour in the abstract," its utility or non-utility cannot possibly come into consideration; we are bidden to "put out of sight ... the useful character of the various kinds of labour" in defining value. Although I have no pretence to be a "Socialist of note," I make bold to say that this quagmire of contradictions and bad metaphysics is no safe foundation for modern Socialism. In a discussion at the Fabian Society, opened by Mr. Hyndman, I challenged him on the contradictions set out above, and as his only explanation was that Marx has used the word value "loosely," I am entitled to suppose that no answer is possible.

May 20 Annie Besant

To the Editor of the Methodist Times

[In this letter Annie Besant took issue with some of the statements in a letter written by George Patterson.]

Dear Sir,

My attention has been called to a letter from Professor Patterson in your issue of October 31. My note — to which it is a reply — was called forth by your direct challenge to myself to investigate the evidence against my friend, Madame Blavatsky, and I had no intention of provoking a prolonged correspondence. It is clear that we are face to face with absolutely contradictory assertions. Professor Patterson says Madame Coulomb was not paid for the letters: Major General Morgan says (pamphlet published in 1884, "Reply to a Report," &c) that the Scottish missionaries "paid them (the Coulombs) Rs. 150 as a commencement." Professor Patterson says every Theosophist who has expressed a wish to see the letters has been permitted to do so. Madame Blavatsky tells me she asked, and was refused; Mr. B. Keightley tells me he asked, and was refused, and that to his personal knowledge other prominent Theosophists met with the same refusal. I do not know Professor Patterson; I do know these Theosophists; and I prefer to accept their word.

But my belief in the forgery of the letters does not rest on these comparative trifles; it rests on a review of the whole case. On one side, a man and woman who had been expelled from a society, the latter for attempts to extort money — four affidavits of such attempts are in evidence; a woman who had been prevented by Madame Blavatsky from obtaining money, and had vowed to be revenged — affidavit giving this threat; a woman who had attempted to blackmail Madame Blavatsky — letter sent by her; a woman who had forged letters from Dr. Hartmann and Major-General Morgan, and who, bringing a suit against the latter for accusing her of forgery, dropped it before it came to trial (the pretence that it was dropped because Madame Blavatsky had left is absurd; what had that lady to do with the forgery of Major-General Morgan's letter?) — a woman who, by her own confession, had been guilty of fraud.

On the other side, the evidence of a committee, including Dr. Hartmann, Major-General Morgan, A. J. Cooper-Oakley, Dr. Gebhard, and ten Indian gentlemen of rank, learning, and proved ability, who investigated every charge at the time, and declared each one to be fully disproved; the testimony of those who saw the letters that they were manifest forgeries; the testimony of Mr. G. Row [Sreenevas Row], "from my experience as a judicial officer of twenty-five years' standing," "I came to the conclusion that every one of the letters was a forgery" (Official Report, 1884); the parallel forgeries on Dr. Hartmann and Major-General Morgan, alleging their disbelief in Madame Blavatsky — forgeries at once denounced and exposed by them on the spot; the internal evidence of the letters, such as the illiterate French, whereas Madame Blavatsky speaks and writes French perfectly, like most educated Russians; the fact that Madame Coulomb was disgraced and expelled, and had everything to gain by currying favour with the missionaries; the fact that the letters were published while Madame Blavatsky was in Europe, that she hurried back to meet the accusation, remained while the matter was investigated, and only left again when the accusations were disproved. (So far from flying secretly, she was assisted into the steamer by the Presidency Magistrate himself, and left at the peremptory order of Dr. Scharlieb, her medical attendant, who feared for her life if she remained in the Madras climate. She had not been called as a witness in the Coulomb-Morgan case, having no concern in it.)

I might add to all this the oath of Madame Coulomb: "I may have said something in my rage, but I swear on all that is sacred for me that I never said fraud, secret passages, traps, nor that my husband had helped you in any way. If my mouth has uttered these words, I pray to the Almighty to shower on my head the worst maledictions in nature." Emphatic, very; but I do not lay stress on an oath from such lips.

As to Professor Patterson's final threat, let him publish. If any compromising documents existed, those who used Madame Coulomb can have no scruples which would prevent the publication. Madame Blavatsky is poor, a worn-out invalid; she is not likely to go to India to prosecute him.

19, Avenue-road, N.W. Annie Besant.

6

Annie Besant on Education

Speeches

Education, as a National Duty

Our subject tonight is the subject of Education, one that is of the most vital moment to every thinker and every lover of his country, for on Education depends the future of the land, and no one who has the interest of his country at heart can afford to ignore the question of National Education. I have worded our subject, "Education as a National Duty?" and this form of words is chosen because I would thus bring home to you that Education is not so much a matter of the Government as it is the duty of the people.

To be really successful it must be taken up, designed, guided, and carried out, by those who are not only the lovers of their country but who are also men who understand its needs and are well aware of its peculiarities, of its characteristics, and of its traditions. To be truly useful, Education must be founded on a knowledge of the past of the country as well as of its present; it must be designed in accordance with the ancient traditions and national habits, and adapted to modern necessities, to meet at every point the growing needs of an ever-increasing nation.

Education, rightly considered, is not a matter chiefly for those who are sometimes called educational experts; I mean, it is not a matter which ought to be exclusively guided and directed by those who are concerned in the carrying out of the work of teaching, i.e., those who form a part either of the Educational Departments, or of the Educational Staffs of the various collegiate and scholastic institutions of the land. There is always a danger of narrowing too much the lines of activity by what may be called the technical specialised lines of work. A man who has been a teacher all his life will give knowledge in a definite groove; will give too much consideration to the minutiae of the appointed subjects and too little to the principles of Education; will think too much of the question of examination and too little of that real Education which turns out men developed on all sides, and able to take up the work of men in the world.

We always find that a specialist is bound to become too narrow, too dogmatic, and too wedded to particular fashions, and for that reason, in dealing with Education, you want to rouse on the question intelligent and popular opinion: the opinions of statesmen, of patriots, of officials, of men of business, of fathers, of guardians of the young, should come into the Councils of all educational institutions. They should bring thither their experience of the world, their knowledge of the country, and their insight into the needs and possibilities of the country, to shape a wide scheme of Education and to carry it out in an effective way.

You will see exactly what I mean by the danger of having Education guided only by a narrow type of experts, when you look at the Education given today in this country. True Education is subordinated to the wants of the examination room; far more time is given to guessing what the examiner is 'likely to set in the way of questions, and trying to cram the boy with "notes" that will give him success in his examination, than to the training of the boy in a way that will make him an intelligent citizen. What is wanted in Education is that such men as I have named above should formulate a correct theory, and then give it to the professional educationists to be carried into practice. We want men of wide knowledge of the country on the one side, and educational experts on the other.

I will put this more definitely. In ray own personal experience I have had some means of judging of the kind of work that is the most useful and proper preparation for dealing with Education. In my own personal life 1 have had experience along three lines. Two in the line of an educational expert, as a Member of the great School Board of London, having had the duty of looking after a large number of schools personally and of debating all questions arising on general educational policy; at another time, for several years. I discharged the duty of teaching classes, under South Kensington, and was exceptionally successful in results. But I consider that those two lines of experience, useful as they were, are comparatively useless as compared with the experience that I have gained as a student of national life, as a student of the needs of different classes in society and of the ways in which those needs may be met, as a student of politics and of social questions; these studies give the most useful results in the shaping of educational schemes. That is the experience which is needed to decide on the knowledge to be given in the classroom, while the method of the giving is rightly within the administration of the Educational Department.

This is why I call Education a national duty. There may be many of you who are not accustomed to preparing the timetables for schools or colleges; many of you have done little work in the drawing up of a definite curriculum. You would find that a very hard task Many of you would be unable, if you were to attempt to make a list of useful text books, to frame such a list with success. But if you study your country and know the kind of men that your country needs; if you have experience, whether in the Government service, whether in administrative work, whether in a judicial capacity, whether in the working of manufactures, commerce or science, that experience enables you to judge the kind of men that India needs; and when you know the kind of men that are wanted, then it is easy to frame a scheme of Education which will provide men to meet the necessities of the land.

I think, then, that every thoughtful man and woman should study the question of Education, and form on it a definite rational opinion. Only thus can Education be rightly guarded and the tendency of its becoming too mechanical, too formal and too separate from the real life of the nation thus be guarded against. Let me illustrate what I mean by one case which will show you graphically the distinction between the technical expert and the man who has wide knowledge of the country and insight into its needs, Take the example of the English Parliament. Its duty is to make laws, and therefore, according to the principle of some of the educationists, only lawyers should be members of Parliament: men of all types should not be found there, and all public criticism and all public advice should be shut out from a Parliament which should be composed only of legal experts.

But every one knows that such a Parliament would be utterly inadequate for the needs of the Empire. What is wanted in Parliament is a body of men who understand the country's needs, its wants, and its powers. The" moat varied experiences, men from all lines of life, are sought. The lawyer-members are a very small minority and they are wanted in Parliament not so much for the decision of the principles of the laws required, as for the technical drawing up of the law itself, and the giving of accurate details for the definite working out of the law. And so for us in Education; we want the technical knowledge of experts for the working out of programme, hut the programme itself should be made by the wisest heads in the nation.

I said just now that Education is not so much a matter for the Government as for the nation. One of the difficulties of Education in India is the fact that it is too-much a Government affair. I was glad to see Sir Michael Hicksbeach, one of the leading English statesmen, lately declaring at Aligarh that the Universities should be entirely free from the Government control, that Government had nothing to do, or ought to have nothing to do, with the Universities. That is the case in England and the system works perfectly well. The Universities of Oxford, Cambridge, Durham, Dublin, Glasgow and Edinburgh have all grown out of private endowments, endowments given by Kings, nobles or gentlemen.

They rest on donations of great and philanthropic men; they were founded by patriots in the past, and are supported by patriots in the present; they do not look to Government for monetary support. For, wherever money is taken from Government, Government has the right and the duty to supervise the way in which that money is employed. What is wanted in Education is that the country itself should build its Universities and support its Schools.

The Universities should have the wisest heads of the country on their Councils, but they should not be under Government You can see how the system works in the United Kingdom. You find there that many a statesman covets the post of what is called the Rectorship of one of the great Universities. A man like Lord Rosebery, a late Prime Minister and probably a future Prime Minister, has stood for the Rectorship of the Glasgow University. He has been elected there as a thinker, a statesman and a patriot, and pot as a Prime Minister of the Empire.

The more in this way you can link the institutions and the nation together, the better for the land; and what we want in the Senates of our Universities now is that they should be bodies recruited from all that is most thoughtful, most cultured, most patriotic and most self-sacrificing in the country. They should not be half filled with nominees who know nothing of Education. That is the kind of reform that you want in Education here. You must have independent, learned and patriotic bodies, which shall make the Education of the young their primary aim.

To pass from that to what ought to be the aim of Education; the aim of Education at the present time in India appears to be the gaining of a degree and when you ask: "Why do people want a degree?" the answer is: "That they may go into Government service or into the learned professions." A man becomes a Bachelor of Arts not that he may know literature, not that he may understand history, not that he may be a student of philosophy, but that he may be a Vakil or a Government; servant. Now the getting of a degree is not the true aim of Education. The aim of Education is to draw out all the faculties of the boy on every side of his nature, to develop in him every intellectual and moral power, and to strengthen him physically, emotionally, mentally and spiritually, that he may turn out at the end of his College career a useful, patriotic, pious gentleman, who respects himself and respects those around him. Education is a failure when it is simply cramming the boy's bead with a lot of disjointed facts, poured into his head as into a basket, to be emptied out again in the examination room and the empty basket carried out again into the world. It is not a good education which, when a boy has passed his examination, eaves him a nervous wreck, exhausted as to his body and overstrained as to his brain. When a boy goes out of his College, be should be full of life, full of vigour, full of energy, and full of delight in his young life, to take up the burden of the work of the world. He should not be nerve-exhausted and nerve-overstrained, when he has finished bis educational career I have often seen boys so anxious about the result of the examination that they were ill. In some cases, when lads failed in their examination they committed suicide. That is a horrible thing — a shocking commentary on the pressure that was put on the lad's young and tender frame To exhaust; the strength, to destroy the energy, to turn out a sickly worn-out man, when the youth should be brimming over with life, has been the result of the system of Education prevalent in the land.

What is the Education that we require? I used just now four words in describing the nature of the boy. First, "physically" unless a boy's body is strong and healthy be cannot, as a man, do all he should in life and for his country. The training of the boy's body is as important part of Education as the training of his mind. His body should be kept frugally and simply, so that he may be strong and healthy, and not indolent and lazy. He should be trained in gymnastic exercises and in games of every kind. He should be trained to regard his body as an instrument for working in the world His duty to his body is a part of his duty to his country and to himself. No school, no college does its duty where physical training is not definitely a part -of its curriculum.

The physical training does not really stop with the body, as when we speak of the training by games. Has it ever struck you, while scrutinising Indian character, what are some of the qualities that most need to be developed in the young? They are quickness of thought, alertness in understanding the situation, swiftness of decision, promptitude of action, and accuracy of judgement. These qualities are wanted to make a good citizen and a useful man, and these are the qualities which are largely, developed on the playing-field, in the games The boy learns in the games alertness and quickness in seeing his opportunity and promptitude in using it he learns to work with others by subordinating himself to a common object, and to subordinate his own success to that of his side. He learns the very Qualities which are wanted in the man of action, in the true patriot. I would rather at present see an Indian boy skilfully playing on the play ground than working in his classroom; because there is no doubt about the brilliancy of his intelligence, but there is a very great doubt about his practical capacity. That is too often lying dormant. House it then by training and development.

Secondly, I used the word "emotionally." It is necessary in our national education to give a most important place to what is called "Moral Education". Let us pause for a moment to consider what is meant by "Moral." Let us see exactly what we mean. We find in ourselves certain things that we call emotions and feelings. As we study emotion, we recognise the enormous part that it plays in life. As we study emotion, we find that out of emotion grow up all the attractions that make a family, a town, a community, and a nation — that bind men together into nations and peoples. We notice also that, on the other side, Crow emotions also grow up all the forces that pull down as well as construct; by emotion families are disintegrated, communities are broken up, and nations are destroyed. While on the one side emotion builds society, on the other side it breaks it down. The moment this is recognised, the culture of emotion is seen to be of vital importance for the State and for the nation, and we find, on further study, that every virtue and every vice has its root in emotion.

Virtuous is the man who discharges to all around him the obligations that arise in his relation with them. The virtuous man performs these duties as perfectly as if love between him and others were the only motive of action. Each father does his duties to bis son because he loves him; each brother does his duty to his brother because he loves him so a man should do his duty to all the weak and the inferior as to bis sons, to all his equals as to his brothers. He recognises the bond of duty to all around him, he recognises that be owes to all that which be gives to his dear ones by the inspiration of love. Thus does the love-emotion work out in our relation with each other; as a permanent mood it is virtue, and it builds up families and stares. But emotion of the opposite kind, the hate-emotion, is the root of all vices, and it breaks up human relations, drives men apart from each other, and leads them to destruction. All the vices that ruin nations grow out of the hate-emotion between man and man. When this is recognised, the culture of emotion necessarily becomes a vital part of Education.

You must teach your boy to cultivate emotion on the side of love, the emotion which grows into virtues. You must teach him to discourage emotion on the side of hate, the emotion which grows into vices. You must teach him to love his fellows as if they belonged to his family, and to love his nation as if it were a part of his family. You must teach him that national life depends on the unity of the organism that we call a nation Take an educated man whose emotional training has been neglected; how can he carry out the work of the world? He thinks of his own gain, his own advantage and his own prosperity, but he does not look to the national welfare. He thinks how he can profit, but not how his nation may thrive. He thinks bow he may grow rich, but not how the nation may be prosperous. That individual, therefore, strikes at the root of the national welfare and brings about the decay of the people.

A father, who has gained wealth selfishly, without regard to the national good, sees the nation growing less and less prosperous, and he knows that his own children and grandchildren have to be members of that decaying nation and that his selfishness has undermined his family as well as injured bis nation. A man who has only thought of his own gain and of his own advancenent finds that the other parts of the nation are suffering, and that he is compelled to share the sufferings with them. A number of men rush into Government service, or into the teamed professions, thinking only of getting on in the world. But what meanwhile happens to India ? Her agriculture gradually grows less and less effective, her industries decay, her manufactures fail, and her wealth is diminished. Does the successful lawyer escape from the result of the general national decay and can he separate himself off from the descent of the people? Agriculture does not affect the agricultural labourers alone, or the landholders alone; every class of the community suffers when the agricultural results are poor. God has bound the classes of the nation together, and the national prosperity depends upon the public spirit of the people, upon the consideration of the whole nation, and upon the subordination of individual gains to the general good and the common prosperity.

These lessons your boys should learn while their minds are plastic, and while their hearts are enthusiastic, in the days of their youth. You must bold up before them the great ideal, you must fire their hearts with love for this land, you must teach them their past in order that they may create the greater future, and you must ask them to love their country in order that country may rise in the scale of nations. Think what these boys are—boys now, they are the coming citizens of the country; boys for the moment, they are the creators of India in the near future. You who are grown up are the India of today, but the India of the future depends on the young boys. . That is why every statesman, every great statesman, concerns himself with the Education of the young. That is why men like Mr. Gladstone and Lord Salisbury concerned themselves with the question of Education. They knew that the future of the nation depends on the boys in the school, and just as those boys are trained the future of the nation will be. Moral education, thus, is vital for the future of India

My third was "mentally." On the intellectual side of education I was speaking to you the other day, and I need not repeat what then I said, I would only remind you that what is most wanted in that intellectual Education is a scientific Education rather than an exclusively literary one, an Education that will add to the productive resources of the country and not lead only to the learned professions. I do not mean that the learned professions are not necessary for the welfare of the State. They are entirely necessary, hut they should not absorb the whole of the brilliant intelligences of the country, and starve the other side of national life, which is equally wanted for the welfare of the people. And let me add to this the bearing of Education on commerce. In the days of old you were a great commercial people; you were great shipbuilders, sending your ships over the whole world and carrying on a great commerce. You may read history, and you will find that, only some three hundred years ago, ships built in India sailed up the Thames to London, and were regarded with envy and admiration because of their admirable workmanship. You will find that you had plenty of good sailors, plenty of enterprising merchants, and plenty of men who carried on the active work of commerce, enriching their country at the same time that they enriched themselves. Unless you educate your trading classes, you will never revive that commerce of the past. Shrewd as the commercial classes are, they are too narrow in their views, and too wedded to their particular fashions, to do what is needed for the nation. We should educate them by tens, hundreds and thousands, and so give back to India the possibilities of active commercial life. Along that line intellectual Education should go, so that India may be what she really should be, a nation with all sides of the national life fully developed. Look at your national life now, and you will see how partial it is, how one-sided it is, and how wanting it is in the manifold activities which are necessary for a great nation.

My fourth word was "spiritually." In India things have gone from bad to worse in this connection. Government colleges teach no religion at all; the missionary colleges teach a religion which is alien to the spirit and genius of the country. The boy has to choose between no religious teaching at all, and the teaching of a religion which is different from his own. That is the worst defect of Education in India, and see how dangerous it becomes. The late Bishop of Calcutta, taking advantage of there being no religious Education of the Indian youth, tried to persuade the Government to introduce into all schools religious teaching based on the Bible, *i.e.*, on Christian lines.

Fortunately that attempt has failed, because popular feeling was roused by it, and the plan was seen to be dangerous. If every religious community gave religious Education to its children, if the Hindu community afforded Hindu religious instruction, if the Musalmans gave instruction in the faith of Islam, if the Parsis gave instruction in the Zoroastrian religion, and so on, leaving Christianity to be taught to the Christians only, then the religious Education of the country would proceed along proper and healthy lines. Again, it is not just to blame Government for want of religious Education. Government cannot give it, and it ought not to give it, lest it should infringe the religious neutrality on which the peace of India depends, Government is pledged to "No religious interference." Government must not do it; you ought to do it yourselves. Every community here should take up the question of religious Education. Now two of the great communities in India, the Hindus and the Musalmans, are beginning to deal effectively with the question of religious Education, The Musalmans have set an example in this direction by the foundation of their college at Aligarh. The Hindus are following in the same important path by the foundation of the Central Hindu College at Banaras. You have thus two educational institutions for the two communities, that is, for two hundred and fifty millions of Hindus and something like fifty or sixty millions of Musalmans! It is but a drop in the ocean, a grain of sand on the seashore. Nevertheless it is a beginning.

Now let me turn for a moment to the Central Hindu College, so that 1 may show you that the theory which 1 have been putting before you is not simply a theory, but is being carried out in practice. I am not so familiar with the workings in the Aligarh College, and therefore cannot speak definitely of that College. As regards the Hindu College, it was supposed, before we began to work, that the question of religious and moral Education was a thorny one; when we began we were told: "You cannot teach religion, because there will be endless sectarian troubles; you will have complaints from the parents of all the youths; it is impossible to teach religion to all the boys." We have not found it impossible, for every day in the College hall the boys gather together listening to the chant of the *Bhagvad Gita*; they also listen to a Pandit expounding some doctrine with some moral illustration from the stories from the *Ramayana*, from the *Mahabharata* and from the *Puranas*.

Where is the Hindu who would object to such moral instruction? Then two or three boys (they take it in turn so that all may have an opportunity) come-forward, and standing, facing their schoolfellows, chant together some *stotra* full of religious feeling and moral instruction. Where is the Hindu who would withdraw his boy from the teaching given in that College ? That is not all that we have done. We have now taken a further step. We have issued two out of a series of three textbooks, and the third will be issued about the end of this month or the beginning of the next. These books give a clear and definite outline of Hindu doctrines, Hindu ceremonies and Hindu ethics.

The first is a little catechism, meant for little boys and girls in the Primary Standards. The second is meant for the middle and upper classes in the High Schools. The third, which will soon be out, is for students in the Colleges. On this third book, of which the others are simplifications, have been obtained the opinions of the leading men in the Hindu community, both orthodox and liberal; we asked them to read and criticise it, and after making any necessary additions or omissions, to send it back corrected. This was done, and we have thus a general consensus of opinion of the leading men of different shades of opinion, endorsing this textbook. It has been a laborious work, and has taken two-and-a-half years altogether in order to complete it.

But what are two-and-a-half years in the national life, if you can thus give to the nation what it wants in religious instruction? Now, all those who want to introduce religious teaching have the means ready to their hands. The Indian States are readily taking this series up, one after another, and are introducing religious instruction in the State schools. Some of the leading Princes in India are cooperating in this righteous work. Wherever there is a private college or school under Hindu management, there these textbooks should be introduced and used as guides for teaching. There is one difficulty about the teacher. We want men who can teach rightly and in an interesting way, and not merely Pandits who will deal with questions of grammar and with the niceties of the commentators. This is one of our needs. Now that the Hindu community has done, others should do.

The Parsi community should provide their children with a similar series of textbooks. The Mussalman and other communities should also supply their children with a similar series of textbooks. I fancy that perhaps it would be possible for each community to take the outlines of the moral teaching from our series of textbooks, and only change the quotations and stories. We have given quotations from the Shastras, supporting morality from the Hindu books, but morality is the same for the Parsis as for the Hindus The Parsis should give quotations from their own sacred literature. Morality again is the same for the Musalmans as for the Hindus and the Parsis. The Musalmans should support it by quotations from Al Quarn. The various quotations from the scriptures of different religions would all support the same virtues. I think, if that is done, that you would begin to build the Indian nation which we so earnestly desire to have. It does not seem quite impossible that, if we give these moral teachings on similar lines, we may gradually build up in the country a body, which will gradually weld itself into an Indian nation.

Moreover, I hope to see, in days to come, a Mussalman University growing out of the Aligarh College, and a Hindu University growing out of the Banaras College, so that these Universities may lead the national life of India, as the Oxford and Cambridge Universities lead the national life of England. I say that it is not impossible, if only all of you will take interest in the matter, and look on it as your own affair and as your own business.

There is one other point which I want to put before you. We have one peculiar thing in the Hindu College. Every boy who comes into the English department is obliged to learn Sanskrit. We have also a Pathashala, and every boy who comes to join it is obliged to learn English, so that the English-educated boys have to know Sanskrit and the Sanskrit-educated boys have to know English. This is a great innovation. You may say: "Why do you do it ? Do you not see that there are two Hindu nations in this land — one of Pandits, profound in their learning, scholarship, thought and knowledge, but knowing nothing outside Sanskrit literature They know nothing of modern thought, modern life, the modern spirit. On the other side there is a Hindu nation growing up, knowing nothing of Sanskrit literature and of the Sacred Books, growing up utterly Westernised. There is a great gulf between them and the nation of Pandits. The Pandit cannot influence the English-educated boy, because he does not sympathise with him in his hopes and aspirations. You cannot influence the young unless you sympathise and feel with them. We want to bridge the gulf between these Hindu nations and we build this double bridge of Sanskrit and English. We lead both classes over it, so that both shall know English and both know Sanskrit; we thus hope to join the two Hindu nations and make them one in the service of their Motherland.

That is the work that we are carrying on in Banaras, and I venture to say that it is a work in which every good Hindu should take the keenest interest. I want you all to think of as and to give us your goodwill. L want you to make a public opinion which will enable the Banaras College to grow into a University, and to have daughter colleges in all the great cities in the land, where the students will learn Hindu religion and Western culture and will know the West without becoming aliens from their ancestral faith. It is the mightiest enterprise for which I ask your sympathy, your goodwill and your financial aid. I know that it will succeed, because the blessings of the great Ones are on it. I know it will succeed, because it is for the benefit of the future of India, which is at the heart of every one of us. But that future depends on Indians, and on no other people and on no other country. The Indian nation will not grow by the influence of any other nation, but by the growth of character within India's own boundary. England can never make you free. You can only make yourselves free by becoming noble and upright, brave and true.

Nations made of such men *must* be free. Your destiny lies in your own hands. Your future is to be of your creating. You must build the basis of noble character, and of the public spirit which shows itself in true citizenship. You must prove yourselves worthy to be a pact of a mighty Empire. As Lord George Hamilton has rightly said, India must be governed on the basis of Indian feelings, Indian traditions, Indian thought and Indian ideas. That is true. It is possible, that if India only grows up to the height of her possibilities, that the time will come when she will send her best and noblest counsellors to take their part in a great Imperial Council, gathered round the Monarch for the ruling of the Empire. 1 dream of a time when India will help to build the Empire with that genius for statesmanship and clear insight which are found from time to time in great Indian ministers.

These qualities will be utilised for the good of the Empire, for the good of the mighty whole of which India is a part. The times are gone by for small nations, for petty States and for little peoples. The tendency now is towards raising a vast realm, united by common aims and common love. India in the future should aid to build such an Empire, should help to bear its burdens and share its responsibilities. I dream of a time when India, England, Australasia and Canada will all join hands in the making of a common Empire, when India's children will bring their priceless treasures to the enriching of that Empire. But for this her children must first build their character, for without that they will never be able to accomplish aught.

Necessity for Religious Education

It is my wish to put before you very plainly and clearly why I believe that religion must be an essential part of all education which is worth the name, why boys should desire it, why teachers should impart it. I propose to set before you certain definite reasons, appealing to your intelligence, why the future of your lives and the future of your country depend chiefly, primarily, on the inclusion of religion in your education, reasons which may impel you, if religious teaching is not already given to you, to earnestly demand it at the hands of those who are responsible for your training. For if the professors in your colleges, the masters of our schools, are so little sensible of the dignity of their high office as to submit to the exclusion of religion from education, degrading education from a preparation for citizenship in this and other worlds to a mere commercial speculation, then must the parents and guardians of students, and the students themselves, imperatively demand that the most important factor in true education should not be omitted therefrom. The law of the State punishes the careless parent who allows his child's body to starve, the law of Karma punishes the thoughtless parent who allows bis child's spiritual nature to be stunted by the withholding of religion.

I am not going today to repeat the well-worn arguments drawn from observations of other countries showing how nations rise as they make religion a part of education, and how they sink as they pronounce an unhallowed divorce between the Spirit and the intellect of man. From those observations, India may well draw a lesson for her own guidance, as to truth she may also draw it from the story of her own past. For when she was mightiest in peace and war, when her industry was most productive and her commerce most enriching, she was then, above all else, a religious nation, and religion interpenetrated every action of her family, her social, her political life.

But today I speak to you ' on other lines, and appeal, not to observations on which you may base conclusions, but rather to your reason itself. Along three lines my arguments will run: first, Religion is necessary as the basis for Morality; secondly, Religion is necessary as the inspiration of Art; thirdly, Religion is necessary as the foundation of original Literature If these three positions can be established and maintained, then is Religion necessary for the greatness of a nation, for what kind of a nation can you have without Morality, without Art, without Literature ?

First, then, *Religion is necessary as the basis for Morality.* When you are teaching the duty of doing the right and avoiding the wrong, when you are trying to persuade people to be virtuous, when you are arguing that a man without civic virtues, a man who is not a good father in the family, a good citizen in the State, is not a man who can help in making a nation great and prosperous, you are apt to be asked in a sort of general way: "Why cannot we teach moral duties by themselves, why cannot we teach men to be truthful add brave, why cannot we teach them to do their duty and to serve their country, without appealing to religion, which is very, very often the cause of turmoil and dissension, which it is desirable to keep in the background rather than draw to the front?"

The answer to that is that, in teaching morality, you must base your precept, to do or not to do, on some principle recognised by those whom you address. It is not enough to say to a man who is eager to amass money, whose one idea of success is the gathering of a great fortune: "You ought to be honest, you ought to be fair, you ought not to cheat, you ought not to take unfair advantage of your rivals in trade." He will turn round upon you and say: "Why ? why should I be honest and fair ? Why should I not take what advantage I can of others by my cleverer brain, if I just avoid coming into contact with the law, and if these unfair ways help me in gaining my object?" You require something on which your 'ought' can find a footing, a basis for your moral precepts.

Three bases of morality have been offered by the great thinkers of the world. One school bases morality on Intuition; the second bases it on Utility; the third bases it on Religion. Let us examine each in turn.

The first school bases morality on Intuition, alleging that a man knows by his own nature, that he ought to do the right, that he ought not to do the wrong; that there is in every man's heart an inner witness which is called Conscience, and which is the voice of God in the human soul; this conscience, it is urged, should be taken as the foundation for morality and to its guidance a nation may safely commit the moral direction of its young. The answer to this is that conscience is a very variable quantity, differing among different nations, among different communities, varying with the varied stages of evolution, useful' only amid accustomed conditions, and failing when applied to new problems.

It is a truism to remark that some of the most evil actions the world has known have been due to conscience. The Spanish inquisition was founded and carried on by men who conscientiously believed that they were serving God by the torturing and burning of heretics, that they wielded the surgeon's knife to cut out from the bosom of society the cancer of heresy, not the brigand's knife to mutilate and murder. There is truth, though truth brutally expressed, in the answer of the Anglican archbishop to a Puritan who pleaded his conscience in defence of bis rebellion against the dictum of the Church: "Verily, thou mayest be acting according to thy conscience; but thou shouldst take care that thy conscience is not the conscience of a fool." That a man should act according to his conscience is right for him, but it by no means follows that his conscientious act is right. By his errors, his conscience is instructed and he learns to avoid pitfalls in the future by the sufferings caused by his conscience flinging him into pitfalls in the present. Out of the pains resulting from his conscientious wrong actions, is made the ladder by which he climbs to wisdom. Why this is so, we shall see in a moment.

The average conscience of the members of a community, as manifested in its public opinion, is behind, not in advance of, the best ethical thought of its time The conscience of average men allows them to do very many things of which a man of noble character will say: "That is against my conscience"; the average conscience is far below that of the greatest thinkers, of the purest saints, of the noblest men of the time. The common average conscience is embodied in the law, and this stamps us criminal the acts which are reprobated at the stage of evolution reached by the large majority of the community But there are many vices, many evils, which the law is unable to touch. The vices which corrupt the trade and commerce of a country, which rot its commercial honesty, and slowly sap its prosperity, are vices which no law can arrest or punish Operations on stock exchanges, by which a few clever men reduce to misery numbers of foolish and ignorant people, is a form of robbery which causes far more suffering than burglary, but the law cannot check it. Public morality condones it, even courts the highly successful destroyer and society smiles on the financier whose operations are on a sufficiently large scale to secure millions, though well knowing that by no morally legitimate means can such gains be heaped together. This shifting, developing, faculty of conscience is no sure foundation for the building of morality.

For what is conscience ? It is true that it exists in all save the very undeveloped, but it is only the result of the experience of the past of each individual and varies *rith* that experience. In past lives, in past births, each man has learned by experience that certain lines of conduct lead to happiness, while others lead to misery. Slowly and gradually, in all the lives that lie behind you, your experience, has shaped itself into definite judgements, and with the tendency to follow these judgements you are born. And as the experiences of each differ from those of others in details, so each man's conscience differs slightly from chat of his neighbour; and as the total experiences of people, at about the same stage of evolution, have their broad outlines in common, so men at about the same grade have broadly similar consciences. And as the experiences that He behind great men are more numerous, more varied, more rich, than those which lie behind the average man, so are their consciences more highly developed than the consciences of their less developed neighbours.

In general morality, you can appeal effectively only to the average conscience, the average moral sense of the hearers; you cannot draw from them a response to the verdict of a more highly evolved conscience, nor impose its decision upon them, any more than you can obtain from a violin string a note higher than that which is yielded by the most rapid vibrations which it is capable of producing. Conscience grows with civilization, with knowledge, with the increasing number of lives; it is quickened by training, by education, by contact with the more highly developed. But not on the shifting sands of conscience can morality be founded. Not from its many-voiced opinions can a categorical imperative be drawn.

Let us turn to Utility, and see whether that can yield us the basis which we need. Of the school which advocates this as a basis, the maxim is: That which conduces to the happiness of the greatest number is right. Many of the most thoughtful people m the West, many philosophers and sociologists, are to be found in this school, and they argue that Utility is the only reliable basis of morality. They argue that you can discover what is right by a study of human experience, by tracing out the results of various lines of conduct. The conduct that results in happiness is right; that which results in misery is wrong. In this there is a great truth; right conduct, in the long run, brings happiness; wrong conduct, in the long run, brings misery. That which brings about universal happiness—not the happiness of the greatest number only — is right; but a result is not a basis, and while the Bight leads ultimately to universal Bliss, the bliss is so distant, and the immediate results of right action are often so painful to the right doer, that the imperative which is based on Utility fails to win allegiance, save from the noblest and the most unselfish, those who need least a moral law outside them, being, in truth, a law unto themselves.

William Kingdon Clifford, a famous mathematical and scientific thinker, and one of the noblest and purest of men, spoke in most eloquent and moving language upon the duty that lay upon every man and woman to pay back to the society of the present the debt they owed to the society of the past. He urged that all the advantages into which we are born, the brains which have been moulded by the thoughts of unnumbered generations, the social order evolved by the efforts of the countless thinkers, statesmen, rulers, labourers, the wealth piled up by innumerable toilers — all these are not for our making but are the gifts of the dead to the living, and should be handed on increased, enriched, as the gifts of the living to the yet unborn Every one of us, he argued was protected, guarded, educated, nurtured, by the whose past humanity, the results of whose labours were summed up in social organisation, in civil order, in the laws of nations, in the comity of peoples. Receiving so much as the accumulations of the past, we were bound, by honour and honesty, to add to those accumulations the results of our own labours, and so bequeath to posterity a larger and richer legacy. He declared that those who would not work for the future, who did not feel and discharge the obligations incurred by receiving benefits is from the past, were men and women unworthy, degraded, unfit heirs of the splendid legacy of the past. Such an appeal stirs to its depths every noble spirit and the highly-unfolded mind and heart respond to it in every fibre of their being, but it leaves cold and unmoved the average man of our time.

I remember now, in a splendid lecture delivered by Charles Bradlaugh, he expressed himself on this with burning eloquence. Answering the statement that a man would not do right unless he looked for a personal reward, for an immortal happiness on the other side of death, he repudiated the idea with all the passionate indignation of a man on fire with love for humanity, with all the beauty of his magnificent oratory. It was not necessary, he cried, to appeal to human selfishness in order to inspire man to the achievement of noble deeds. "Enough for me, if the great citadel of truth, into which I may not enter, shall have its possession by humanity made the nearer because I have fought; enough for me, if my body, failing into the most which surrounds that castle, helps to make the bridge over which mankind shall march to victory." There is no doubt of the splendour of that conception. There is no doubt of the greatness of the soul which could find sufficient reward for sacrifice, for suffering, for renunciation, in the hope that in the future, when he was dead, when nothing — as he firmly believed — remained of him, when his life had vanished as a blown-out flame, as the brightness of rusted steel, the world would be a little nearer to happiness because in the past he had struggled, because he had lived.

But how few there are who, by such a hope, could be inspired to a life as heroic as was his. Only the world's great ones can live nobly, upheld by such a thought. The average man remains cold before the appeal for posterity's welfare. He says in act what a witty Frenchman said in word. "What has posterity done for me, that I should work for posterity?" If he repudiates his obligation to pay to the future the debt contracted by his receipts of benefits from the past, what moral law can utter an imperative that he will recognise as cogent, a command that he will fee) compelled to obey ? The weakness of the utilitarian basis lies in the fact that your imperative fails, save where you appeal to the noble minded, to those who need it least. These respond to it, but others shrug their shoulders, and care not for the welfare of the race. The present pain to be incurred by themselves is not, for them, balanced by a future welfare in which they will not partake, and the slight ill-doing of the present, bringing to them a personal gain, is not checked by the idea that it injects a moral poison into the shadowy bodies of generations yet unborn.

If intuition fails as a basis for morality, if Utility, devoid of immortality, also tails us, we are forced to our third basis — Religion.

In most countries of the world, religion has been made the basis of morality, for the founders of religion were occultists, who understood the nature of men, who intended religion to guide their evolution and who, knowing that the motives which appealed to men at one stage, failed to appeal to them at another, graded their teachings to suit the grade in evolution of their hearers. In each great religion, the sayings of its founder, his precepts, his commands, have been accepted as the moral law of his people. The Jew obeys the laws of Moses; the Christian bows to the sayings *of* Jesus, although — owing to the fact that His esoteric teachings became exoteric — he ignores those which he regards as impracticable in the life of the world; the Hindu looks back to Manu as his lawgiver; the Buddhist accepts the precepts of the Enlightened One, the Buddha; the Mussalman sees in the teaching of his Prophet the rule of his conduct.

In each of these religions the moral law comes from an authority divinely commissioned or itself regarded as divine, the law which the believer must obey. The world has grown up along these lines. The morality of the nations of the world has been fed from the breasts of their religions. Religions have yielded the categorical imperative necessary for the moral education of mankind. These have used praises and threats, rewards and punishments, suited to the age and intelligence of their adherents. Ignorance may have distorted the sure sequences of moral law into a rewarding and avenging deity; ignorance may have prolonged a term into an everlastingness, and have distorted the self-made scourges of passions into the fire and brimstone and fiends of bells.

The sure truths of nature and of natural sequences may have been twisted by ignorant and self-seeking priesthoods for the terrorising of the simple and the timid. But none the less have the religions of the world trained their believers into a practical and useful morality, by which nations have been builded, civilization has been rendered possible and a social order has been secured. It bag been said in mockery, but the saying embodies a truth, that religions have been the police of society. And, however much modern sentimentality may shrink from it, fear is one of the motives which curb the strong and the oppressive, and spread a shield over the otherwise defenceless victims of their greed.

But now, for the first time, the very basis of religion has been undermined; its authority has been challenged, its ancient world, scriptures rent in pieces. More and more insistently the sceptical intellect of man is asking: "Why should I obey? Where is the justification for your claim to authority?" The critical reason is demanding a sure basis for a compelling power, a categorical imperative which can be enforced by logic and by an appeal to undeniable facts. Such a basis, is to be found only in that supreme fact of nature which is asserted alike by revelation, by philosophy and by science — before the unity of the Self, the one life universal clothed in an illimitable diversity of forms. Dr. Miller has truly said that the great gifts of Hinduism to the world are the teachings of the Immanence of God and the solidarity of mankind. But every religion has taught these great truths more or less clearly, has proclaimed them in language more or less definite, according to the intelligence of the people to whom they were addressed. Hinduism has taught them with supreme lucidity, because its religion and its philosophy were shaped by occultists addressing the subtlest and keenest brains that humanity has yet evolved.

The unity of the Self — that, and that only, is the sure foundation for morality, the rock which can never be shaken, the basis which no logic can impugn, which experience continually re-verifies. The Unity of Life — revelation proclaims it, philosophy demands it, science affirms it. The ancient truth, the Truth of truths, intuited by the Pure Reason, is being ever more insistently asserted and demonstrated by science. Experiment confirms what intuition and reason demand and no surer guarantee of truth is attainable by humanity. On this irrefragable, impregnable Truth, may morality be built surely and fearlessly! It is the Rock of Ages, eternal, stable, secure.

Many names are given by the different religions to this sure fact. Some say, God, the universal Father, and mankind, His children; some say, the one Self dwelling in the heart of all; some say, the Life Universal, the all in all, the source of being and of beings. Names matter nothing; they are all but labels for one fact, the Unity.

We are all one in the unity of the universal life, we are all one in the unity of the Self, who knows no 'other.' But if you and I are one, one Life, one Self, though in two forms, then if I injure you, 1 injure myself; if I lie to you, I am lying to myself, and the lie will deceive me and I shall fall; if I cheat you, I am cheating myself and that cheating will defraud me and I shall suffer. I cannot get away from you. I cannot separate myself from you. We appear as two, but one life unites us, and the blow that I aim at you inflicts pain on myself. This is the truth which, denied, asserts itself as pain; which, accepted and lived by, reveals itself as bliss. This is the law which destroys civilizations which ignore it, which crushes into fragments, into dust, every society which refuses to obey it. It has destroyed scores of civilizations, and only a civilization built upon it shall endure.

So is every community, every nation, one body, a smaller within the larger Self. It is in verity, not only in name, a body politic and there is a real unity in a nation's life. If men pour into that national life, cowardice, and lies, and cheating, and knavery, the whole nation is poisoned, the vitality of the nation is lowered, and good men and evil men alike suffer from the common ill. A nation is so truly constituted as one body, that its evildoers poison the lifeblood of that body, and all the citizens suffer, for all share the national life. The whole morality of the nation is lowered by the presence in it of a number of dishonest men, whether their dishonesty be legally punishable or not. They spread through the nation like a subtle poison, for we cannot be separated the one from the other, since we are all clothed in one matter, and are all living by one life.

Nor can injustice be done to one part of the nation, without the rest of the nation suffering. All nations have a degraded class of people belonging to them, in whose persons the Unity of the Self is outraged. In England this class is called 'the submerged tenth,' and it is a continual disgrace and peril to the nation, a constant menace to the stability of the State. Here also is a similar class of people, though not degraded to the same point of brutality as in England — the class called the Panchamas, or Pariahs, or outcastes. Some five and a half millions of these people are living on Indian soil, the remnants of the conquered aborigines of the country, submerged by the waves of the Aryan conquerors. For many generations you have sought to push these people away, to keep them separate, and have thought: "I can get rid of these inferior people, I can keep; them out of those among whom I move: I will not allow them to come into my house; they shall go off the road on which I am walking".

True, you can turn your backs on the outcaste people, and deny in them practically the presence of the all-pervading Self, the presence which you pride yourself on acknowledging in words. But what happens ? The enemies of your faith take pity on them. Christian missionaries go to them, and turn them into Christians. Muhammadans go to them, and say: "Come into Islam; we shall treat you as brothers, and not as outcastes." The Christian missionary allures them; the Mussalman allures them with promises of better social condition, and thus a vast population is turning against Hinduism, and threatens the stability of Hindu society. The very Hindus who refuse to allow them to enter their homes, allow them to enter when they are Christians or Mohammedans, thus aiding to bribe them to turn against the religion to which they had naturally gravitated. Has this denial of the Unity of the Self profited the Aryan conquerors or has not the karma of conquest and oppression worked itself out, has not Nemesis trodden on the heels of wrong ? The. Aryans who conquered the elder races, now, in their turn, are conquered by their youngers, and they are forced to drink of the bitter cup which they have held to other lips. The liberty they have denied to others is denied to them; the hospitality they refused to others is refused to them; the oppression wherewith they hive oppressed others falls upon these, but in far smaller measure than they meted out to the races they conquered.

My brothers, see in this hard lesson the working of the Unity of the Self, bringing oppression to the oppressor, loss of liberty to those who have denied it to others. You complain and justly, of the harsh and rude manners often shown to you by your English rulers, but are they one-hundredth part as insolent to you, as you are insolent to this race whom you, in the past, brought under your yoke ? If you would have courtesy from the conquerors, yield your courtesy to these, your conquered; if you would win liberty, give liberty to these, the downtrodden of many countries; lift up these whom, in your pride, you have trodden under foot, and karma, ever just will lift you up, and will return to you, in fullest measure, the blessings you have showered upon those whom you had wronged. It is not to the point that you are, intellectually and morally, the equals of your conquerors, while these people were an inferior, as welt as a conquered race. Oppression is oppression, on whomsoever it is wrought; insolence is insolence, whether shown to high or low; the very fact that these were your inferiors, helpless in your hands, rendered them the more worthy of your compassion, of your pity; it is the tears of the weak that rot the foundations of empires.

Thus do we see that religion is the only sure foundation for morality, as the fundamental truth of Religion, the Unity of the Self, is that on which alone a science of ethics can be built. How, then, shall we venture to rob our boys and girls of this essential element in true education.

Religion is the Inspiration of Art. — Many people do not consider, do not understand, how important is the part played by Art in the life of a nation and how impossible it is for a nation to reach a full-orbed greatness unless Art plays its part in the shaping of the nation's growth. The Art of a nation is the expression of that nation's conception of the Beautiful, of its love of harmony, proportion and order. The Beautiful is that which refines and polishes a nation, gives it dignity and grace and self-restraint. Inevitably vulgar becomes the nation which has no true Art, in which passion begets no poesy, and love delights not in grace of outline, in splendour of colour. There, passion changes to brutality, and love puts on the hideous mask of lust. Study nature, alike in the masses with which she constructs a world, and in the details with which she crowds the smallest nook in her vast realcus, and you will understand that one of the pillars on which the Great Architect of the Universe constructs His Universe is beauty.

India, the country whose life has everywhere been permeated by religion, has wrought beauty into the daily life of her people, and hence the refinement which is the common possession of her children. Look at the vessels in daily use in an Indian home, in which Western influence has not vulgarised the ways of living, and you will find them all beautiful in form and colour; the kitchen utensils, the brass and pottery, would serve as ornaments of an English drawing-room; the woman's dresses, the hangings, the carpets, are all lovely from an artistic standpoint; beauty meets you at every turn in the domestic life, a constant delight to the eye, a refining influence on every member of the household. Go into a country village, and you see the peasant woman draped in a sari exquisite in colour, falling in graceful folds round the erect and supple form; she bears on her head a brazen vessel of noble outline, or an earthen one of brownish red, harmonising with the trees she passes, a veritable picture, though but a village lass or dame. That beauty of the life surroundings softens and mellows the life, and lends it a charm of dignity and grace which refines and educates.

But even into the village life the vulgarising influence is spreading, and sometimes the peasant woman going to the well, still wearing the graceful sari, still carrying her head with queenly dignity, bears on that head neither the brilliant brass, throwing back the glory of the sunray, nor the glowing red of the village potter's handiwork, but the stiffly outlined, unlovely kerosine oil tin. You may think it does not matter, but that is not so. It matters, because the subtly vulgarising and coarsening influence of the replacing of beauty by ugliness in common life drags the whole nation to a lower level. The peasants catch their colour from their environments, and the slouching, clumsy, round-shouldered walk of the English ploughman, in such striking contrast to the springy, alert, erect gait of the Indian peasant, corresponds to the ugly clumsy vessels of his cottage and his village alehouse. The English peasant of two centuries ago had also his things of beauty, his carven wooden vessels and his well-carved bench, as the Norwegian peasant has still. It is the advent of the age of machines that has cursed the countryside, and deteriorated the manhood of the English peasantry.

Hence, in England, the most thoughtful people are trying to bring beauty back to the country life, to restore handicrafts and to revive the arts which make common life beautiful. What William Morris and his followers have done for the middle classes, others are seeking to do for the poorer people, so that England may regain the beauty of the common life, the refinement and the grace lost in the coming of machinery and the passionate struggle for wealth. The early Victorian age in England is now a synonym for ugliness, and her manufacturers try to palm off upon Indian Princes the atrocities for which there is no longer sale among their English customers, thus degrading and vulgarising the once exquisite Indian taste.

There is nothing in nature untouched by man that has not its own beauty and its own grace. The forest depths and the mountain solitudes, the tossing waves of ocean and the shimmering ripples of the lake, the little out-of-the-way valley, cradled in the bosom of the hills and carpeted with flowers, the snow-clad peak, the brilliant blue and the summer noon, the dark star-spangled depths of midnight, the white radiance of the moon, the dancing shadows cast by the sunbeams — what are these but signs of the eternal beauty, the sign-manual of God ? Nature, which is . His expression in matter, in her contact with the ugly and the formless, is ever moulding into new forms of beauty the chaotic matter which is the plastic material for her artist fingers. Beauty is a real power, and each religion, in its day of supremacy, has generated some great Art. The faith of Islam, conquering Northern India, gave to its new home the exquisite lines of the Taj Mahal, the beauty of the Pearl Mosque, the marvellous courts of the Delhi Palace; in Spain, the victorious Moors reared the splendour of the domed and minaretted Alhambra, and left the deathless memory of their art in Cordova, and in many an Andalusian city. In Greece, the massive but delicate lines of her architectural genius modelled buildings which modern Art reproduces, but fails to improve, and she sculptured marble with a skill and power that have made immortal the names of her artist sons.

In Rome, her Art built with the strength of a Titan and her temples, her pillars, her theatres, proclaim the majesty of her vanished past. In Egypt, her sombre religion bodied itself forth in grandiose and gloomy fanes, mighty in their power, impressive beyond all other architectural types. Christianity, in medieval Europe, gave birth to the marvel of Gothic architecture, wherein the springing lines of pillar and arch seem to carry the soul upwards, as though it would climb the very heavens from the slender strength of the upward-soaring shaft. And who that has seen it can forget the glory of the Florence Duomo, where the green and rosy marbles have imprisoned the hues of the sunbeams, and tier on tier, carven figures carry the charmed sight upward, till the crowning images are outlined against the blue of the Italian sky. Did not Christianity give to the world the canvases on which the brush of Raphael limbed the immortal beauty of the Virgin and the Child, the marbles which the chisel of Michael Angelo carved into the Lawgiver and the Laocoon?

Everywhere has religion given birth to Art, the cult of the Beautiful, and faith has been the inspiration that gave life to the brush and the chisel. If our modern days have no great Art, it is because they have no might of faith. They copy, but they cannot create. And not until the great spiritual impulse now sweeping over the earth, that we call the Divine Wisdom, Theosophy, gives birth to a new ideal and conception of beauty, will the Art of the future be seen among us, the Art which shall be the expression of Beauty for our age. If you would preserve what is left of Indian Art, if you would create the Indian Art of the future, you must revive the religious spirit which is the mother of Art, you must welcome the latest — and the most ancient—expression of that spirit, Theosophy, the Supreme Science. Then and then only will Indian ideals of Beauty draw again the hearts of mankind, and give through the most spiritual of religions, the highest expression of Art.

Religion is the Foundation of Great Literature.— Where religion is not an essential part of the education given to the youth of a nation, there the nation has no literature, worthy to he called great. By 'great' literature, I mean literature that is original literature produced by the creative, as distinguished from the imitative, intelligence. Trace back your own literature, and you will see that its most splendid-age was that which was profoundly religious. Hinduism inspired the Vedas with, their Upanishads, wrote the ancient Puranas, lived and then immortalised in deathless verse, the epics, of the *Ramayana* and the *Mahabharata;* from its fertile womb sprang the six great schools of philosophy, the science of Yoga, the ancient treatises on medicine, on grammar and astronomy. These writings, which are the admiration and the study of the foremost nations of the present day, for the depth and sublimity of their thought and the stateliness and beauty of their diction, were all flowers on the mighty tree of Indian religion.

Later, as religion weakened, India had great commentators, great grammarians of the second order, great philologists; but these cannot raise a nation to the pinnacle of literary fame. Creative literature. Not commentative and imitative literature — India is barren of that today And she will never again become creative in her literature, any more than she will become exquisitely beautiful in her Art, until religion is incorporated in her education and her children grow to manhood within the inspiration of her faith. Nor is this fact confined to India.

The great literature of Islam, philosophical and scientific, in Europe, grew out of Muhammadanism in the few centuries which succeeded the death of the mighty Arabian Prophet. The masterpieces of Christian literature were written in an atmosphere of religion; the Renaissance was the child of the Moorish teachers; the Elizabethan age followed the religious struggles of the Reformation. Everywhere history testifies to the close relationship between religion and literary genius.

And this is natural. For the nobler part of the human intellect is an aspect of the spirit in man, and the lower mind contacts the spirit only as it is fed and nourished by religion As that contact opens the avenues to the spirit, the spirit shines down these avenues and illumines the mind. When the mind is illumined by the spirit, and the brain is able to respond to the swift and subtle vibration of that mental world, then we have the radiant and splendid manifestation that man calls genius.

Thus great and imperative, then, is the necessity for religion as an integral part of education. Do not tell me that religious training may be given in the home, in voluntary classes, on special occasions. If you leave it out of education, you shut it out of life. The boys will learn the things which are in the educational curriculum, and will treat outside subjects of study with the same indifference that you show by placing them in an inferior rank—will treat them with indifference, if not with contempt. Nor will they turn in later life to the study ostracised in the school and the college. Then the world will have hardened them, then social ambition will have fettered them; the brains will be less plastic, the hearts less warm, than in the eager and passionate days of youth. Life's ideals must be wrought in the soft clay of youth, and they will harden into firm material with maturity. Train your boys and girls in religion, and then only will they become the men and the women that India needs.

See how the great men of your past were religious men. To take even modern times, see how Baber and Akbar were penetrated with the religious spirit. And, later yet, see Shivaji, bowing at the feet of his Guru, ere be drew the sword to free his native land.

Those of you who would have India great, those of you who would see her might, remember that the condition of national greatness is the teaching of religion to the young. Teach them to be religious, without being sectarian. Teach them to be devoted, without being fanatical. Teach them to love their own faith, without decrying or hating the faiths of their fellow-citizens. Make religion a unifying force, not a separative; make religion a builder-up of nationality, not a disintegrator; make religion the fostering mother of civic virtues, the nurse and teacher of morality. Then shall the boys and girls grow up into the great citizens of the India that shall be; then shall they live in an India, mighty, prosperous and free; then shall they look back with gratitude to those who, in the days of darkness, lifted up the light, and gave the religions teaching which alone makes good citizens and great men.

Vital Necessity for Religious Education

Religion is necessary as the basis for Morality .... as the inspiration of Art.... as the foundation of original Literature. . .. So is Religion necessary for the greatness of a nation, for what kind of a nation can you have without Morality, without Art, without Literature ? . . .

As the Basis for Morality

In most countries of the world, religion has been made the basis of morality, for the Founders of religion were occultists, who understood the nature of men, who intended religion to guide their evolution, and who, knowing that the motives which appealed to men at one stage, failed to appeal to them at another, graded their teachings to suit the grade in evolution of their hearers. In each great religion, the sayings of its Founder, His precepts, His commands, have been accepted as the moral law of His people.. .. The religions of the world trained their believers into a practical and useful morality, by which nations have been builded, civilization has been rendered possible, and a social order 'has been secured... .

The great gifts of Hinduism to the world are the teachings of the Immanence of God and the Solidarity of Mankind.. .. Hinduism has taught them with supreme lucidity, because its religion and its philosophy were shaped by occultists addressing the subtlest and keenest brains that humanity has yet evolved. The unity of the Self—that, and that only, is the sure foundation for morality, the rock which can never be shaken, the basis which no logic can impugn, which experience continually reverifies.... On this irrefragable, impregnable Truth, may morality be built surely and fearlessly It is the Rock of Ages, eternal, stable, secure.. ..

We are all one in the unity of the universal life, we are all one in the unity of the Self, who knows no "other." But if you and I are one, one Life, one Self, though in two forms, then if I injure you, I injure myself; if I lie to you, I am lying to myself, and the lie will deceive me and I shall fall; if I cheat you, I am cheating myself, and that cheating will defraud me, and I shall suffer. I cannot get away from you. I cannot separate myself from you. We appear as two, but one life unites us, and the blow that I aim at you inflicts pain on myself. This is the truth which, denied, asserts itself as pain; which, accepted and lived by, reveals itself as bliss. This is the law which destroys civilizations which ignore it, which crushes into fragments, into dust, every society which refuses to obey it. It has destroyed scores of civilizations, and only a civilization built upon it shall endure.

So is every community, every nation, one body, a smaller within the larger Self.... If men pour into that national life, cowardice, and lies, and cheating, and knavery, the whole nation is poisoned, the vitality of the nation is lowered, and good men and evil men alike suffer from the common ill... . The whole morality of the nation is lowered by the presence in it of a number of dishonest men, whether their dishonesty be legally punishable or not. They spread through the nation like a subtle poison, for we cannot be separated the one from the other, since we are all clothed in one matter, and are all living by one life.

Nor can injustice be done to one part of the nation, without the rest of the nation suffering. All nations have a degraded class of people belonging to them, in whose persons the Unity of the Self is outraged.. . . Here also is a similar class of people, . . the class called the Panchamas, or Pariahs, or outcastes. Some five and a half millions of these people are living on Indian soil, the remnants of the conquered aborigines of the country, submerged by the waves of the Aryan conquerors. For many generations you have sought to push these people away, to keep them separate.. .. Has this denial of the Unity of the Self profited the Aryan conquerors, or has not the karma of conquest and oppression worked itself out, has not Nemesis trodden on the heels of wrong ?

The Aryans who conquered the elder races, now, in their turn, are conquered by their youngers, and they are forced to drink of the bitter cup which they have held to other lips. The liberty they have denied to others is denied to them. ... It is not to the point that you are, intellectually and morally, the equals of your conquerors, while these people were an inferior, as well as *a* conquered race. Oppression is oppression, on whomsoever it is wrought; insolence is insolence, whether shown to high or low; the very fact that these were your inferiors, helpless in your hands, rendered them the more worthy of your compassion, of your pity; it is the tears of the weak that rot the foundations of empires...

As the Inspiration of Art

Many people do not consider, do not understand, how important is the part played by Art in the life of a nation, and how impossible it is for a nation to reach a full-orbed greatness unless Art plays its part in the shaping of the nation's growth. The Art of a nation is the expression of that nation's conception of the Beautiful, of its love of harmony, proportion, and order. The Beautiful is that which refines and polishes a nation, gives it dignity and grace and self-restraint. Inevitably vulgar becomes the nation which has no true Art... . There, passion changes to brutality, and love puts on the hideous mask of lust. Study nature, alike in the masses with which she constructs a world, and in the details with which she crowds the smallest nook in her vast realms, and you will understand that one of the pillars on which the Great Architect of the Universe constructs His Universe is Beauty.

India, the country whose life has everywhere been permeated by religion, has wrought Beauty into the daily life of her people, and hence the refinement which is the common possession of her children. Look at the vessels in daily use in an Indian home, in which Western influence has not vulgarised the ways of living, and you will find them all beautiful in form and colour; the kitchen utensils, the brass and pottery, would serve as ornaments of an English drawing-room; the women's dresses, the hangings, the carpets, are all lovely from an artistic standpoint; beauty meets you at every turn in the domestic life, a constant delight to the eye, a refining influence on every member of the household.

Go into a country village, and you see the peasant woman draped in a sari exquisite in colour, falling in graceful folds round the erect and supple form; she bears on her head a brazen vessel of noble outline, or an earthen one of brownish-red, harmonising with the trees she passes, a veritable picture, though but a village lass or dame. That beauty of the surroundings softens and mellows the life, and lends it a charm of dignity and grace which refines and educates.

But even into the village fife the vulgarising influence is. spreading, and sometimes the peasant woman going to the well, still wearing the graceful sari, still carrying her head with queenly dignity, bears on that head neither the brilliant brass, throwing back the glory of the sunray, nor the glowing red of the village potter's handiwork, but the stiffly outlined, unlovely kerosene oil tin. You may think it does not matter, but that is not so. It matters, because the subtly vulgarising and coarsening influence of the replacing of beauty by ugliness in common life drags the whole nation to a lower level. The peasants catch their colour from their environments.. . .

There is nothing in nature untouched by man that has not its own beauty and its own grace. The forest depths and the mountain solitudes, the tossing waves of ocean and the shimmering ripples of the lake, the little out-of-the-way valley, cradled in the bosom of the hills and carpeted with flowers, the snow-clad peak, the brilliant blue and the summer noon, the dark star-spangled depths of midnight, the white radiance of the moon, the dancing shadows cast by the sunbeams—what are these but signs of the eternal Beauty, the sign-manual of God ? Nature, which is His expression in matter, in her contact with the ugly and the formless, is ever moulding into new forms of beauty the chaotic matter which is the plastic material for her artist fingers.

Beauty is a real power, and each religion, in its day of supremacy, has generated some great Art. The faith of Islam, conquering Northern India, gave to its new home the exquisite lines of the Taj Mahal, the beauty of the Pearl Mosque, the marvellous courts of the Delhi Palace.. . . Everywhere has religion given birth to Art, the cult of the Beautiful, and faith has been the inspiration that gave life to the brush and the chisel. If our modern days have no great Art, it is because they have no might of faith. They copy, but they cannot create. And not until the great spiritual impulse now sweeping over the earth, that we call the Divine Wisdom, Theosophy, gives birth to a new ideal and conception of Beauty, will the Art of the future be seen among us, the Art which shall be the expression of Beauty for our age. If you would preserve what is left of Indian Art, if you would create the Indian Art of the future, you must revive the religious spirit which is the mother of Art, you must welcome the latest—and the most ancient—expression of that spirit, Theosophy, the Supreme Science. Then, and then only, will Indian ideals of Beauty draw again the hearts of mankind, and give through the most spiritual of religions, the highest expression of Art.

As the Foundation of Great Literature

Where religion is not an essential part of the education given to the youth of a nation, there the nation has no, literature worthy to be called great. By "great "literature, I mean literature that is original, literature produced by the creative, as distinguished from the imitative, intelligence. Trace back your own literature, and you will see that its most splendid age was that which was profoundly religious. Hinduism inspired the Vedas with their Upanishads, wrote the ancient Puranas, lived, and then immortalised in deathless verse, the epics of the *Ramayana* and the *Mahabharata;* from its fertile womb sprang the six great schools of philosophy, the science of Yoga, the ancient treatises on medicine, on grammar, and astronomy. These writings, which are the admiration and the study of the foremost nations of the present day, for the depth and sublimity of their thought and the stateliness and beauty of their diction, were all flowers on the mighty tree of Indian religion. Later, as religion weakened, India had great commentators, great grammarians of the second order, great philologists; but these cannot raise a nation to the pinnacle of literary fame. Creative literature, not commentative and imitative literature —India is barren of that today. And she will never again become creative in her literature, any more than she will become exquisitely beautiful in her Art, until religion is incorporated in her education and her children grow to manhood within the inspiration of her faith....

And this is natural. For the nobler part of the human intellect is an aspect of the Spirit in man, and the lower mind contacts the spirit only as it is fed and nourished by religion. As that contact opens the avenues to the Spirit, the Spirit shines down these avenues and illumines the mind. When the mind is illumined by the Spirit, and the brain is able to respond to the swift and subtle vibrations of that mental world, then we have the radiant and splendid manifestation that man calls genius.

Thus great and imperative then, is the necessity for religion as an integral part of education. Do not tell me that religious training may be given in the home, in voluntary classes, on special occasions. If you leave it out of education, you shut it out of life. The boys will learn the things which are in the educational curriculum, and will treat outside subjects of study. . with indifference, if not with contempt. Nor will they turn in later life to the study ostracized in the school and the college. Then the world will have hardened them; then social ambition will have fettered them; the brains will be less plastic, the hearts less warm, than in the eager and passionate days of youth. Life's ideals must be wrought in the soft clay of youth, and they will harden into firm material with maturity. Train your boys and girls in religion, and then only will they become the men and the women that India heeds.

See how the great men of your past were religious men. To take even modern times, see how Baber and Akbar were penetrated with the religious spirit. And, later yet, see Shivaji, bowing at the feet of his Guru, ere he drew the sword to free his native land.

Those of you who would have India great, those of you who would see her mighty, remember that the condition of national greatness is the teaching of religion to the young. Teach them to be religious without being sectarian. Teach them to be devoted without being fanatical. Teach them to love their own faith, without decrying or hating the faiths of their fellow-citizens. Make religion a unifying force, not a separative; make religion a builder-up of nationality, not a disintegrator; make religion the fostering mother of civic virtues, the nurse and teacher of morality. Then shall the boys and girls grow up into the great citizens of the India that shall be; then shall they live in an India, mighty, prosperous, and free; then shall they look back with gratitude to those who, in the days of darkness, lifted up the light, and gave the religious teaching which alone makes good citizens and great men.

—Lecture delivered 26 February 1908, *The Birth of New India*

Education of Indian Youth

From the cradle onwards, should come ... the education of boys and girls. .. from the example and the lips of fathers and mothers who are themselves full of spirituality, thus forming a spiritual atmosphere which shall permeate the dawning mind. No after-training can compensate for the lack of religion in the home, the saturation of children's minds and hearts with pure religion and with the exquisite stories with which Indian literature abounds—tales of heroism, devotion, self-sacrifice, compassion, love, reverence. A man should not be able to remember a time when he was not familiar with the melodious names of Indian Saints and Heroes, both men and women.. . .

An effort should be made to substitute a detailed knowledge of Indian *history and geography* for the excessive amount of foreign history and geography now learned. A sound and broad knowledge of universal history widens the mind and is necessary for culture, but every man should know in fuller detail the history of his own nation, as such knowledge not only conduces to patriotism, but also enables a sound judgement to be formed as to the suitability of proposed changes to the national genius.. .. Stories from the *Mahabharata* and the *Ramayana*, well translated, should form reading-books both in English and in the vernaculars.

Indian history is a thing which seems to be written as though with the object of disgusting every boy who has to pass an examination in it. Nothing more dry, nothing more uninteresting, nothing more uninspiring, than the school histories of India; nothing to enable the people to realise what India was in her far past, in her near past; yet this is of vital importance for the building of character today. How many of your boys and girls know anything really inspiring about the great history of the last two thousand years in India ? They may have a few glimpses in their homes of those heroes and saints whose names shine out in the far distant past; but how much do they know of the story of Maharashtra or Rajputana ? How much do they know of the great kingdoms of the South, which were mighty and civilized when Europe was still in medieval barbarism ? That is the history that would inspire your boys and girls... You must give Indian boys Indian heroes and not English ones.

Moreover, you must make them realise—most important of all, and for that you will have to rewrite your history— that all the great men of India, no matter what their religion, what their blood, whether they be Musalman or Hindu, that they are all builders of Modern India, and that they have to share in the future building of India.. .. Many forces go to the building, to the making, of a people, and all who have -fought and struggled in the past are builders of the Nation of the present, and our boys should learn to love them all. The Hindu should learn to love Akbar; the Musalman, Shivaji. Only so will you make them realise that, out of past divisions, a Nation is being born, and we must honour all the strivers of the past who have made possible the splendours of the future.

And your history lessons have also to be remodelled, so as to contain plenty of Indian matter and less of other Nations. Indian boys should learn Indian history chiefly, and the others only to widen out, to strengthen and illuminate the mind.

—Lecture delivered 17 April 1914, *The Birth* of *New India*

Failure of the Educational System

The aim of Education at the present time in India appears to be the gaining of a degree, and when you ask: "Why do people want a degree ?" the answer is: "That they may go into Government service or into the learned professions." A man becomes a Bachelor of Arts not that he may know literature, not that he may understand history, not that he may be a student of philosophy, but that he may be a Vakil or a Government servant. Now the getting of a degree is not the true aim of Education. The aim of Education is to draw but all the faculties of the boy on every side of his nature, to develop in him every intellectual and moral power, and to strengthen him physically, emotionally, mentally, and spiritually, that he may turn out at the end of his College career a useful, patriotic, pious gentleman, who respects himself and respects those around him. Education is a failure when it is simply cramming the boy's head with a lot of disjointed facts, poured into his head as into a basket, to be emptied out again in the examination room, and the empty basket carried out again into the world. It is not a good education which, when a boy has passed his examination, leaves him a nervous wreck, exhausted as to his body and overstrained as to his brain. When a boy goes out of his college, he should be full of life, full of energy, and full of delight in his young life, to take up the burden of the work of the world. He should not be nerve-exhausted and nerve-overstrained, when he has finished his educational career.

I have often seen boys so anxious about the result of the examination that they were ill. In some cases, when lads failed in their examination they committed suicide. That is a horrible thing—a shocking commentary on the pressure that was put on the lad's young and tender frame. To exhaust the strength, to destroy the energy, to turn out a sickly, worn-out man, when the youth should be brimming over with life, has been the result of the system of Education prevalent in the land.

—Lecture delivered 9 March 1903, *The Birth* of New *India*

Mass Education

First you have to decide what you are going to teach, and then how you are going to get the means to teach it... .

What to Teach?

Elementary education ought to be the same for every child, and by elementary, I mean that knowledge which is necessary for the whole life of the future. Reading, writing, arithmetic and so on, these ought to be learnt by all alike. But . . . I submit that every boy and girl who goes to an elementary school should learn some of the common things of life, which will later inevitably come into the everyday life, whether it be of the shopkeeper, of the merchant, or of the professional man. Children ought all of them to learn those simple things which are carefully left out of our education: how to bind up a cut; how to bind up a sprain; what to do if a burn happens in the household; what to do in more serious cases until a doctor can be called in.... Every child should learn' the common lessons of everyday life. A large number of your men and women would not be able to tell me how you should put on a bandage if there were a bad bleeding — which was threatening the life of a person before a doctor could be brought — in order to save that life. You would' not, most of you, know where to put on the bandage, above or below the' wound. The man's life may depend upon it, and it is a common and a simple thing . . . . I was able to save the life of a woman in the London streets by the simple fact that I knew how to put on the kind of bandage which would stop the flow of blood. ... If there is a common burn, people run about and wonder what they shall do, because of the absence of such kind of education, and this ought to be a part of the teaching in every elementary school.

How to Teach?

Some say children are hard to teach. It is because you do not know how to teach them. Every child is always asking questions, which means that he wants to know something about the queer world in which he suddenly finds himself; but when the children ask questions, you say: "Don't bother." When the child says "Why ? "you say: "Oh, be quiet," and so you make the child afraid and stop his longing to learn. Teach the child what it wants to know, and not what you want to teach it, and you will very soon find your elementary schools crowded by eager children anxious to learn. . . .

Medical Examination

Wherever there is a school, there should be a medical man to look to the examination of the children in the first instance; not the kind of doctor who cures disease when it is there, but one who prevents little defects from growing into permanent and large defects. . ..

Financing of Mass Education

How to found these elementary schools. ... That is your big problem, and I can only suggest one or two ways. First, the cooperative movement is spreading. Wherever there is a cooperative society in a village, a village school should form part of that cooperative society... . Wherever you have a cooperative panchayat, add one or two men more for the educational department of it. That you can do without the help of any Government, You can do it ire areas of such small size that the cost of it will not be crushing to any particular community.

Restore the Panchayats: Then the next step is to appoint village panchayats everywhere, whether the cooperative movement is there or not. Now, in this, Government is willing to help you. The panchayat saves litigation and heavy expenditure. It saves the Collector rushing about from one place to another, and deciding twenty or thirty suits perhaps in as many minutes for lack of time. It makes over the disputes of the villagers into the hands of people who know the men, who know the rights and the wrongs of the case, as no visitor can possibly know them, however clever he may be; and I believe that by the establishment of the village panchayat system of rule in India, which will from the village unit grow upwards in graded ranks, as also by the establishment of the cooperative societies, you will be able to solve piecemeal the problem of mass education, which is too huge, as I said, for any Government to deal with effectively. ... Your villagers have the genius for Self-Government. They have shown it for thousands of years. But they have not now the initiative to begin it.... So I would ask the more self-sacrificing of the town-dwellers, those who are able to give some time to it, to put their hands to this plough of national education, to found cooperative societies, .. to establish panchayats everywhere. .. . Then your cultivated villagers will form the strength of your nation, and will pay you back in intelligent patriotism that which you spend upon them today in effort and in labour.... In your mass education, take village by village, and solve the question slowly, beginning in small manageable areas, building up from the village schools to the University.

Summing up: . . in your literary education you want to bring the Indian side out, and use the Western to supplement, except perhaps in matters of science, where the line of teaching in the West is more effective than the line of teaching here. But do not forget that you also have science, and do not let the West entirely drive you out of it. You have an indigenous medicine. You have a knowledge of many scientific facts, you have a psychology greater than the western, and you should not let these go while you are acquiring scientific knowledge from the West. Make the subjects that relate to India first in education, and to other nations second. Then, in the technical education which you give, take the other side of providing a field of employment for the trained young men you turn out, otherwise they become bitter and discontented and add to the difficulties of the country.

—Lecture delivered 17 April 1914, *The Birth* of *New India*

WRITINGS

Education

Duty of the Brahmana

What is the first problem that is pressing on every nation ? That of the education of the young.... How should that be solved? There is one way—though no public leader yet has suggested it—that has within it the power of solution and that is by the recognition of real castes, and among them the cast of teachers. Your Dharma as Brahmanas—those of you who are Brahmanas — is not the gathering of wealth and the holding of places of power; but the gathering of knowledge and the imparting of that knowledge to the people. If the Brahmanas would only do that duty as Brahmanas, then there would be no educational problems in India today. But the Brahmanas, instead of doing their duty by imparting instruction, are busy in administering justice—which is properly the function of the Kshattriya; they are busy gathering wealth—which is properly the duty of the Vaishya ... If we had true Brahmanas in India, all educational problems would be solved....

—1917, The *Ancient Ideal* of *Duty*

Child is a Spirit

Reincarnation must reconstruct our educational system and our penology. The child must be seen as a Spirit, evolving from within latent powers, and bringing with him definite faculties, his creation out of his experiences in past lives. His education must be based on a study of the individual child and fitted to his intellect and his temperament. Not only a "religious "has a "vocation "; each child has a vocation, is "called of God," the Hidden God, to serve the larger Life in the smaller. As I have said elsewhere: "The Education must be made to fit the needs of the child, not the child be made to fit the education." Education here is a Procrustes' bed; the short are pulled out, the tall are lopped off, to fit it. The School is a place of fear, not a place of joy; the pupils are ruled by punishment, not by love. Initiative is crushed out; home lessons lengthen the school hours; the body and mind are overstrained, and the healthy riotousness of all young things is checked. The western Nations are remodelling their educational systems and we in India must do the same. We need a National system under Indian control.... —1 June 1917, *The Theosophist*

Ideals in Education

Nothing is more necessary in education than the holding up of Ideals before the minds of the young. One of the greatest defects in the education of boys in India is the: absence of this presentation of Ideals, and the consequent absence of enthusiasm. A really noble manhood cannot grow out of a boyhood which is left uncultivated on the emotional side. Much of the patriotism of Englishmen, which makes possible the growth of the Empire, is sown during their schooldays, when their highest feelings are constantly evoked by the holding up of the memories of great Englishmen—great in religion, in self-sacrifice, in love of country. Indian boys are even more sensitive than are English lads to the compelling power of such examples, but these must be drawn from the past of their own country.

One of the most remarkable things about the Central Hindu College in Banaras was the swift response of the students to the great national Ideals constantly held up before their eyes. It was one of my greatest joys there to see the young faces brighten and glow, as I spoke to them of self-sacrifice for the Motherland, of love of country and of service. And here, in Madras, I have found the same thing in every address which I have given to students; there is always the same lighting up of the eager faces, the same swift response to the appeal. But there is apparently no School here which makes such evocation and training of right emotion part of its regular instruction, as was done at the Central Hindu College. Yet people complain of the lack of enthusiasm and of self-sacrifice in the men ! As well might the husbandman complain of his barren field when he has sown no seed-therein.

—November 1913, *The Young Citizen*

You will only prove yourselves trueborn if you five again as your sires did. —1901, *Ancient Ideals in Modern Life*

Religious Duties of the Student

- *Study of the Doctrines of Religion:* There is no knowledge more necessary for a boy than the knowledge of the fundamental doctrines of his religion. This knowledge should therefore be imparted to him in a simple elementary form in school, and in further detail in college. No controversial points should be raised, no philosophical disquisitions should be imposed; a clear definite statement of the main doctrines is all that is needed. Half an hour a day throughout school-life would be time sufficient to equip the lad with this knowledge and to enable him to answer intelligently any questions addressed to him about his religion.
- *Worship:* Everybody should worship, recognising with gratitude the Source of life and strength and joy. The Hindu boy should daily perform his Sandhya, after bathing, according to the custom of his caste and family; if he does this, with concentrated attention and devotional feeling, he has fulfilled the duty of worship suitable to his state. He may also, if he likes, read and think over a shloka of the *Bhagavad Gita.* The duty of meditation belongs to later life, and he will gain such training of the mind in steadiness as is fitted for his youth, by the careful and attentive performance of his Sandhya.
- *The Life of Love:* This is the religious duty which the boy must discharge all day long, and it is this which makes a life a truly religious life whatever may be its occupations. Let us see how a boy should lead the life of love in school and college, the dharma of the student:

He must show his love to his parents and his teachers by diligent study and by prompt obedience. Youth is the time for study, and a youth wasted in idleness cannot later be made good. A man's usefulness to others depends largely on his education; the ignorant man cannot be a good and wise husband, father, or citizen. A diligent, industrious boy is showing a religious spirit by this diligence and industry; if he practises these qualities from love and from a sense of duty, he is performing the dharma of his state. And he must be obedient, with the obedience of love, which is as complete out of sight as under the eyes of authority, which is prompt, cheerful and ungrudging, not slothful, carping and unwilling.

He must show his love to those around him by helping them in every way he can; if he is clever, he should help the dull boys with their lessons; if he is strong, he should protect the little lads, and never tyrannise over them. He should be brave, gentle, truthful, courteous; these qualities are all fruits of the fair tree of love. He must be chaste and must always be clean in his own speech and actions; and he must strongly protest against any coarseness of speech or actions in his fellow-students, and should especially be careful to protect the younger boys from bad talk and bad ways.

A boy who lives in this way during his school and college-life, will, when he goes out into the wider world of men, practise there the virtues that in his school and college days he learned as part of his religion. For there is no division' between true religion and noble living; a religion that does not express itself in nobility of living is an empty shell; a noble life without religion is shorn of its fairest grace.—1903, *Central Hindu College Magazine*

True Object of Education

What after all is the object of Education? *To train the body* in health, vigour and grace, so that it may express the emotions in beauty, and the mind with accuracy and strength. To *train the emotions* to love all that is noble and beautiful; to sympathise with the joys and sorrows of others; to inspire to service ever widening in its area, until we love our elders as our parents, our equals as our brothers and sisters, our youngers as our children, and seek to serve them all:

> to find joy in sacrifice for great causes and for the helpless;
>
> to feel reverence for all who are worthy of it, and compassion for the outcast and the criminal.

To evolve and discipline the mind in right thinking, in right discrimination, in right judgement, in right memory.

To subdue body, emotion, and mind to the *Spirit, the* Inner Ruler *Immortal,* making the mind the mirror of the Ego, the emotions the mirror of the Intuition, the body the expression of the Will. To put all this in a single sentence:

> To *make the man a good Citizen* of *a free and spiritual Commonwealth* of *Humanity.*
>
> —1926, *India: Bond or Free?*

Education of Youth

In teaching *Science,* vigilance must be exerted to shut out many of the ways in which some branches of science are taught in Europe. No experiments on living animals should be permitted; they brutalise the heart and generally mislead the intellect. Reverence for life, compassion, and tenderness to all sentient beings, should be inculcated in the school, by precept and example.

Moral education should form part of the curriculum. Daily, in every class, a brief portion of some sacred book should be read and explained, and its moral lesson enforced by illustrations; their bearing on individual, family, social, and national life should be shown, and the evil results of their opposed vices should be expounded. Occasion should be taken with the elder youths to explain the scientific basis —the basis in nature—on which moral precepts are founded and to point out the wisdom of Hindu religious practices. They will thus acquire an intelligent appreciation of the value of religion and morality.

Sanskrit should be a compulsory subject in every school, as Latin is in European schools. It is the mother of many Indian vernaculars and of Pali; all the greatest treasures of Indian literature are enshrined in it and a knowledge of it should be a necessary part of the education of every Indian gentleman. Such a knowledge should also serve as a national bond, for a common language is one of the strongest elements in nationality. . . But it must be taught in the modern way, that a competent knowledge of it, sufficient for reading and conversation, may be acquired in the short time available for learning it. The fashion in which it was taught in more leisurely ages is not suitable to the needs of the time, and even if it be still used for the training of specialists, it can never be adopted as part of the curriculum in modern education. To insist on teaching it only in the old way is to doom Sanskrit to extinction as a living language universally known by educated Indians. —9 March 1903, *Education as* a *National Duty*

II

It is ... exceedingly important that English should be introduced into Sanskrit Schools in which Pandits are trained . For the growing gulf between English-educated Indians who know no Sanskrit and the Pandits who know no English is a danger alike to religious and national life. These two classes understand each other and sympathise with each other less and less; and the legitimate influence which religious men should wield over worldly men is an ever-diminishing factor in the national life of India. These classes must be drawn nearer together, and this object will largely be gained by all educated men knowing Sanskrit, and all Pandits, the Sanskrit specialists, knowing English and being a little more in touch with Western thought. A course of Western philosophy should form part of a Pandit's education and it would make him all the better able to appreciate and defend the unrivalled philosophic systems in his own literature. Indian thought has influenced the thought of the world, and the effects of this influence should be known and appreciated by those who are its natural custodians. Men, to influence the world, must be in touch with it, and the Pandits are, with each generation, becoming less and less in touch with it, and more and more isolated from their educated countrymen. The difficulty of making Sanskrit part of the necessary education of every gentleman is much overrated. Every Muhammadan gentleman knows Arabic, and can read the *Koran.* Why should the Hindu be more backward in reading the Vedas? To be ignorant of the language in which all his religious ceremonies are performed is to be doomed to irreligion or to unintelligent religion, and such ignorance should be regarded as disgraceful to a man claiming to be educated.

Hindu boarding-houses should be established wherever there are school and college students who come from a distance, and these should be conducted on religious lines; the boys being taught there to observe their religious duties as if living in the atmosphere of a religious Indian home. Here again Muhammadans are ahead of us in their care for the religious training of the young, for such Muhammadan boarding-houses are found near colleges attended by Muhammadan students, whereas Hindu boys are ruthlessly exposed to purely secular or even proselytising influences at the very time when they are most impressible. Are there-no wealthy Hindus who care enough for their faith and their country to help in the care and protection of the young ?

—March 1897. *Theosophist*

It is an honourable and ancient rule of Sanskrit teaching: that the pupils should be taught without fees. Any innovation on this ought to be resisted if you wish to keep up the revived ancient feelings .. . *Every* son of India who desires to know the ancient tongue should find teaching open to him without the necessity for payment, as it was in the ancient days; and not only so, but there ought to be provision made for the maintenance of the students, so that they may be able to pursue their studies without any anxiety, and may be able to learn in order to be fitted to teach afterwards what they have learnt. —1901, India

Education of the Indian Girls

Let us turn to the education of girls, the future wives and mothers of Hindus, those on whom the welfare of the family, and therefore largely the welfare of the nation, depends. Until the last two or three generations the education of Hindu girls was by no means neglected. They were trained in religious knowledge and were familiar with the great Indian epics and with much of the Puranas, to say nothing of the vernacular religious literature. They would' learn by heart thousands of lines of these, and would also have stored in their memory many *stotras.* Hence their children were cradled in an atmosphere full of devotion, fed on sacred songs and stories. Further, they were thoroughly trained in household economy, in the management of the house, and the knowledge of the duties of dependents and servants. They were skilled in medicine and were the family doctors, and many were highly skilled in artistic needlework and music.

If a woman knows medicine, if she knows the value of foodstuffs, if she knows how to deal with the difficulties of a large household, if she has learnt literature by listening to it, not necessarily by reading it, such a woman is a truly educated woman, whether or not she has passed any examinations or holds any University degrees. And that education was very largely spread among those aged grandmothers and great-grandmothers of the immediate past. —17 April 1914, The Birth of *New India*

II

Their education was directed to fit them to discharge their functions in life, to render them competent to fulfil the weighty duties belonging to them in Indian family life. This "old-fashioned education" has now almost entirely disappeared, and the present generation is for the most part singularly incompetent and helpless, too often trivial and childish, unable to train sons and daughters in the noble simplicity and dignity of true Hindu life.

To remedy this admitted deterioration, attempts are being made to introduce "female education," but unhappily, the kind of education mostly essayed, being founded on the needs of Western life, is mischievous rather than beneficial to Indian womanhood. . . . The higher education of women in England and America is mainly directed to fitting women to compete with men as breadwinners in the various professions and Government employment... . Needless to say that in India there is no prospect of such a complete revolution in social life as would break up the family system, drive the women out into the world to earn bread and make them competitors with men in every walk of life. The province of women in India is still the home; such a thing as an unmarried girl is scarcely known, and the joint family system offers a secured shelter to every girl and woman of the family. Their life is a family life, of what avail then to waste the years during which they should be educated to play their part well in the family, in giving them an education suited for Western social life but entirely unsuited to their own ? The school-life of the girl in India must necessarily be brief, and it is therefore the more important that she should spend that brief time to the best possible advantage...

When parents wish their daughters to follow the same course of education as their sons, they can readily secure for them that which they desire. But the *national* movement for the education of girls must be one which meets ' the national needs and India needs nobly trained wives and mothers, wise and tender rulers of the household, educated teachers of the young, helpful counsellors of their husbands, skilled nurses of the sick, rather than girl-graduates, educated for the learned professions.

Let us, then, put down in order the essentials of the education which is desirable for Indian girls.

Religious and Moral Education: But above all else must the Indian girl be trained in the devotion and piety to which her nature so readily responds. Not only should she read, but she should learn by heart, stories and poems from the best Indian literature, *stotras,* and sacred verses. No girl should leave school without becoming familiar with the *Bhagavad Gita,* and knowing much, if not all of it, by heart....

Every girl must be taught the fundamental doctrines of her religion in a clear, simple, and rational method. *The Sanatana Dharma Series I and II,* in the vernaculars, will suit Hindu girls as well as Hindu boys, and girls thoroughly grounded in these will be able to study the *Advanced Text-Book* after leaving school, as they are not likely to remain there to an age fit for such study. The *Mahabharata* and the *Ramayana,* in the vernaculars, should be largely drawn on for moral instruction, as well as *Manu-Smriti,* and Tulsi Das' *Ramayana* should be read by all Hindi-knowing girls.. Girls belonging to the Islamic and Zoroastrian faiths should be similarly instructed, the books of their respective religions taking the place of the Hindu works named above. There is an abundant wealth of beautiful devotional verse in Persian, to culture and elevate the mind of the Muslim girl, to whom also should be opened the stores of Arabic learning. The Zoroastrian has also ample sacred treasures for the instruction of his girls, and can utilise selections from the Avesta, Pahlavi, and Persian...

They should be taught to worship, and simple plain explanations of the worship followed should be given, and, while the devotion so natural to an Indian woman should be nurtured, an intelligent understanding should be added to it, and a pure and enlightened faith, their natural heritage, should be encouraged in them. Where any girl shows capacity for deeper thought, philosophical studies and explanations should not be withheld from her, so that opportunity may be afforded for the reappearance of the type of which Maitreyi and Gargi and the women singers of the Vedas were shining examples....

All the great heroines of Indian story should be made familiar to her with their inspiring example and elevating influence. The Indian ideal of womanhood should be made living to her in these heroic figures, and she should be taught to regard them as her exemplars in her own life. With heart thus trained and memory thus stored, she will be fit to be the "Lakshmi of the House," and the hearts of husband and children will safely trust in her. Girls thus educated will make the Indian home what it ought to be — the centre of spirituality, the strength of the national religious life. Among them we may hope to see revived the glories of the past, the tenderness and fidelity of Sita and Savitri, the intellectual grandeur of Gargi, the all-sacrificing spirituality of Maitreyi....

Literary Education: A sound literary knowledge of the Vernacular should be given, both in reading and writing. Vernacular literature, in Hindi, Urdu, Bengali, Marathi, Gujarati, Telugu, and Tamil, is sufficiently rich in original works and translations to give full scope for study, and to offer a store of enjoyment for the leisure hours of later life. A colloquial knowledge of some Vernacular other than her own would be useful to a girl, if time would allow of the learning. A classical language, Sanskrit or Arabic or Persian, according to the girl's religion, should be learned sufficiently to read with pleasure the noble literature contained therein, and the quick Indian girl will readily master sufficient of one of these tongues to prove a never-failing delight to her in her womanhood, and to listen with intelligent pleasure to the reading of her husband as he enjoys the masterpieces of the great writers.

Indian history and Indian geography should be thoroughly taught.... serving as a basis for future study. It might also, in the higher classes, include the broad outlines of universal history and geography, and of the greatest literary masterpieces of foreign nations... While their minds will be thus widened and their ideas enlarged, at the same time they will be led along lines purely national and in consonance with immemorial ideals. If the Westernising, in a bad sense, of Indian men be undesirable, still more undesirable is such Westernising of the Indian women; the world cannot afford to lose the pure, lofty, tender, and yet strong, type of Indian womanhood. It is desirable, also, seeing how much English thought is dominating the minds of the men, and how many sympathetic Englishwomen seek to know their Indian sisters, that the girls should learn English, and have thus opened to them the world of thought outside India; in later life they may make many a pleasant excursion into that world in the company of their husbands, and the larger horizons will interest without injuring.

Scientific Education: Nothing is more necessary to the Indian wife and mother, ruler often of a household that is a little village, than.

A knowledge of sanitary laws: The hygiene of the household should be thoroughly taught, the value of fresh air, sunlight and scrupulous cleanliness; these were, indeed, thoroughly understood and practised by the elder generation, and must still, if learned in the school-room, find their field of practice in the home; but the latest generation seems to be in all this far behind its grandmothers.

The value of foodstuffs: Essential again is a knowledge of the value of foodstuffs, and of their effect on the body in the building of muscular, nervous, and fatty tissues, of their stimulative or nutrient qualities.

Simple medicines, "first aid" in accidents, nursing the *sick:* Some knowledge of simple medicines is needed by every mother, that she may not be incessantly calling in a doctor. .... She should be thoroughly instructed in medicine, botany, the preparation and use of herbs.... She should also be able to deal with accidental injuries, completely with slight ones, and sufficiently with serious ones to prevent loss of life while awaiting the surgeon's coming; simple nursing every girl should learn, and the importance of accuracy in observing directions, keeping fixed hours for food and medicine, etc.

Cookery of the more delicate kind: A knowledge of cookery has always been part of the education of the Indian housewife, and this should still have its place in education, or there will be little comfort in the houses for husband and children. The Indian cook—like cooks in other countries—does his work all the better if the housemother is able to supervise and correct.

Household management, and the keeping of accounts: Sufficient arithmetic should be learned for all household: purposes, for quick and accurate calculation of quantities and prices, and the keeping of accounts.

Artistic Education: Instruction in some art should form part of the education for a girl, so that leisure in later life may be pleasantly and adequately filled, instead of being wasted in gossip and frivolity. South India is leading the way in musical education, and the prejudice against it is disappearing. The singing of *stotras,* to an accompaniment on the vina, or other instrument, is a refining and delightful art in which the girls take the greatest pleasure, and one which enables them to add greatly to the charm of home. Drawing and painting are arts in which some find delight, and their deft fingers readily learn . .. artistic embroidery and needlework of all kinds... The exquisite Indian embroidery. . with its delicately shaded gradations of colour and its graceful forms . . . trains the eye and the taste. Needless to say that all should learn sewing, darning and the cutting-out of such made-garments as are used in their districts. In all of these, the natural taste of the pupil should be the guide to the selection of the art, though almost all, probably, will take part in singing.

Physical Education: The training and strengthening of the bodies of the future mothers must not be left out of sight, and, to this end, physical exercises of a suitable kind should form part of the school curriculum. In Southern India, the girls are very fond of exercises in which they move to the sound of their own songs, performing often complicated exercises, in some of which patterns are woven and unwoven in coloured threads. .. All these are good; and there are games which give exercise of a pleasant and active kind. These conduce to the health of young bodies, and give grace of movement, removing all awkwardness. Nothing is prettier than to see a group of girls moving gracefully to the sound of their own young voices, in and out, in mazy evolutions, with clapping of soft palms or clash of light playing-sticks. The lack of physical exercise leads to many chronic ailments in womanhood and to premature old age.

Such is an outline of the education which would, it seems to me, prove adequate to the needs of the young daughters of India, and would train them up into useful and cultured women, heads of happy households, "lights of the home."

There will always be some exceptional girls, who need for the due evolution of their faculties a more profound and a wider education, and these must be helped to what they need as individuals, each on her own line. Such girls may be born into India in order to restore to her the learned women of the past, and to place again in her diadem the long lost pearl of lofty female intelligence. It is not for any to thwart them in their upward climbing, or to place unnecessary obstacles in their path.

Of this we may be sure, that Indian greatness will not return until Indian womanhood obtains a larger, a freer, and a fuller life, for largely in the hands of Indian women must lie the redemption of India. The wife inspires or retards the husband; the mother makes or mars the child. The power of woman to uplift or debase man is practically unlimited, and man and woman must walk forward hand-in-hand to the raising of India, else will she never be raised at all. The battle for religious and moral education of boys is won, although the victory has still to be made effective all over India. The battle for the education of girls is just beginning, and may Ishvara bless those who are the vanguard, and all beneficent Powers enlighten their minds and make strong their hearts! —Lectures delivered 1897 and 1904, The *Birth of New India*

Indianise the School

It is not customary for young children—boys and girls and especially girls—to be perched on long benches with their little legs dangling and not able to touch the ground. It is bad from the standpoint of health and it is uncomfortable and they are unaccustomed to it. We propose to introduce nice little mats with little low tables on which books-can be put, and there will not be the strain of unaccustomed and foreign ways of fitting a child to a bench. Mother earth fits every body and that is a great advantage of sitting on the ground. If they have little chowkies they will be far more comfortable than they are at present and far more healthy. It is in that kind of direction that we shall move in Indianising the school. When you come here a little later, you will see the little girls dressed in their beautiful National costume with the saree, and not in the way in which they are dressed at present. It is a mistake to copy foreign fashions when you have beautiful fashions. For over a quarter of a century I have set my face against ugly copies of half-English dress. We shall try to get the children here to honour their country and follow her ways and to grow up to be the mothers, wives, and guides of truly Indian homes. That will be our object in education: to help the girls to grow up and to be what the Indian woman used to be and still to a very large extent is, but adding to that such an amount of the culture which her husband follows that she may be able to be what an Indian woman was in the past — a sympathiser with him in the whole of his life. That is the ideal which we shall put before ourselves.

— 10 July 1918, *New India*

Two things I do not like: the wearing of the English dress by the Indian girls and the use of the Harmonium. The English dress is not hygienic and spoils the beauty, and the harmonium spoils the voice. Indian girls must wear beautiful Indian sarees. Give your girls the Indian atmosphere at home and at school. English painters . .. very much like to paint an Indian lady in her Indian dress. —21 January 1918, *New India*

Organising National Education

> "You may dig your gold wherever you like—in Australia, America, or India—but you must stamp it in the Indian Mint." —21 January 1918, New *India*

Passing to education, there an immense amount has been done and far more has yet to be done... We have only begun the very A.B.C. of the educational reform which is necessary in order to make India what she should be.. . Education is a matter that belongs to the nation when understood. Fathers and guardians are the people who ought to fashion the national education. How long have I been urging upon you to take this matter of education into your own hands, and not leave it for others to guide and plan.. . The things that make a nation great, from the material standpoint, are not the learned professions and Government service, but scientific agriculture, well-devised manufactures, thoughtfully planned arts and crafts, and the innumerable forms of workmanship that go to the building up of national wealth. But along the lines on which education has been carried on, this has been left on one side, and mind you, the blame for that does not lie on the Government; it lies on the people... If, instead of sending your boys to Government college and missionary schools, you built your own schools, and had your own teachers, you might guide education exactly as you would.

A Balanced Education

Classical

Arabic and Sanskrit, these are the two classical languages for India, not Latin and Greek. Instead of French or German, you should teach English and one vernacular, one common language which would serve everywhere as a means of communication between educated and uneducated alike. ... If you had Sanskrit or Arabic according to the religion of the boy, Hindi as a common tongue, a thorough knowledge of his own vernacular, and then the necessary English for all dealings with foreign countries, and in Government and Court matters, you would have an education, so far as languages are concerned, that would make a boy ready for the future, and enable him to take up his work in the world as soon as he goes into it.

Technical

The most important thing, which I have often urged, is *Technical Education*, and, above all, thorough education in agriculture. .. . Famines are preventible things, and things that ought to be prevented. But they can only be prevented by a wiser system of agriculture on the one hand, and by the building up of manufacturing industries throughout the land on the other.

But, mind you, the manufactures that you want are the manufactures of this country. Here arts and crafts are fast dying. Your weaving craft is dying out of existence, because its products are not bought. That brings me to the next point, for education here slips into economics. Why is it that the weavers of cloths, the potters, and metal workers, and the makers of beautiful objects of all kinds, the weavers of shawls in Kashmir, and of muslims and silks in other parts of the land, why are they slowly disappearing ? These people, who by heredity are fitted for the work, are swelling the ranks of the agricultural labourers, starving the land and overcrowding the fields. Why this ? Because for many years you have been wearing foreign goods in preference to home-made ones.. .. Fashion has been more powerful than patriotism. Now, thanks to the Partition of Bengal, poor patriotism has a chance. But the present enthusiasm for Swadeshi goods will only be a flare like the blaze of twigs, easily lighted and quickly dying out, unless a principle underlies the movement and not a passing political irritation. No durable things are built on violent passion. Nature grows her plants in silence and in darkness, and only when they have become strong do they put their heads above the ground... Without home manufactures, there is no prosperity; without home manufactures, there are recurring famines; without home manufactures, there are overcrowded, unproductive professions and undermanned industrial pursuits ...

Help this movement in every way that you can, save by ways that are wrong, for remember that the Devas are behind all national policies, and therefore that the wrong way is always the long way, and useless. ... Be a little patient.. .. Governments are not perfect, any more than the governed. After all, Governments are only men, just as you are, with the same faults and the same shortsightedness. Therefore the Government should learn to be patient with the governed and the governed with the Government. . . . Politics are constantly changing, one burning question today and another tomorrow. Go on quietly and steadily without any fuss, building up your Indian manufactures, educating your sons. You think brains are wanted for pleading; much more are brains wanted for carrying on large agricultural and industrial concerns. We want the brightest brains for the building up of Indian industries at the present time. If an Indian Prince wants to have an electrical plant installed in his capital, he has to go to Europe to find an engineer who will set up for him his electrical machinery. That must be so until you educate your boys on the right lines. Educate them on all the lines of learning wanted to make a nation great.... A calling which helps national prosperity is more-respectable than a calling which does not. That is a lesson that has to be learned in modern India . . . — 1910, *India's Awakening*

In giving technical education more completely, do not forget that you must have employment for your own educated *men,* and that you must make a public opinion which will cry shame on the Indian Prince or the Indian man of wealth who gives preference to the foreigner rather than to the man of his own country when he is equally well educated. ...

—17 April 1914, *The Birth of New India*

.... What is really needed is to make education cheap, widespread, scientific, literary, and technical: to change the policy which draws the intelligent Indians only into Government service, and to get them to take up other lines of work which affect the economic future of their country; to educate them in arts and manufactures; not to leave the direction of industry to people who are of the ruling nation, but to draft into industrial undertakings large members of the educated classes—that is the kind of education that is wanted, and the kind of education that England does not give to India, and will not let India give to herself.

—1903, *England and India*

A System of National Education

Our method ... is to classify each part of Education in ... four departments, Physical, Emotional, Mental, and Spiritual. .. .

We would divide up the life of a student into certain distinct parts:

Up to 14 Years — General Education

Up to 5 years of age: Training at Home during which the physical body is to be developed, and his emotions to be burned to the unselfish side instead of the selfish one.

We hold that the training, the nurture, the nourishing of the body is the chief thing for a young child.

From 5 years to 7: A training in Primary school based on the child's desires, the child's curiosity, the child's questions, for thus you find what the child likes, what he wants to know, and along what lines his faculties lead him. To such schools children come very gladly . . . because they are going to a place where they are happy, and where, in that happiness, true education is possible.

From *7 to 10 years:* The child should be in the Lower Secondary School.

From *10 to 14* in the Higher Secondary. These seven years see the growth of the emotional nature, the mind also developing but being dominated by emotion. From 10 years of age should come the training of the feelings, which is so vital for the future, so that the surging emotions which accompany and follow puberty may be directed and brought under control instead of poisoning the life. The moral teaching is directed to the developing of the virtues which make the good man and the good citizen. The physical education includes, for the individual in relation to his body, instruction in the physiology of sex — plant, animal, human — the individual and National need of Brahmacharya in student life, the danger of errors in the great transition from boyhood to manhood. The body to be trained in muscular strength, hardness, and athletics, before the danger-zone is entered. Indian exercises to be practised daily. Carpentry basketwork and the use of tools to be practised. First Aid to be taught. In the relation to the outer world, the individual must learn his duty to the Motherland of making and keeping vigorous health. The self-control of true-manliness, the training of the playground in cooperation, discipline, obedience, and the leadership of merit — all are important. From very childhood the eye, the ear, and the mind, is trained. Make the boy a complete and useful citizen of the country, so that he begins to love the work he does, and one sees how in a few months the faculties develop surprisingly.

After 14 Years — Specialisation

Through two years in

- An Ordinary High School, with its Art, Science and Teachers' Training Division;
- Commercial High School;
- Technical High School;
- Agricultural High School.

A year of University Preparatory Work. Three years in the University, if the students are to go still further.

A requisite for advancement into collegiate grade—that the student should be shown how to do things which afterwards he will continue to study.

Underprivileged Children must go into special schools where they will be taught the elements of civilization, of decent living, and only when they have reached a suitable stage will they then go along with the others. —1919, *Problems* of Reconstruction

National University

The first ideal of a National University is that of service to the Motherland, the training of the national character. ... The next great ideal is that it must be a centre of an all-round Culture for the Nation. By culture I mean knowledge plus emotion. A man should be trained in emotion by music, by drama, by poetry, by literature, etc. They are all needed to produce culture. They purify the emotions. Where intelligence and emotion are balanced and both active, the man is truly cultured. The National University must also be a centre of Research, must be a centre of men trained to develop knowledge and to desire knowledge for its own sake.. .. The University has also a duty to the Nation. It should communicate to the adults of the Nation, in a form more popular than the teaching and training in a college, in comparatively untechnical language, the results of research ... so that they may keep themselves abreast with the knowledge of the day. . .. The University should set a standard of education ... and by its own methods it should discourage false lines of education and encourage good lines. There must be in the future at least one university for each of the great vernaculars.

On this the whole of National Education turned.. .. We should throw open the way from the village school to the University. A degree or diploma should be based not on the results of a particular examination but on the result of the study of the student through the whole period of which that examination was the close. Students' merit should not be judged by strange examiners, by somebody outside the College but by the Professors themselves. A University Professor might be added to the Board of Examiners in each subject. ... From the elementary school right up there should be a double line of teaching, intellectual teaching and practical manual training . . . The training of the senses is as essential as the training of the brain...

The elder men have to train the younger men as citizens of a free country to prepare them for the heavy burden of national responsibility, to make them strong physically, mentally, emotionally, and spiritually. Hence the necessity for National Education. —1 March 1918, *New India*

Do you want a denominational or a National University ? Will you have a University built up by Hindus for Hindus, another by Musalmans for Musalmans and another perhaps by Parsis for Parsis and so on; or will you have a system of a National University which shall affiliate alike denominational and undenominational colleges ? I am in favour of a National University and not a denominational University. I am in favour of denominational schools or colleges, but a National University that unites them together. —21 January 1906, Calcutta, reprinted January 1918, *New India*

[Dr. Besant dreamt of a great *National University with daughter colleges in all the great cities in the land "wherein the great gulf between the West and the East could be bridged, wherein its students will know the West without becoming aliens from their ancestral faith."]*

It is the mightiest enterprise for which I ask your sympathy, your goodwill, and your financial aid. I know that it will succeed, because the blessings of the Great Ones are on it, know it will succeed, because it is for the benefit of the future of India, which is at the heart of every one of us. But that future depends on Indians, and on no other people and on no other country. The Indian nation will not grow by the influence of any other nation, but by the growth of character within India's own boundary. England can never make you free. You can only make yourselves free by becoming noble and upright, brave and true. Nations made of such men must be free. Your destiny lies in your own hands. Your future is to be of your creating. You must build the basis of noble character, and of the public spirit which shows itself in true citizenship. You must prove yourselves worthy to be a part of a mighty Empire ... India must be governed on the basis of Indian feelings, Indian traditions, Indian thought, and Indian ideas. That is true.

It is possible that if India only grows up to the height of her possibilities, the time will come when she will send her best and noblest counsellors to take their part in a great Imperial Council gathered round the Monarch for the ruling of the Empire. I dream of a time when India will help to build the Empire with that genius for statesmanship and clear insight which are found from time to time in great Indian ministers. These qualities will be utilised for the good of the Empire, for the good of the mighty whole of which India is a part. The times are gone by for small nations, for' petty States, and for little peoples.

The tendency now is towards raising a vast realm, united by common aims and common love. India in the future should aid to build such an Empire, should help to bear its burdens and share its responsibilities. I dream of a time when India, England, Australasia, and Canada will all join hands in the making of a common Empire, when India's children will bring their priceless treasures to the enriching of that Empire. But for this her children must first build their character, for without that they will never be able to accomplish aught.

—9 March 1903, *Education as a National Duty*

Mother Tongue

I can think of no young generation happier than the present. It is the leaders today who are battling for the freedom of the Motherland, and it is the younger men who will inherit the power and the responsibility that the victory of the leaders will secure to India. Not into the hands of the elder fighters will pass as it were, the spoils of the victory. They fight for the future, not for themselves; although they know that in a later generation they also should return to the land that they have liberated in order to enjoy the blessings which in the present life they struggle for. But it is on the young men of today, the young men in schools and colleges, the young men at present scarcely known at the Bar, the young men who will carry on the industry, trade and commerce, that will fall the glorious responsibility of freedom, and it is on them the country looks with eyes of hope and eagerness. It is no light thing to be a citizen of a country that is free.

Many of us may think of the joy and the glory of it. It is well to remember the burden and the responsibility. On the free citizen in a free State lies the whole welfare of the country, and as he lives, so will the country prosper. As he leads and guides, so shall the country go forward among the Nations of the world; as he develops wisdom and courage, so shall his country rise in the scale of Nations. To that great end, there lies on the younger generation, especially those who are still in school and college, that supreme duty of service. There are things that the young men can do which the elders are too much occupied to perform. The study of the condition of the country, the going about among the poor, the learning how the poor live, making friends with them, trying to alleviate their sufferings and teaching them to uplift themselves—these are all the practical ways in which social service could be rendered. The young men must study their vernaculars and make them the media of their thought and daily actions in life.

They must' realise that the mother tongue is the great instrument for the uplift of the country, and that no foreign tongue can ever reach the people as well as their vernacular language which moves their emotions and thrills their hearts. Our younger men, while still in their schools and colleges, should study their vernacular and have it as the medium of full) expression. It is not true that modern thought cannot be expressed in the vernacular of the provinces — vernaculars in which a great literature exists, so great enough and rich-enough as to touch the spring of patriotism, to inspire the: hearts of the people, and to make them realise their dignity as citizens of the country. If you cannot reach the masses by your vernaculars, you will never reach them at all by any other method. So, I would urge on you young men to cultivate the vernacular and not to look on it as a burden.

—16 April 1,918, *New India*

Cornerstone of the New World Order

How is . . inequality to be reduced in our new social order ? Clearly by education, by giving an education which will draw out everything which is in the child, not allowing it to be withheld because of poverty. . . .

What you are giving them in schools to a great extent today is not education, not a drawing-out of faculties in the child already, but a forcing into his memory of large numbers of facts which you take out of him again in the examination room. That is not education; it is cramming and not very successful cramming either.

Individual Education

What you want first of all to do . . . is to study the child and find out what qualities he has, what capacities he has, and what powers he has, and you can only do that by giving him a very large amount of freedom, by not forcing him into a groove with children who you think are like him, whereas they are most unlike. Hence you want individual education . . .

Essence of Good Teaching

Instead of having teachers who will have a certain number of children around them whom they teach and of whom they ask questions for the children to answer, you will have the children asking the teacher questions: not what the teacher wants them to know, but what the children want to know themselves. That is the essence of good teaching . .. continually placing before the child all the things he wants to know and wants to learn, so that education may develop the faculties he has, instead of trying to force upon him the faculties he has not. If that were done the schools would become a place of joy and happiness; as it is we transfer them into forcing places. .. .

One great rule of our social order should be: Every child who is born into a civilized nation will be certain of the circumstances which bring out of him to the full every faculty which he has brought with him into the world. That is the cornerstone on which I would found the new Society . . . Education should be free, paid for out of the taxes. —August 1928, *The Theosophist*

Education of the Depressed Classes

"Children ought to grow like flowers in the sunshine and not like weeds in the cellar. In every nation we find as the basis of the social pyramid, a large class of people, ignorant, degraded, unclean in language and habits, people who perform many tasks which are necessary for society, but who are despised and neglected by the very society to whose needs they minister.... In India this class forms one-sixth of the total population and goes by the generic name of the "depressed classes." It springs from the aboriginal inhabitants of the country, conquered and enslaved by the Aryan invaders, but has a civilization behind it. ... The scavengers, sweepers, husbandmen, and the followers of other simple crafts who make up the huge bulk of the depressed .. . are gentle, docile, as a rule industrious, pathetically submissive, merry enough when not in actual want, with a bright though generally very limited intelligence; of truth and the civic virtues they are for the most part utterly devoid — how should they be anything else?—but they are affectionate, grateful for the slightest kindness, and with much "natural religion." In fact they offer good material for simple and useful, though humble civic life, very much better material than is found in the lowest strata of western lands... .

Shall they Attend the General Schools?

Here, as everywhere, education is the lever by which we may hope to raise them, but a difficulty arises at the outset, for one class of the community moved by a noble feeling of compassion and benevolence, but not adding thereto a careful and detailed consideration of the conditions, demands for the children of the pariah community admission to the schools frequented by the sons of the higher classes, and charges with lack of brotherhood those who are not in favour of this policy. It becomes, therefore, necessary to ask whether brotherhood is to mean levelling down, and whether it is usual in a family to treat the elder children and the babies in exactly the same way. It is a zeal not according to knowledge—and not according to nature—which would substitute equality for brotherhood, and demand from the cultured and refined that they should forfeit the hardly won fruits of the education of generations, in order to create an artificial equality, as disastrous to the progress of the future as it would be useless for the improvement of the present.

The children of the depressed classes need, first of all, to be taught cleanliness, outside decency of behaviour, and the earliest rudiments of education, religion, and morality. Their bodies, at present, are ill-odorous and foul, with the liquor and strong smelling foods out of which for generations they have been built up; it will need some generations of purer food and living to make their bodies fit to sit in the close neighbourhood of a schoolroom with children who have received bodies from an ancestry trained in habits of exquisite personal cleanliness, and fed on pure foodstuffs. We have to raise the depressed classes to a similar level of physical purity, not to drag down the clean to the level of the dirty, and until this is done, close association is undesirable. We are not blaming these children, nor their parents, for being what they are; we are stating a mere palpable fact. The first daily lesson in a school for these children should be a bath, and the putting on of a clean cloth, and the second should be a meal of clean wholesome food; those primary needs cannot be supplied in a school intended for children who take their daily bath in the early morning, and who come to school well fed.

Another difficulty that faces teachers of these children is the contagious diseases that are bred from dirt; to take one example, eye-disease, wholly due to neglect, is one of the most common and "catching "complaints among them. In our Panchama schools in Madras the teachers are ever on the alert to detect and check this, and the children's eyes are daily washed and the disease is thus prevented. But is it to be expected that fathers and mothers, whose daily care protects their children from such dirty diseases, should deliberately expose them at school to this infection?

Nor are the manners and habits of these forlorn little ones desirable things to be imitated by gently-nurtured children. Good manners, for instance, are the result of continual and rigid self-control, and of consideration for the comfort and convenience of others; children learn manners chiefly by imitation from well-bred parents and teachers, and secondarily by suitable precept and reproof. If, at the school, they are to be made to associate with children not thus trained, they will quickly fall into the ways which they see around them. For until good habits are rendered fixed by long practice, it is far easier to be slipshod than accurate, to be careless than careful. Ought the children of families in which good manners and courtesy are hereditary, to be robbed of their heritage, a robbery that enriches no one, but drags the whole nation down ? Gentle speech, well-modulated voice, pleasant ways, these are the valuable results of' long culture, and to let them be swamped out is no true brotherhood. Rather should we try to share them with our younger brothers by training them as we have ourselves been trained....

A man in England who proposed that ragged school children should be admitted to Eton and Harrow would not be argued with, but laughed at. Here, when a similar proposition is made in the name of brotherhood, people seem ashamed to point out frankly its absurdity, and they do not realise that the proposal is merely a violent reaction against the cruel wrongs which have been inflicted on the depressed classes, the outcry of an awakened conscience, which has not yet had time to call right reason to guide its emotions ... It is scarcely likely that I urge this on my Indian brethren from indifference to the suffering: for thirty-four years I have worked for those who suffer; but, perhaps, because I have so long been in close touch with them, I know that they are not at present fit to come into association with children of happier surroundings . . .

Hence the duty and responsibility which lie upon us of improving both the surroundings and the characters of the depressed classes by every means in our power, shortening the period of their lives in this stage, and utilising our knowledge in their favour. By teaching their children the elements of right living, we draw out and cultivate the germinal powers of the soul; and by checking and repressing the faults which are manifest, by improving their food and their environment, we help to build better bodies suitable for the more unfolded souls. This is the help we both can give and ought to give to these our successors on the stage of the world, and small will be our claim to the help of the Greater Ones, if we refuse our help to these little ones of the human race. How shall we dare to plead to the Lords of Compassion to stoop to us and help us to rise, unless we, in our turn, stoop to those below us, and seek to raise them up.

—1909, The Birth of New India

Night Schools

There is no duty more pressing and more incumbent ore all men and women who love their country than an attempt to spread education among those whose circumstances in life make it difficult for them to obtain it without much help from outside.. .. The fact that certain classes of the population who are most in need of help . .. send to the schools people of different ages makes their work the more difficult and demands more exertion from those who guide it. If a young lad comes to a night school who is also employed in the day it is clear that his longing for knowledge is of the very strongest kind and that some scheme should as far as possible be adopted which will make the gaining of that knowledge easy to him, which will make it attractive and easily assimilated.... In England, they are proposing that even where the child is employed in some form of livelihood he shall still be kept under some educational control up to the age of eighteen. Such a proposal shows a very great advance....

In the case of the younger children that come to these schools, dealing as you are with children earning a livelihood, you have to consider whether you cannot make your education helpful to them in the vocation which they have taken up. The great fault to a large extent of the education of the children, especially of the poor, has been that instead of making it vocational, it has been entirely apart from the ordinary life, and the result is that the brain is not trained in a fashion which will enable it to apply the training intelligently to life. The effect of the education upon the poor is to drive them to the most underpaid and overworked class of the community of the semi-educated clerk. It is not that class that you want to increase. You want to give to the boys and girls a means of earning their bread which will increase the wealth of the country as well as the wealth of the individual and enable them to earn a livelihood which will put them beyond a continual struggle for bread.

From the beginning, you must train the hands of the children, the senses of the children, as well as the intelligence of the children. The lessons given in a night schools should be short and varied. The attention of a child, especially of a child that has been working during the day is difficult to hold. When you are dealing with young children, you will find that the very moment the attention begins to wander it is well to change the subject of the teaching. With regard to the older pupils who come to these night schools and who belong to the labouring classes, you will find that they are very little interested in learning how to read and write. They are not only interested in information that bears upon their ordinary work and life, but in village schools you find that they are eager to learn by taking part in repetition of what is read, rather than learning in modern fashion. Enormous good would be done by having talks with such pupils on subjects such as sanitation, hygiene, conditions of the body, and things which interest them in everyday life.

One of the most promising things is the inclination for Cooperative Societies to grow up among the pupils in the night schools. There is no quicker way to help people crushed by debts borrowed at exorbitant interest than to start such societies and help them to pay off their debts at easy rates of interest.

There is one thing that is universally true: the measure of service that you can give to your fellow men is the measure of happiness in your own life. Instead of seeking happiness for yourself, if you seek to spread happiness among those less fortunate than yourself, you will wake up to find that your life is full of happiness and that it flows back to you The deepest thing in us is the unity which grows out of the One Life in which we are all rooted. We cannot bring out that life and expand it, as happiness expands life, without sharing the expansion that we have made possible for the life of another.

Sacrifice, to the life within us, is a joy and not a sorrow. It may be sacrifice looked at from the standpoint of the body, but it is joy looked at from the standpoint of the spirit that gives, and the life in you lives by sacrifice. The life of your body lives by taking—it is the essence of matter and it grows by what it takes and assimilates. But the life of the spirit is just the reverse of it; it grows by giving and not by taking, by spreading to others and not by accumulating in itself, and it is a splendid truth as regards all that is non-physical that it increases as you give and does not diminish. If I am imparting knowledge and if I am sharing happiness and striving to give life and share it with others, as I give away it increases in myself, and the more I give, the more I have to give.

As you grow older and older you will find the truth told in so many scriptures and proved to be true in so many experiences that such work as is being done to help the poor, the attempts that are made to instruct the ignorant, to feed the hungry, to spread happiness among the miserable, will come back to the givers in ever-increasing measure and they will find a joy than which no joy on earth is greater, that in the realisation of Brotherhood they have found that unity of the Self which it is the effort of all to realise and live in, knowing that in that alone is bliss, in that alone is rest.

—30 April 1918, New India

To What End, Education?

Why should I speak to you about education, and urge you to make it a matter for the Nation, and not only a matter for the Government ? I speak to you on this, because there is one thing that we all are hoping and working for, that great building up of India into one mighty Nation, United India. It is towards that all our efforts should be turning, and we must build up young men and women of character, of courage, of patriotism, and of self-sacrifice, because only out of these elements can a nationality be built.' People sometimes say... that India is only "a geographical expression." ... The prophet creates the ideal, and the thinker places it before the mass of the people; with the fire of his genius he lights the flame of patriotism, which from the altar of his heart is to spread to the hearts of the people. Now the prophecy of the dreamers that India shall yet be a mighty nation is proving true today; forces are at work which are drawing together the people from the Himalayas to Tuticorin, from Assam in the East to Kathiawar in the West; the India of the future lives in our hearts and hopes today, and she will come down into actuality when her children are worthy of her....

In the genius of the Indian people it is the woman, it is the mother, who is raised above all others, and the love for the mother is the deepest in the heart of every man. And so he calls India the Motherland, and not the Fatherland. And when the Indian home is ready, then the Mother shall come to her place; built as she is now as an ideal, she shall become a reality.... That is the India that is coming, that is the India that is building, and you are the builders who are training the young for her service. They shall reap what you are sowing; they shall build in actuality what you are building in hope and in ideal. You remember what Mr. Gokhale said, words so noble that they can never weary us in their repetition: "It will be for others in the future to serve India by their successes; we must be content to serve her by our failures." I know of no nobler words spoken by nobler patriot, for greater are they who in the dark believe in the dawning, than they who stand in the glory of the sunlight; those who know in the depths of their strong hearts that the dawn shall come and the shadows disappear.

Sometimes I look forward to the happier days of tomorrow, when all roads shall be open, when all ways shall be clear, when a vast Empire shall look round on her children filled with patriotism; then men and women in other lands will look back to the days in which we are, and they will say: "We thank them that in the days of fear they still were brave; that in the days of ignorance they still looked forward to the hope; that in the darkness they never forgot the coming light." For it is a grander thing to serve while others stand back, than to take part in the progress of a mighty nation, when all the Empire welcomes the children born of her womb. —17 April 1914, *The Birth of New India*

7

Tributes to Greatness

Mahatma Gandhi

Cultivate the great qualities of Dr. Besant, namely, firmness, simplicity, self-control, etc. She is one of the greatest orators of the world, because she speaks what she believes and acts according to what she speaks. She has the courage of her convictions and always puts her words into action. .. Imitate her unflinching determination and simplicity of life .... Obtain the same strength and indomitable will that she possesses which alone will bring Swaraj. India is not fit for Swaraj without these qualities. Remove India's chains and then alone will we achieve our goal. Religion is interwoven in Dr. Besant's life and she has built a bridge between politics and religion. Swaraj without religion is of no use. It is Dr. Besant who has awakened India from her deep slumber and I pray that she may live long to witness a free India.

—2 October 1928, *New India*

Gurudev Tagore

(To a Friend)

In your letter you seem puzzled at my conduct in sending a message of sympathy to Mrs. Besant. I am afraid, compared with your own troubles, it may appear to you too-small, but yet sufferings have not lost their keenness for us, and moral problems still remain as the gravest of all problems in all parts of the world. The constant conflict between the growing demand of the educated community of India for a substantial share in the administration of their country and the spirit of hostility on the part of the Government has given rise, among a considerable number of our young men, to methods of violence, bred of despair and distrust. This has been met by the Government by a thorough policy of repression. In Bengal itself hundreds of men are interned without trial, a great number in unhealthy surroundings, in gaols and in solitary cells, in a few cases driving them to insanity or suicide.

The misery that is carried into numerous households is deep and widespread. What I consider to be the worst outcome of this irresponsible policy is the spread of the contagion of hatred against everything western in minds which were free from it. In this crisis the only European who has shared our sorrow, incurring the anger and derision of her countrymen, is Mrs. Annie Besant.

This was what led me to express my grateful admiration for her noble courage. Possibly there is such a thing as political exigency, just as there may be a place for utter ruthlessness in War; but I pay my homage to those who have faith in ideals and, therefore, are willing to take all other risks except that of weakening the foundation of moral responsibility.

—25 September 1917, *New India*

Lokamanya Tilak

You have adopted India to be your Motherland; you have suffered a great deal for her, and found her almost triumphant. India is united for the commonwealth, and all our efforts are directed towards reaching the goal of Swaraj. Our reception may not be as magnificent as from others you may have obtained. But I may assure you it comes from the inmost of our hearts. If India is nearer the goal, it is due to your strenuous efforts, and, if I may be allowed to add also, largely to your internment. Regarding you as an embodiment of our principles and our success, we offer you our welcome and wish you long life and inexhaustible energy.

—15 October 1917, New India

M.A. Jinnah

No other person has worked and served our cause with that singleness of purpose, devotion, and transparent sincerity as has Mrs. Besant. She has sacrificed all that she could. What for ? For the freedom of India. —20 February 1918, *New India*

Sir S. Subramania Iyer

The Empires which have hitherto been built in the world have been built either by military commanders or by statesmen .... The time has now come when Empire-building must have a different basis .... The Empire-builder of today must have qualities vastly different from previous builders and statesmen, if today he is to carry out the plan of the Supreme. That means building with the power of religion and without the power of the sword....

The new type of Empire-building, which the world now requires, is most strikingly exemplified by Dr. Besant, and the type is seen in her work for India. Her work will best be understood by those who realise the unusual task involved in building India to be a vital part of the British Empire. Here in this land we have many languages and many forms of religion, which separate the peoples into many communities. Now all these must be welded into one whole and unless that work is done here, the British Empire is bound to fail, for without India there is nothing in the British Empire but a name and if the British Empire does not perform the high role before it, the future of the world will be seriously handicapped for ages. Therefore, Brotherhood as an essential principle in Empire-building in India is imperative. The Hindus must be united with the Muhammadans, and the Jains and Buddhists...

Now India is not a *tabula rasa;* the Empire-builder is not dealing with primitive peoples with no traditions or culture. India is a land of many communities who cherish a hoary civilization. They have their own religions, sciences, arts, and literatures. Therefore, the Empire-builder cannot do his work with the sword, but must appeal to reason and spirituality, in order to suit the new conditions of building. Who can accomplish this task except a soul of the type of Dr. Besant ? The required elements of love and sympathy can only be provided by one of her sex; no man, however great, could show these qualities as finely as a woman. That is why the ego we know as Dr. Besant has been put into a woman's body to do her work in India. She has, however, at the same time, an iron will which supplies the element of the male sex. It is this will that was made manifest... in her refusal to concede by way of compromise any deviation in the matter of principle, even for the sake of obtaining her liberty and escaping from persecution that was likely to endanger her life, thus revealing the trait of the martyr.

Dr. Besant's whole life is so spiritual that, as an Empire-builder, she is not aiming at a political institution but a spiritual organisation. The especial characteristic mark of that organisation may be said to be Aryan, for Dr. Besant represents the Indo-Aryan type in perfection. She has in her nature all its elements; when lecturing in Christian countries she is recognised as an exponent of Christianity; in India well recognise her as an authority on our religion; and it is the same when she lectures to Buddhist or Muhammadan audiences. Dr. Besant has the power of combining the various elements of Indo-Aryan culture and producing from them a beautiful mosaic.

This is important, for if an Empire is to be built in India it must have this character of a mosaic, and unless the builder is himself of this nature of a mosaic, the work cannot be done. Undoubtedly, Dr. Besant stands in a peculiar relation to the people of India. She has repeatedly stated her own belief that in her previous lives she has again and again been born in India, and that her present Western birth is only for the purpose of supplementing her Indian character with something of the Western, in order that she might do better her work of organisation for India .... There is no instance of a single Western person, except herself, who has called forth ... such universal love and sympathy from every part of India. The educated and the uneducated, the English-speaking and those who know not a word of English, have all united in one profound admiration and reverence, and many are the prayers that go up from temple and shrine on her behalf today.

It is interesting to note how Dr. Besant began her work of Empire-building. When she came to India, she did not at once work in the political field. She expounded one religion after another, emphasising the common unity of faith and aspiration. In India, where religion may degenerate into fanaticism, with its concomitant of bloodshed, Dr. Besant's first work was to make fanaticism impossible, and today the whole attitude of Hindus to Muhammadans and vice versa has changed, so far as religion is concerned.

Her next work was to put education upon a religious basis. A lasting monument to her education work is the Hindu University, which she organised as the Central Hindu College of Banaras.... The Central Hindu College, under Dr. Besant's guidance, was the first large institution definitely to embody the teaching of religion as part of its curriculum. The impulse she gave has influenced hundreds of schools to make religious teaching and worship an integral part of education. And to crown all her labours, she has... organised the National Board of Education, comprising many of the leading men in India, to put education on a thoroughly national basis.

The next unique thing that Dr. Besant has done is to bring together the Hindus and the Muhammadans as brothers in one common National work. This is a miracle, the significance of which only those living in India can understand; and though many have helped in this union, she stands supremely as the worker of the great miracle. No less marvellous is the fact that this stupendous work has been achieved in the course of three years, since she took up political work. There are few Empire-builders who can show such a record of work in so brief a time. Not less noteworthy is her bringing together once again into a common political body the "Extremists" and the "Moderates" of the Indian National Congress. Many had prophesied that these two bodies would never unite, but Dr. Besant has done it.

Dr. Besant has brought about union, because of the force of the ideals which she has lived in her own life. One of the prominent Muhammadan leaders, the Hon. Mr. Syed Wazir Hassan, Secretary of the All-India Muslim League, referred the other day in a public meeting "to the spiritual side of her life, and how ennobling from that point of view her influence has been." "I look upon Dr. Annie Besant," he said, "as an embodiment and external symbol of what is my ideal of existence. Life is not worth living without such ideals, and we should resist with all our power attacks threatening the fulfilment of our hopes and the attainment of our ideals." ...

All through Dr. Besant's work in India she has continually emphasised the inseparable bond between India and England, Indeed, her insistence upon this essential element of the future has made her to be sharply criticised by those in India who have not believed as firmly in the ideals of the British Empire as she has done.

It is just because she has this ideal conception of the British Empire that she has been so anxious to emphasise the unique nationality and worth of the Indian peoples to the British Empire, It is this that has made her preach Home Rule against the wish of ninety-nine per cent of her race in India. The sincerity of her purpose could not be evinced better than by her unflagging work of uplifting the peoples of India in spite of every misrepresentation and even vilification.

One noteworthy characteristic of her political work is its constitutionalism. Never for a moment has she hesitated to denounce violence in every form.... She has not been merely critical, she has actually shown the methods of construction. The "Madras Parliament," which she organised for training in Parliamentary method and debate has to its credit ... a number of carefully worked-out Acts....

Dr. Besant is a profound mystic and when, after twenty-one years of strenuous life in India, she entered into the political field, it was as a practical mystic of a unique type. ... Dr. Besant is unique in that she only uses peaceful persuasion; she achieved her work by calling forth the powers of faith within men. It was well said by Sir Arthur Lawley, when he was Governor of Madras, "Her voice is never raised save to move her hearers to some nobler impulse, to some loftier ideal, to some higher plane of thought."

—1 October 1917, New *India*

C.Y. Chintamani, Editor, 'Leader'

Where can one find the like of this marvellous personage in the combination of the qualities of enthusiasm, eloquence, power of organisation, courage, energy, determination, purposefulness, optimism, and faith in her mission ? Truly is she a living wonder. To how many millions has she not been the inspiration and the unapproachable example?

If Irish in body, Mrs. Besant is Hindu in spirit and faith, and she has looked upon and served India as her Motherland with a devotion and at a sacrifice equalled by few and surpassed by none. We pay her today our tribute of admiration and respect, and are proud to be able to do so.

8

Golden Words of Annie

- Liberty is a great celestial Goddess, strong, beneficent, and austere, and she can never descend upon a Nation by the shouting of crowds, nor by the arguments of unbridled passion, nor by the hatred of class against class.
- Refusal to believe until proof is given is a rational position; denial of all outside of our own limited experience is absurd.
- No philosophy, no religion, has ever brought so glad a message to the world as this good news of Atheism.
- Better remain silent, better not even think, if you are not prepared to act.
- Never forget that life can only be nobly inspired and rightly lived if you take it bravely and gallantly, as a splendid adventure in which you are setting into an unknown country, to face many a danger, to meet many a joy, to find many a comrade, to win and lose many a battle.
- For centuries the leaders of Christian thought spoke of women as a necessary evil, and the greatest saints of the Church are those who despise women the most.

- I will suggest that the great aim of our education is to bring out of the child who comes into our hands every faculty that he brings with him, and then to try to win that child to turn all his abilities, his powers, his capacities, to the helping and serving of the community which is a part.

9

Great Life at a Glance

1847, Oct. 1: *Annie Besant*, nee Wood, the rationalists' rationalist, the 'militant Annie' was born in England, but her destiny was linked to India.

1867: Annie married Frank Besant, a clergyman, when she was nineteen year old.

1874: Bradlaugh formed a partnership with Annie Besant. Highly intelligent, attractive and an effective speaker, Annie had left her husband, Frank Besant, Anglican Vicar of Sibsey, after losing her Christian faith.

1885, Jan.: Becoming a friend of George Bernard Shaw, Sidney and Beatrice Webb, Annie Besant joined the Socialist Fabian Society. She and Shaw were also on the executive committee of the Social Democratic Federation. She agreed with the Fabians' gradual approach to reform as evolution, instead of revolution. Besant wrote pamphlets on why she was a socialist and on the socialist movement.

1888, Jun. 23: Annie Besant, a campaigner for women's welfare and rights, published an article called 'White Slavery in London'. She revealed the terrible conditions and poor wages suffered by the match girls employed at the Bryant and May factory in the east-end of London. The match girls worked for long hours at very low wages, and could lose part of their wages in fines for such offences, as arriving late or talking. Still worse, their working conditions were dangerous.

1889, May: Long before Annie Besant joined the Theosophical Society, she had established herself as a leading figure in London's social activism scene, as a champion for the rights of the poor and dispossessed as a strong defender of freedom of thought and expression. She made history on taking up the case of the matchmaker girls by exposing before society and the judicial system. The appalling working conditions, those young women endured.

1893: After joining the Theosophical Society Annie Besant not only took up the cause of India with renewed vigour, but also, made her permanent home in the country. During her first visit Mrs. Besant travelled 6000 miles into many parts of the subcontinent and delivered 120 lectures and addresses in public.

1895: Jiddu Krishnamurti was born and adopted by Annie Besant, President of the Theosophical Society, who brought him to England to live and be educated, and raised with the expectation that he would be the predicted "World Teacher." Unfortunately for this expectation, he rejected this role, and disbanded the organisation built for him.

1902, Sept. 26: Annie Besant, a prominent champion of women's rights, especially for the poor and underprivileged, a leading figure in the Theosophical Society, and the first woman and the only non-Indian to become President of the Indian National Congress, was initiated into the Co-Masonic Order in Paris.

1907: Mrs. Annie Besant, who was British by birth, became the President of the International Theosophical Society after the death of its founder, Col. Olcott, who had started many schools for the young children in the city of Madras and its suburbs.

1909: The Hidden Side of Lodge Meetings,' by CW Leadbeater; 'Extracts of Lectures' by Annie Besant, given in Paris in *1909*. (The future that Awaits Us; the Second Coming of the Christ; the End of a Cycle and the Beginning of a New Era) published by the Lodge Annie Besant of Havana, Cuba, for Lodges and members speaking the Spanish language.

1916, Sept.: Dr. Annie Besant, inspired by the Irish rebellion, started a Home Rule Movement in India. The movement spread rapidly and branches of the Home Rule League were established all over India. Bal Gangadhar Tilak wholeheartedly supported the movement. He joined forces with Dr. Besant and persuaded the Muslim League to support the programme as well.

1917, June: The movement was intensified, when the Madras Government interned Annie Besant. Leaders like Moti Lal Nehru, Tej Bahadur Sapru, Munshi Narayan Prasad, CY Chintamani and Asthana joined the Home Rule League to protest against the arrest of Besant.

1920: The District Congress Committee was reorganised as the Kerala Provincial Congress Committee at the fifth District Conference held at Manjeri in Ernad taluk. The conference witnessed a conflict of opinions between two factions, one led by Annie Besant and supported by the landlords, while the other faction was led by local leaders from the region and supported by the Mappila peasants.

1922, Feb. 19: An alliance between Mrs. Besant's Co-masonry and the Grand Orient of France was celebrated at the Grand Temple of the Droite Humain in Paris. Annie Besant's involvement with Co-Masonry continued. Co-Masonry was closely associated with the Adyar Society. Of course, Freemasonry was far older than the exposition of Theosophy.

1928: Dr. Annie Besant provided Rukmini with her ideal vision and life's mission. In public announcements, both in India and abroad, Annie Besant declared that young Rukmini had been chosen and ritually prepared to lead the World Mother Movement, started as a parallel movement to the World Teacher movement led by J. Krishnamurti.

1933, Sept. 20: Mrs. Annie Besant passed away, peacefully at her Adayar home.

Bibliography

Agnew, Elizabeth N.: *From Charity to Social Work: Mary E. Richmond and the Creation of an American Profession*, University of Illinois Press, Urbana, 2004.

Anne Taylor: *Annie Besant: A Biography*, Oxford University Press, Oxford, 1992.

Annie Besant: *Annie Besant: An Autobiography*, T. Fisher Unwin, London, 1893.

Arthur Hobart Nethercot: *The First Five Lives of Annie Besant*, University of Chicago Press, Chicago, 1960.

Axinn, June and Mark Stern, J.: *Social Welfare: A History of the American Response to Need*, Pearson/Allyn and Bacon, Boston, 2008.

Balgopal, Pallassana, R.: *Social Work Practice with Immigrants and Refugees*, Columbia University Press, New York, 2000.

Barker, Richard: *Making Sense of Every Child Matters - Multi Professional Practice Guidance*, Policy Press, Bristol, 2009.

Besant, Annie and Blavatsky, H.P.: *Memory and its Nature*, Theosophical Publishing House, Madras, 1935.

Besant, Annie: *Man and his Bodies*, Theosophical Publishing House, London, 1911.

Besant, Annie: *Man's Life in this and Other Worlds*, Theosophical Publishing House, Adyar, 1913.

Besant, Annie: *Study in Consciousness - A Contribution to the Science of Psychology*, Theosophical Publishing House, Madras, 1907.

Besant, Annie: *The Building of the Kosmos and Other Lectures: Delivered at the Eighteenth*, The Path, 1894.

Besant, Annie: *The Devachanic Plane*, Theosophical Publishing House, London, 1895.

Besant, Annie: *The Future of Indian Politics: A Contribution to the Understanding of Present-Day Problems P252*, Kessinger Publishing, LLC, 1996.

Besant, Annie: *The Life and Teaching of Muhammad*, Madras, 1932.

Butler, Ian and Gwenda Roberts: *Social Work with Children and Families: Getting into Practice*, Jessica Kingsley Publishers, New York, 2004.

Chandrasekhar, S.: *A Dirty, Filthy Book: The Writing of Charles Knowlton and Annie Besant on Reproductive Physiology and Birth Control and an Account of the Bradlaugh-Besant Trial*, University of California Berkeley, California, 1981

Davies, Martin: *The Blackwell Companion of Social Work*, Malden, Oxford, 2002.

Fischer, Joel and Kevin Corcoran, J.: *Measures for Clinical Practice and Research: A Sourcebook*, Oxford University Press, Oxford, 2007.

Frederick Marion De Mello: *The Indian National Congress: An Historical Sketch*, Oxford University Press, 1934.

Geoffrey West: *The Life of Annie Besant*, Gerald Howe, 1929.

Gertrude Marvin Williams: *The Passionate Pilgrim: A Life of Annie Besant*, Coward-McCann, New York, 1931.

Greene, Roberta, R.: *Social Work with the Aged and their Families*, Transaction Publishers, New Brunswick, 2008.

Grinnell, Richard, M. and Yvonne Unrau, A.: *Social Work Research and Evaluation: Foundations of Evidence-Based Practice*, Oxford University Press, Oxford, 2008.

Grover, Verinder and Ranjana Arora: *Annie Besant: Great Women of Modern India – 1*, Published by Deep of Deep Publications, New Delhi, 1993.

Harish Kaushik, P.: *Indian National Congress in England*, Published by Friends Publications, 1991.

Iqbal Singh: *Indian National Congress: A Reconstruction*, Nehru Memorial Museum and Library, Published by Riverdale Company, 1988.

Jagdish Saran Sharma: *Indian National Congress: A Descriptive Bibliography of India's Struggle for Freedom*, Published by S. Chand, 1959.

Jim Masselos: *Struggling and Ruling: The Indian National Congress: 1885-1985*, Published by Sterling Publishers, 1987.

John Riddick, F.: *The History of British India: A Chronology*, Greenwood Publishing Group, 2006.

Kumar, Raj Rameshwari Devi and Romila Pruthi: *Annie Besant: Founder of Home Rule Movement*, Pointer Publishers, 2003.

Lutyens, Mary: *The Life and Death of Krishnamurti*, Krishnamurti Foundation Trust, Bramdean, 2003.

Madhvi Yasin: *Emergence of Nationalism, Congress and Separatism*, Raj Publications, 1996.

Mahendra Prasad Singh: *Split in a Predominant Party: The Indian National Congress in 1969*, Abhinav Publications, 1981.

Manikrao Hodlya Gavit: *Indian National Congress: A Select Bibliography*, Published by U.D.H. Pub. House, Attar Chand, 1989.

Manvell, Roger: *The trial of Annie Besant and Charles Bradlaugh*, Elek, London, 1976.

Moin Zaidi, A. Shaheda Gufran Zaidi: *The Encyclopedia of Indian National Congress*, Indian Institute of Applied Political Research, Published by S. Chand, 1987.

Nethercot, Arthur H.: *The First Five Lives of Annie Besant*, Hart-Davis, London, 1961.

Om, P. Gautam: *The Indian National Congress: An Analytical Biography*, Published by B.R. Pub. Corp., 1985.

Pande, B.N. Nisith Ranjan Ray, Ravinder Kumar, Manmath Nath Das: *Concise History of the Indian National Congress: 1885-1947*, Published by Vikas Pub. House, 1985.

Pattabhi Sitaramayya, B.: *The History of the Indian National Congress*, Working Committee of the Congress, 1935.

Pitambar Datt Kaushik: *The Congress Ideology and Programme, 1920-1985*, Published by Gitanjali Pub. House, 1986.

Pran Nath Chopra, Ram Gopal, Moti Lal Bhargava: *A Century of Indian National Congress, 1885-1985*, Published by Agam Prakashan, 1986.

Rajan Mahan: *Women in Indian National Congress, 1921-1931*, Published by Rawat Publications, 1999.

Ralhan, O.P.: *Encyclopaedia of Political Parties: India, Pakistan, Bangladesh: National, Regional, Local*, Anmol Publications PVT. LTD., 1996.

Ramparkash Dua: *Social Factors in the Birth and Growth of the Indian National Congress Movement*, Published by S. Chand, 1967.

Reamer, Frederic, G.: *Ethical Standards in Social Work: A Review of the NASW Code of Ethics*, NASW Press, Washington, 2006.

Richardson, Virginia, E. and Amanda Smith Barusch: *Gerontological Practice for the Twenty-First Ccentury: A Social Work Perspective*, Columbia University Press, New York, 2006.

Roger Manvell: The Trial of Annie Besant and Charles Bradlaugh, Elek Pemberton, London, 1976.

Sowers, Karen, M. and Catherine Dulmus, N.: *Comprehensive Handbook of Social Work and Social Welfare*, Hoboken, New Jersey, 2008.

Taylor, Anne: *Annie Besant: A Biography*, Oxford University Press, US, 1991.

Theodore Besterman: *Mrs. Annie Besant: A Modern Prophet*, Kegan Paul, Trench, Trubner & Co., London, 1934.

Wessinger, Catherine Lowman: *Annie Besant and Progressive Messianism, 1847-1933*, Edwin Mellen Press, New York, 1988.

Index

D

E

N

O

P

Q

R

❑❑❑